Jean Calvin, Thomas Stocker

Two and Twentie Sermons of Maister John Calvin

In which sermons is most religiously handled the hundredth and nineteenth Psalme

of David, by eight verses aparte according to the Hebrewe alphabet. Vol. 1

Jean Calvin, Thomas Stocker

Two and Twentie Sermons of Maister John Calvin
In which sermons is most religiously handled the hundredth and nineteenth Psalme of David, by eight verses aparte according to the Hebrewe alphabet. Vol. 1

ISBN/EAN: 9783337318314

Printed in Europe, USA, Canada, Australia, Japan

Cover: Foto ©Lupo / pixelio.de

More available books at **www.hansebooks.com**

Two and twentie
Sermons of Maister
Iohn Caluin.

In which Sermons is most religi-
*ously handled, the hundredth and nine-
teenth Psalme of Dauid, by eight
verses aparte according to
the Hebrewe Al-
phabet.*

*Translated out of French into
Englishe by T.S.*

❧ *Imprinted at London*
for Iohn Harison and
Thomas Man.
1580.

To the right worshipful Sir Robert Ier-
myn, Knight, and to the right worshipful his godly
and vertuous wife, the Lady Iudith Iermyn, Thomas Stocker
wisheth continuall increase of all spirituall and earthly good
thinges in this life, with an earnest zeale to the
glorious Gospell of Christe Iesus, and perseueraunce of
practise thereof vnto the ende and in the
end, and after this life, euerlasting ioy and
blisse in the life to come through the
same Christ Iesus our
Lorde.

Lbeit the whole Scripture vniuersally (Right Worshipfull) is as it were a diuine Maistresse, teaching bothe vertue and true faith: yet notwithstanding the Booke of Psalmes hath ouer and besides that in a manner an expresse image of the state and condition of soules, and therfore very necessary for all people in generall. Howbeit this hundreth and ninteene Psalme, namely conteyneth a perfect art and a woonderfull vehemencie of the Kingly Prophet, in setting foorth and highly extolling the prayse of Gods lawe and the excellency thereof: wherein hee cannot satisfie himselfe, nor yet sufficiently expresse the affection which he beareth therunto, adding moreouer many notable complaintes and consolations, wherfore it is most meete

☞.2. for

The Epistle

for all the children of God to haue it alwayes bothe in their heartes and mouthes, and so continually meditating thereon as this holy Prophet did in his distresse, they may also finde the like comfort, whensoeuer and whatsoeuer affliction shall assaile them, and also to flie and abhorre that which is wicked and euill in the sight of the Lord.

Which Psalme beeing deuided into twoo and twentie partes, by eight verses aparte, according too the Hebrew Alphabet, the godly and learned Father and moste famouse furtherer of the glorious Gospell of our Sauiour and Redeemer Chriſte, hath according to that order, very religiously handled and drawne into as many Sermons, too the benefite and comfort of all the true aud faithfull Scholers in the Schoole of God, which shall diligently reade them, and earnestly striue to followe the same direction in their life and conuersation.

Which Sermons according to my poore skill, I haue englished frō the French, and haue taken boldnesse to dedicate and offer this my simple trauell vnto your Worships, as a speciall token of my good will in Christ: beseeching you to accept of this my labor, not according to the rude translation, but the goodnesse of the matter which they propound, and my heartie affection vnto you. And the rather haue I beene enbodened this to doe: both for that I haue beene crediblly informed off, either of your greate paines taking in reading ouer such like godly works as also that my selfe am *Testis oculatus*, of your dayly presence and diligent attention at all Sermons and godly exercises vsed in this countrie of Suff. Whose good & godly beginnings with the rest of the right

worshipful

Dedicatory.

worshipfull both men and women in these partes (and all others of what state and condition so euer they be) I heartely beseech our good God and mercifull father, euen for his Christ, his trueth, & mercyes sake, to increase, strengthen, and continue witth dayly practise of the same, in some measure in your liues and conuersation, with full perseueraunce vntoo the end of your dayes here, without which all the rest is but labor lost. For as the Apostle witnesseth, we are made partakers of Christ, if wee keepe sure vnto the ende that beginning wherewith we are vpholden. The Lord God therefore by his holy spirit work these effects in you and in vs all that professe his gospell, and leade our aduersaryes (when it shall please him) into the trueth, as he is God of trueth: that whē his sonne Christ our Sauiour shall appeere in glory, wee may be founde to haue walked without halting in whatsoeuer hee hath thought meete to open to vs for our saluation.
From Mildenhall the 4. of
Nouember, 1579.

Your worships to command
in the Lorde

Tho. Stocker.

¶ To all faithfull Readers.

HE Reading ouer of these present Sermons, will sufficiently declare what commoditie and profite they may bring with them: As in very deede the Author of them right wel sheweth throughout all his woorkes, in what sorte the Lorde GOD hath heeretofore beene serued, and also how ordinarily hee is serued by him. And therefore for a full recommendation aswell of the Author, as also of the woorke it selfe, I intende through GOD his assistaunce too sette foorth none other thing, then the same fruite and profite, which they haue already gotten, that haue read them, and that fruite which they may make reporte of, that shall heereafter reade them. For this may very well be thought that nothing in the whole worlde maketh a man more blessed, then the liuely and continuall meditation of the holy lawe and good will of our heauenly father. Nowe then this is the Psalme, which is framed, and wholly serueth too this ende and purpose, dayly to exercise our selues heere in, and although that hee so oftentimes repeateth these woordes, Lawe, Ordinaunces, Statutes, Edict, Commaundements, Decrees, and other such like: yet are they no vaine repetitions: but vsed to this intent and purpose, too let vs throughly vnderstand, howe meruelous peruerse and frowarde our nature is causing these so necessary thinges, too too easily to melte (like waxe against the Sunne, as wee say) cleane away from vs, and also to make vs too bee touched at the quicke, that we might feele howe feruently we ought too sigh and grone, after the lawe and ordinaunce of God, how zealously too desire to put the same in execution, and also how greatly too be greeued

with

with beholding the moste proude and villanous contempt of the
vngodly treading the same vnder their feete.
 And because there are some who rather desire too haue
such Bookes as they may easily carry aboute with them, I haue
the rather to please all parties beene very willing too sa-
tiffie them herein, alwayes reseruing this good
affection, that GOD might bee honoured, and glorified, by this my small
trauel, and the building vp of
his Church aduaun-
ced.

Farewell.

The first Sermon of M. John Caluine, vpon the hundreth and ninteene Psalme, of the Kingly Prophet Dauid,

The first eight Verses vpon ALEPH.

1 Blessed are al those which are vpright in the way: and walke in the lawe of the lorde.
2 Blessed are they which keepe his Testimonyes: and seeke him with their whole heart.
3 Surely they worke no iniquitie: that walke in his wayes.
4 Thou hast commaunded to keepe thy Preceptes diligently.
5 O that my wayes were directed too keepe thy Statutes.
6 Then should not I be confounded: when I haue respect vnto all thy Commaundements.
7 I will prayse thee with an vpright heart: when I shall learne the iudgements of thy righteousnes.
8 I will keepe thy Ceremonies: ô forsake mee not ouerlonge.

Eloued, we ought to be greatly ashamed of our selues, when as our good God and heauenly Father, goeth aboute by all meanes possible too drawe vs vnto him, and yet wee in no wise will come nighe him, but rather as is commonly said, do pul our heads out of the coller and hale backwarde. If there were none other testimonie heereof againste vs, but this

A.   Psalme

The first Sermon of M. Jo. Cal.

Pſalme which I am heere nowe in hand about to handle, it might ſuffice. The ſumme whereof is this, to ſhewe vnto vs what grace the Lorde our God offereth vnto vs, when as we are taught the ſtraight rule and order, by which wee may rightly and truely ſerue him, wherein conſiſteth the whole effect of our ſaluation, and the ſame to bee the very way and meane to com therunto. When as God then granteth vnto vs his grace, to be thus inſtructed by his woorde, beholde he hath now giuen vnto vs an vnſpeakeable treaſure, and impoſſible too bee ſufficiently valued. By this Pſalme is declared vntoo vs, that this is the very vſe of the lawe of God, and alſo of all the holy Scripture: and that we are inſtructed and exhorted too profite our ſelues by that which is there offred vnto vs. But becauſe that when any talke is miniſtred of drawing vs to God, wee are ſo blockiſhe and dull, that it is pittie and lamentable to ſee: and albeit that God approcheth neere vnto vs, and that wee haue many and ſundry times cleerely forgotten all whatſoeuer wee haue vnderſtoode and learned of him, ſee heere what an ayde and helpe he hath added for our behoofe: which is this, that his will and meaning is, that this Pſalme ſhoulde bee drawne and framed into an order of eight verſes aparte, and that all the verſes of euery eight aparté, ſhould begin with a ſeuerall letter, after the order of an A.B.C. As if he ſhould ſay, It ſhall not be materiall that we be profounde learned men, for our inſtruction in that which is neceſſary to our ſaluation: But that the doctrine is common aſwell to the learned as to the vnlearned. Are our wittes and memoryes growen ſo ſhort? Let vs then recken and tell vpon our fingers, when as wee haue learned our A.B.C. Let vs then ioyne eight verſes togither, and ſo eight by eight, & go through the whole croſſerow, and wee ſhall haue the whole Pſalme at our fingers endes. What ſhall we farther ſay? If wee will heereby profite our ſelues no way, neither yet vouchſafe to hearken vnto our good God, ne yet ſuffer vs to be ſo familiarly guyded by

him

him, yea euen vnto that thing which is more then necessary, may it not be very well sayd, that we are al most accursed? True it is that the verses in deede beginne not either with the Englifh or yet the Latine letters: but with the Hebrue: wherin Dauid made and wrote this Psalme. Notwithstanding so it is, that the wil and purpose of the holy ghost, is to make vs to feele and vnderstand that which before I haue declared: to witt, that the doctrine herein conteyned, is not onely set downe for great Clearkes which haue gone to schoole ten or twentie yeeres: but also for the most simple: to the ende none shoulde pretende any excuse of ignoraunce. And heerewithal let vs note this by the way: That we al, ought too knowe and vnderstand this Psalme as perfectly as our Pater noster as we vsually say. But here we must not say as a number of men doo, that our wit & capacities are not so excellent and fyne, as to comprehende & vnderstande the holy scriptures: and besides, that oure memorie will not serue too reteine and keepe that whiche sometymes is preached vntoo vs. A straunge case: wee will easely retaine and keepe in minde not onely vayne and foolishe songes and ditties, but also such as are both wanton & dissolute, & euen such as S. Paule sayth, doe corrupt and poyson good manners, for this horible infection is alwayes shutte vp for an euil intent and purpose. For if wee shall heare any villainous and ribaudrous song, which shall only stirre vs vp to all filthy lust and shamelesnesse: the same by and by we retaine with greate ease.

 Beholde nowe, how the Lorde our God heere teacheth vs as it were by an A. B. C. a moste excellent song emongst the rest, by which we may learne to rule & order our liues; whereby also he exhorteth vs to well dooing, to comforte vs in all our afflictions, to ratifie vnto vs the promisses of saluation, too open vnto vs the Gates of his euerlasting Kingdome, that wee might enter into euerlasting life: and all this is contayned within this A. B. C. of this present Psalme, and yet wee will all say that our memory

The first Sermon of M. Jo. Cal.

is ouer shorte, and our witte too too grosse, or weake to holde it. Nowe I beseech you tell mee this, will this excuse goe for payment or not? Verely I beleeue not, wherfore let vs learne to bestowe our whole indeuour and study to recorde the lessons which are heere taught vs: & that we may be heerafter throughly acquainted with this Psalme, if we wil be repured & take to be the children of God. And seeing we see our nature to be giuen to many vngodly and pernicious, or at the least to very vnprofitable thing: let vs yet retaine and holde that which shall be moste profitable for vs, and the rather becaufe that God so abaseth himselfe to the moste rude, simple, and ignorauntest emong vs. For mine owne parte, because I will frame my selfe to that manner and order which the holy Ghoste hath heere set downe, I shall inforce my selfe to followe as briefely as I can the plaine and true meaning of the text: and without continuing in longe exhortations, I will onely doe my beste too mince or shred, as we say, the wordes of Dauid, becaufe wee may the better digest them. For performance whereof, I determine by the grace of God, too finishe eight verses aparte in euery Sermon, and to holde my selfe with in such a compasse, as that the most ignoraunt shall easily, acknowledge and confesse that I meane nothing else but to make open and playne the simple and pure substaunce of the text. And nowe let vs come to the contents of the first viii. verses apart, beginning with the first letter Aleph: *Blessed are they* (saith Dauid) *which are vpright in the way: and walke in the Lawe of the Lorde*. First of all, he doth vs heere to witte, that we vnderstand not wherin our chiefe blessednesse consisteth, and the reason is, because that wee are blinde, and doe liue in the worlde as sauage and wilde beastes, vtterly voyde of sense and reason: and suffer our selues to be ledde and carryed away of our brutishe and swinish affections and lustes. And because it is so, that we are thus carryed away, it is a manifest signe and token that wee discerne not good from euill: or else that the

Deuil

vpon the Cxix. *Pſalme.* 3

Deuill hath ſo bewitched vs, that wee thinke thereof no whitte at all. True it is that the moſte wicked wil confeſſe and ſay, that they deſire too bee ſaued but yet in the deſire thereof, they cleerely flye from it, and goe as cleane away from it, as they can for their liues.

But what is the cauſe whye they ſo greately withdrawe them ſelues from that which they ſo highly proteſte too loue? Yea they drawe as neere vnto it, as they can poſſibly flye from it. By this it ſeemeth that they haue conſpyred too reiecte and make little accounte of that good which GOD meaneth to doe for them. And heere we are too note, that Dauid in this firſte verſe accuſeth vs of horrible blindeneſſe, as if he ſhould ſay, Surely you are all ſenſeleſſe and without witte. And to ſay the trueth if there were but one droppe of reaſon in vs, without doubte, wee would not ſo reiecte and refuſe our ſaluation of a ſett purpoſe as wee doe. See heere howe mercifully our good God dealeth with vs, who ſheweth vs howe and in what manner we may be bleſſed, and yet we for all that drawe altogither backwarde. Doth not Dauid then of very right, iuſtly condemne vs? But becauſe euery of vs proteſteth to knowe the right way, hee addeth, *They which walke in the way of the Lorde.* Hee hath ſayde: *Bleſſed are they which are vndefiled in their way*: that is, whiche walke aright. And who are they? It is very true in deede as before I haue ſayde, that there are a greate number, which will boaſt them ſelues too walke aright, and that in ſuch ſorte, as that it can not be much amended: and yet notwithſtanding, if they be aſked who made their way, and who it is that aſſureth them that they ſhoote at the true marke, they knowe not what aunſwere to make. For there is but one way which leadeth to ſaluation, which is the law: as Dauid heereof ſpeaketh, wherefore as many as walke in the Lawe of the Lorde, ſayth he, goe not out of their way. We haue in this firſte verſe twoo notable leſſons: The one is, that God heere acuſeth vs, that euery of vs ſtrayeth and

A.3. erreth

erreth from the way of saluation, and although wee proteste that we are willing and desirous to bee saued, yet for all that our wicked affections doe in such sorte carry vs away, as that we desire nothing else but that wee may bee farre from that felicitie and blessednesse which is set before vs. For there it is sayde, *Blessed are they which walke in the right way.* And thus much for the first poynte. The seconde is, That wee may inuent and deuise many and sundry kindes of life, and so think that we go the best & surest way that may be, and by this meane deceiue our selues, for there is but one way that leadeth to saluation. What way is it? It is not that which wee of our owne braine doe imagine: For when Isaiah sayth, that euery one hath declined from his way, he meaneth that we all runne into euerlasting destruction. The Law of God then is the way which must rule and order our life, and when we will hearken vnto it, all thinges shall goe well with vs, but whosoeuer swarueth from that, the same is like vnto a sauage and wilde beaste, which can doe nothing else but gallopp and flinge ouerthwart the fieldes. There is none of vs all but that may haue many motions which may seeme good to vs, as wee may see by the poore and silly vnbeleeuers, which are very feruent and earnest to doe this or that, which too their thinking seemeth very good and profitable: but yet the spirit of God is not their leader and guide.

Esay. 53. 6.

Nowe it is sayde, That when wee haue the lawe of God before vs, it shal go wel with vs: & that without it, it is impossible, but that our life must needes bee confounded and come to naught. He sayth a little after, *Blessed are they which keepe his Testimonies: and seeke him with their whole heart.* Dauid now vseth another worde, then this word the law, to wit, testimonies. This word in it self importeth a couenant or cōtract, & it is not to be vnderstood otherwise than to be ayplyed to this end: to wit, that God couenanting with vs, declareth, that his meaning is to pull & draw vs vnto him, and also howe we ought to order our life, because

cause it is a mutuall Contract betweene him and vs. As if he should haue saide: Goe to now, vnderstand you that heere I make a couenaunt with you, that you acknowledge mee to bee your GOD: That you doubte not of my loue towards you, and in louing you that I am your Sauiour, and that you call vppon mee in this affiaunce and trust, and besides that you bee also my louing & obedient Children, that I doo protect and gouerne you, and that you are my housholde Seruauntes. When the Lorde our GOD thus abaseth and offereth him selfe vnto vs, and that hee vseth suche famyliaritie and gentlenesse towardes vs, as to talke with vs, It is sayde, that hee giueth vs his Testimonyes of his loue and fauour towardes vs.

Heere nowe Dauid declareth, That they are blessed which keepe the Testimonyes of GOD: and seeke him with their whole hearte. As if hee shoulde say that the Lawe of God consisteth not onely in this, that it sheweth vnto vs what wee ought too doo, but that it carryeth also with it another speciall Doctrine: too weete, to assure vs that hee will bee our Father, that hee loueth vs so deerely that hee desireth none other thing of vs, but that wee woulde bee his sonnes and heyres. And heereunto tende all the Ceremonyes, whereof wee shall speake heereafter more at large. Yet this is true, that aswell in this place abouesayde, as also by the reste of the names couched in this Psalme, as of Statutes, Decrees, and Ordinaunces, Dauid alwayes meaneth the doctrine of the Lawe. Howbeit it is to be noted, that this diuersitie of woordes, it is not heere sette downe without good cause. For it expresseth moste plainely vnto vs, what varietie of consolation wee receiue by that which GOD sheweth vnto vs in the Lawe of Moyses, and in all the Prophetes, who are as it were Expositors thereof. For many times when wee speake of the Lawe, wee suppose that there is nothing else meant but that which GOD

A.4. comman-

The first Sermon of M.Io.Cal.

commaundeth vs to do. But there is a great deale more to be considered: to witte, hee assureth vs of his fauour and grace, and willeth vs to staye our selues thereon, that wee might be assured of our saluation, and that also we might be certaine of his loue by his sacraments therein ordeined. Moreouer, that wee shoulde addresse our selues to Iesus Christ, and by that meanes be instructed to runne vnto him who is our onely and alone Sauiour. When God then speaketh vnto vs, we must consider that hee saith not onely, doe this, or that, but declareth himselfe vnto vs, what manner of one wee should thinke him to be, and what one also he sheweth him selfe on his parte too be towardes vs, both by experience and effecte. This diuersitie of woords vsed heere in this Psalme by Dauid is not superfluous: For it sheweth vs that the Lawe of God doth not onely commaunde vs how wee should liue, and after what sorte; but doth also certifie vs of the good will of God, promiseth vs saluation, leadeth vs too Iesus Christe, stirreth vs. vp too call vpon the name of God; giueth vs Ceremonies to confirme vs therein, and moreouer, that it guideth, & holdeth vs within our limits. And surely there is not one verse in all this Psalme (although there are very many) wherein there is not mention made of one of these wordes, too witte, either of the lawe of God, or of his Commaundementes, either else of his Ordinaunces, Statutes, or Testimonyes, or of his voyce, Iudgementes, or Iustice. These wordes are heere so many times repeated, as that there is not one verse, but that there is one or sometimes twoo of them in it: as heereafter wee shall see throughout the whole Psalme.

And now let vs come to the matter heerin contayned: *Blessed are they which keepe the Testimonies of the Lorde: and which seeke him with their whole heart.* First Dauid declareth heere (as afore said) that wee haue greatly profited in the lawe, when as wee shall acknowledge and confesse what affection and loue God beareth vs; and how we ought

vpon the Cxix. Pſalme.

to aſſure our ſelues of his good will and fatherly loue. And afterward he telleth vs to what end and purpoſe it is, that God graunteth vnto vs ſuch an aſſurance, bicauſe (ſaith he) we ſhould ſeeke him. For this is moſt ſure, when as we ſhall vnderſtand God to be ſuch a one, as he declareth himſelfe vnto vs by his worde, it is impoſsible but that wee ſhoulde ſtirre vp our ſelues, and be moued to giue our ſelues wholy vnto him. And to proue that this is true, behold the ineſtimable bountie and goodnes declared vnto vs in our God, what man is hee that is ſo peruerſe and voide of ſenſe and reaſon, which wil not be contented to place him ſelf there, where he thinketh his whole bleſſednes and felicitie conſiſteth and lieth. Euen ſo likewiſe, when as we become careles in ſeeking after the Lorde our God, it is a ſigne and token that we haue vnderſtoode nothing of that which he hath ſhewed vnto vs of his goodnes and mercie, and of all his fatherly affection, which is witneſſed vnto vs in the law, and in the holy ſcriptures. But becauſe it ſhall be no great adoe for a number of men, to make a countenance of ſeeking the Lord, Dauid ſheweth that wee muſt not ſeeke him with our feete and handes, with the outward geſtures of the bodie alone, but with a true and pure affection. And therefore, he ſaieth, *Bleſſed are they which ſeeke him with their whole heart*. As if he ſhould ſay, I would not haue you to doe as the hypocrites do, which beare of religion with ſtrōg hand, no, I meane not ſo: but I would haue your loue to be found and true. As touching that ſaying, *With their whole heart*, it is to declare vnto vs, That God cannot away with parting of ſtakes, as we men many times doe: For we are well contented to beſtowe ſome part vpon God, and would be at free libertie to holde vs with the world, and to ſerue God by halfes. But Dauid teacheth vs here to ſerue him with our whole heart: to wit, in all integritie and foundnes, and not with two faces in one hood. He would not haue vs parted in ſunder, to ſaye, Well, I am contented to ſerue God, howbeit I would not that he ſhould require my whole ſeruice to him ſelfe: but that I might after ſatiſ-

A 5   fie and

The first Sermon of M.I.Cal.

fie and followe my owne lustes and pleasures, that I might be at libertie to serue the worlde. No not so (saith he:) It must be brought into a true and perfect soundnes, and not to deuide man after such a maner. True it is that wee shall neuer be able to seeke God with such a perfection, but that it may be greatly amēded: neither doth the holy scripture meane by this saying, *With their whole heart*, ful perfection, but only opposeth it selfe against the hypocrisie of a great nūber of men, and which would be in vs al, were it not that God him self did remedy & help it, That is, we would with good wil serue God by halfes, if so be he would let vs alone with the rest, to do what we thought good. As for example, Wee shall haue very many which will not sticke with God, to come to the Sermon on a Sunday, and to be present at the prayers of the faithfull, and to make some shewe of religiō: and yet they would haue God to giue them free choise to do what they listed al the rest of the wecke after: or if they come to a Sermon oftener then on the Sunday, it seemeth to them that they haue done very well, that they are throughly discharged of their dueties if they tarrie there but one houre. But because they might be set at more libertie, they will not sticke to saye, that they will bee free from some one vice, one will say that he will be no whoremaister, Another, that he will be no drunkarde, Another, that he wilbe no blasphemer: & yet euery one of these wil haue his particular vice, and thinke that God ought to beare with them, seeing that for his honour, and to do him pleasure, they absteined from some synne, and that they obeyed him in some point. But the scripture telleth vs that all this is nothing, but that euery one ought to examine him selfe throughly and in all pointes, and finding in him selfe any thing which is against the wil of God: to be vtterly displeased therewith, clerely to renounce it, and to desire nothing but to be cleansed thereof. See nowe, this is that perfection, whereof Dauid here speaketh. Nowe let vs see what is the summe of the second verse, to weete, that wee

should.

should doe nothing els but study in the lawe of God, not onely to knowe what is forbidden or commaunded, but to be certaine what maner of one GOD is towardes vs, and what affection he beareth vs, that we might put the trust of our saluation in him, and call vpon his holy name. And besides, there is declared vnto vs, that when we haue tasted of the mercies of God, that hee hath certified vs of his loue and grace, that the same ought to stirre vs vp to seeke him, and to cleaue wholy vnto him, and to yelde our selues wholy to his seruice: and that not in the outward shewe, and in hypocrisie: but with a pure and sound heart and affection, and not by halfes: so that there bee founde true soundnes and integritie, as before I haue touched, Now it followeth,

Surely they woorke none iniquitie that walke in his waies. First Dauid here sheweth in this present verse, what the cause is why all men abounde in euill and iniquitie: to weete, for so much as they will not bee ruled by the Lorde their God. See here the spring head of the outrages, of all the disorder, and confusions in the worlde, to weete, that God is prest and ready to guyde and gouerne vs, but what? we may not awaye to beare his yoke, euery man refuseth it, and wilbe exempt from it. Loe here whereupon ariseth our dissolute and wanton life, to weete, bicause we will not suffer the authoritie which God hath ouer vs, to leade and guide vs, as he is alwayes ready to do, and as he also sheweth vs by his lawe. Let this then be an Item for vs.

And it followeth further. For Dauid meaneth to confirme the woordes before spoken, to weete, howe it commeth to passe that wee are blessed, that is, if wee keepe the testimonies of our GOD, and walke in his lawe. For, sayeth hee, they which doe no wickednesse walke in his wayes: contrarywyse, wee doe nothing but prouoke his heauy wrath and displeasure against vs, in committing of synne and iniquitie.

When

when as God then standeth against vs, & becommeth our enemie, must not our life be vnhappy and accursed? It can not be otherwise chosen. Heere then is one proofe of that which before hath beene said: to wit, that our whole felicitie consisteth in this, that God is our instructer and teacher, and that we holde our selues too the doctrine which wee receiue from him And what is the reason? For loe, sayth Dauid, they will abstaine from euill dooing. When then wee abstaine from dooing of euill, wee prouoke not God his heauy wrath against vs: and so let vs conclude, that herein consisteth our chiefe felicitie. Moreouer, here is to be noted, that as many as walke not in the law of God, cannot but runne into mischiefe and destruction: yea how soeuer they thinke of their well doing, and persuade them selues to liue holily and godly, yet hath God tolde them that it is cleane contrary. And here this parcell of scripture is worthie the marking, for hereby we may see the pryde of vs men, in that wee make all the worlde beleeue, that all things goe with vs as well as is possible, when as we follow our own fantasies, being thus arrogant to say, whatsoeuer we do it is all well done. But behold what God (the onely iudge hereof) hath certainly set downe, which we can no way, repeale or call backe, neither shalbe possible to be retracted as we lust, to wit, that no man can abstaine from euill doing, but such onely which walke after this heauenly doctrine. They then which walke after their owne pleasure, must needes runne into euerlasting perdition. Now then there are two maner of wayes wherein men doe erre. For one sort exceede in open and most manifest transgressions and sinnes: and although they very well knowe that they are euill and wicked, yet take they leaue, continually to followe them. As a whoremonger can not iustifie his wicked doing: no more can a theefe, a swearer, nor a dronkard. And yet it is so with them, that they alwaies giue them selues leaue to goe from better to worse. Howbeit there is another maner of way of euill doing, which is mere dāgerous, ānd a great deale more to be feared, bicause it is

more

more couert and secret to weete, when as men will not acknowledge them selues to be worthy of condemnation, and that they thinke that there is none that can detecte or condemne them, hauing a foolish and diuelish opinion which blindeth their eyes. These men then (as it is the maner of all hypocrites) may well iustifie them selues: but yet the case so standeth, that God condemneth them, as here we may see. It remaineth now, that we vse nothing for the whole rule and order of our life, but the law of God alone: for without it, all our life must needes bee dissolute, and there shalbe nothing in it but confusion and destruction, It followeth next after, *That God hath commaunded vs too keepe diligently his precepts*, That is, alwayes, according to the truth which Dauid holdeth. For it is very sure, that God is so carefull ouer our saluation, that he procureth and furthereth it, as much as is possible for vs to desire. Nowe if God be thus touched with vs, and beareth vs such a good will and loue: let vs vnderstand that when he chargeth vs to keepe his ordinances and preceptes, that he thereby signifieth vnto vs, that the same is our whole blessednes and felicitie. And to prooue it to be so, God requireth not our seruice, bicause he hath some busines for vs to do: For he hath not, nor needeth any helpe of his creattres. When then we are not able do that which he commaundeth vs, we can neither do good nor hurt vnto our creator. What is it that moueth him to bee so carefull ouer vs as he is, and what is it that pricketh and thrusteth vs foreward to keepe his commandements? Surely, since neither his profite nor gaine leadeth him to be thus careful, doutles he respecteth onely our saluation. By this we may conclude, that there is none other blessednes which we can enioy, but to walke in his lawe, as he hath before said. But in the meane while we may see how villanous and wicked a thing our vnthankfulnes is: for God sheweth not vnto vs onely in a worde what is our duetie to doe, but vseth also a familiar & gentle doctrine, to drawe vs vnto him. And afterward he exhorteth vs, bicause he seeth vs to be very cold and vntoward, And

for

The first Sermon of M. Io. Cal.

for the selfsame cause he vseth much diuersitie, and pursueth it diligently as we see: to the ende wee might pretende no excuse of ignorance, when we haue not performed that which he hath set downe vnto vs by his lawe: but that we should be conuinced of malice, and that wee might vnderstand and knowe that wee are well worthie of euerlasting condenation. And so much the more ought we throughly to marke this doctrine, where it is declared vnto vs, that no excuse shall serue vs, whē as euery of vs outrageth so much and followeth his owne lust: seeing that God hath preuented vs, and that he hath declared vnto vs, that the right rule to walke by, is to follow his cōmandementes: neither that he hath done the same slightly, but that hee hath persisted and continued therein, as much as was possible for him to do. Thirdly, that by this meane hee hath shewed vnto vs his great loue towardes vs, and what care he hath of our welfare & life. Dauid thē goeth on forward, & saith. *O that my wayes were directed to keepe thy Statutes.* Here Dauid pricketh him selfe forwarde, and sheweth the desire hee hath to come to that blessednes and felicitie whereof hee hath spoken before. And we must be sure to obserue this order, for it is not enough for vs to vnderstand and knowe wherein our felicitie and blessednes consisteth, and the way to come thereunto, as God hath appointed vs: but we must also enter into our selues, For euery man must thinke thus with him selfe. What maner of man am I? Seeing my God is so louing and mercifull that he seeketh me, & that he requireth nothing els of me but that I should come vnto him, is it reason that I should sit still? shall I become a blocke? shall I become a sensles and witles creature? shall I not be moued with such fauour and grace as my GOD sheweth vnto me, and maketh me to feele.

See here what Dauid meaneth to teach vs in this verse, O that my wayes were made so direct, that I might keepe thy commaundements. When as he speaketh of his waies, he meaneth al the actiōs of his life, for the life of mā is called a Waye: And that not without cause, for all our thoughtes

upon the Cxix. Pſalme. 8

thoughtes and affections, are as wayes, and as our footeſteppes. Nowe he ſayeth, O that my wayes were made ſo direct, that I might keepe thy commaundementes. Herein he declareth, that a faithful mã, after he hath knowẽ this mercie of God in guiding our life, ought to enter into him ſelfe, and thinke that there is neither reaſon nor wiſedome in him how to gouerne him ſelfe: but that all proceedeth from the good will and louing kindnes of the Lorde. Sythens then that wee are ſo enclined to roue in our owne wayes hether and thether, by reaſon of the fooliſhe preſumption and vaine confidence which we haue of our own wiſedome, let vs vſe ſuch remedy as God hath aſsigned vs: to weete, that we forſake our ſelues, and treade vnder foote this carnall reaſon which deceiueth vs: that wee ſet at naught all our luſtes and vngodly affections that God only may beare rule, and our life be guided according to his his lawe.

It followeth, *Then ſhould I not bee confounded, when I haue reſpect to all thy commaundementes*. Here Dauid confirmeth him ſelfe in the doctrine next before: for hee declareth what the marke is whereat he aymeth. O Lorde, ſayeth hee, when as thou ſhalt doe me that good, that I may be directed according to thy word, I ſhal neuer be cõfounded. When Dauid now hath ſuch a deſire, he thereby right well declareth, that euery man ought to be careful & to endeuour himſelf therũto, or els he ſhall neuer obey the will of God, cõſidering that there are ſo many gainſayings in our fleſh & nature, as is moſt pitifull to thinke vpon. For looke how many our affections & thoughtes are, we haue euen ſo many enemies rebelling againſt God, and which hinder vs to walke after his will. Wee ought therefore to praye vnto him that he will holde vs in, that he may be our maiſter, & we his vaſſails. Moreouer, let vs conſider wel of that which is here ſpoken, to weete, that in keeping the cõmaundementes of God, we ſhall neuer be confounded. By this he doth vs to vnderſtãd that ſo many as followe their owne luſtes & fantaſies, which looke this way & that way,

and

The first Sermon of M. Io. Cal.

and do imagine them selues a marke, & forge them selues such away as seemeth good in their owne sight, that they shalbe confounded and deceiued. No doute when men do that which best liketh the selues, they streightwayes thinke all things shall goe so well with them as is possible to bee wished, glorying in their owne vaine imaginations: but what followeth thereof? God confoundeth them in their owne arrogancie wherwith they were puffed vp for a time: Woulde wee eschewe this confusion of the vnbeleeuing persons? Let vs haue an eye to the commaundementes of God: to wit, let our eyes be setled on them, and looke not on our owne reason, nor of our naturall sense, neither yet of any other thing that lieth in our owne power, which may turne vs away from them. And it is a necessary point for vs to be enfourmed thereof. For as often as men will giue them selues leaue to imagine and thinke what they list to haue done, there shall a thousand thoughtes forclose their mindes, and so will turne them away from God, and wholy estraunge them from the doctrine of saluation. And for this cause Dauid declareth that there is but one onely meane, to wit, that we should wholy settle our eyes vpon the Lawe of G O D, without turning away from it either on this side or on that, as commonly and vsually we doe. Afterward he goeth on and sayeth, *I will prayse thee with an vpright heart : when I shall learne the iudgementes of thy righteousnes.* Dauid sheweth in this verse how we may praise the Lord our God, and that is continually following the plainnes of his matter. For wee must all confesse that our life is miserable, if it tende not to the prayse and glorifying of God. Let vs now see how we may prayse him : We must be exercised in his iudgementes, that is, in the rule which hee hath set downe vnto vs. For this word *Iudgements,* importeth that wee are taught and instructed of that which wee haue to do For our life is outragious if we passe the limits and boundes which he hath appointed vs : and contrariwyse, we keepe a true vprightnes in obeying of him. Now then he sayeth, that when he shall haue learned the righte-

ous

teous iudgementes of God, that then he will thanke him with an vnfained heart. By this hee signifieth vnto vs, that although men perſuade them ſelues to loue GOD as much as is poſsible, neuertheles that it is but fained, vntill ſuch time as they are vnfainedly inſtructed in the lawe. And thus much for that. Moreouer, here is to be noted, that that is not all which wee haue learned that God ſheweth vnto vs in his word: but Dauid ſpeaketh here of an inſtruction which taketh roote, and is ſettled and abideth in the heart of a man, according to that which hath heretofore beene ſaid. For a number may imagine of their own braine what the lawe of God is, but in the meane while it ſtandeth ſo with them, that when we beholde their life and conuerſation, it appeareth that they haue profited no whit at all in his ſchoole. It is meete therefore that our heart be brought to the ſchoole of God, to weete, that whatſoeuer hee teacheth vs, it may bee throughly imprinted and engrauen within. And this is that maner of learning, whereof Dauid here ſpeaketh. For if we haue beene exerciſed in this ſort, that we haue holden the doctrine and law of God, we may very well glorifie his bleſſed name: to weete, we may truly praiſe him as he hath commaunded vs.

When he ſaieth, *I will keepe thy Statutes*: that is, That he is ſo reſolued and confirmed in the doctrine of the lawe, that he hath ouercome all the affections and luſtes of the fleſh and the worlde, which might reſiſt and hinder him in the ſeruice of God. He hath ſayd before, O that my wayes were made ſo direct. He deſireth, as a man which when he cannot haue that which he wiſheth for, is in great paine and trauell. It behoueth vs alſo to poure out ſuch ſighes & groanes, conſidering the rebellion of our fleſh, which is ſo cōtrary to the righteouſnes of God, that all our thoughtes and affections (as is aboueſaid) are ſo many gaineſayinges, that they turne vs cleane away from his obeyſaunce. Wee muſt therefore ſaye with Dauid, Alas: howe is it poſsible that I ſhould be euer able to come to the perfect ſeruing of my God? to truſt vpon him, and wholy to ſettle my ſelfe

B   vpon

The first Sermon of M. Jo. Cal.

vpon that rule and order which hee hath set downe vnto me? Loe I say, these should be our wishes and desires. But this is not sufficient enough, to haue a desire that we might serue God.

But there is yet much more, as when we shall desire that God will pushe vs forward and stirre vs vp thereto, and yet we must not stay there neither. What must we then do? Let vs step forth with Dauid and protest, that we will keepe the commaundements of God: to wit, when wee haue fought against our inordinate affections, and that wee are assured to haue victorie ouer them, that we then make this conclusion: God shall so conduct me, that I shalbe able to keepe his Statutes. As for the rest, bicause we can not haue this as of our selues, we are alwayes to pray as Dauid did:

O Lord forsake me not vtterly. For if God withhold his holy hand from vs, alas what shall become of vs? Is it possible for vs to haue one good desire or thought in vs? No, it is impossible, but we shall wholy decline to all euill and mischiefe, yea and we shall become his enemies and aduersaries. We must therefore, hauing all our refuge from God, beseeche him with Dauid, that he wil not forsake vs. When he saith, *O Lord forsake me not ouerlong*, He signifieth vnto vs, that God many times suffereth vs to go wrong, & suffereth vs to fall, or els to stuble. And why doth he so? Because hee would humble vs: for what is he which goeth not out of the waye, or at the least halteth not, and which oftentimes falleth not flat downe? But yet for all that hee would not haue vs discouraged. When then we see our weakenes, and that there are many faultes and imperfections in vs. Let vs beseech the Lorde our God that hee will not forsake vs for euer: for there is no difficultie which Dauid woulde not but that we shoulde knowe, and hee knew a great many of faultes in himselfe: But yet he hoped that God would not forsake him for euer. And he knewe also that though he happened oftentimes to fall, yet that he would relieue him by his grace.

And this is his meaning also what we must doe: for we
knowe

knowe this, that there is no man which wholy keepeth the lawe of God: we are al tranfgreffors thereof, we are all miferable finners. We muft therefore runne vnto our good God, and befeeche him that when we are fallen, that he wil relieue vs through his fatherly goodnes, as hee is alwayes ready to doe, and that he hath promifed hee will gouerne vs, in fupporting of vs, vntill fuch time as he hath defpoyled vs of all the imperfections of our flefhe. And according to this holy doctrine, let vs proftrate our felues before the face of our good God in confefsing our faultes, befeeching him that it would pleafe him to giue vs a taft that we may feele what a pleafure he doth vs, when he communicateth his word familiarly among vs, and that hee will inftruct vs thereby, not onely to vnderftand to difcerne betwixt good and euill; but that we may alfo be fure and certaine of his loue and good will towardes vs: to the ende that we liuing vnder his charge and conduction, might runne vnto him, that in the middeft of the miferies and wretchednes of this world, he will make vs bleffed, that wee may come to euerlafting bliffe, and the glorie immortall, which hath beene purchafed for vs once for all by our Lord & fauiour Chrifte Iefus his fonne. And that when he hath once fet vs into the right waye, that he would keepe vs therein more and more, vntill the time that he hath brought vs into his heauenly kingdome. That not onely, &c.

B 2.   The

The second Sermon of the hundreth and nineteenth Psalme.

BETH.

Wherewithall shall a yong man redresse his waye? in taking heede thereto according to thy word.
With my whole hearte haue I sought thee: let mee not wander from thy commaundementes.
I haue hidde thy promise in my heart: that I might not sinne against thee.
Blessed art thou O Lord: teach me thy statutes.
With my lippes haue I declared all the iudgements of thy mouth.
I haue had as great delight in the waye of thy testimonies: as in all maner of riches.
I will meditate in thy commaundementes: and consider thy wayes.
My delight shalbe in thy statutes: and I will not forget thy wordes.

Pon Sunday last past I declared vnto you in summe the argument of this Psalme, the vse thereof, and the instruction that we may gather by it: to weete, that a faithfull man is here taught to stirre vp himself to the reading of Gods word, and thereby to confirme himselfe accordingly. Dauid himselfe hath doone this, who of all others was the most excellent: how much more then ought we to do the like? euen we I say, which are so rude and ignorant, and farre from so much profiting in the schoole of God as he? But bicause

we

vpon the Cxix. Psalme. 11

we are so colde, and haue neede to be spurred forward like Asses: Beholde why Dauid here sheweth vs, what profite and commodity we may receiue by this continual study, if euery of vs wil apply our selues to see and heare that which God hath manifested vnto vs in his lawe, and in the holie Scriptures: As here he sayeth,

Wherewithall shall a young man redresse his way? in taking heede thereto or standing vpon his gard *according to thy word.*

He sheweth vs here, that if we be desirous to order our life as it becommeth vs, to haue it rightly gouerned, and to be pure and simple, we must holde that way which GOD hath set before vs. For wee must not trust vnto our owne wits. Neither frame & fashion vnto our selues such a way as shall to vs seeme best: but to suffer God to rule and conduct vs, and to obey him simply and playnely. To bee short, Dauid signifyeth vnto vs, that all the wisedome and perfection of our life, is to followe GOD, and cleaue vnto his will. True it is, that this sentence at the first sight may seeme to vs too to common, and as it were more then needeth. For we will say, what is he that knoweth not this, & wil not confesse it, I will not deny but that it is an ordinary thing to confes it. But in the mean while, how few are ther which are persuaded of that which is here spoken: or if we imagine such a thing in our head, where is the practise of it? I feare me, we shal finde it in a very smale number of vs. Let vs not therefore thinke that this rule which the spirit of God hath set before vs, is in vaine, for it is for the amendement of our life according to his worde, and to make vs to vnderstande, that without it, all is but doung, & filth, that we haue al erred, & that we hold no way, although we think al to the contrary. But we are to consider, why he especially speaketh here, of a yong man. For we are sure that God hath geuen his law aswel for the great as the smal, for the olde as the yong: that when we shal begin to be taught it euen frō our youth, we must hold & continue it to the graue. Wherfore then doth Dauid straine this doctrine of the lawe too yong men? It is not for that it reacheth not vnto the aged:

B 3   but

The second Sermon of M. Io. Cal.

continue and holde vs in this study all the daies of our life. Let vs not then tarry vntill we come to the graues brinke to become wise in this behalfe, as wee see these scorners, which make them selues mery, and outrage in mocking of God, saying, Well sir, wee shall haue leisure to repent time enough. For if we may haue but one hearty sighe, care away. Sithens then this is most sure that it is Satan which eggeth thē thus greeuously to abuse the patiēce of God: let vs beware that we be not so bewitched. But let vs follow that which is here set downe, to weete, that wee may be Gods schollers euen from our youth. And aboue all things let vs consider, that yong mē haue here a speciall lesson to learne, as before hath beene touched. For Dauid here declareth vnto them, that they haue a great deale more neede to bee restrained, thē any of the rest. It is very true that we are before God alwayes, euen as yong childrē: Yea, I say that the elder sort of greater experience, and such as appeare graue and wise to the world, are without all dout before the maiestie of God very fooles and idiotes. We heare also what Dauid confesseth of him selfe in an other place, where he saieth, that he was like a calfe, and a beast, without reason or wisedome. And if it went so with him, with him I say, that was so excellent a Prophet, what shall become of vs? I say then that the elder sort ought greatly to profite in this schoole of Gods wisedome: and yet this is no vaine thing, whereunto Dauid here especially exhorteth the yongemen. And why so? For as I haue already sayde, this age is so without any consideration, as nothing can be more, and is much subiect to the temptations of Satan, and of the flesh. And on the other side, ouer and besides that, there is neither iudgement nor wisedome in yongmen, in so much that they are so stirred vp with heate, as that their boiling affections breake out: Yet in steade of hauing some modestie, & to take in good part the admonitions which might be giuen them, they will be the more loftie and stubborne, which might take better occasion to be more grieued in beeing reprehended or rebuked.

Psal. 73. 22.

And

And that this is true, we see at this day howe all things are out of order. This is sure, that the true vertue which should be in youth, is modestie: and that the younger sorte ought to knowe that since they are not furnished with wisdome and discretion as the elder sorte are, they ought to heare them, and not to be giuen ouer to their owne will and wit. This is the moste principall wisedome that ought to bee in young men. But what? they are at this day past all shame. By this we may see that the worlde is euen as it were vtterly desperate, and that we are growen to the fulnesse of all mischiefe and iniquitie. For wee shall see these beastly and gracelesse boyes and wenches, which scarsely are able too wype their owne noses, as we say, yea and that might yet be vnder the rod ten yeeres, like peeuish wretches as they are, that when so euer they shalbe spoken vnto, wil make no reckoning of whatsouer is said, but poute and mowe at it, counterfaiting the very Apes and Monkeyes, as dayly wee may see. And when we see such extreame pride in this people, what shall wee say but that Satan hath euen possessed them? and that they will shew themselues as in deede they are, to weete, without all amendment? So then, this point is so much the more to be wel considered of, when as hee saith: *Wherwithall shall a young man addresse his wayes by taking heede thereto according to thy worde.* True it is, that a great many which haue neede heere to be tolde this geere, care not for filling of their eares with any such matter, they haue knowledge inough too keepe them selues from the Church: For they haue the thing which they desire when they may be at the Tauerne, playing and Dauncing. But what? It is certaine that this doctrine will not leaue them vncondemned when as God cryeth vnto them, as hee witnesseth by Solomon, where he bringeth in Wisedome saying, I haue cryed out, and put foorth my voyce in the streetes, I haue bidden both great & small, to the end that men might heare mee, and none hath vouchsafed too receiue me, ne yet to giue me lodging. When God declareth vnto vs, that our life shall be well ordered if wee keepe his words,

Prou. 1. 20.21.22.23.

The second Sermon of M. I. Cal.

word, surely as many as flye from this doctrine and admonition, shall render an account at the last day, because God hath called them. And also because they haue not only bin deafe, but also haue added this mischiefe, to flye from the admonitions, which Gods word admonished them off, to bring them againe into the way of saluation, from whiche they were strayed. It is especially sayd, *Yea, by taking heede thereto according to thy worde*. Dauid his meaning is heere to expresse vnto vs, that we may make our selues beleeue, that we haue wisedome and discretion inough. But yet it shall profite vs no whit at all, without we will bee gouerned and ruled by God, according to that which hath beene before saide. Nowe it followeth:

With my whole hearte haue I sought thee: let mee not wander from thy Commaundementes.

Dauid heere maketh a notable confession, which is not common to all men, That hee hath sought God with his whole heart. For although we haue a desire to goe to God, yet it is so feeble as is lamentable, seeing we are withdrawn with so many vanities; by reason the world hath such dominion ouer vs, and yet ought not to retire our selues frō any good deuotion, whē as we haue had a through feeling therof. There are very few of vs that are able to say with the prophet Dauid, that we haue sought God with our whole hart: to wit, with such integritie and purenesse, that we haue not turned away from that marke, as from the most principall thing of our saluation. It is very true, that Dauid had not yet any such perfection, but that hee slacked in the fight against the prickings of the fleshe, and went back.

Rom. 7. 19. 20.

Saint Paule also confesseth that hee went too God as it were halting, that he did not that good which hee woulde & desired, but that he was encompassed with his naturall vices, to doe the euill which he condemned. Dauid was not without such temptations: but howsoeuer it was, it is most certaine that the principall matter wherto he bent himself, was to serue God. Now as I haue before said, we are all farr from this example. For as many of vs as at this day are best affected

affected, may be letted and hindered by a number of vices, vaine cares of this world, & with lusts & desires of the flesh, that if we should remoue our foote euery day too goe one pace forward, it were much and yet it may come so to passe often times, that we would drawe back againe to the place from whence we came. And yet notwithstanding, Dauid, after hee had protested that he sought God with his whole hearte, besought God that he would not suffer him to decline from his Commaundementes. Heereby let vs see what great neede we haue to call vpon God, too the ende he may holde vs with a mightie stronge hand. Yea, and although hee hath already mightely put too his helping hand, and we also knowe that he hath bestowed vppon vs great and manifolde graces: yet is not this all: But there are so many vices and imperfections in our nature, and wee so feeble and weake, as that we haue very greate neede dayly to pray vnto him, yea and that more and more, that hee will not suffer vs to decline from his Commaundementes: For although Dauid protested that hee sought God with all his heart, neuertheleffe, hee addeth, yet suffer mee not O Lorde too goe wronge from thy Commaundementes: What shall we doe then? Let vs also learne to walke carefully: for since hee is the God which giueth vs that good minde to wil, and that also giueth vs the power too performe, and all of his meere fauour and grace: wee ought (sayth Saint Paule) to walke in feare, and to keepe good watch, too the ende that Satan taketh not vs vnprouided, and that he enter not within vs. *Phil. 2. 18.*

And loe what is the cause that wee haue seene some men which haue made a greate shewe of holinesse for a time, and haue seemed too bee more like Angels then men, which at length haue growne too outrage: and haue so greatly excceded their boundes, as that G O D euen forsooke them, like desperate men. And whence then proceedeth this? Verily from their owne securytie and negligence, becaufe they thought them selues to bee very perfect. But Paule is cleane contrary to this, for thus he
sayth,

The second Sermon of M.I.Cal.

Phil.3 12.

sayth, I haue not attayned as yet to that ful perfection, neuerthelesse I haue doone what in me lyeth. When he saythe, I haue doone what in me lyeth, he declareth that there was that humilitie in him, whereof he spake in the place before by me already alleaged: and this humilitie importeth, that we should call vpon God as Dauid did, as he sheweth vnto vs heere in this place.

It followeth: *I haue hid thy promise within my heart: that I might not sinne against thee.*

When Dauid speaketh after this manner, I haue hid thy word or promise in mine heart, he wel declareth that if we haue but only a wandring knowledge, that the same wil not holde vs in, but that the Deuil hath by and by woone vpon vs to oppresse vs, with temptations, and in the ende to cast vs downe hedlong. What must wee then doe? It is not inough that we haue beene at church, and heard what hath bin there said vnto vs, and that euery of vs hath mumbled vp vnto himselfe some one thing or another, but the word of God must be setled in vs and be hid in our heart, to wit, that it may there be resiaunt and continually abyding: and to haue receiued it with such an affection, as that it bee as it were imprinted in vs. If this be not so, sinne will reigne in vs, for it hath by nature his habitation with vs: For all our senses are wicked and corrupt, all our willes and desires are enemyes vnto God, vnlesse Gods woord be wel hidden in our heartes. Moreouer, we are to vnderstande, that Dauid heere vaunted not himselfe of his owne power & strength, as though he were in admiration thereof: but the spirite of God speaking by his mouth, entendeth to giue vs a glasse, wherein we must be confirmed, to weete, that we must not haue onely our eares beaten with the Doctrine of saluation, and receiue it in our braine: but that it should be hidden in our heart, to wit, that we should lay it vp as in a Treasure house. For this saying, to hide, importeth that Dauid studyed not to be ambitious to set foorth him selfe, and to make a glorious shew before men: but that he had God for a witnesse of that secret desire which was within him.

Hee

vpon the Cxix. Psalme. 15

Hee neuer looked to worldly creatures, but beeing content that he had so great a Treasure, he knewe full wel that God who had giuen it him, would so surely and safely garde it, as that it should not be layd open to Satan to be taken away. Saint Paule also declareth vnto vs, that the chest wherein this treasure must be hid, is a good conscience. For it is said, that many beeing voyde of this good conscience, haue lost also their faith, and haue beene robbed thereof. As if a man shoulde forsake his goods and put them in aduenture, without shutting of any dore, it were an easy matter for theeues to come in and to reaue and spoyle him of all: Euen so, if wee leaue at randon too Satan the Treasure which GOD hath giuen vnto vs in his word, without it be hidden in this good conscience, and in the very bottome of our hearte as Dauid heere speaketh, we shalbe spoiled thereof. He addeth immediatly after:

1. Tim. 1. 19.

Blessed art thou O Lorde: O teach me thy statutes.

After he had sayd, I haue sought thee with mine whole heart: hee addeth, *Blessed art thou O Lorde: O teach mee thy Statutes.* Dauid sheweth in this verse, that the request which he made here afore, is not founded or grounded of any merite or desert which he pretended to haue. In very deede, at the first sight it might be said, that Dauid ment that God would not forsake him, because he had sought him, & thervpon conclude that man must first beginne to goe on, too preuent Gods grace, and then that God wil afterward aide him. Yee see heere what men may imagine, but this is not Dauids meaning and purpose. And to proue it to be so, it is moste sure, hee attributeth it not to his owne power and strength, that he had sought God with his whole heart, for we must first be touched with the spirite of God, when as we haue any such affection. And why so? For by nature we haue all strayed from God, and all our force, power, and study, bende them selues to estraunge vs from him. And therefore wee must come vnto him in such sorte as is declared vnto vs in many places of the holy Scripture. Dauid then was preuented already by Gods grace, and hee onely

requireth

The second Sermon of M. Io. Cal.

requireth of God to continue the same in him which hee hath begunne, for he knewe right well that hee had greate neede thereof. As if he should haue said, I know very wel O Lord, that thou hast already mightily put too thy helping hand by thy holy spirit, when as I sought thee: in very deed I had neuer done it, without I had beene conducted by thy holy hand, neither is this yet inough, except thou continue the same in me: & when thou shalt so doe O Lord, all praise and glory shalbe thine for the same, because thou hast done it of thy meere fauour and grace.

   By this then we may see, that Dauid heere meaneth not to glorifie himselfe as beeing puffed vp with his owne vertues and merites: But because God deserueth to be blessed and exalted to the end that we shoulde render vnto him all honor and glory. See now wherefore hee assureth himselfe that he will teach him, and that he shall be more and more confirmed in that doctrine which he hath already learned. For when he sayth, Teach me thy Statutes O Lord: it was not because that he was altogither rude and ignorant, that hee coulde bee nowe a Nouice, which was a Prophet, had charge to instruct others, and was also a King. Dauid then spake not as one that was vnlearned: but hee knewe well inough that all this was not sufficient, without hee profited still more and more. Now if Dauid spake after this manner, I beseech you what ought we to do? When soeuer then that we would obtaine this grace at Gods hands, to be instructed in his statutes, let vs bring this reason vnto him, & ground our selues vpon this, to wit, that he be blessed and prayfed. And aboue all things, let vs vnderstand the great neede we haue heereof: that is, that although wee haue already beene instructed in the holy Scripture, that wee must be Scholers vnto the ende, and too pray vnto God dayly to encrease our fayth: I meane such chiefely as are appointed too preach the woorde. True it is, that it were a meruelous great presumption for any man too come into the Pulpit, and to vsurpe the office of a Preacher, excepte hee were well studyed in the holy Scripture. But so it is that

wee

vpon the Cxix. Pſalme. 16

wee goe vpp in the Pulpit dayly, with this condition too learne, when as we teach others. And beeing thus, I doo not onely ſpeake that I might bee hearde: but for mine owne parte I muſt alſo bee the Scholer of God, and that the word which proceedeth from my mouth might profite my ſelfe likewiſe, otherwiſe curſed am I. Let vs then note this by the way, that they which are moſte perfecte and ready in the Scriptures, are arrogaunt fooles, except they acknowledge that they had neede too haue God for their Schoolemaiſter all the dayes of their life, and to bee more and more confirmed, after the example of Dauid.

In very deede theſe things very well deſerue to bee ſpoken of more at large, but that I reſpecte one thing, that in handling of this Pſalme by parcels, it may be imprinted the better in our memory. For as I haue ſayde in the firſt Sermon which I made on Sunday laſt paſt, that it is not without cauſe, that the ſpirite of God would haue this Pſalme to be made according to the Letters of an A. B. C. becauſe euery one ſhould learne it as perfectly as their Pater Noſter, as wee commonly ſay. Seeing then that our Lorde God would that we ſhoulde haue this Pſalme perfectly, and for our owne vſe, it is alſo good and neceſſary that the handling of it be pure and ſimple, and ſo to follow the plainneſſe of the text, as that wee might vnderſtand as it were worde by worde, whatſoeuer is contayned therein. It remayneth now, that euery of vs vnderſtand what hath byn handled, without looking after any longer repetition. Neuertheleſſe I will ſo endeuour my ſelfe to be ſhorte, as that (God willing) the woords which I ſhal vtter ſhall not bee very darke, eſpecially to thoſe which be attentiue.

It followeth: *With my lippes haue I declared all the Iudgementes of thy mouth.*

Dauid ſheweth heere the accorde which ought to be betwixt God & vs: to wit, that god hath inſtructed vs, & when we haue heard that which hath bin ſaide vnto vs, that euery one ſhould ſay Amen, & that there bee a ſweete harmony & accorde betwixt him & vs, without iar or contradiction.

Loe

The second Sermon of M. Io. Cal.

Loe heere in summe that which is ment in this verse. Nowe in the meane while we haue to note, that Dauid declareth that he contenteth not himselfe alone with following of God and cleauing vnto him: but that he laboureth and desireth asmuch as in him lyeth, to stirre vpp his neighboures likewise, and to bring it so to passe, as that God might bee serued with a common accorde, throughout the whole worlde. He then that will haue a true zeale to honor God, will not thinke onely of himselfe, but will haue an eye euery where, and seeke by all meanes possible that he can, too redresse those which are wickedly giuen, to stirre vpp those which are colde and negligent, to strengthen those which are weake and feeble, to entertaine those which are already in a good forwardnesse, and to make them more forwarde. Loe heere whereunto all the faithfull haue an eye. For the Lord our God teacheth vs vpon this condition, that euery of vs thinke not onely particularly of himselfe, but that wee should also haue a mutuall care one of another, and whensoeuer we shall haue this zeale, let vs vnderstand, that God hath created the whole worlde vppon this condition, that we all should be obedient vnto him. But we must wel way the order that is heere set downe: For Dauid beginneth not with this sentence, That with his lippes he hath tolde of all the Iudgementes of the Lordes mouth. For he hath sayde before, that he hath hid them in his hart. The thing which Dauid said to be hid in his hearte, he soone after declareth it with his mouth, wherin he sheweth that euery of vs ought to beginne with himselfe. When wee meane too instruct and teach our neighbours, we must not say vnto them, Go you before: but, Come next after me, or else harde by me: and hauing care all to goe the right way, wee should all atonce labour to goe togither to our God, to be conioyned vnto him in true fayth. And I speake it too this ende, because wee shall see many who in this behalfe can very well prattle and babble, and would seeme to be the greatest doctors in the world. But what of all this? Let vs in the meane time locke into their liues and conuersation, and wee shall
finde

vpon the Cxix. Pſalme. 17

finde in them nothing but infection and ſtench, nothinge elſe but mocking of God in all they goe about and doe.

We muſt therfore followe the order which Dauid here holdeth: to witte, that the word of God bee hid as a Treaſure in the bottome of our heart: and afterward when as we ſhall haue this affection, let vs indeuour our ſelues to draw others alſo thereto, and goe altogither with one accorde to honour our Lorde God: and that hee which hath beene better taught then any of his neighboures haue beene, let him confeſſe that hee is ſo much the more beholden and bound vnto God, to doo that which is heere ſhewed vnto vs by Dauid. For although wee are not all Prophetes as hee was, yet for all that, this was ſpoken to vs all in general, Admoniſh ye one another. Saint Paule ſpeaketh it too all the faithfull and to all Chriſtians. And that we ſhould alſo knowe that this belongeth and appertaineth too vs: and chiefely as I haue before ſayde, that they which are moſte forwarde, ſhoulde lay foorth the grace which was giuen vnto them for the common building vpp of the Church, and inſtruction of their neighbours. It followeth:

1.Theſſa.5. 14.
Collo.3.16.
Heb.3.13.

I haue had as great delight in the way of thy teſtimonyes, as in all manner of riches.

Heere Dauid declareth that hauing wayned him ſelfe from his earthly affections, wherwithall we are ouer greatly intangled, he wholly traueleth to come to God. For it is impoſſible for vs too taſte the ſweeteneſſe conteyned in the worde of God, to take pleaſure in this doctrine of our ſaluation, and to bee altogither giuen therevnto, before ſuch time as we haue cut off from vs, all our wicked luſtes and affections which reigne too too much in our mortall bodyes. It is like as if a man woulde haue land to bringe foorth Corne, which were altogither full of thornes and weedes. Or what is he that would haue a Vine growe vpon ſtones and rockes, wherein is no moyſture? For what is the ſtate of the nature of man? Forſoth it is as barré land as poſſibly can be. What are al our affectiōs, but buſhes, thornes, and weedes, which choke and make all the good ſeede of

C. God

The second Sermon of M. Jo. Cal.

God nothing worth? So then, it is not without cause that Dauid heere matcheth riches with the worde of God, and this auarice wherwith we are led and inflamed, against the desire that hee had too followe God, and too walke after his word. As if he should haue sayd, Alas Lord, it is true that I am giuen to the vanities of this world aswel as others are: But yet haue I chiefely desired thy word, & haue euen striuen with my self to subdue al the euil affections of my flesh. Here we see what doctrin we haue to gather vnto our selues out of this place: to wit, that if we wil be the good scholers of God, and take delight in the way of his testimonyes, we must first subdue the lustes of our fleshe, & not learne to be giuen to worldly things, neither yet to bee nousled in that which we imagine to be the highest pointe of our felicity: but that we might vnderstand to conténe riches, & al other things whatsoeuer, which might withdrawe vs from our God and our sauiour Iesus Christ, to make no more accoūt of it then of doung and dyrt, as S. Paule saith, And yet it is most sure that Dauid contemneth not the riches which he had. For beeing a mightie rich king, as we know, yet he cast not his Golde & siluer into the bottō of the sea, but vsed of the abundance & store which God had giuen him: yea wee see what an excellent and beautiful house he had, as the holy history telleth vs. But yet he followed the rule which the Scripture setteth downe vnto vs: which is, that hee so vsed the goods of this world, as though he neuer had them. We must therfore passe through this world, without staying our selues altogether in it, as S. Paul exhorteth: that if God giue vs abundāce of riches, we might know how to vse thē, with out hauing our harts imprisoned in them: & yet notwithstāding to be pore in spirit: to wit, to be redy to forsake all whatsoeuer, as often as god would haue vs to be rid of thē, & to haue alwaies one foote redy lifted vp to go vnto him, whēsoeuer it shalbe his wil & pleasure to take vs out of this world. But it is not without cause that Dauid hath spoken heere of the abundaunce of riches. For wee see it maketh men couetous, which is the springhead of all mischiefe, as

Phil. 3. 8.

1. Cor. 7. 31.

Saint

Saint Paule faith. Forafmuch then as we are so much giuen 1. Tim. 6.10. to the goods of this worlde, and that we holde our selues accurfed if we haue not wherwithall, and them to bee blessed which are wel furnished with them: let vs keepe well the lesson which is heere taught vs: to wit, that all our desier must be in the way of the testimonyes of God, as in all manner of riches: to wit, that all our delight and contentation be wholly in them. Now in the end Dauid goeth on and fayth, *I will meditate in thy Commaundementes and consider thy wayes.*

My delight shalbe in thy statutes: & I wil not forget thy words. This is the conclusion, to confirme the matter which we haue already spoken off. For Dauid heere speaketh of no newe matter, but protesteth as he hath begun: That his delight shalbe alwayes in the commandements of God, & in the doctrine conteined in the holy Scripture, and that hee wil bestowe his whole study therin, & so continue the same and neuer forget the desires which he hath to profite in the obedience of God. If Dauid nowe hath thus saide, let vs vnderstand that it is not inough for vs to be wel affected to serue God, and that for the performing thereof that wee haue already sufficiently traueled: but we must also be pricked forwarde, that we might alwayes goe on. For euen the very faithful, neuer runne with so feruent and hote a desire, but that they continually draw one leg after them, & neuer come vnto God but in halting wise. What is there then for vs to doe? Forsooth wee must protest with Dauid, neuer to forget that which God hath once declared vnto vs, and also neuer to ceafe to pricke our selues on, to the ende there might be greater vehemencie in vs to goe vnto him, with a more feruent desire and boulder courage. So that at the last we may growe to this perfection, whereunto God calleth & allureth vs: that is, that beeing vncased from out of our flesh and nature, hee might fully conioyne vs vnto his righteousnesse, that thereby his glory may shine in vs.

And according to this holy doctrine, let vs prostrate our selues before the face of our good god, acknowledging our

innume-

The third Sermon of M. Jo. Cal.

innumerable sinnes, by which we continually prouoke his heauy wrath, and indignation against vs. Beseeching him that it would please him to make vs to feele our sinnes and iniquities, more then euer tofore we haue done, to the end we might seke for such remedies as he hath ordained for vs in exercising our selues about the reading of his holy word, and the dayly Preaching thereof which hath graunted vnto vs. And furthermore not to forget to stir vs vp to call vpon him, to the end that by his holy spirite he might to put his helping hande euen in our heartes, and not too suffer the doctrine which we heare by the mouth of his Preachers, to become vnprofitable vnto vs, but that it may haue the full power & strength: so that we may from day to day be confirmed therein: and more and more learne to forsake the worlde, and all what souer may withdrawe vs from the vnion and coniunction of our Lord and Maister Iesus Christ, who is our heade. And that hee will not onely shewe vnto vs this fauour and grace, but also vnto all people and nations of the earth. &c.

The third Sermon of the hundreth and nineteenth Psalme.

GIMEL.

Bee beneficiall vnto thy Seruant: that I may liue & keepe thy woorde,

Open mine eies, that I may see the wondrous things of thy lawe,

I am a straunger vpon Earth: hide not thy commandements from me.

My hart breaketh out: for the desire vnto thy iudgementes alwaies.

Thou hast destroyed the proude: cursed are they that doo erre from all thy Commaundements.

Remoue

vpon the Cxix. Pſalme. 19

Remoue from mee ſhame and contempte: for I haue kept thy Teſtimonyes.
Princes alſo did ſitte and ſpeake againſt mee: but thy Seruant did meditate in thy ſtatutes.
Alſo thy Teſtimonyes are my delight and my counſaylers.

IT ſhall greatly haue profited vs, if ſo be wee haue learned what the ende of our life is. For, for that cauſe, hath God placed, and bringeth vs vpp in the worlde: and yet fewe there are which thinke vpon it. True it is, that euery man will ſay, that it is good reaſon wee ſhould doe homage too GOD for our life and beeing, becauſe wee holde all of him: and that wee ſhould glorifie him with ſo mnch of our goods as he hath largely beſtowed vpon vs. But what of all this? When as wee haue confeſſed that, it is but to ſhewe our ingratitude and vnthankfulneſſe: and yet no man maketh any account heereof. Loe heere, wherefore the holy Ghoſte, ſeeing vs ſo tyed to the worlde, putteth vs in minde too what ende wee liue heere. As heere Dauid maketh this requeſt to God too obtayne that benefite of his Maieſtie: *That hee might liue and keepe his woorde*: As if hee ſhould haue ſayde, I deſire not O Lorde to liue for my ſelfe alone in this worlde, to receiue heere my pleaſures and commodyties: but deſire it too an other more precious and excellent end than that: to wit, that I might ſerue thee. Euen ſo then, as often as we are deſirous to liue, we muſt remember vs of this requeſt which Dauid maketh: That is, that we ſhoulde not be like vnto brute beaſtes, lyuing wee knowe not to what end: but that we ſhould alwayes ayme at this marke, to honour GOD. For without this wee

C.3.   are

are more miserable then all the rest of his creatures. Euery creature will followe his owne naturall inclination: and albeit that brute beastes haue an hard and irkesome life, yet notwithstanding they are not in their kinde so tormented & greeued as we are. We know & feele by experience, that our euill desires and lusts, are like hot burning furnaces, so that we neede no body to persecute and vexe vs, for ther is none of vs all, but can tel wel inough how to greeue & vex our selues one with ambitiō, another with couetousnes, & some with fornication & adultery. So thē our life should be very accursed if we looked no farther. But we must alwayes aime at this marke, to serue God, & to keepe his word. For when as all our affection and loue shal reste in it, then shall our life be blessed. But contrariwise, when we are so brutish as to desire nothing else but to liue heere a long time, & to haue none other care but of our body, and this temporall life: the longer we liue heere in the world, the more do we heape vppon vs the malediction and curse of God. Let vs then keepe in minde this prayer which Dauid heere maketh: to wit, that he beseecheth God to bestowe that benefite vpon him, that he might keepe his commandement all the dayes of his life. As if he should haue said, Alas my God, I see vs to bee so peruerse and frowarde, as that none of vs all thinketh to what ende we liue. And we are so giuen to all sinne and wickednesse, that wee doo nothing else but more and more prouoke thy heauy wrath and indignation against vs. Suffer me not O Lorde to be one of that company, but graunt vnto me thy grace, that my life may bee ruled and gouerned as it ought to bee : that is, That I may employ my selfe wholy to serue and honour thee. It followeth by and by after.

> *Open mine eyes, that I may see the woendrous things of thy lawe.*

Heere he declareth that it was not without cause, that he made this request vnto God: For if it were in our power to follow the word of God, and keepe it, it were meere hypocrysie and feyned holinesse to make any such prayer. For

For we craue at Gods hand that which we haue not: and in our Prayers we must alwayes confesse our pouertie and want. Were it not a mockery thinke you, too craue of God the thing which I haue already? I shall beseech him to giue it me, and I haue it already in my possession?

It is moste true, that wee must craue that at Gods hande which already wee haue. And why so? Becaufe wee are certaine that wee cannot inioy it, nor yet vse the same without his grace and fauour: And that the vse thereof shall neuer profite vs without he blesse it, euen as we desire of him our dayly Breade. And although the table be couered, and the meate sette ready on the boorde, yet we desire of God to make it noutishment for our bodyes. Wherby, as I haue before sayde, it shall profite vs no whit at all, without God blesse it through his grace and liberalitie. It is very so that we doe craue it, by reason of our continuall confessing of our want and neede.

So then, it cannot possibly bee, that this was in Dauid his owne hand and power, to keepe the woorde of God. And he sheweth it to be so in this which followeth, *O Lorde open thou mine eyes*. As if hee should haue saide, Alas deere father, it is so farre off that I am able to keepe thy worde, as that I should not be able to vnderstand any whit thereof, if thou guidest mee not thereto: For it is thou which must both beginne the same, & also performe it wholy in me. This is the way and meanes for vs to vnderstande what to doe: For many there are which knowe the thinge that is good, and yet for all that they vtterly refuse it. Nowe Dauid declareth, that he is not onely voyde of all power too keepe the word of God: but also that hee is without all vnderstanding, except it be giuen him by the holy Ghost. Let vs note well who it is that speaketh Euen Dauid a most excellent Prophet. And yet for all that wee see that hee declareth (yea and that boldely) him selfe to bee ignoraunte, without GOD instructeth him. Neither dooth hee heere speake of any worldely instruction, as wee woulde imagine of the thinges whiche wee knewe not

The third Sermon of M. Io. Cal.

of before. Dauid confesseth, that all that, would serue him to no purpose at all, without God, added therunto a notabler or more excellent thing: to wit, that hee did enlighten him with his holy spirite.

Sithens then it is so that Dauid, who was an excellente Prophet, did knowe, that hee could neither by reading nor preaching vnderstand that which was requisite vnto saluation: what shall become of vs, which are yet farre from that forwardnesse that was in him? And let vs not thinke that through our owne labour and industrie, and by our owne sharpnesse of wit, to come so farre as to vnderstande the secretes of God, but let vs knowe that wee had neede to be inlightned with the grace of his holy spirit, to open our eyes, for without it we are poore blinde soules. Nowe if this were wel vnderstood, we should neuer see such a pride amongst vs as is, that euery of vs is wise inough too gouerne himselfe. It is an easy matter for vs to make protestation that God hath giuen vs his word: and yet for all that we shall still be blinde, and knowe nothing, vntill such time as he openeth our heartes and mindes. For when nothing else shal gouerne vs but our own sense and naturall reason, what beastes and Calues shall wee then bee? See then how we shall be better instructed in humilitie, when as the doctrine shalbe imprinted in our heartes. True it is, that this was not spoken in vaine, but to the end, that we shoulde be admonished after the example of Dauid, too present oure selues before God: and in confessing our selues that we are not capable to vnderstande any thing, without that he put to his helping hand, let vs beseeche him too open our eyes by his holy spirit. And bicause it should not seeme straunge, that Dauid desired to haue his eyes open, he declareth, that the wisdom conteined in the lawe of God, is too high for our capacities, yea although we think oure selues to haue neuer so sharpe and fine wittes. And therefore hee sayeth, *O Lorde open myne eyes: that I may see the woonderous thinges of thy Lawe*. Wherefore vseth hee this woorde woonderous? It is, as if he would haue ~~fane~~ saide: Although

the

the world taketh the lawe of God to be but a light thing, and seemeth to be giuen but as it were for simple soules, & yong children: Yet for al that there seemeth such a wisedom to bee in it, as that it surmounteth all the wisedome of the worlde, and that therein lye hidde wonderfull secrets.

As much is saide of the Gospell, and that not without great cause. And in very deede, that which at this daye is most plainely declared in the Gospell, was before conteined in the lawe: onely these were darker shadowes, then they are, which were since the comming of our Lord Iesus Christ. And yet notwithstanding, there is no chaung or alteration in this wisedome, as God also is not mutable. It is not then without cause that all the holy scripture is called wisedome, and that the Angels of heauen theselues do wonder thereat. If then the Angels be astoyned at the secrets conteined in the holy scripture, I beseeche you tell mee, what reuerence deserueth it to haue among vs mortall men? For we are but poore wormes vpon earth, creeping here belowe. If there be comparison made betwixt vs and the Angels, what shall it be? See howe the Angels are wonderfully rauished to see the wisedome of the word of God, and yet we make no accompt of it, but esteeme of it as a base and childish thing. The more therefore ought wee throughly to marke this saying of Dauid, that the doctrine of the lawe is not as wee take it to bee: to wit, a thing of small valure, or a common and ordinarie doctrine, but a wonderfull wisedome, wherein are such secrets as ought to rauish vs with admiration, bicause they farre surpasse our wit and reason. But what is the cause that we so lightly esteeme of the lawe of God? that is to say, his whole word? Herein the common prouerbe is verified when we saye, A foole regardeth nothing. Which prouerbe we declare to be rightly verified in vs! For many of vs make no estimation of the holy scripture, & it seemeth to vs, that, that which we reade there, is tooto comon. and this is the reason, bicause we know not what it is, ne yet the great and abundant treasure hidde therein. But such as haue once knowen what

Ephes. 3. 10.
1. Pet. 1. 12.

the

the Maiestie of God is, which hee sheweth and declareth him selfe to be there, and do see whether it is, that God calleth and allureth them, and do also vnderstand and knowe the large and sweete promises offered vnto them therein, such I say, will say with Dauid, O Lorde, thy law is wonderfull. And so consequently will desire that their eyes might be lightened, confessing them selues to be blind, vntill such time as God hath ayded them with his holy spirite. Now it followeth,

I am a stranger vpon earth: hyde not thy commandementes from me.

When Dauid did put to this verse, he ment to confirme the matter which before he touched, that is to say, that he desired not simply to liue, as if his life had beene deare and precious vnto him, without any other respect: but he had a further meaning. For he saith by and by after, I am a stranger in the world: therefore hyde not thy commandements from me: They which make their continuall nest here according to their owne fansie, and thinke to make their heauen in this world, these men I say, haue nothing to do with the commandementes of God for their saluation. For they are safe enough if they may eate and drinke to be glutted, that they may take their pleasures and delightes, that they may be honoured, that they may be in estimation and credit: loe here is all that they desire or wysh to haue. Yea forsooth: For they looke no further, but to this corruptible and transitorie life. These men I saye are not greatly troubled, ne yet haue any care of the commaundementes of God, but when as they shalbe taken from them, all shall be one to them. When as the couetous man, the whoremonger, the dronkarde, the ambitious person, shall heare no preaching of the word at all: neither any talke of God, ne yet of Christianitie, nor of life euerlasting. He in the meane time ceaseth not to pursue his owne waye. Yea, and it is to them a lothsome and vnpleasant kinde of speach to heare God spoken of, but had rather haue no mention in the whole worlde made of him. And therefore it is not without cause why Dauid requireth, not to haue the cōmandements

ments of God taken from him, & this is his reason: to wit, bicause he is a stranger on the earth. As if he should haue sayd, O Lord, if I had none other consideration but of this present life, I should be euen accursed, and it had beene better my mother had beene deliuered of me as of a dead body, and that I had beene an hundred times plunged in hell. And why so? For we are here in this world but as pilgrims and wayfaring men: and we passe to a more excellent life: as to that also wherein we repose our whole trust. Seeing then, O Lord, that I am a stranger in the world, let not thy commandementes be taken away from me. Nowe in this part is conteined a very profitable doctrine, and exhortation for vs, for we knowe how cold wee are, wherein deede we ought to haue an ardent desire to be taught the worde of God, and to be more and more confirmed therein. And I beseeche you how carelesse are we? But what is the cause hereof? No doubt of it, we must alwayes euen searche and looke into the depth and bottom of this corruption and mischiefe: for when we see any vice in our selues, we ought to enquire from whence the cause proceedeth, to the ende we might finde remedy for the same. Now the reason is, bicause we are blynde, and do suppose our abode should bee here still vpon earth, and euery man imagineth him selfe to haue here euerlasting life. Wherefore when we are thus giuen to the world, & thinke our selues to haue here an euerlasting enheritance, loe this is the cause of our thus contēning of God and his word, or rather that we care no whit at all for the seeking out of the doctrine of our saluation. What must we then do? Forsooth wee must looke a great deale farther then to the world, if we will come vnto God, and be exercised in this study wherof mētion is here made, and to say with Dauid, O Lord, bicause we are strangers in this world, to wit, that we are to passe here only, & that nothing can be shorter then our life is here, let not thy commandements be taken away from vs. On thother side, Dauid his meaning here, is to signifie vnto vs, that he was but as a poore pilgrime and wandring man, without he were conducted and guided by the worde of God,

And

The third Sermon of M. I. Cal.

And this is a very fit similitude for the purpose. We know that a man in a straung countrey, will thinke him self to be a straung and forlorne man, so that if he hath not a conduct and guide, he knoweth not what shall become of him. Euē so fareth it with vs, if we be not directed and conducted by the hand and power of God. And why so? Bicause we are as strangers here in this world. It is very true, that wee are but too too much tied vnto our affections and wil, and yet out alas, our sense and wittes are so confounded, that wee know not what way to take or holde, except we be shewed it. Loe here the meaning of the similitude which Dauid here vseth, in saying that he is a strāger in the world: which is, that he complaineth that he is a strang and forlorne mā, and therefore beseecheth God to guide him by his worde. Now it followeth.

My hart breaketh out, for the desire, vntoo thy iudgementes alwaies.

When hee sayeth, that his soule breaketh out, it is too protest, that hee desired not that thing of God which wee haue hearde, either for fashions sake, or countenance, as many doo, which beseeche God very often too inlighten, confirme, and guide them, in the trueth of his woorde: but in the meane tyme, they neuer seeke after it as they should do. Now, this is but after a sorte, and God wil not be thus mocked. For in thus doing, we doe nothing els but profane his holy name, whē as we make such requestes, as proceede not from a true affection and desire. Loe here, wherefore Dauid saieth, that his soule brake out: For this worde emporteth as much as if his soule had vtterly fainted. My soule then fainteth for the desire which it had to thy cōmaundementes. Wherfore here are three things to be cōsidered off.

The one is, that if we will obtaine at Gods handes to be conducted by him, and to haue his worde to be our waye and direction, we should not make such an hypocritical nor cold prayer vnto him, with mocking of him thereby: But with such a true desire as carieth vs euen out of our selues, and to make no such accompt of this present life, but to be

well

well aduifed, to fhoote at an higher matter. And thus much as touching the firft point, which here we haue to note.

The fecond is, that this defire, ought not to be onely as a wauering defire, but an ardent and an hoat defire. For he faith, That his foule hath fainted. And why fo? Let vs here a little confider, what our appetites and luftes are, when wee turne our felues away from God, and giue our felues wholy to worldly things. They are fo excefsiue and inordinate, that it is euen pitifull, being without end and meafure. But if we haue a leane defire, & fuch a one as I know not what, to walke according to the will of God: this defire woulde be as foone alayed, as a droppe of wine put into an hundreth times fo much water. I befeeche you what fhall that be? fhall it tafte any more as wine? Euen fo forcible fhould the good affection of a faithfull man be. If this affection be not feruent, and very vehement, it fhalbe foone choked by the corruptions of our carnall pafsions & affections which (as I haue before faid) haue neither meafure, modeftie, nor temperance. See then for the fecond point what we haue here to note in this behalf, to wit, that it is not enough that we haue a meane defire to ferue God, for that woulde bee very foone quenched in vs, and be made nothing woorth. But we muft be fo attentiue thereto, as that we may be able to fay that our foule fainteth, and languifheth, that our power and ftrength droppeth and melteth away as it were vntill fuch time as God relieueth vs, in graunting that vnto vs which we require of him.

The third point which we haue here to note, is, the firmenes and conftancie in this our defire. And fee here why Dauid is not contented with this faying, that his foule is broken out: but he faieth, *Alwayes*, As if he fhould haue faide, this was not a blafte of wynde, but a rooted affection in his heart, and that he perfeuered therein. Nowe thefe three things are moft neceffarie: For we fee in the firft place that we are as it were by nature enclined to vanitie, bicaufe that being fo addicted vnto the world, we thinke no whit at all of heauen. We ought therefore to bee fo much the more

very

very attentiue to this doctrine, & to haue a burning desire to follow the word of God: and besides this our affection ought to be so vehement, as that it might be able to haue the dominion ouer all our affections, which hinder vs to cleaue vnto our God, and euē to be marueilously rauished therewith. Now it had neede to be mightely strengthened with the power of the spirite of God: For our lustes beeing too too mad and furious, if God stretched not foorth his arme vnto it, what should become thereof? And put the case that we had a good desire, surely it woulde very soone vanish away in vs. We must then be wōderfull feruent therin, and afterward, when wee shall haue such a good and stedfast affection, we must be wonderfully in loue with the word of God, not for a day, nor yet for a short time, but euen so long as we liue. It followeth soone after.

Thou hast destroyed the proud: cursed are they, that do erre from all thy commaundementes.

Dauid addeth hereto an other reason, whereby hee is more enflamed to praye vnto God, and to addresse him selfe vnto him, to be taught in his word: to wit, when hee seeth that he hath so rebuked the proude: For the chastisements and punishementes which God layeth vppon the faithles and rebellious, shoulde bee a good instruction for vs: As it is said: That God hath executed iudgement, and that the inhabitantes of the land should learne his righteousnes. It is not without cause that the Prophet Esay also hath so said: for he signifieth vnto vs, that God hath by diuers and sundrie meanes drawen vs vnto him, and that chiefly when he teacheth vs to feare his maiestie. For without it, out alas, we shall become like vnto brute beastes, if God laye the bridle in our neckes, what licence we will giue vnto our selues, experience very well teacheth vs. Now God seeing that we are so easily brought to runne at random, sendeth vs examples, bicause he woulde bring vs to walke in feare and carefully.

And for our part, when wee see God to chastise the wicked and disobedient, we should by them take example and instruc-

instruction. Loe here (in summe) what Dauid saieth. Thou O Lorde, hast chastised the disobedient: as if hee shoulde haue saide, True it is, O Lord, that I haue desired, euen with a vehement affection, and true constancie, to cleaue vnto thee, and to thy holy comandementes: But yet had I neede to be more throughly instructed, that I might beware of the punishementes which I haue seene with mine eyes. When I haue seene that thou chastisedst the proude, I haue beene by and by humbled thereby: so much discipline haue I receiued by it, see then nowe why I do beseeche thee, that I might be more carefully and diligently instructed in thy law. If now it was behoouefull for Dauid (who was already so well instructed in the law) to be thus aided for the drawing of him selfe to God, to wit, that hee seeth the vnbeleeuers punished, and God to laye his hand vpon them: I beseeche you tell me, had not we neede of such instruction, & also of a great deale more? And so, as oftentimes as we shal plainely see, God to send his chastisements into the world, to punishe sinne, we ought greatly to consider thereof, and to vnderstande that it commeth not by aduenture or chaunce (as we commonly saye.

And when GOD so striketh the proude and disobedient, let vs consider that he meaneth not to punish their persons, and bodies onely, but to teache vs, to haue a greater regarde to our selues: that wee might bee humbled, to the ende the like fall not vppon vs. For God doeth vs great pleasure, when hee punisheth others, thereby to teache vs to take heede: as also it is great wisedome for a man to beware by the harme of an other according to the olde prouerbe. And so also meaneth God. Let vs then consider of the fauour and grace which he sheweth vnto vs, when as he setteth foorth his iudgementes before vs, it is to aduertise vs of our faultes, to the end we should the better walke in his feare, to obey him: yea, and that he punisheth others for our amendement, as I haue already sayd. And especially he addeth; *Cursed are they, that erre from thy commaundementes,* or that goe wrong.

By

The third Sermon of M. Io. Cal.

By this hee farther declareth and expresseth that which wee haue already shewed, to witte, howe hee hath beene taught to walke according to the will of God, by the punishmentes which lighted vpon the proud and disobediét. And here he maketh this generall conclusion, That all they which erre from the commaundement of God are accursed. Whereupon we are to gather first of all, that the particular iudgementes of God ought not to serue vs for one deede alone: but that we should apply it for a generall instruction all the dayes of our life. As how? When as we see God punish one person:, O, wee must not stay our selues vpon such an act, to say, that God punisheth but one person which deserueth it: but wee must conclude and say (according to that saying of S. Paul) There is no respect of persons with God. Now when he hath punished such a fault, we must then say, that this fault displeaseth him in as many as do committe it. As in an other place he sheweth. Sir hens that God so grieuously punished the children of Israel for Idolatrie, we must conclude that he vtterly abhorreth Idolatrie. As greatly also abhorreth he Lechery, murmuring, & disobedient persons, and horrible & wicked couetousnes. And all this (saith S. Paul) should serue vs for an Image or paterne, to the end, that when we see the like come to passe, we should remember vs of that which is conteined within the holy scripture, and applie it wholy to our own vse and profite. And thus much as touching the first point, which we haue here to note: to wit, that if God punisheth a man, we must gather out of it a generall instruction, and conclude, that all they which go wrong from the commaudementes of God are accursed.

Now we haue to touch the second point, which is also notable: that is, we must not tarrie vntill such time as God scourgeth vs, but beeing aduertised by that which hee hath shewed vs a farre of, wee might preuent the punishmentes and corrections which might light vpon vs in the end.

And this is it which wee must gather vnto our selues in generall, of that which hath beene spoken. That all they which

Rom. 2. 11.

1. Cor. 7. ver. 7. 8. 9. 10.

vpon the Cxix. Psalme.   25

which erre from the commaundementes of God, are accursed.

Moreouer, let vs also in the third place learne, that all the happinesse which we imagine, when wee are farre from God, is nothing but accursed, and that in the ende the sentence of our Lord Iesus must be accomplished, Cursed are ye which laughe, for ye shall weepe, and your laughter shall be turned into gnashing of teeth. Let vs then vnderstand, that whiles the poore worlde maketh it selfe mery, and that it seemeth to be come euen to the full aboundance of the wisshes and desires, and that it hath obteined the chiefe felicitie, that it is euen then vnder the greatest and chiefest curse. And why so? For all they which stray from God, are accursed, bicause that hee is the fountaine of all goodnes, and without him there is nothing but all miserie. True it is, that for a time hee suffereth the infidels and vnbeleeuers to make them selues mery, that we might thinke them to be the happiest people in the worlde, but what of that? It will all returne to their greater confusion. It followeth soone after, *Luk. 6, 1. 25.*

Remooue from me shame and contempte: for I haue kept thy testimonies.

Here Dauid commenceth a newe suite vnto God, to wit, that he would hold him in his innocencie and puritie. And it is not without cause that he so doeth, for we see that they which serue God with their whole heart, are contemned, and despised, yea, they are most shamefully slaundered. For we see euen at this daye, that he which walketh simply, he shall by and by be called an hypocrite. All they which would serue God, are thus cried out vpon, O these hypocrites! O these mortified! See here how the puritie & simplicitie of the faithfull is despised & naught set by. For the deuil possesseth the contemners of God in such sort, as that they vomit out their blasphemies, not onely against those whome they purpose to oppose them selues, but euen against God him selfe.

But this mischiefe and corruption is not of a dayes hatching:

D

ching: and therefore wee are throughly to confider the faying which Dauid here fetteth downe:

O turne from me rebuke, to wit, fuffer mee not O Lorde, to be lightly efteemed of men, bicaufe I haue kept thy teftimonies. Wee fee then that the fumme of this verfe is this; That Dauid defireth GOD to vpholde and mainteine his puritie. Now the caufe is incontinently added,

For Princes alfo did fit, vnder the fhadowe of Iuftice, *and fpeake againft me*.

Nowe this was a great temptation to Dauid, that hee was not onely mocked and fcorned at the Tauernes and Innes, beeing there blafoned by diffolute Iefters and Scoffers, and talked of in the ftreetes and market places, but euen in the place of Iuftice (which ought to bee holy) it could not therefore bee chofen but that they alfo woulde vtterly defame and flaunder him, and condemne him to be as it were a moft wicked and curfed man. When Dauid then did fee, that he was thus vniuftly intreated and handled, hee maketh his complaint vnto God: and fayeth, O Lorde the Princes and Gouernours them felues doe fit and fpeake euill againft me: *And yet for all that I haue kept thy Teftimonies.* Here in fumme we are to gather out of this place, that if it fo fall out, when as wee haue walked vprightly and in a good confcience, to bee falfely flaundered, to bee accufed of this and that, whereof we neuer once thought: yet ought we to beare all thinges paciently, for let vs be fure of that, that we are not better then Dauid, although we would make neuer fo great proteftation of our integritie and puritie.

Dauid walked both before God and men fo faithfully as none of vs all is able to doe, and yet wee fee that he was fubiect to thefe flaunderous reportes. Let vs then be patient, when the like fhall happen to vs. But let vs alfo follow his example in that hee fayeth, that is, that wee fhoulde not be difcouraged: feeing our felues to be fo euill and vniuftly recompenfed at mens handes, that we forbeare not for all that to exercife our felues in the commaundementes of

God

vpon the Cxix. Pſalme.

God. And howe ſhould we come by that patience? wee muſt come to that which he there ſpeaketh off, to wit, that wee take all our whole delight and pleaſure in the commaundementes of God. It is the thing which hee often beateth vpon before by me touched, and therefore it ſhall not be needefull to ſtaye vpon it any longer.

Let vs onely vnderſtand this, when Dauid ſayeth, that all his pleaſure was in the commaundementes of GOD, that we (after his example) muſt doe the like. Hee added,

They are my Counſellers. Loe here a ſentence worthy to be wayed of vs, when Dauid calleth the commaundements of God his counſaylers: For in the firſt place he meaneth, that he might ſcorne at all the wiſedome of the moſt able and moſt expert men in the worlde, howe goodly and gay ſhewes ſoeuer their counſailes ſeeme to be to thoſe, which ſo exceedingly commend them, and are alſo commended of all in that he was conducted by the word of God, & gouerned therby. Lo what he meaneth here by the firſt point.

The ſecond is, That when he ſhalbe ſo gouerned by the word of God, he might not onely ſaye that hee was truely wyſe, but that it was ſo much, as if he had all the wiſedome of all the men in the worlde, yea and a great deale more, put euen in one man. When any one man miſtruſteth his owne witte, hee will aſke councell, and arme him ſelfe the better, and when he ſhall haue vſed ſuch counſell, as euery one ſhall ſoundly giue him, hee will holde him ſelfe a great deale the better reſolued.

Dauid then declareth vnto vs, that if wee will not bee without good counſell and aduiſe, we muſt follow the ſtatutes and ordinances of God. But what? fewe men at this day are able in truth thus to ſaye. Euery man will ſaye the beſt for him ſelfe he can, and yet it ſhalbe all but a mere mockerie. Howe many of vs are there which will be contented to be gouerned as hee was, by this counſell? Wee ſhall hardly finde one amonges an hundreth. Howe do we iuſtly promiſe our ſelues rightly to knowe that GOD hath ſpoken vnto vs?

The third Sermon of M. Jo. Cal.

And let it be that we are in the right way, what assurance haue we of it? It cannot be chosen but that the least let in the world will trouble vs: Our spirite alwayes greatly desireth to be contrary to God, we haue greater regarde to the vayne opinions and fantasies of men, then to the heauenly doctrine, so that we lende our cares to whatsoeuer men bable, and are so caried with euery wynde, that we knowe not what it is to holde our selues to the counsell of God.

And so let vs bee aduised to make our profit of this sentence, beseching the Lord to graunt vs that his grace, that we may be gouerned by him, and that with such humilitie and reuerence, as that whatsoeuer is set before vs in this world, we may alwayes go on our wayes, in true and inuincible constancie. And according to this holy doctrine, let vs prostrate our selues before the face of our good God, in acknowledging our faultes: beseching him that it woulde please him to gouerne vs in such sorte, as that we looke not downe here on the earth, ne yet stoope downe to the corruptible things of this world, but that we might continually aspire vnto this heauenly life, whereunto hee daily calleth vs by his worde: And for performance thereof to suffer vs to be truely vnited to our Lord Iesus Christ, yea, and that with an inseparable bond, as wee may alwayes followe the waye which he hath shewed vnto vs, vntill such time as wee be come to that immortall glorie, whereunto he hath gone before vs, to gather vs all vp vnto him, and to make vs partakers of that blessednesse, which hee hath gotten and purchased by his death and passion, and whereof he will make vs enheritours with him in the kingdome of heauen.

That he will not onely graunt vs this grace
and fauour, but also vnto all people
and nations of the earth, &c.

The

The fourth Sermon of the hundreth and nineteenth Psalme.

DALETH.

My soule cleaueth vnto the dust: quicken me according to thy word.

I haue declared my wayes, and thou heardest mee: teache me thy statutes.

Make me to vnderstand the way of thy commandements: and I will meditate of thy wonderous workes.

My soule melteth with very heauines: rayse me vp according vnto thy word.

Take from me the way of lying: and graunt me graciously thy lawe.

I haue chosen the way of truth: and thy iudgements haue I laid before me.

I haue sticken vnto thy testimonies: O Lord confound me not.

I will runne the way of thy commaundements: whē thou shalt enlarge mine heart.

Auid sheweth vnto vs in these eight verses what the ioye and contentation of the children of God ought to bee. And this is a doctrine for vs, most profitable. For there is not that man which longeth not too haue the thing that may content and delight him: but there is none of vs which holdeth the true meane. So much the more therefore ought we rightly to recorde the

The 4. Sermon of M. Io. Cal.

the lesson heere conteined: to wit, that all our reioycing is accursed, and will come to an euill end if wee looke not to God and to his worde. Loe wherefore here he sayeth,

My soule cleaueth vnto the dust: quicken me according to thy word.

Dauid confesseth here that hee was driuen to an extremitie. For behold what hee meaneth by this saying, That his soule (or life) cleaueth vnto the dust: As if hee shoulde haue said, O Lord, there is nothing that I more looked for then my graue, I am like to a poore castaway and forlorne creature. Nowe whether or to whome should he haue recourse? Euen vnto God, hee desireth to be restored. And how may that be? according to the promisse which he hath receiued. We see then whether, and to whom we must haue recourse in all our necessities, And thus much for the first point. The Second is, when that wee shall haue had our refuge to God, we might finde in him wherewith fully to reioyce vs. Thus much then for the second. The third is, That if we will obteine to be restored at Gods handes, wee being as it were dead and confounded, should looke vnto his promises: For behold he will giue vs encouragement to come vnto him. We haue here then a good admonition and very profitable: that is, That as often as we shall be ouerwhelmed with all the miserie that can be, we should yet looke vnto God, bicause that then hee will seeke after vs more then euer he did before, willing vs to come vnto him. But here we are to note, that there is not any so great a miserie which ought to let and stay vs from comming straight on vnto him: For Dauid confesseth that he was become as a dead man. When then wee shalbe euen as it were at the last cast, as we say, that we can no more, that we should bee as a man would saye, oppressed and ouercome with sorowe and griefe, yea and that the graue euen gapeth to swallowe vs vp, let vs not for all that cease to beseeche God to restore vs. For it belongeth properly vnto him, when he hath appealed and brought vs to deathes dore, to restore and quicken vs againe.

But

But we are to vnderstande that we must not come vnto him after an hypocriticall maner: we must not require him too restore vs, and yet haue our mindes wandering here and there, neither yet must we seeke for that thing in the worlde, which wee make countenance to seeke for at his handes: We must not make vs two wayes to the woode as we saye, but our whole delight and contentation must bee in God and in his grace, that it suffiseth vs to haue him onely, and to feele his mercie and compassion towardes vs; and when wee haue gotten that, to bee contented onely therewith. But bicause we can not come vnto God, without he him selfe draweth vs, when as wee desire him to restore vs, and to stretche out his hande vnto vs, wee must adde thereto this saying here expressed, to wit, that he will quicken vs according to his word. Now by this, as I haue already sayde, wee are taught that in the middest of death we finde saluation and health, bicause the promises of God neuer fayle vs. It followeth in the second verse,

I haue declared my wayes, and thou beardest mee: teache me thy statutes.

Here Dauid alledgeth another reason that GOD heareth him, to wit, that this is not the first time that he had heard him, neither yet that God is mercifull and liberall, to graunt vnto his faithfull, their petitions and requestes. But wee in very deede must, in continuing the matter which wee are here in hande to open, be throughly assured and resolued, that it is not in vayne, when as we make our prayers vnto God, neither yet that wee lose our labours, but that our prayers shall profite vs. We must therefore be fully resolued herein. And howe must that bee? Forsooth, Dauid euen very now alledged vnto God, his promises assuring him selfe that hee receiued them through his meere mercy and goodnesse.

And this is no foolehardinesse. Euen so then, let vs in no case feare to come vnto God boldly and cherefully vpon this condition, yea so long as wee builde vpon his promises. We

D 4

ses. Wee must not come vnto him according to our owne fantasies: neither must we allege and saye, my God, I present my selfe here before thy maiestie, bicause I thinke or suppose that thou oughtest to heare me: this were too too fonde and lewde arrogancie: but to saye, Alas my good God, it is very true that I am not worthy to come neare vnto thy presence: and although it shall seeme to me that I might approche to thee, yet must I pull back that foote againe: Neuerthelesse, since thou biddest me to come vnto thee, and hast commaunded me to call vpon thee, and promised also for to heare mee: Loe here my God the cause which maketh mee so bolde, not to doubt to come vnto thee, bicause I beleeue thy worde. And now O Lorde, I stand in no doubt that thou wilt not receiue mee, when as I thus buylde vpon thy promisse.

After Dauid hath vsed this kinde of speech, to stirre him selfe vp to praye vnto God, and also to obtaine his request, he addeth, *O Lorde, I haue acknowledged my wayes, and thou heardest mee.* As if he should haue saide, Ouer and besides thy promise, my God, there is another reason which enboldeneth and encourageth me to come vnto thee: to wit, the experience which thou hast shewed vnto me of thy great goodnes. I neuer required any thing of thee in my necessitie, but thou diddest heare me: to witte, but that thou satisfiedst my request, but that I haue felt howe thou hast relieued thy seruauntes, and hast alwayes beene ready to succoure them in their distresse: Yea, O Lorde, and that thou hast not tarried nor wayted vntill they came vnto thee, but hast euen offered thy selfe first vnto them.

Seeing then it is so that thou hast shewed thy selfe to be so good and liberall, O, I nowe doubt not but that thou wilt continue the same thy goodnesse: Wherefore I beseeche thee teache mee thy statutes. See here a text worthy the marking: For, as I haue before sayde, wee must not come vnto God doubting and wauering: but with full resolution, that hee will heare vs.

And howe is that? O, we haue a most sure and infallible

testi-

testimonie: too wit, he hath promised too bee neare vnto al those which shal craue and begge of him in trueth: we may then say, wee beseeche thee, O Lord, to haue regarde vnto vs according too thy woorde. It is very true, that wee are vnwoorthy that thou shouldest bee careful ouer vs: But so it is, that hauing thy woorde and promise, wee may boldly come vnto thee: and besides, let vs adde theretoo the experience which God hath already shewed vntoo vs: that hee neuer forgetteth his, but preserueth and keepeth them, and alwaies watcheth ouer them. And why so? That wee ought to be much more heedful then wee are of al the benefits of God, too the ende wee might come too this consideration of the reason which Dauid heere bringeth in: too wit, that wee might say vntoo God, that hee hath hearde vs. Nowe there are very fewe of vs that can doo this. And why so? Bicause that when we are in any distresse, wee neuer thinke to cal vpon God, yea although the griefe or disease presse and grieue vs neuer so much. And yet if wee doo then cal vpon him, it is so, that assoone as we haue escaped the danger, we wil not acknowledge it too bee God that hath had pytie and compassion vppon vs, but is quyte out of memory and troden cleane vnder foote. Bycause then we remember not the benefites of God, Loe what is the cause why we cannot say, when wee come afresh to pray, O Lord, thou hast heard mee. For (as I haue before saide) our vnthankfulnesse hindereth vs that we cannot haue any such experience & practise too pray vntoo God incessauntly. And see also what is the cause of our so colde and faynt prayers: for if wee were ready too cal to minde the graces of God: O, we should be sure and certaine to bee alwaies fenced, when as we meant to present our selues before him, to say, Alas my God, this is no noueltie vnto mee: neither ought I, Lorde, to thinke it straunge too present my selfe before thee, for thou hast graunted mee free accesse and libertie: this is not the first tyme that thou hast doone mee good, no, I haue felte thy fauour by experience euen from my youth: and when as I shal speake of the number of tymes which thou hast hearde

D 5   mee, I

The 4. Sermon of M.I.Cal.

me, I shall finde them infinite: I may very well then repose and put all my trust in thee, hoping that thou wilt continue thy goodnesse towardes me, as thou art alwayes ready so to doe. Nowe because we are so vnthankfull vnto God, as not to acknowledge his benefites as becommeth vs, and as to him apperteyneth: Loe here, why we cannot benefite our selues by this confession in truth, to confirme our hope to come vnto him, as should be good for vs.

Moreouer, we are to note, that we must not deale with God, as with mortall men. For if any man hath doone vs a pleasure, we may truely say, as we commonly do: I shalbe the more beholding vnto you, because you haue already bound mee thereto, this shall come in amongst the rest: But yet if we shall haue borrowed much of any man, wee shall be ashamed that we haue troubled him so often. But the case standeth not so betwixt God and vs. And why so? For God is neuer weary of well dooing as men are, and besides he neuer diminisheth his substaunce when hee dooth vs any good. If any man bestoweth his goodes liberally vpon vs, hee hath so much the lesse: if he giue his woorde for vs: hee will say, this is all that I can doe for you. But God so aboundeth in riches, that it is like too a Spring which can neuer be drawne dry: & the more that is drawn out of it, the greater abundance is to be seene.

So then, wee must not be affrayde too come vnto God, when as he shall haue bestowed vpon vs store of wealth, & that we shall be so much bounde vnto him, as is possible to be thought: but the same ought to make vs the boulder, as Dauid heere declareth vnto vs. And of this are many like sayings in the Scripture. *O Lorde* (sayth Iacob) *I was neuer woorthy of the benefites which thou haste bestowed vpon me: but yet thou haste so bountifully dealte with thy seruaunte, as that I must needes call vpon thy name continually.* See then, howe GOD moueth vs to come familyarly vnto him, by reason that he sheweth him selfe so liberall, and hath his hands wyde open, to the ende hee might giue vs whatsoeuer wee stand in neede off. And when as hee shall haue

Gen. 32. 10.

continued

continued thus all the dayes of our life, wee ought the boldelyer to call vpon him as Dauid him selfe sheweth vs heere by example. And now let ys mark his saying:

I haue declared my wayes, and thou heardst mee : teach mee thy statutes.

Dauid heere protesteth that God hath giuen eare vnto his particular matters, to wit, when as he was perplexed and full of sorowe, hee then called vpon God. Loe what this worde, *Way*, in the Hebrue meaneth, where it is sayde, I haue acknowledged my wayes, and thou answearedst me: to witte, heardst me. Heerevpon hee desireth that God woulde teache him his Statutes: to witte, that hee woulde shewe him the right rule to liue wel. Heere we are to note, that God yeldeth his consent euen ynto vs, and that hee will assist vs in all our seuerall needes. We see that our Lorde Iesus hath taught vs too aske our dayly breade, which importeth all that concerneth this transitory life. Euen so when we haue any thing to doe or too treate off, God graunteth vnto vs this priuiledge and licence too come vnto him: yea if wee should steppe on but one pace, or but remooue our hand, we may come vnto God, beseeching him to direct and conduct vs.

Let vs then marke this inestimable goodnesse which God vseth towards vs, when hee seeth well that wee haue shewed vnto him all our wayes: to witte, all our desires and smallest matters. If a man had his brother or deere companion, he durst hardly shewe him selfe so familyarly, for feare he would be importune vpon him, as God giueth vs leaue too come vnto him. What bountie is this? Nowe when wee see that God maketh himselfe so familyar in our small affayrs: so much the more ought we to beseech him, after the example of Dauid, that he would conduct vs according to his lawe: to witte, that hee will graunte vs his grace to liue in such sorte, as that wee may followe the rule which hee hath sette downe heere vnto vs. See then, howe that by the lesse, wee muste come too the greater, as by particularityes wee muste come to generalities.

From

The 4. Sermon of M.I. Cal.

From the lesse too the greater, say I, is this, That if God giueth vnto vs our dayly breade, let vs also craue of him health for our soules. If God will so humble him selfe, as to aduise vs: when we haue any thing to doe amongst men, about the earthly affaires of this transitory life, let vs also beseech him to doe vs this good, as to conduct vs likewise according to his lawe. Loe heere how we may come from the lesser to the greater. Wee may also discend from particularities to generalities, when as we shall say, O Lorde, thou hast hearde me in such a thing, which is a speciall matter: now by a more forcible reason, I may call vpon thee for a thinge which may serue me all the dayes of my life, which is, that whē thou hast set me into the way of saluation, thou wouldst keepe me therein, and that thou neuer forsake me, vntill such time as thou hast brought mee vnto that ende and perfection, whereunto thou hast called me.

It followeth, *Make me to vnderstand the way of thy commaundementes: and I will meditate of thy woondrous woorkes.*

Marke heere the thirde reason which Dauid alledgeth to obtaine of God, that he might bee taught in his lawe. O Lorde (saith he) *make me to vnderstande the way of thy commaundementes, and so shall I talke of thy woondrous woorkes.* As if hee should haue sayd, O Lorde, if it be thy good pleasure instruct me according to thy will, and it shall not serue for my selfe onely: but also for my neighbours: for I will indeuour my selfe to bring also others vnto thee. And thus we ought to vse the graces and giftes of God: to wit, that they be not as it were buryed in vs, but that wee may also profite our neighbours: and to communicate them vnto such, as they may doe good vnto, to the ende that God may be honoured, and that they all may serue to the common saluation of the members of our Lord Iesus Christ.

But heere we haue in this Texte too note, that it is impossible for vs to instruct others, except we haue beene before the disciples and Scholers of God. There are a greate many which will put foorth them selues, as if they were sufficient

sufficient and able Clearkes inoughe too teach others: And in so thrusting in them selues, they haue not once knowen what they ought to vnderstand, either for themselues or yet for any others. Let vs then consider the order which is heere obserued: to wit, that euery of vs doe acknowledge our owne ignoraunce. Dauid was a moste excellent Prophet, and yet notwithstanding he besought God that he woulde make him too vnderstande the way of his commaundementes. Yea, but had not he the Lawe written? Wherefore then desired he that which hee had already in his handes? For he knewe well inough that to read, to preach, and to heare, was not all that was needfull: For vnlesse God open our eares, we shall neuer be able to vnderstād it. And therfore it behoueth that he inlighten vs, or else we shall neuer be able to see the brightnesse thereof, albeit it lye wide open before our eyes. If Dauid made this request (as we haue already heeretofore intreated) I beseech you what shall we doe then? Let vs then euen so confesse our ignoraunce, and beseech God that it would please him to teach vs. See now that we must needes bee first scholers: before we vsurpe the office of a Maister: and before wee thrust our selues in, too speake vnto others, that we heare God first speake vnto vs, and that we bee grounded in his woorde, that we may protest as Saint Peeter telleth vs, that 1.*Pet.* 4. 11. it is the woorde of GOD which commeth out of our mouthes. *Whosoeuer speaketh,* (sayeth hee) *let him speake the woord of God,* For it is no reason that a mortall man shoulde extoll himselfe, and preferre his owne dreames and fantasies. And although that this sacriledge be ouercommon in the worlde, it behoueth vs too haue greate regarde therto: & that we al keepe silence, & that both great and small, ignoraunt and wise, the simple and learned, giue eare to the word of God, & suffer them selues to be taught by him: and after that, euery man according to those graces which he hath receiued, to communicate them vnto his neighbours. And when any of vs shall be better instructed in the word of God then any of our brethren, we ought

to

so much the more to exhorte them that haue neede therof to reprehende and rebuke those which make defaulte, and to instruct the ignoraunt and vnlearned. For our Lorde God bestoweth not his graces liberally vpon vs, to the end we should holde them fast locked as it were in a chest: but that we should make them common to others, to set forth and commend them to other according as opportunitie shall serue, and also according to the dispositions of those to whome we addict our selues to teach, are contented to heare vs.

Moreouer when Dauid sayth, *That hee will speake of the woondrous woorkes of God*, Let vs marke that he dooth it not of any ambition, or vaine glory, as many doe, which could be very wel contented that we should heare them, when as they shall doe nothing else but babble at randon of the worde of God. And why is that? It is because they prophane it, without hauing any reuerence thereto. For wee see that the moste ignoraunt will be most bolde, according to the olde saying, None so bolde as blinde Bayard, or, A foolish man doubteth no perill. When soeuer any would goe about to teach them, O by and by the word of God shall be nothing with them: For ye shall haue them alwayes to haue answeares ready coyned in their sleeues. There are then which woulde be accounted great Clarkes, who notwithstanding shewe them selues not to knowe what holynesse, and Maiestie the worde of God carryeth with it. But contrarywise Dauid telleth vs, that if we will instruct and teach our neighboures, that wee ought firste to vnderstand the lawe of GOD to be full of woonderfull and straunge secrets: to be so high a wisdome, as that we ought not to presume to take on hande too handle it without all modestie and sobrietie. Let vs then learne, if we will be good Doctors and teachers, to proceede in all humblenes and feare, knowing that the least sentence in the scripture surmounteth our vnderstanding, and that wee are too too dull and blockish to attaine vnto so high wisdome, except the Lord our God guideth and leadeth vs thereto. Lo how

that

that both scholers and maisters & as many as are hearers, and speakers, ought to come with great reuerence when as they meane to handle the word of God. It followeth soone after: *My soule melteth with very heauinesse: raise me vp according to thy woorde.*

Heere Dauid more cleerely expresseth that which wee haue already touched: to witte, that the abundaunt ioy of the faythfull consisteth wholly in this, that God is merciful vnto them, and knowing him to be such one, they are comforted by his grace, nothing douting of his good will. And to proue it to be so, Dauid saith in the first place, *My soule melteth away with very heauinesse,* as if hee should haue said, that all his power and vertue was cleane gone from him. For this similitude heere, is also very well set downe in diuerse places of the Scripture. We haue gushed and burst out like water. So then, see how Dauid is heere become as a forlorne man, so throwne downe and humbled, as that he is cleane voyde of all strength, and all other things whatsoeuer, and therevpon beseecheth God to comfort him. Now heere we are to note that he speaketh not of the feeblenes of his body, to say that he was humbled by sicknesse, & yet his soule to be lusty and strong: but he sayth that he is melted away with very heauinesse, as if he should haue said, that he was vtterly ouerthrowne. And therevpon he desireth to be comforted, and that by the worde of God. Heere then we see, that when God shall mortifie vs, we shall be as men forlorne: and that not onely all our force and strength in this present life shall be of no value, but also our soules and spirites shalbe as it were humbled and cast downe, too this ende that we might boldely call vpon God after the example of Dauid. Let vs not feare then that God wil forsake vs, but let vs rather learne to beseech him to comforte vs, for Dauid hath shewed vs the way vnto it, neither went hee so on of his owne proper motion, but it was the spirit of God which pushed him forward thereto. Wherefore, hauing so good a guyde, let vs not feare, to be frustrate and voyde of our petitions and demaundes, so long as wee followe the doctrine heerein conteyned. Now

The 4. Sermon of M. Io. Cal.

Nowe returneth hee to the firste Argument which we haue already touched: to wit, *according to the woord of God*. Wherein we see, that all the assurance and certaintie which we ought to haue in our prayers to God, is, to looke vnto that which hee hath promised vs. For they which trust vnto themselues, and think there is sufficient in them, why God should heare them: it is most sure that they shal neuer open their mouthes to desire any thing of God: or if they doe, it shall be all but meere hypocrisie: As in Popery, where wee are not taught the promises of God. True it is that they wil babble much, mumble ouer a number of Pater Nosters with a mixture of Aues, yea and will also direct their Paternoster to the Puppet of S. *Agatha*, or some other Saint, as if it were to God. Nowe this is nothing else but beastly to profane the name of God. And therefore I haue sayde that the principalest poynt that we ought to vse in praying vnto God, is to lay before him his promises saying: O Lord God it is true that we rightly deserue to be reiected of thee, but seeing thou inuitest and callest vs, shall wee goe from thee? Is it not meete that we should doe thee this honour, as to giue credite vnto thy worde, and to holde it for stedfast and sure? Sithens then it is so, that we haue thy promises, we may boldely trust vnto them, considering that they are true, and because wee cannot but haue them graunted vnto vs, we onely rest and stay our selues vpon them. Loe heere the meaning of Dauid in this verse. Nowe hee goeth on and sayth,

Take from me the way of lying: and graunt mee gratiously thy Lawe.

Heere he acknowledgeth, that although hee were already exercysed in the lawe of God, and in his knowledge, and that although he were a Prophet to teach others, neuerthelesse, that he was yet subiect to a number of wicked thoughtes and imaginations which might alwayes wickedly leade him from the right way, except God had helde him with his mightie and strong hande. And this is a poynte which we ought heere rightly to note: For wee see howe

men

upon the Cxix. Psalme.

men greatly abuse them selues. When any of vs shall haue had a good beginning, we straight wayes thinke that wee are at the highest: we neuer bethinke vs too pray any more to God, when as he hath shewed vs that fauour too serue our turnes: but if we haue doone any small deede, wee by and by lift vp our sayles, and woonder at our great vertues. To be shorte, wee thinke straightway that the Deuill can winne no more of vs. This foolish arrogancie causeth God to let vs goe astray, so that wee fall mightily, yea that wee breake bothe armes and legges: and are in greate hazarde of breaking our neckes. I speake not now of our naturall body, but of the soule. Let vs looke vpon Dauid him selfe: For he it is that hath made proofe heereof. It came too passe that he villanously and wickedly erred, when as hee toke Bethsabe the wife of his subiect Vry, to play the whoremonger with her, that hee was the cause of so execrable a murder, yea & that of many: For he did asmuch as in him lay, to haue the whole army of the Lorde and all the people of Israell to bee vtterly ouerthrowne. Loe then too too great negligence and securitie in Dauid: and see also wherefore hee sayth, *Alas my good God, I beseech thee so to guide me, as that I may forsake the way of lying.*

1.Sam.11.

This is the whole summe, that Dauid (although he exceedingly profited in the lawe and word of God) acknowledgeth that he was subiect and apt to be carryed away and abused: that the deuill might sundry wayes beguile and deceaue him: that hee might bee seduced through many temptations: allured by the lustes of the fleshe: and oftentimes fall, were it not that God did take from him the way of lying. Loe heere a poynte which we ought thorowly too mark, *O Lord,* saith he, *take from me the way of lying.* It is spoken to this ende, that euery of vs might knowe our owne wante: to wit, that we should enter into our selues, and meditate after this manner. Goe to now, I am as a poore, wretched, and so fraile a creature as is possible: my faith so very weake, and the lustes of my fleshe so stronge, as that they might haue sudenly oppressed me. Alas my God, sithens I

E. am

am so weake and feeble, I must needs be assisted by thee and by thy power and might. And againe howe many are our enemyes which molest and greeue vs? howe mightie and strong is the Deuil? How great and infinite are the meanes wherewith he assayleth vs? and when hee shall assayle vs with his Dartes and arrowes, it is impossible for vs too escape them, we shall become then like vnto the Lambe in the throte of the Lyon. Whē we shall thus haue vnderstood these our wantes and needes, then may we say with Dauid, *O Lorde take from me the way of lying.* Nowe he sheweth the remedy when he sayth: *Cause me to make much of thy Lawe, or graunt me thy grace that I may keepe thy law*: For the word which Dauid vseth, importeth meere fauour and free gift: As if he should haue said, it commeth of thy meere fauour and grace, that thou giuest me thy lawe.

See heere the remedy which our lord and Sauiour vseth, when he would withdraw vs from the law of lying, to wit, that we should keepe his truth: For the truth of God is sufficiently able to encounter al the subtelties and slye practizes of Satan, to withstande al temptations, and to vanquishe and ouercome al the lustes of our flesh. The trueth of God then wil suffice against al this. And this is it whiche Saint Paule speaketh of, that when we shal be strēgthened in the doctrine of the Gospel, that then we shal haue wherwithall too bee lusty and strong, and become valiant Champions too fight vnder the signe of our Lord Iesus Christ, and triumphe ouer al our enimies. So then, wil we bee farre from hypocrisie? wil we be deliuered from lying, from al the subtelties of Satan, and from al the deceits of the world? Let vs beseeche God then to graunt vs his law, and to doo vs that good that we might be instructed therein, as wee are heere taught by the example of Dauid. Now after al this he maketh his protestation:

Ephe. 6. 10, 11, 12, &c.

That he hath chosen the way of trueth, and hath cleauen vnto the testimonies of God, that he hath folowed his iudgements: and heerevpon he beseecheth him, *not too bee confounded.*

Heere

Heere now we see, that when we beseech God to giue vs his law, to deliuer vs from temptations, to suffer vs not too be deceiued neither by Satan, nor the woild, that we doe it with such a true desire, as Dauid sheweth vs heere, in this place. For there are many which may say with their mouth, O Lord I would gladly resist all temtations. But what? They compound with the Deuil, conspire with him too set themselues against God, flatter them selues in all their iniquities, and desire wholy to giue themselues to all wickednes. Are not heere I beseech you faire and proper petitions which we make with the mouth, when as the hart bendeth it selfe altogither to mischiefe, and iniquitie. Is not this I pray you to mock God? what other thing else is it? Let vs then learne to say with Dauid, *O Lord, I haue chosen the way of trueth, and haue sticken to thy testimonies*. When he sayth, that hee hath chosen the way of trueth, hee meaneth that he desired nothing else, but to follow that which was right and good, as God had shewed it vnto him. When he saith, that he cleaued to the testimonyes of God, he declareth what trueth that is whereof he made mention: For men many times imagine vnto them selues certaine fantasies in their heads, and think the same to be the best & most sure foudation in the world, and that there is no other reason, trueth, nor wisdome, but that which they haue conceiued in their owne braine. Let vs now beware of that, and assure our selues that trueth it selfe is inclosed within the word of God, & that that is it, which we must seeke: And not to haue vs thinke that to bee the trueth, which wee in our owne fantasies doe iudge too bee good: but euen then haue wee chosen the way of trueth, when as we shall sticke to the testimonies of God, when we shall vnderstand and knowe that it is hee onely which may leade vs straight, and that we haue doone this honour vnto his woorde, to be ruled thereby all the dayes of our life. Loe, howe we shoulde followe the way of trueth.

    Nowe when Dauid hath made all these protestations, hee desireth that hee may bee confounded. As if hee shoulde haue sayde, My G O D, since that it is so that I

The 4. Sermon of M. Io. Cal.

desire to obey thee, suffer me not now to bee confounded, that I be not scorned, and supposed to bee as a vacabonde and without a guide. Loe heere a place which ought dilygently to be marked: For I beseech you, when we shall bee desirous to cleaue vnto God and his word, when wee shall haue preferred the same before all our lustes and pleasures, yea aboue all whatsoeuer shall seeme good and right in our owne eyes: if wee shall then I say bee put to confusion and shame, what shall become of vs when we shall laye the raine of the bridle in the necke of all our desires, and take from God all his authoritie? Deserue we not to bee vtterly confounded? No doubt we doe. So then, let vs way the firste parte of this doctrine, that wee muste not let our tongues walke against God: For he knoweth how to bee right well auenged thereof. How many doe we see at this day too become after this manner so beastly, as that it is shame to see their brutishnesse? and what is the cause? They haue cast of the yoke of God, they haue not vouchsafed to do him that honor, as to bee gouerned by him: It is meete then that they be confounded in the open sight of the worlde, that they may be pointed at, that euen young Children may perceaue their beastlynesse, and are very well woorthy so to be serued. And so least wee fall into such shame: let vs pray with Dauid, that it woulde please God to make vs so too stick vnto him and his woord, as we neuer be confounded. Nowe too conclude with these eight verses aparte, Dauid sayth,

I will runne the way of thy Comaundements: when thou shalt inlarge mine hearte.

When he sayth, That when God hath set his hearte at libertie, hee will runne: it is too shewe vnto vs, that when our heartes are inclosed and fast shutte vp, that wee are not able so much as too remoue one of our fingers to well dooing, vntill such time as GOD gladdeth vs, and sheweth vs a mery countenaunce. Nowe Dauid in this firste place declareth vnto vs, that wee are able to doe nothing except God stirreth vs vpp thereto.

And

vpon the Cxix. Psalme.

And although he hath already solicited & admonished vs, yet that is not all. We should cry out and Alas: & poure out some sighes and grones. But becauſe God will be ſerued with a cheerefull minde, and not with an euill will, ſo long as we are faſt ſhut vp, we cannot once ſtirre out of the place, to goe on forwarde in the way of ſaluation. And how can we then runne? When as he ſhall haue ſet our heart at libertie: to wit, that he ſhal haue ſo diſpoſed & ordered vs, as that we ſhould freely bend our ſelues, & fully & wholy yeeld our affections vnto him, For otherwiſe, we hauing our harts faſt ſhut vp ſhal alwaies become the bondſlaues of ſin. It is very true, that while we are in this world, we neuer run ſo faſt ne yet ſo perfectly, as is required, yea wee ſhall many times go as it were halting, where in deede we ſhould make haſt. But thus it is with vs, that whenſoener he ſhall gouern vs with his ſpirit, and that we ſhall be vnder the conduct of our head & Captaine Ieſus Chriſt, we may ſay with Dauid, that we doe not onely walke in his commaundements, but that we alſo runne in them: Yea, ſo that our affection bee not hypocritical, and that our zeale be alſo feruent to addict our ſelues vnto our good God, ſince he hath placed vs in the world to this end, to obey him, and too glorifie his holy name.

And according to this doctrine, let vs proſtrate our ſelues before the face of our good God, in acknowledging our ſinnes: beſeeching him, that it would pleaſe him to make vs to feele our ſinnes and iniquities more and more, & that it would alſo pleaſe him to make vs ſo to remember them, that we may learne to acknowledge how neceſſary it is for vs to be more & more encreaſed & confirmed in his graces which he beſtoweth vpon vs, to the end that in allowing & eſteeming of his benefites as it becommeth vs, we may render vnto him our humble and hearty thankes: beſeeching him alſo to continue vs in ſuch ſort in his holy vocation, as that we may be glorified in the latter day in hauing fought a good fight, and that we may inioy the prize & rewarde of the victorie, to triumph in our Lorde Ieſus Chriſte. Let vs

The 5. Sermon of M. Io. Cal.

vs beseech him that he will not onely giue vs this grace, but also all the people and nations of the worlde, &c.

The fifth Sermon of the hundreth and nineteenth Psalme.

HE.

Teach me O Lord the way of thy statutes: and I wil keepe it vnto the end.
Giue mee vnderstanding and I will keepe thy lawe: yea I will keepe it with my whole heart.
Direct me in the path of thy Commandementes: for therein is my delight.
Encline my hearte vnto thy testimonyes: and not to couetousnesse.
Turne away mine eyes from regarding vanitie: and quicken thou me in thy way.
Stablish thy promise to thy seruant because he feareth thee.
Take away thy rebuke that I am afrayde off: for thy Iudgementes are good.
Beholde I desire thy commaundements: quicken me in thy righteousnesse.

Hese eight Verses heere conteine the Prayers which wee haue already before seene: to witte, that Dauid prayeth too be taught in the lawe, that he might the better serue God. Nowe vpon this wee haue to note, that this is not all to heare

and

and to be taught by preaching vnto vs, that the same is as it were from the trueth of GOD: but wee must also be taught by the holie Ghoste, yea and that twoo manner of wayes. For when God shall haue inlightened vs, to the end we might knowe that it commeth from him, it behooueth that he imprinte in our heartes a desire too cleaue vnto it, for without that wee shall doe cleane contrary, as naturally we are enclyned.

So then, although it bee not superfluous too reade and heare: yet wil it profite vs nothing at all, excepte the holy Ghoste teacheth vs: yea and that to discerne aswel betwene good and euill, as also to be wel and rightly affected, too walke according to the Commaundementes of GOD. Which thinge is sufficiently confirmed vnto vs in the person of Dauid: For (as wee haue heeretofore declared) hee was a moste excellent Prophet.

Nowe it appeareth that hee was not onely sufficiently instructed for him selfe, but GOD hadde also ordayned him too gouerne and instructe others: this was the Doctor of the whole Church. And yet notwithstanding, hee confesseth him selfe too be vtterly ignoraunt and blinde, except God directed him by his holy spirite. Yea, and hee declareth vnto vs moste plainely, that hee had neede of these twoo partes of the grace of GOD, heere by vs touched: to witte, to bee taught too knowe that which is good: and afterwarde too haue his minde framed to continue therein.

This circumstaunce also is specially too bee noted, that Dauid in making his requestes heerein conteyned, was no Nouice: For God had already instructed him by his holy Spirite. And that which is more, he declareth that hee had already desired too followe God, and too obay his Commaundementes. Wherefore then is it, that hee prayeth afreshe, but onely that hee felte in him selfe greate weakenesse in this point, and that hee was but in the mid way?

E.4. Let

The 5. *Sermon of* M. Io. Cal.

Let vs thevnderstand, that euen they which are inlightened by the spirit of God, & are wel affected, ought not to content themselues heerewith, as if they were already come to a ful perfection: but rather to acknowledge their weakenes, that they are not growne to that forwardnes, but that they may faile, and that it is God which causeth thē to perseuer and to be more and more confirmed. Loe heere, what wee haue yet to obserue, by the example of Dauid. Nowe let vs follow the words which he vseth, to the end the effect of this doctrine may the better be imprinted in our memoryes:

Teach me O Lorde the way of thy statutes: and I will keepe it vnto the end.

Heere Dauid declareth that he hath well begun to serue God, but he right wel feeleth that we are so frayle, that wee can neuer come home to the mark, without God stregtheneth vs: wherfore he hath recourse vnto this high & mighty power, by which God remedieth the vices that are in his chosen, which he knoweth, not to be in their nature. We see then, that when God stretcheth out his hande vnto vs, so that we haue alredy bin instructers & teachers of our neighbours, yet that we must not presume of our owne power & strength, but stand alwaies vpon our garde: beseeching god with all humilitie and reuerence, that as he hath wel begun in vs, so he wil performe & go through with the same. Dauid said not, O Lord, I haue strayed. But he hath very well said heretofore, that he was by nature a wandring shepe: & so shall we see him to be: And yet notwithstāding our Lord had already brought him into the way of saluation, yea and had bestowed vpon him excellent graces. But yet he knowing that he might erre an hūdreth times in a minute, without God held him with a mightie hand: prayeth to be instructed anew, as if all the rest which hee had done had bin nothing. So then, when as God shal haue bestowed vpon vs his graces, let vs not be negligent & secure to lul our selues asleepe, as though our state and condition were not to bee amended. But let vs rather think with our selues and consider, that he which hath bin taken and holden for a good &

vertuous

vpon the Cxix. Pſalme.

vertuous man for the ſpace of ten or xx. yeeres might bee ſeene ouercome in a matter of nothing, were it not that God aſſiſted him.

Loe here how the faithfull, after that God hath liberally beſtowed vpon them great graces, ought alwaies to walke in feare and humblenes, knowing that they are ſubiect to many temptations, which they are neuer able to reſiſt if God continued not the ſame in them, as well to inſtruct them, as alſo to ayde them with his power and ſtrength, & to fortifie them more and more, as before I haue ſaid.

And here we are diligently to marke this ſaying, *And I will keepe it vnto the end.* As if he ſhould haue ſaid, My God, I haue already followed thy commaundementes for a certein time: but what ſhall become of it, if thou doeſt not alwayes put too thy helping hand vnto me, as thou haſt already done? I may in one minute fall into a great and horrible confuſion. O Lord, I beſeeche thee therefore, that as thou haſt begunne well in me, ſo to perfourme the ſame throughly. By this we ſee what a dieueliſh arrogancie that of the papiſtes is, wherewith they are puffed vp, when as to their ſeeming, that a man, after God hath once ſtretched out his arme vnto him, can by and by worke wonders of him ſelfe: and is ſufficiently able too ouercome all temptations. But let vs rather vnderſtand and knowe, that euen as it is God that muſt beginne to ſet vs in the right way, ſo likewiſe that we cannot continue and abide therein, without he alwayes holde vs by his mightie hand, and neuer to ſuffer Satan to ſeduce vs, neither yet to bee wickedly led, by his ſubtelties and wyles. And thus much as touching the firſt verſe. Now it followeth:

Giue me vnderſtanding and I will keepe thy lawe: yea I will keepe it with my whole hart.

Here Dauid declareth vnto vs in the firſt place, what our true wiſedome is: to wit, that we ſhould walke in the feare of God: as alſo it is ſaid in the ſcripture, That the feare of God is true wiſedome: In ſumme, wee haue here the confeſsion of Dauid, that al they which withdrawe themſelues

E 5 from

from the obediēce of God, are people voide of wit, iudgement, wisedome, and reason. In very deede wee shall neuer haue the worlde to iudge thus of it: For wee will saye, loe this is a witty fellow, this man is very wyse, when hee is able to beguile his neighbours, and craftily inuent, how to giue himselfe too all iniquitie. Such is the vvysedome of this worlde. But in the meane whyle let vs note this by the way, that these woordes are not spoken without cause, too witte, that al our wysedome and reason consisteth heerein, that wee walke in the feare of God, and seeke after his wil, yea and too holde vs too it. In the second place as Dauid hath already protested, that wee are not capable to vnderstande the lawe of God, and the contentes thereof, if wee bee not taught from aboue, that is, by the holy ghost: hee also addeth, that hee can haue no good affection nor desire to giue himselfe thereto, vntil such tyme as his heart bee reformed.

The law of God may seeme to be but a common thing, yea we our selues do see, that the proude men of this world contemne it as a thing tootoo common: But yet, as Dauid hath before said, God hath set downe vntoo vs in his lawe wonderful secretes, which hee heere repeteth not in vaine, that it must needes bee that in receiuing the spirite of God from heauen, hee shoulde bee conducted, to the ende to followe the commaundementes of God. Nowe he namely saith, *That I will keepe, yea that I wil keepe it with my whole hart.* This is no superfluous repetition, when he saieth, That I wil keepe, yea that I wil keepe it with my whole harte. For beholde what it is that abuseth a great number of men, so that they cannot be reprehended by men, that their life is not so dissolute as that they may bee pointed at, and bee not brought to rebuke and shame: Loe these men bee lyke little Angelles. They make themselues belieue, that they are more then iust before God: they feele themselues guiltie in nothing. For this cause then Dauid hauing said that he wil kepe the lawe of God, declareth, that it is not so common a thing to doo as we take it.

And

vpon the Cxix. Psalme.   38

And why so? For saith he, he must keepe it with his whole heart. When he meaneth to shewe vnto vs what the good keeping of the law of GOD is, and such an obseruation as God requireth of vs, it is not onely meant that our feete and handes should be seene to bee well ruled and compassed, that our sinnes and iniquities should be so apparaunt, as that they might be cōdemned in the sight of the world: this sayI, is not all, as to vse such an obseruation. But wee must (saith Dauid) keepe the lawe of God with our whole heart. When as we shalbe neuer so litle affected or desirous thereto, it shalbe a great deale more worth then all the substance in the worlde. But we must beware that we haue not a double heart, that our desire be so colde and feeble, as to say, very well, I would gladly that God would bestowe his grace vpon me that I might followe his commaundemēts: and thereupon, to shewe our selues wearie and slougthfull: but we must haue a true sinceritie to walke therein with all fulnes and integritie. But I beseeche you what is he that is able to attaine to that perfection? It is so farre of that there should be any such vprightnes in vs, as that we are not able to thinke once a good thought, except God chaūgeth our peruerse nature, which before should be repugnāt and contrary vnto his righteousnesse. Wherefore, in summe, Dauid, after that he had prayed vnto God that he woulde instruct him, to the ende hee might keepe his commaundementes: addeth, for a more ample confirmation:

That I may keepe thy commaundementes with my whole heart. As if he should haue saide, O Lorde I knowe that we men, as we are puffed vp with pride and arrogancie, doe thinke vs too haue accomplished and fulfilled all the whole lawe, when as wee haue set a good countenaunce of the matter, and haue made some apparaunce or shewe to the worlde: if there were no more in it but this, yet shoulde it be enough for mee, considering that all our members doe so rage in wickednesse, as that it is very harde too holde them in. But all this shoulde bee nothing. For it shoulde be all but meere hypocrisie: and bycause that thou
                                                                     hast

hast respect to the heart, all my carnall passions and affections must be pulled down & my selfe in such sort renued, as that I may be wholy conformed vnto thy righteousnes. Alas my God, and if I must be brought to that, I see it to be an impossible matter. And so thou must needes put thy helping hand vnto me, that I might be taught by thy holy spirite. It followeth in the thirde verse,

Make me to goe in the waye of thy commaundements: for therein is my desire.

Here we see that which hath beene touched, to wit, that Dauid prayeth not vnto God that he would beginne to set him in a good way: For he was already entred into it, hee had already walked in it a good long season. And in deede, this desire is a very great furtherance vnto vs, when as wee may praye vnto God to beseeche him to gouerne vs, and we ought to preferre this felicitie or blessednes before all the things in the worlde. And herein let vs shewe our selues to haue greatly profited. Now Dauid protesteth, without hypocrisie, that he hath kept the comaundements of God: Neuerthelesse he beseecheth the Lord to graunt vnto him power to perseuer therein, and that hee may come to the perfection thereof. Wherein wee see that it is not enough that whē God hath begunne and set vs in a good way, that we may euer after doe what soeuer seemeth good in our owne sight. We see here to the contrary, that when God shall haue taught vs, and that we haue beene apt to learne from the beginning: neuerthelesse that his grace shoulde be made voide euery minute, without hee did continue it. And so in the first place, when as God shall haue instructed vs, to make vs to come to a good vnderstanding and knowledge, he must also graunt vnto vs a good affection and desire. And hath he giuen vs that? It is also meete that he continue the same in vs, and make vs desirous to walke in his commaundementes. Finally after that he hath giuen vs to will, he must also giue vs to perfourme as S. Paul saith, that he doe all in all, but not to rewarde this good will or any other good preparation which is in vs, but to doe it according

ding to his pleasure, to wit, of his free mercie.

Moreouer, let vs on our behalf consider, when as wee would obteine any such grace at Gods handes: to witte, to leade vs into the way of his pathes; that our hearts be there setled as that we be not so accursed as to forsake God, and to set light by him, to queche this light which he shal haue put in vs. For otherwise, if wee bee alwayes giuen to the vanities of this world, as commonly we are, and that wee make no accompte of the graces which God shall bestowe vppon vs: it is good reason, that hee take them from vs, and set vs cleane without them, yea and that hee take his holy spirite from vs, although we had bene before endued with the same. He added soone after,

Encline my heart vnto thy testimonies: and not vnto couetousnesse.

Here we see how it hath already byn taught, that God must haue the gouernement of all the partes of man: that it is not enough that he giue him a good witt, to the ende to iudge that which is good, but his courage and minde must also be tied thereto. He hath said before, Giue me vnderstanding: and by and by, Encline my heart vnto thy testimonies. And to what ende should he encline it? Let vs here note that it is the office of God, to encline our heartes vnto his ordinances, or els, they would goe cleane against the haire. For if we were disposed of our selues to walke according to the wil of God, to hold & conceiue whatsoeuer is written in his worde, Dauid needed neuer to haue made this request, or els he should speake it faynedly and after a lying maner. When then he besought God to encline his heart to well doing: it is as much, as if he had confessed & said, It is not in me, O Lord, neither yet in any mortal creatures, to walke as thou hast commaunded, for our heartes are altogether peruerse and wicked. There is nothing in vs but rebellion and treason against thee, wee shall neuer be able to walke in thy obedience, nor neuer place our selues therein, except thou puttest to thy hand, and enclinest our mindes and heartes thereto. We see then what the condicion

dicion and disobedience of mans nature against God is, vntill such time as hee hath softened our stony and flinty heartes and that we haue learned to beare his yoke: to bee short, that our heartes be so abased and humbled, as that wee haue learned to hate that which is euill, and to desire that which is good. Loe, what is declared vnto vs in the first place.

Nowe when Dauid speaketh here of couetousnes, hee sheweth vnto vs that these thinges can abide no fellowship together, as to followe the word of God, & to be giuen to the goodes of this world. In very deede, he putteth in here one kinde for al the whole. But in the first place, let vs note, that in opposing against the keeping of the commaundements of God, that, which he knewe to be cleane contrary vnto it: he meaneth to declare that wee are intangled with so many vices and desires, as is most lamentable. And to say the truthe, what are the appetites and desires of men? when as we shall haue called out euery of them by their selfe, we shall finde nothing in them but a mere contrarietie to resist the Lorde our God. For looke howe many thoughtes and affections are in vs, they are euen so many mē of warre to fight against God. So then Dauid acknowledgeth, that he can not serue God, vntill such time as he be clensed, from all his euill desires, and vitious affections, and therefore he beseecheth God to expell out of him, that peruerseneſſe which he felt in him selfe, that he was ouermuch giuen to couetousnes, and to such other like things. And thus much for this first point.

Euen so, when as wee would followe God, let vs vnderstand that we can not do it without great conflict: to wit, vntill such time as all our passions are mortified. For our heart will neuer place it selfe rightly, vntill such time as our nature be brought vnder. True it is, that wee must not serue God either by force or constraynedly. Yea, but let vs see howe wee doe serue him, Are wee thereunto enclined as of our selues? Alas, it is nothing so, vntill such tyme as
he hath

vpon the Cxix. Pſalme. 40

he hath renued in vs our minde and will. For ſo long as we remaine in this our nature, all our ſenſes are ſtirred vp to doe euill: ſo that, as I haue before ſaid, wee ſhall neuer bee able to ſerue God, in captiuing our affections, and holding them in, as pryſoners: to the end wee be not letted to follow that which God hath commaunded vs.

Let vs now come to the ſecond point. Bicauſe that ſome vices are greater then other ſome, and ſithens that euery man may be giuen more to one vice then to an other: let vs keepe good watche, and warde, and ſtande vppon our garde. If there be any man that feeleth a vice to reigne in himſelfe, let him vnderſtand and ſaye, loe a combat euen ready at hand: and ſo let euery other man doe the like. As how? If a man haue a great number of ſeruants vnder him, he wil appoint euery one his taſke: hee will appoint to one man this thing, to another that thing, and euery of them muſt beſtowe himſelfe accordingly as hee is appointed. Euen ſo is it in an army: Some are appointed to wayte vpon the ordinaunce, ſome other are harquebuziers, ſome are horſemen, and other ſome armed pykes, or otherwiſe. Now euery of theſe muſt haue regarde whereunto to applie himſelfe, and the ſame is looked for at his hand, Euen ſo it is with vs, when as any vice warreth againſt vs: for it is as much, as if God addreſſed vs to be exerciſed therewith, to the ende wee might fight againſt it. No doubte, there is not that man which hath not in himſelfe ſome one roote of all kinde of wickedneſſe, and this is a bottomleſſe pitte wherein we are all confounded. But yet, as I haue before ſaide, there are vices which more plentifully doe abounde in one more then in another. Euery man therefore ought to haue great regarde, whereunto his nature is moſt enclined, and ſo much the more enforce him ſelfe to reſiſt all thoſe temptations, wherewith hee may bee moſt cruſhed and ſhaken. And that which is more, wee muſt haue reſpect to thoſe wicked affections and thoughtes, which might in any wyſe deceiue vs by occaſions offered vs.

It is

The 5. Sermon of M. Jo. Cal.

It is not like to be true that Dauid was naturally couetous, neither yet do we finde that he was so. But wee reade that he was a king, that he had a fertile and plentifull countrey, and that he might haue gathered together excedingly, as we also see he did. When men come to wealth and riches after that maner, it is great perill, but that they will giue them selues too too much thereto, where before they had them in contempt. Euen so then, it may be that Dauid had a care to desire to be more welthy then he was, although as the scripture witnesseth, that Gold and siluer was then little set by: For he had such plenty of them, as that golde and siluer were no better accompted off the leade or earth. He then seeing him selfe to haue so great occasions to bee giuen and drawne vnto couetousnes, was the more carefull to pray vnto God to deliuer him from it. Wee haue now to gather out of this place a good and holsome doctrine, that they which are chosen to dignitie and honour, ought to haue great regard that they bee not ouertaken with ambition, whereby they might shew the selues to be both mightie and noble touching the worlde. And againe, that they which are welthy and riche, bee not giuen ouer vnto their wealth, as in another place of the Psalme is said. If thou abound in riches, set not thine heart on them. And also that they which might bee ouertaken with their pleasures and delightes, should keepe an hard hand on the bridle, and be well aduised that they abuse not the goodes which G O D hath bestowed on them.

Loe here, say I, in the first place how euery man ought to bridle his nature, to the ende to resist and withstande the vices and sinnes, whereunto he is enclined. And next, as euery one hauing lettes or occasiōs to cause thē to exceede, they ought to keepe so much the better watche ouer them selues. For, as I haue already saide; albeit that euery of vs is giuen more to one vice then to another, yet for all that, we are euery of vs contagiously infected with them all, & there is not that man which can exempt him selfe from the same. Now it is true in deede, that Dauid here speaketh namely

of coue-

vpon the Cxix. Pſalme. 41

of couetouſnes. And why ſo? Bicauſe it is a vice which breedeth exceeding many miſchiefes. And it is not without cauſe, that S. Paul calleth it the roote of all euill: For after that a man is once giuen to the peſtilent couetouſnes of the goodes of this world, he maketh an Idol of his money, riches, and poſſeſsions. He is ſo violently carried away with them, as that he will neuer be ſatiſfied. Hee is like vnto a bottomleſſe depth which neuer wilbe filled. And afterward it maketh him to be full of crueltie, hauing neither pitie nor compaſſion of his neighboures, making neyther conſcience nor doubt to fal out with God and the worlde, ſo that he may haue them, al ſhalbe one to him. Let vs note then, that if there bee any vice which hindreth vs from the ſeruing of God, this is it: to wit, this couetous deſire of getting worldly goods. Now Dauid (after he hath ſpoken ſpecially of couetouſnes) ſaith,

1.Tim.6.10.

Turne away myne eyes from beholding of vanitie: and quicken me in thy way.

When as Dauid prayeth that his eyes might bee turned away, leaſt he beheld vanitie: It is as if he ſhould haue ſaide, Alas, my God, I had neede too withſtand a thouſande teptations, yea and they are infinite which may come before me, and that the deuill may preſent me with: to the ende I might bee wickedly ledde, from ſeruing of thee, if there were nothing els but this, it muſt needes bee that I muſt haue beene vanquiſhed a thouſand times, if thou haddeſt not inſtructed me, and that I had beene ſtrengthened with thy mightie hand: And yet O Lord, behold two gates open to receiue in the enemies. I beſeeche thee, O Lorde, that whenſoeuer we ſhalbe aſſailed with an huge armie, and beeing not of our ſelues able to reſiſt them, and that in ſteade to be in ſome moſt ſure place, where we might repulſe and beate backe our enemies, the gates ſhall ſtande wyde open to let them in: to what purpoſe were all this? Euen ſo is it in this caſe, for the two eyes of man are as it were the twoo gates whereat the enemies enter. And to what ende ſhall it be,

F

The 5. Sermon of M. Jo. Cal.

it be, when as wee shall haue neither power nor abilitie too resist, and goe out against them. And so, since we haue enemies euen lurking within our selues, and that wee are not onely weake, but that there is nothing els but weakenes in vs: and are also thrust out as it were for a praye too Satan, when we shall see these twoo gates stand so wyde open vnto all the assaultes wherewith he assaileth vs, wee haue very great neede to praye vnto God (after the example of Dauid) to turne away our eyes, least they behold vanitie. Let vs then vnderstande, that the meaning of Dauid is to declare vnto vs in this place, that the eyes of men are alwayes bent to beholde vanitie: that is to saye, that they are euer carried away to all euill, to all wicked concupiscenses, vntill such time as God turneth them away. Yea, and our eyes are not onely gates to receiue all euill: but are euen messengers also. As if the gates were not only open, but that there were also traytors within, to giue intelligēce to instruct the enemies. Loe where and which waye you must come: and which waye you must enter. Euen so is it with our eyes: our eyes receiue on the one side the enemies, and on the other side, they sende messages euen from the bottom of the heart, to enuenime and poyson vs all ouer. So then, we see howe necessarie this request is for vs all, as Dauid hath made before vs. But according as euery man most profiteth in the knowledge of God: so much the better comprehendeth he this doctrine: and they which knowe and vnderstande least herein, shall be they which will presume greatliest of their owne power and strength. But contrariewise, when God shall haue giuen, and liberally bestowed vpon vs many of his graces, it should be to this ende, that wee might so much the better vnderstande our miseries and calamities: beseeching him to remedy the same, and too make prouision for vs against all our euils and vices. Nowe he addeth,

Quicken thou me in thy waye, as in the ende hee sayeth, quicken thou me in thy rightuousnesse. This may be interpre-

vpon the Cxix. Psalme. 42

terpreted twoo maner of wayes: *Quicken thou mee in thy waye*, to witte, O Lorde, make me to walke in thy woorde, that I may lyue. Or els: O Lorde, giue mee strength, to the ende I may followe thy woorde. We knowe that when we withdrawe our selues from God, we can not but committe all iniquitie, for which is the waye of life but euen that which God sheweth vs, and calleth vs vnto? All they then which forsake the worde of God, goe astraye, and runne headlong vnto death, and into euerlasting destruction. Euen so, it is not without cause, that Dauid desireth to bee quickened in the waye of the Lorde: as if he shoulde haue sayde, that all they which forsake the Lorde, and the waye which hee sheweth them, are vndone, and vtterly ouerthrowne. But according to the true meaning of the place, wee are to note that Dauid his meaning is rather to signifie vnto vs, that all men of them selues, are as it were dead, that they haue no power nor strength when there is any question of walking according to the will of God.

True it is, that in all euill, wee are therein too too puissaunt and strong, and so diligent in it as in nothing more: to be short, there is not that hee, which is not therein too too able: But when wee meane to walke according to the commaundementes of God, wee are not able once to remoue a finger: our armes and legges shalbe cleane broken: to be short, wee are not onely weake in this, but also vtterly dead therein.

The Papistes will confesse, that men are weake, and not able to satisfie the lawe of God, except they be ayded: and thinke it sufficient enough, if God giue them a signe to ayde their weakenesse, as if a man shoulde reache his hande to a young infant, and saye vnto him, come hether my prety childe, and hee commeth, and the other maketh semblāt as though he would take him by the hād to leade him, & yet suffereth him to go alone by himselfe. Loe howe the Papistes haue diminished the graces of GOD. But contrariwise, the scripture telleth, vs that

F 2 we

thereto. Euen lo, O Lord, since thou grauntest vnto mee a cleane contrarie kinde of life: to witte, that I endeuour my selfe to serue thee, graunt me now, O Lord, that I be earnest and feruent, where before I was very slow and dull, yea, euē altogether weake and impotent. Nowe hee goeth on and sayeth:

Establishe thy promise to thy seruant, bicause he feareth thee.

When as he desireth God to establish his worde in him, and with this addition that he may feare God, hee confirmeth the requestes which he had before made. Nowe wee ought to carie this point alwayes in minde, that when wee meane to praye vnto God, wee must laye our foundation vpon his promises. We must desire nothing of him, but that we are already assured that hee will giue it vs, that hee hath of his owne good will promised vs without our requiring thereof first. For it were foolehardines to present our selues before the Lord our God, and to make our petitions after our owne pleasures: but it is mete that God himselfe preuent, and speaketh first vnto vs. Herevpon then we may assure our selues to praye when as wee haue his woorde for it.

According to which reason, Dauid after he had made his requestes as we haue heard, addeth, *O Lord, establishe thy worde in thy Seruant.* As if he shoulde haue saide, O Lorde, I desire nothing of thee, but that which thou hast promised. And loe it is it that maketh mee so bolde too come vnto thee, bicause I knowe that thou art faithfull, and wilt too doe vnto mee euen as thou hast promised. Wherefore as the promisses of GOD ought to giue vs an entrance into our prayers, and alwayes to go on: euen soo also after that wee haue prayed, lette vs call too minde his owne promisses, to the ende wee may bee

assured

vpon the Cxix. Psalme. 43

assured that it shall not be in vaine, that wee haue required of him. And why so? Bicause that God of his owne free good will hath bounde him selfe vnto vs, there is no doubt but that we shall obtaine, considering that he will accomplishe whatsoeuer he hath saide, for he can not fayle vs. Loe then the meaning of the beginning of this verse.

Nowe when Dauid saieth *that he may feare the Lord*, he meaneth not that he would here alledge his merites: but he doth it to this ende, to declare that hee hath followed the same vocation whereunto he was called: and yet notwithstanding hee sheweth, that hee coulde not walke in the feare of God, but by the vertue and power of the holy ghost, which was continually in him. And euen so must we also do. For whensoeuer we shall feele any good zeale in vs, wee must not bragge vpon it: for what haue wee that wee haue not receiued: according to the saying of Paul? For what is it that should separate vs, that we should not be like vnto the most wicked? commeth it of our owne nature? no surely. It must needes be then, that it is God which hath put to his helping hand. And so, whatsoeuer goodnesse is in vs, it is a testimonie of the good will which God beareth vs, and that he wilbe our father and Sauiour. Loe here why Dauid setteth this foremost, as though he would ratifie the promisses of God. Now he concludeth.

Take away my rebuke that I am afraide of: for thy iudgements are good.

Behold I desire thy commandements: O quicken mee in thy righteousnesse.

We shal neuer be able to knowe, what the rebuke which Dauid here speaketh of is, except we haue regard whereunto all his whole drifte heretofore tendeth, and too what ende: to witte, that God would defende and keepe him, and also guide him, as it were with his hande, to the ende that as he had begunne well, hee might also in like maner perseuer and continue. Nowe the shame which all the faithfull ought to feare is, that God suffereth them not to be confounded: that when they haue for a certaine time walked

The 5. Sermon of M.I. Cal.

walked well, they might not in the ende giue them selues to wickednesse: that the latter part of their life might manifest that it was not well and surely rooted within, but was hypocriticall and dissembled.

Behold the rebuke which Dauid feared, to wit, that after he had walked well, that God would not leaue him as a confounded man: And namely he sayth, *for thy iudgements are good*. As if he should haue saide, Alas, my God, so that I followe the same which thou hast commaunded mee, although that men speake euill of me and slaunder me for it, all is one to mee, when as my conscience shalbe pure and cleane, and that thou art my warrant and witnesse, it is enough for me. Behold then, O my God, the rebuke from which I desire to be deliuered, to witte, that thou suffer me not to be wickedly giuen, nor that I depart from thy commaundements: but let my life and conuersation be agreable to thy worde. O that suffiseth me: and let men speake what them liste, their iudgement is false, and I appeale from them.

Then to conclude he saieth; *My delight is in thy commaundementes: O quicken me in thy righteousnes*. The righteousnesse of God oftentimes is taken for the grace which God vseth towardes his children, or at the leastwise wherewith he conducteth them. But he setteth downe righteousnesse here, for right, and equitie. Hee hath saide before, *quicken me according to thy woorde*: Nowe by and by after followeth *righteousnesse*. Neyther must we thinke this to bee straunge, for we haue shewed here before, that Dauid speaking of the commaundementes of GOD, after that he hath vsed his terme namely of these woordes, ordinaunces and statutes, he taketh other wordes. As in this place, after he hath said, *quicken me in thy worde*, he sayeth soone after, *In thy righteousnesse*. And he maketh also this request, *that hee might bee conducted in the way of the Lord*. Whereby hee would shewe, that it is not enough that we be wel affected, but that God must encrease the same in vs, yea, hee must conduct and quicken vs, as here he telleth vs. For it is so farre off, that of

our

our selues we can doe any good, that we are not able once to thinke a good thought, as S. Paul saith.

Loe then, how Dauid desired to be quickened: but that was in protesting that he was as touching him selfe and his owne nature, but as it were a condemned man.

And herein must we also do the like. For wee must goe vnto our good God as men condemned in our selues, beseeching him that he would quicken vs. And when he shall haue caused vs to feele his grace, and that wee haue stayed our selues thereon, let vs say, we beseeche thee O Lord, that since it hath pleased thee to beginne in vs well doing, that thou wouldest also perfourme the same in vs. And according to this doctrine let vs prostrate our selues before the Maiestie of our good God, in acknowledging our faultes: Beseeching him that it would please him to make vs feele our miserie and wretchednesse, whereunto wee are giuen whiles we liue here in this world: to the end we may walke so fearefully and carefully as that wee may be able to perceiue that wee haue receiued some fauour and grace from our God, and that in following the right way which hee hath shewed vnto vs, wee may daily more and more aspire to the ende which he hath set before vs, which is to attaine to that immortall glorie, to conioyne vs vnto our head and captaine our Lord Iesus Christ, after that he shall haue despoyled vs of all the vices and imperfections of our flesh, and cloathe vs with his righteousnes. And that he will not onely graunt vs this grace, but also vnto all people and nations of the world, &c.

The

The sixth Sermon of the hundreth
and nineteenth Psalme.

VAV.

And let thy louing kindnes come vnto me, O Lord:
and thy saluation according to thy promisse.

So shall I make answere vnto my blasphemers: for
my trust is in thy word.

And take not the worde of thy truth vtterly out of
my mouth: for I waite for thy iudgements.

So shall I alwaies keepe thy lawe: yea for euer and
euer.

And I will walke at libertie: for I seeke thy commaundementes.

I will speake of thy testimonies also euen before
kinges: and will not be ashamed.

And my delight shall be in thy commaundements:
which I haue loued.

My handes also will I lift vp vnto thy commaundements, which I haue loued: and my study shalbe
in thy statutes.

HE beginning of these eight verses côteine a request which Dauid made vnto God, that he felt the accôplishment and performance of the promises which god graūted vnto him, and after which he hoped. As if he should haue said, O Lord, declare vnto me, that the promisse which thou hast made vnto me to do me so much good, be not in vaine, but that thou wilt make me feele in deede, that thy word and promise is most certaine and true. Now, that he founded him self vpô the promises of God, appeareth by his thus saying:

And

Wherein also we see that Satan craftely goeth aboute to ouerthrow his faith, as if God had made it nothing worth. So then, First of all we are to note, that Dauid feeling him selfe pressed downe, runneth vnto the promises of God. And this is a poynt very profitable for vs. For beholde how we must put the word of God in practise, when as we haue learned it, that when we come to the fight, and Satan assaileth vs on euery side, in such sort as that it might seeme that all the worlde had conspyred against vs; and that wee see nothing but destruction rounde about: Euen then, I say, must we run vnto the promises which God hath made vs, and make accounte of them, and so apply them to our own vse, that then wee may feele the power and strength of them. Nowe it shall be an easy matter for vs, when as wee are at rest and quiet, to receiue whatsoeuer God hath saide vnto vs. And why so? Because our Faith all that while shall not be exercised and troubled, so that we shall neuer bee able to feele whether we haue beleeued in good earnest, vntill such time as we are tryed. Loe, Why I haue said that this place is worthy the marking, that Dauid speaketh not without cause when he sayth, So shall I make answere vnto those that go about to shae me. For by these words he protesteth, that the wicked conténed, despised & mocked him, as if he had bin a very foole, in trusting so much vnto God, but yet for that, his faith was not shaken. And see how Satan assayleth vs with temptations, when as the wicked and vngodly speake reprochfull woordes of vs: insomuch as wee haue thought it to be woonderfull straunge geere, because that we hauing hearde the so honourable & excellent promises of God, thought our selues straightwayes to bee rapte and caryed aboue the cloudes, and yet this same our persuasion proued nothing at all so, as it made a shewe to the outward apparance: Euen so likewise came it to passe in Dauid, as wee

The 6. Sermon of M. Io. Cal.

we may especially see in the twentie and twoo Psalme.

And our Sauiour Christ also, who is the very true paterne and mirrour of all the Children of God hath sustained & abiden such combates. Very well (said they vnto him) hee trusteth in God, Let him nowe see whether God will heare him or not. Let vs then note, that Dauid hath not deuised and made heere any vaine speculations, as an idle body might doe, which neuer had beene tempted nor distressed. But beeing so mocked by his enemyes, that his faith seemed to be ouerthrowne, and he him selfe in great hazarde vtterly to be destroyed, then came he for refuge to the promises of God, saying: My God, thou haste giuen mee thy worde, which cannot fayle me: Loe wherein is all hope and trust. Euen so also ought we to followe this doctrine, too wit, when the worlde on the oneside shall deride and scorne vs, because we haue ouer lightly credited God, and that Satan shall trauel all he can too turne vs cleane away from the certaintie which wee haue had : yet let vs not cease too say, O Lord, it is thou which hast spoken, and in thee is all our hope and trust.

Moreouer, as wee are to call too minde the promises of God, when as wee are assayled by Satan and the vngodly: Let vs also note (as hath beene heeretofore treated of) that this is it whereon we must builde al our requests: For if we will earnestly pray vnto God, and obtaine that which wee pray for, we must not pray in the ayre, & say, O Lord I pray vnto thee for such a thing, and I would it might so come to passe. For this were ouer rash and too too great boldenesse to think to make God subiect to our willes, to bridle him as we list, and to desire him to graunte vs whatsoeuer shall please our appetites: but it is his worde that must leade vs, and be our Cresset: and we must referre our selues wholy to it, and altogither rest thereon. Beholde, say I, after what sort our prayers are allowed, to wit, whē as we pray not to God for that which seemeth best in our owne eyes, but when as we be fenced with that which he hath promised vs.

And this is it, wherein we differ from the Painimes and Infidels,

Infidels. For wee see that the Turkes and Idolaters doe greatly pray vnto God. But after what manner pray they? Forsooth euen at all aduenture: so that they knowe not what they doe. But contrariwise wee must pray vnto him, with full assuraunce that he will heare vs. But from whence shall this certaintie proceede, if wee haue not the trueth to goe before vs, and say: beholde the Lorde, who calleth vs vnto him? And then when wee come vnto him, this is no foolish presumption: But we come in such sorte vnto him, as he hath commaunded vs.

    Let vs then see what wee haue yet to note in this place, when Dauid setteth downe heere the promises of God, by which he is bounde vnto him: *O Lorde*, sayth he, *let it bee doone vnto me according to thy worde*. Nowe heere is a very profitable poynt to be considered off: to witte, after that we are once assured, that God hath promised too doe that for vs which we shall aske of him, we must no more doubt, that it shall be so: but that the thing is fully concluded vpon, so that we are euer sure and certaine thereof. For when God speaketh vnto vs, we are very sure, that he will not deceiue vs: hee will not giue vs faire woordes, and then deceiue vs, as men many times doe, dealing very liberally with their tongues, but yet notwithstanding very close sifted: But God dealeth not in such sorte. Let vs then come before him without distrust, Haue wee his woorde? Let vs then holde the thing as already performed. And so when Dauid sayth, *according to thy word*, hee signifieth vnto vs, that hee was not onely assured, that God is faithfull and liberal, that he meaneth not to abuse vs when as wee truste to him: but sheweth vs, that this certaintie which wee haue of the trueth of God, should not make vs weary, to say, that wee bee as it were euen ouerwhelmed. But wee must rather be carefull and diligent to pray vnto him.

    There are some men which will in deede say, that they beleeue the promises of G O D, but since, say they, hee knoweth what wee haue neede of, what neede wee to bee importune vppon him.

Now

The 6. Sermon of M. Io. Cal.

Nowe these men indeede, very well declare, that they neuer vnderstood what faith and hope are For if we receiued the promises of God without hypocrisie we ought to be thus earnest and zealous, to pray, and haue recourse vnto him, saying, O Lorde God, when as thou hast assured mee of thy bountie and mercie, it is to this end, that I should call vpon thee in my neede. And that I see the necessitie which vrgeth and presseth mee, I muste needes come vnto thee as thou haste called mee by thy worde. Beholde then, that all the promises of God should serue vs in stede of so many spurres to prick vs forwarde, in making our prayers vnto him. Let vs nowe come to the woords of Dauid.

Let thy louing mercyes, or thy graces, come vnto me O Lord, and thy saluation.

After that he hath layde his foundation whereuppon too builde, he desireth one selfe same thing in two words, which to the outwarde apparance are diuers and sundry: to wit, the graces of God, and his saluation. And yet notwithstanding Dauid meneth nothing else, but that god would shew him selfe to be his Sauiour. Neither is there any thing heere spoken superfluously: For it is asmuch as if he had sayd, O my God, I besech thee that according to thy promise, thou wilt make me feele thee to be my sauiour and father. But yet in the meane while, he expresseth vnto vs whence this saluation which we must wayte for, and whiche God hath promised vs cometh, and that is, of his meere good will. For men cannot otherwise choose: but that they wil euer wrongfully take vpon them some thing or other, which apperteineth nothing vnto them, and alwayes to be foolishly and arrogantly bounde vnto them selues. Nowe Dauid, cleane contrary, sheweth heere, that all the saluation which he hopeth after & desireth, commeth from another springheade, then from the vertue and dignitie of men: to wit, euen from the meere goodnes of God, So then wee see, that as before he hath spoken of the promise, euen so also hee heere addeth and expresseth the cause, which moued God to bind himself so vnto vs: to wit, *his meere mercy.*

By this we are admonished, that when we are to call vpon God, we should alwayes haue regarde vnto these twoo things: to wit, the grace of God and his free mercie, and after that his promise. God is good and liberall, and see why it is; that he with pitie looketh vppon vs: and beholding vs with his eyes of cōpassion, vouchsafe th to receiue vs, yea and calleth and allureth vs vnto him, and also imboldeneth vs to craue of him, to the end he would help and succour vs in all our needes and necessities. Now this goodnesse should lye hidden in God, were it not that hee made vs to feele it by his promise: For God sheweth himselfe vnto vs, to be such a one as in deede he is, he layeth his heart wide open, when he rendreth vs a testimonie of the loue hee beareth vs.

Loe heere why I haue said, that in all our prayers wee ought to haue these two considerations: The one is, that God is so good and louing, that although wee bee poore and miserable creatures, and nothing else but doung and stench, yet for all that hee ceaseth not too loue vs, and to haue greate care of our saluation. And since wee are come too the promise, which is a sure testimonie that God is such one, we should no more doubt what affection he beareth vs, whether he be our friend or enemie, seeing it is so that he is very well willing to bee bounde vnto vs, in declaring vnto vs that he is our father, and taketh vs to bee his Children.

Nowe Dauid maketh such a request as we haue already touched, to the end he might answere those which wrought him shame. Although he sayth word for word, *To the ende I may answeare these which woorke me shame.* Heere Dauid declareth, that when God shall haue ayded him, that then he shall be able to withstand all his enemyes, put by all the iniuries & scornes of the vnbeleuers and faythlesse which they did lay before him, to the end too shake and crush the faythful and to destroy them, yea and vtterly to make their fayth nothing woorth, if it were possible for them to do it. By this we are let to vnderstande, that if we make our prayers

The 6. Sermon of M. Io. Cal.

ers to God, whensoeuer it shal happen al the world too assaile vs, and that it might seeme wee shoulde be plunged in hel an hundred thousand tymes, yet wee might stande sure against al our enemies: yea verely, for God wil neuer fayle vs, whensoeuer we shall desire & pray him to performe his promises vnto vs, and make vs feele his goodnesse for our saluation. Moreouer if we haue wherewithal too resiste the wicked and vngodly which come vppon vs too daunt and quaile our fayth, we shall haue also wherwith to withstande Satan. For whē men shal persecute vs, or deride the promises of God, and labour al they may to turne vs away from them, it commeth not of themselues, but it is the Deuill which pusheth them foreward. Euen so then, wee may fight and winne the victorie against al the combats of Satā, if we wil pray vnto God, after the example of Dauid.

This is also to be considered and noted which heere hee addeth, when he sayeth, *My delight is in thy woorde*. Hee declareth what signes and tokens he desired of God here before, that he would doo vnto him as he had promised. For I haue delight therein, saith hee, would wee then haue God his promises to take place in vs, to open the gate that wee might come vntoo him, that they might bee as keyes too giue vs in entree, too the ende our requestes and petitions might bee receiued? wee must then ioyne hope therewith. And loe what is the cause why wee feele not the power of the promises of God as wee ought: the reason is, for that we haue no hope nor trust in them. It is most true, that god for his parte is alwaies true of his woord: and although we are miserable faythlesse people, yet wil hee neuer falsify his fayth which he hath giuen to vs. But what? Surely wee are vnwoorthy ones too feele such a pleasure. In very deed, god hath promised to powre his grace vpon vs, as also hee offereth it vntoo vs: But yet are wee vtterly vnworthy thereof, without we belieue his promises, would we that god shold do vnto vs according to his word? we must then receiue his word, and imbrace it by fayth: as also the Apostle treateth thereof.

Heb. 4. 2.

vpon the Cxix. Pſalme.

thereof. And thus much as touching theſe two firſt verſes.

Nowe it followeth: *Take not the woorde of thy trueth vtterly out of my mouth: for I waite for thy iudgementes.*

When Dauid ſayth, *O take not the word of thy trueth out of my mouth:* He meaneth not, that it ſufficeth too magnifie God with his toung: and to make many goodly proteſtations before the worlde: but he preſuppoſeth, that when he hath witneſſed of the trueth of God with his mouth, that it muſt alſo be graffed within his hearte. And in deede, Dauid ſpeaketh not heere like an hypocrite, as they do which would ſeeme to make a goodly ſhew before him: and think them ſelues wel inough and in good caſe, when as they are openly ſuppoſed too bee very faithful, well thought off, and taken to be very honeſt men, this think they is all that is to be required. But Dauid hath not proceeded after this manner: For when he ſayth, *Take not the woord of thy trueth out of my mouth, O Lord.* It is aſmuch as if hee had ſayde, O Lorde, doe me not onely this grace, that I truſt ſecretly in thee, that I ſtay me vpon thy promiſes, that I ſtand ſure againſt all the aſſaultes of mine enemyes, but namely and cheifely euen before the face of men: that my faith might declare it ſelfe, that by this meane I might guide and inſtruct all thoſe which would come vnto thee: & contrarywiſe that I might withſtand all thoſe which ſhall goe about to ouerthrowe this ſpirituall hope of mine, which I haue in thee and in thy trueth. And when thou O Lorde ſhalte haue deepely rooted thy worde in mine hearte, let it alſo bee often times in my mouthe, that I may magnifie thy name before men.

Wee haue then to learne out of this place, that in the firſt place we muſt be aſſured of the trueth of God, yea al. though that men perceiue it not in vs: And againe although euery man would keepe it ſo ſecrete too him ſelfe, as that no man in all the worlde knewe thereof, yet GOD and his Angels doe knowe, how true and certaine

we

The 6. Sermon of M. Io. Cal.

we esteeme it to be, and also how we yeelde therto, the honor which vnto it appertaineth, and to be such in deede as deserueth to bee holden for true and faithful. And thus much for the first poynt. Now for the seconde, Let vs aduisedly consider to edifie our neighbours, that they might be confirmed by our example, and all with one accorde to trust in God, that the wicked and vngodly might bee ashamed that we might vexe them, that we haue wherin to glory, notwithstanding all their windelasses, priuy deuises, and whatsoeuer mischiefe else they are any way able to imagine against vs, and thinking to make vs as prophane as themselues, yet that we may be able to cast them of, after the example of Dauid. Lo then, the worde which he desireth to haue alwayes in his mouth, too confirme all those which would trust in God, and to confound all them which deride and scorne his worde and trueth. But what meaneth he by this saying, *For euer?* That is, that he beeing as it were forsaken of God in all his afflictions, was as one that were dumbe and coulde not speake, as he complayneth in another place. And in deede, so long as God sheweth vnto vs no token of his grace, although our enemyes deride vs with open mouth, yet we are not at that libertie to confute them and stop their mouthes. Dauid then beeing thus tempted a long time, desireth that the confession wherewith hee might be able to magnifie God, might not to be taken frō him for euer. Wherein we are to obserue, that if God sometimes leaueth vs confounded after the maner of the world, in steade of beeing dismaied, wee ought too beseech him that hee woulde not suffer our mouthes too be stopped for euer.

Nowe he repeateth it ouer againe: *For my hope is in thy iudgementes.* It is not without cause that Dauid stil maketh this protestation: For as I haue already saide, behold what power and efficacy the woorde of God causeth vs to feele (according to that place which I haue alledged out of the Epistle too the Hebrues.) when wee haue therewith hope also, which hangeth vpon faith. It is true that God stretched out

vpon the Cxix. Psalme. 49

ched out his hand vnto his people, when he brought them out of the land of Ægypt, to the ende hee woulde bringe them into the promised land. But what? the people stayed not them selues vpon God, and therefore it was meete that that promise should be voyde, yea and that iustly vnto such a faythlesse people. God had no long time to finde out such a woonderfull & meruaylous straunge meane as that man could not possibly cōceiue, how that might be brought to passe which hee had spoken. But this auayled them nothing which were faithlesse: For loe they beeing excluded from such a benefite: are depriued of that promised inheritaunce. Let vs then learne, that when wee woulde haue God to open his hand vnto vs and deale liberally with vs, to haue vs to feele his mightie power, and that wee might perceiue the fruite and benefite of his promises. It is meete that we plant them deepely in our heartes: that wee may say after the example of Dauid, *My hope O Lorde is in thy iudgementes.* For this woorde *Integritie* or *iudgement*, wee haue heere before already declared, signifieth nothing else but the doctrine conteined in the law of God, yea although he heere vseth diuerse and sundry woordes, yet doe they tende alwayes to one and the selfe same ende. Loe then whether we must refer the iudgements of God: to wit, that that which we reade in the word of God, and that which is preached vnto vs out of the same, we must vnderstand and knowe to bee sure and certaine Statutes and ordinaunces, and so well ordered as that they cannot bee bettered, and therfore to haue all our hope and trust in them. Now he goeth on and sayth,

So shall I alway keepe thy lawe: yea for euer and euer.
And I will walke at libertie: for I seeke thy commandements.

Dauid heere maketh protestation not onely of his good affection & integritie, but also sheweth the fruite and benefite that might come vnto him, when as God shall haue so holpen him and that he shall haue put in proofe the fruit of his faith. Loe then how this place must be expounded: O Lord, when I shall once haue knowen thee to be my sauiour

G. and

and felt by proofe thy mercie: then will I keepe thy lawe a greate deale better: As if he should haue said, I shallbe continually confirmed in thy obedience: and that shall greatly helpe me, to make alwayes forward. And to say the trueth, all the graces which we receiue from God, should conduct and leade vs a great deale further, that if wee haue already beene in a good way and forwardnesse, it is to this end that wee shoulde continue in it, and goe on more and more, vntill such time as we come to the end.

It is very true that God in conducting vs, looketh not for any recompence. For he will lightly passe it ouer: but this is spoken for our vse and instruction. And when we pray vnto God, we ought to seeke after all the thinges that can be which might confirme vs, that we should not doubt but that God would heare our requests, and that we should also vnderstand and knowe to what ende wee ought to referre those benefites which he bestoweth vpon vs, and that we receiue at his hands. Now then, when Dauid saith, *I shall alwayes keepe thy lawe, yea for euer and euer.* By this wee haue to note, that accordingly as God liberally bestoweth his benefites vpon vs, that our faith should be so much the more strengthened in him, that we ought the rather too be inflamed with a true desire & zeale, to yeelde our selues fully and wholly too him, to cleaue to his righteousnesse, and to keepe his lawe and woorde. And I woulde it pleased God that this might bee deepely imprinted in our minde. But what? we see the vnthankfulnesse, which is as it were in vs all. For God neuer ceaseth to doe vs good, and will dayly giue vs newe matter to trust in him, to loue and serue him. But whatsoeuer he doth for vs, it auaileth vs nothing, for we are alwayes colde as yse: there is no zeale in vs, no not so much as any motion, so that it seemeth wee are altogither senselesse. And the rather ought we to meditate vpon this Doctrine: For it is the right remedy to amend our so great litherneffe and coldenesse.

Let vs then learne, that when Dauid sayth, *I shall keepe thy Law, O Lorde,* that by this he meaneth, that accordingly as

ly as God putteth vnto vs his helping hande, and that wee
haue had proofe of his graces, that we receiue the fruite &
commoditie thereof, which we haue hoped for in his promises: that it ought to serue vs for a more ample and large
confirmation, and that we ought a greate deale rather too
be stirred vp to loue God, and to serue him, and too yeelde
vs vnto his worde; in summe as heere it is saide, too keepe
his lawe. But yet there is a great deale more to be consi-
red. For Dauid speaketh not heere of a blast of winde,
as some shall be very forwarde for a little time. But hee
sayeth, *I will alwayes keepe thy lawe : yea, for euer and euer.*
Wherein he sheweth, that we ought to haue such a remembraunce of the benefites of God, that it neuer slip from vs.
For as I haue heereof already spoken, wee shall see some in
this behalfe, which shall be moued for a little while, when
as God shall haue deliuered them from any daunger, and
hath bestowed vppon them some fauour and grace: they
shall haue a very good taste and feeling, and say, Alas, howe
greately am I bounden and beholden to my God! A ma-
man woulde thinke that these men were well affected. But
in the turning of a hand, no doubt it is soone forgotten,
or at the least if they remember it a little while, they waxe
colde againe and thinke no more of it. Since then it is so,
let vs mark, according to that which is spoken in this place,
that it is not meete that the remembrance of God his benefites should at any time be wiped out of our heartes: but
let vs beseech him to make vs to keepe his lawe for euer and
euer: and in such sort to instruct vs, as that wee desire none
other thing of him, but to stick vnto his maiestie, and to his
righteousnesse. It followeth:

That hee will walke at libertie : because hee seeketh his
Commaundementes.

To walke at liberty, signifieth to go at a mans owne will &
pleasure: For like as when we are in a narrowe & straight
rowme, we know not which way to turne vs, but thinke our
selues cleane pend vp: Euen so also, are wee once narrowly
held in, or else surely we look about vs to see if wee can finde

G.2. which

which way to get out, and so doe remaine in perplexitie or doubte. And is this the assuraunce and ioy that wee must haue in the lawe of God? What? is this it? Dauid contrariwise sayth, *That he will walke at libertie* : to wit, that hee will boldely walke the brode beaten way, as we say, after he hath sought the Commaundementes of God. This is also a thing which we ought wel to obserue and keepe. For the holy Ghost by the mouth of Dauid meaneth rightly to shewe vs, that when we are desirous to haue our life ruled by the commaundementes of God, to suffer him too bee our leader and guide, and giue vnto him the conducte of all our affayres and businesses, that hee will so frame himselfe vnto vs, so farre foorth as hee shall knowe to bee good and expedient for our saluation.

And this benefite which wee receiue by the knowledge heereof is inestimable: to wit, that we may walke at liberty, That is to say, that wee are deliuered from many doubtes and griefes : that we cannot bee vtterly ouerthrowne and caste downe, although we happen to be pressed with some griefes : because we alwayes conclude thus, that wee cannot bee ouercome, seeing God holdeth vs with a mightie and stronge hande. And in very deede what is the cause, I pray you, that men are so oftentimes tormented, but onely that they submit not them selues vnto God? It is very true, that there are very fewe which knowe this, but this is the very cause : For when as wee shall haue looked somewhat neerer the matter, wee shall find that nothing so much hath hindred vs, as our owne vnthankfulnesse: But because we wil be ouerwise, in not yeelding vnto God the honor to gouerne vs, & wholy to rule our life, ne yet become his subiects, it is meet we should receiue the hier due for the same. For men whē any thing is in question that they haue to do, wil straight wayes enter into their owne speculations, they neuer make question to haue recourse vnto God, nor to cal vpon him, but euery man wil doe what semeth best to himself. And therfore it is meete that God pay vs in such mony as we deserued, that he put vs, I say, in such doubt as that

wee

wee shall neuer be able to knowe what shall become of vs, so that the anguishes shall force vs too say, What shall become of this matter? Which way shall I beginne? And what shall bee the ende and issue heereof?

Beholde howe wee see the miserable and wretched worlde, dayly so fast shutte vp in streights, as that it seemeeth that wee are more then cast away. And what is the cause heereof? Euen the men which haue built vnto them selues such Mazes. For it is euen they them selues that are the cause of their so greate tormentes. For Dauid hath heere declared vnto vs, that as many as seeke the Commaundementes of God, doe walke at libertie. It is very true, that the faithfull although they indeuour themselues all they can, to obey God, and suffer him to gouerne them, yet for all that they are not voyde of merueylous griefes & vexations that they are many tymes at their wittes end and knowe not what to doe, but yet they come vnto God, and lay all their care vpon him, as it is written in the thirtie and seuenth Psalme. And there they finde them selues discharged and vnburdened. And so goe they dayly on: for they are assured that God can neuer fayle them. Beholde then, howe we may bee very well tempted with many sorrowes and griefes, neither can wee be exempt from a great number of disquietnesses: but yet God will alwayes vnburden vs of them, as it is sayd in an other place of the Psalme, that when we haue beene for a while fast shut vpp, yet God will set vs at libertie: as also Saint Paul sayth in the second to the Corinthes: *It is very true,* sayth hee, *that wee are oppressed with many tormentes and griefes, but yet we continue not in sorrowe and payne: For God will alwayes deliuer vs, and will giue vs a good and ioyfull issue, so that in the ende wee shall bee able to ouercome them.*

See then what is declared vnto vs in this place, where it is sayde, *I will walke at libertie, O Lorde, because I seeke thy Commaundementes.* Euen so let vs knowe, that when our life is miserable and wretched, and that we must needes liue

The 6. Sermon of M. Io. Cal.

liue in payne, torment, and sorrowe: that all commeth by reason of our sinne, because wee present not our selues before GOD, suffer vs not to be conducted by him, put not our liues into his handes, neither doo wee come willingly too seeke for remedie, after wee haue once knowen our griefe: that is too say, too desire God that it woulde please him to take vs into his custodye, without hoping or wayting for any other thing, but forthat which he telleth vs out of his woorde. For when wee shall so doo, there is no doubte, but that he will make vs too walke at libertie. Nowe it followeth:

I will speake of thy Testimonyes also euen before Kinges: and will not be ashamed.

Beholde a declaration of the matter which wee haue already touched heere before: For Dauid making this request, not to haue the woorde of trueth to bee taken out of his mouth for euer, had regarde to twoo thinges: that is to say, beeing able too speake, after that GOD in bestowing his grace vpon him, had opened his mouth, had confirmed the Children of GOD by his example, and brought them vnto him in shewing them the way, and in the meane whyle had foyled the wicked and despisers of God and of the Lawe, the scorners of his hope, and the blasphemers of God: yet was hee able, I say, too beate them backe, and make his parte good againste them all. And this matter hee manifestly declareth, whereas hee sayeth, *I will speake of thy Testimonyes*, because GOD shoulde no more take the woorde of trueth out of his mouth.

Nowe besides this, that God giueth vntoo vs matter whereof to speake freely, yet must that come from him, as we heare, that our Lord Iesus Christe hath spoken off: that it is the holy Ghoste which guideth our tongues, that it cometh not of ourselues, to be able to answere our enemies that there neded but a small gale of wind to ouerthrow vs. So then, it is meete that God shoulde vse his power that

wee

vpon the Cxix. Pfalme.

we might be confirmed by him: For when as he shal put his woorde in our mouth, we may speake before Kinges and Princes, and neuer be ashamed. As if he should haue sayde, O Lorde, thy woorde ought to be of such power vnto vs, as that wee may foyle our enemyes, yea howe greate and mightie soeuer they bee: albeit they should bee suche as were able to astonish and feare all the whole world, yet let our Fayth be ouerthrowne, through their mightinesse, and pompe: knowing that when as they shall thinke too swallowe all vp, yet that we be left stil alwayes as Conquerors, yea euen becaufe we haue regarde to it.

Nowe heere wee are too note, that when God maketh his trueth forcible in vs, it shall bee sufficient too holde vs vpp, yea, notwithstanding all the Combates that the Deuill shall stirre vpp agaynst vs, and that the whole world opposed it selfe too the contrary. And it is not without cause that this is spoken, for whereon is our fayth setled? Euen vppon the trueth of God. Let vs nowe compare God with men, and with all their woorkes and vertues. Let vs take Emperours and Kinges: and let all their glorie and pompe bee set foorth too the shewe, and let God be set right ouer agaynst them: too witte, whether men with all their mightinesse and great boasting, are able too surmounte God, too reuerse his will, or too make voyde his power and vertue? Oh, it is very sure they can neuer be able to doe it.

So then, let vs consider with whome wee haue too deale, and remember this saying of Saincte Paule, *Thou knowest* (sayeth hee) *to what ende thy beliefe serueth*. When then wee shall haue our eyes so fixed vppon GOD, who hath armed vs with his infallible trueth, wee may bee able too withstande and fall out with all whatsoeuer that lifteth it selfe vpp too the contrary: Wee shall haue no occasion too feare the worlde, for GOD is sufficiently able too ouercome all the scruples and griefes which the Deuill shall rayse vppe agaynste vs. And thus muche as concerning

concerning this poynte.

Moreouer we see that when there is any question to make confession of our faith, it cannot be that men shalbe able to abash and feare vs with al their power and might: As at this day we see, when as they woulde gladly make vs too tremble. What I beseech you Sir? (wil they say) you are but euen a handfull of people. Doe you thinke your selues wiser then all the Kings and Princes of the world? You see that all the world, are against this doctrine which you holde & professe: and what doe you thinke to doe? True in deede, that at the firste sight, this were euen inough too shake vs, yea were it not that we knewe, and were very certaine: but when we looke vnto God, then all this geere vanisheth intoo smoke: these are but Bladders pufte full of winde: and the leaste pinnes poynte, will emptie them. In very deede these will bee greate fraybugges, but yet it will all prooue nothing. Beholde these Frogges, beholde these Pismeres, yea, beholde these Flyes and Gnattes, for they are all no better then very vermine and wormes, when as they shall lifte them selues vp thus against God.

So then let vs learne, yea let vs learne to stay our selues so vpon God, as that when we shall be called too make confession of our faith, since it is so that it is GOD whiche hath spoken, let all the creatures in the worlde be nothing to vs warde: let vs not bee ashamed, and let nothing hinder and stoppe vs, from mainteining of his woorde. In the ende Dauid concludeth and sayth,

My handes also will I lifte vpp vnto thy Commaundementes, which I haue loued: and my study shallbee in thy statutes.

These twoo verses heere neede no long declaration, for wee haue already had the same sentences: and yet notwithstandinge Dauid sheweth vs, that it is not inough to thinke of this Doctrine for a time: but wee muste all the course of our life profite our selues therein more and more.

Loe

vpon the Cxix. Pſalme.

Loe here the principall point which we haue to note, that we muſt take pleaſure in the commaundementes of God which we haue loued: to wit, that wee ought to learne to conceiue ſuch an affection and deſire to followe the worde of God, and to ſticke thereto, as that we ſhould be fully reſolued to ſay, In very deede, this is the moſt ſweete and amiable thing that poſsibly can be, to ſubiect our ſelues vnder the yoke of our God and to beare it; and therefore wee muſt drawe in it, and obey him. Haue we done this? Wee muſt then in ſteade of a number of fooliſh vanities wherevnto we are enclined, yea, and in place of the wicked affections and allurementes of Satan, learne to take pleaſure in the worde of God, ſo that we may proteſt in trueth (after the example of Dauid) that they are the commandements of God which we haue loued. Moreouer let vs marke well this ſentence, when he ſaith, *My handes alſo wil I lift vp vnto thy commaunndementes.* For this is as much as if he had ſaid, O Lord, I will not onely proteſt with my mouth that I loue thy word, but I will alſo lift vp my hands: yea, as wee commonly ſay, I will lift vp my handes to the caky God. By this he letteth vs to vnderſtande, that if we would ſerue God as becommeth vs, that it is not enough for vs to witneſſe the truthe of God with our mouth, but we muſt alſo ſhewe by our good and godly life, that which wee proteſt with our mouth, and that there be an accorde and ſweete harmonie betweene the one and the other. True it is, wee ſhall finde ſome doubtes when as there ſhalbe any queſtion of following God: but this ſentence is to bee noted, when hee ſayeth, I will lift vp my hands. And to know that when God ſhall ſee, that it ſhall ſurpaſſe our force and ſtrength, let vs pray vnto him to graunt vs that grace, that we may lift vp our handes vnto his commaundementes, to witte, ſo high as we can poſsibly, to the ende wee may take holde of his grace and vertue, better then heretofore we haue done. Lo in what maner we ought to doe in this caſe, that not preſuming of our owne power and ſtrength, we might praye notwithſtanding this good God, to make his grace ſo forcible

The 6. Sermon of M.I.Cal.

cible in vs, as that it may settle and reigne there, and to haue vs know that it is not in vaine that hee calleth vs vnto him & giueth vs his truthe. Which thing no doubt he will doe so that wee reiect not his grace, which hee so freely offereth vnto vs. And according to this holy doctrine let vs prostrate our selues before the maiestie of our good God, in acknowledging our faultes, beseeching him that it would please him to open our eyes, to the ende wee may know our wretchednes, & the miserable conditiō wherein we stande, that wee might returne to him : yea, and that with a certaine confidence, that hee will perfourme that which he hath promised vs : that we be not frustrate of our hope, when as it shall stay vpon him, and in his truthe, but that hee will more and more strengthen vs therein, vntill such time as we come to the perfect knowledge of thinges, which we yet knowe not but in parte. That not only he will grant vs this grace, but also vn-to all people and na-tions of the world, &c.

The

The seuenth Sermon of the hundreth
and nineteenth Psalme.

ZAIN.

Remember the promise made vnto thy seruaunt:
 wherein thou hast caused me to put my trust.
The same is my cōfort in my trouble: for thy worde
 hath quickened me.
The proud haue had me exceedingly in derision: yet
 haue I not declined from thy lawe.
I remember thine euerlasting iudgements, O Lord,
 and receiued comfort.
I am horribly afraid for the vngodly which forsake
 thy lawe.
Thy statutes haue beene my songes: in the house of
 my pylgrimage.
I haue thought vpō thy name, O Lord, in the night
 season: and haue kept thy lawe.
This I had: bicause I kept thy commandements.

Auid here, maketh a request vnto God, which wee are all wonted to make: but not with such affection as hee doeth. For wee can not protest, after his example, that all our ioye, in the middest of our aduersities, is in meditating and studying of that which God hath shewed vnto vs by his woorde. And that it is so, we see that whensoeuer any of vs shall endure and abide
any

The 7. *Sermon of* M.I.Cal.

any grief, whether runne wee then for refuge and ayde? Forsooth euery of vs faineth him selfe a comfort, as best pleaseth him. For very fewe of vs rest vppon God and trust in him, ne yet leane vpon his promises: yea, we shall finde none almost which doth it. And see why wee can not craue of God, as Dauid doth, *Which remembreth him of the promises, that he hath made vs.* And therefore it can not be that this was set downe in vaine. Let vs therefore note, that God sheweth vnto vs, from whence wee must receiue our comfort and consolation in all our afflictions: to wit, bicause he hath bound him selfe vnto vs, and that hee hath witnessed vnto vs, that he will haue pitie and compassion vpon those which will call vpon him in their miseries, and holding vs to that, we should be as it were quickened: that is to say, that although we were oppressed with afflictions euen to the vttermost, so that wee were as it were almost dead, that this onely point might suffice vs: certainely to knowe that God will not forsake vs. And for doing hereof, we are to obserue twoo pointes: The first is, that we rest neither vpon our selues ne yet vpō creatures, setting our hope too fondly here and there: but let vs know, that our life and all our felicitie consisteth in God, and that there it is which we must seeke after. Loe then the ende, whereat we must beginne, if we will haue true comfort in our aduersities. And contrariwyse, we see how our mindes wander & go astraye, and that is, bicause euery of vs faineth vnto him selfe foolish and vnprofitable confidences: for if we knew the thing that is in God, it should make vs neuer to turne away from him, we should neuer more wander after creatures, for in them is nothing els but vanitie. And therefore we ought to haue the greater regarde vnto this doctrine: to wit, that if we wil be deliuered from all euill, wee must still looke vnto God. The second is, that we are to craue of God, that hee would haue pitie and compassion vpon vs, and deliuer vs from all our afflictions: yea and that we may come vnto him by reason of his promisse. For without God call vs vnto him, wee can not come vnto him but vnaduisedly. For it should bee

too

too too great presumption for mortall men to take vppon them such boldnes, as to come vnto God, without he gaue them leaue, and exhorted them so to doe. Wee must then haue the word which God giueth vs, by which he testifieth vnto vs, that he is ready to receiue vs, and willeth vs also to come vnto him. Loe what this verse emporteth, when Dauid sayeth, that the comfort which hee receiued in all his aduersities, was, that hee was quickened by the woorde of God. By this he sheweth, that hee not onely wayted vppon God, to be saued by him, but that he had respect, namely to his promise: for without it (as I haue already said) we can haue no accesse vnto God.

In the meane time, wee are to note, that this woorde, *to quicken*, importeth a great matter: to wit, that the word of God should haue this power & strength, that if wee should be as it were forlorne and desperate, that it would comfort and restore vs, and that wee should receiue life through it. In very deede, this is a hard matter to put in practise: but we must not thinke that Dauid hath spokē any thing here, but euen as in deede it was. For in making of such a protestation, his meaning is to instruct vs after his example, what our duetie is. And that which is more, the holy Ghost meaneth here to shewe vs, that the word of God hath not taken deepe roote in vs, except it quicken vs: to wit, that it plucketh vs as it were out of the graue, when we are cast downe and that wee can doe no more; giuing vs freshe force and strength, to be as it were men brought backe out of hell, as if he tooke vs by the hand lifting vs vp into a lusty courage. And thus much for this verse.

Now here aboue, Dauid maketh his request, *That God would be mindefull of his word, which he had giuen him: wherein* (saith he) *thou hast caused mee to put my trust*. Here Dauid sheweth vs, that when the faithfull doe glad and comfort them selues with the promises of God, and be as it were restored, it is not done to the ende that wee shoulde become cold and blockish: but that we ought rather to be stirred vp the more to pray vnto God. Whensoeuer then wee shalbe

oppres-

oppressed with any aduersitie, loe what the remedie is that we must take: to looke vnto the promises of God, and to thinke of that which hee hath testified vnto vs of his owne good will. Herevpon let vs boldly confirme our selues, and returne as it were to life, if that we haue beene in death. But after that we haue made the promises of God so forcible, as to take courage, and to be fortified therein, wee must oftentimes fall to our prayers and offer them to God, beseeching him to perfourme his woord. And since it is so, that he is faithfull, let vs be sure that we shall not go away empty, if we beleeue his word: but that he will performe whatsoeuer he hath promised. See then, that after we haue meditated of the promises of God, and trusted to him, let vs make our prayers many times and runne vnto his maiestie for ayde, beseeching him to accomplishe that, which through his infinite goodnes he hath shewed vnto vs, and neuer forsake vs, but too declare the same too bee so in effect and deede. This is it that Dauid here meaneth by this sentence, *Be mindefull, O. Lorde, of thy word and promise.* Dauid speaketh here according to the grossenes and weakenesse of mans vnderstanding. For it is most certaine, that God neuer forgetteth that which he hath said, so that he needeth to be solicited, to be put in minde of it as mortall men are, which promise much at randon, and neuer remember it after. Now we must not imagine God to be such one, but suffereth vs to stammer after our owne fashion, when he deferreth the accomplishment of his promises, so that wee knowe not who is the cause of the let: God, I say, then suffereth vs to speake after our owne guise, and saye, *be mindfull, O Lord*, that is, we beseech thee to shewe vnto vs by the effect, that thou hast not forgotte the promises which thou hast made to vs. Thou O Lord, art not like men, who after they haue determined vpon any matter, neuer thinke after of that which they haue said. Wherefore, O Lord, shew not thy selfe to be like mortall men: but when thou hast spoken the worde, let it be done, and forthwith executed.

See

See then howe wee muſt proceede, that after we haue once knowne to ſtaye our ſelues vppon the promiſes of God, we muſt beſeeche him to ſhew vnto vs by proufe, that ſo many as put their truſt in him, ſhall not be deceiued. Nowe hee ſayeth, *Thy worde towardes thy ſeruant*. And this ſentence is worthy to be well wayed, bicauſe that there are very fewe, when any mention is made of the woorde of God, which vnderſtand and knowe that it is ſpoken to them, and without they knowe that, all is to no purpoſe. Wee may reade the Bible an hundreth times ouer, but wee ſhall neuer haue any taſte of the promiſes of God, or certainly if we learne any thing out of it, that ſhall no whit aſſure vs, to conceiue a true certaintie of our ſaluation except we knowe that it is to vs which God ſpeaketh, that it is wee euen wee, I ſaye, whome hee woulde make to feele his mercy and fatherly loue. If we conceiue of the promiſes of God as hanging in the ayre, that God hath ſpoken, & we know not to whom, to what purpoſe ſhall this bee? What benefite ſhall wee reape by this? So then, let vs throughly conſider of this doctrine, *Be mindful, O Lord, of thy ſeruant according to thy word*. Dauid applieth vnto him ſelfe the promiſes which he had receiued, for he knew that they appertayned vnto hym, bycauſe he doubted not that he was the childe of God: for hauing receiued them with ſuch a faith, hee ſayeth, O Lorde, Thou haſt not ſpoken to this body or to that body, as though I knewe not to whome: but I am out of all doubt, that thou meaneſt to call me vnto thee, and haſt declared vnto me that I ſhalbe partaker of all the benefites which thou haſt promiſed vnto the faithfull. Loe then, after what maner we muſt do herein.

So likewiſe, when it is ſaid in the holy ſcripture, that this is a true and vndoubted ſaying, that God hath ſent his onely begotten ſonne, to ſaue all miſerable ſinners: wee muſt include it within this ſame ranke I ſaye, that euery of vs apply the ſame particularly to him ſelf: when as we heare this generall ſentéce, that God is merciful. Haue we heard this? Then may we boldly call vpon him, and euen ſay, although

1.Tim.1.

I am

*Iohn.*3.16.
*Rom.*8.32.

loued the world, that he spared not his onely begotten sonne: but deliuered him to death for vs. It is meete I looke to that. For it is very needefull, that Iesus Christ should plucke mee out from that condemnation, wherein I am. Since it is so, that the loue and goodnesse of God is declared vnto the worlde, in that that his sonne Christe Iesus hath suffered death, I must appropriate the same to my selfe, that I may knowe that it is to me, that God hath spokē, that he would I should take the possession of such a grace, and therein to reioyce me.

We see now, how we must practise this sentence, that we may say vnto God, *Thinke vpon thy seruant, O Lorde, according to thy word.* If any man wil reply, that it can not be said, that God hath spoken to him, when as he speaketh to al in generall: let vs consider, that God offereth his grace too men in common, to the ende that euery man might afterward enter into him selfe, and not to doubt being a member of the church, but that hee hath a part and portion of that, which is common to all the faithfull. And where it is sayd, *Reioyce thou daughter of Syon, for behold thy king commeth towardes thee,* all the faithfull in generall ought to receiue this promise, & that al also, euē frō the greatest to the least, might knowe that God offereth him selfe vnto them, and allureth them, to the ende that this promise might be performed and perfited vnto them. And see why the sacraments are not administred vnto vs in common: but to euery one seuerally. We will neuer baptize the whole Churche with one baptisme: but euery one wilbe baptized in the name of our Lord Iesus Christe. And what other thing is meant by baptisme, but a cōfirmatiō, of al the promises of God, which he hath giuen in common to the whole body of his churche. See then, howe the promises are speciall in the vertue of baptisme. And so is it in the Supper. For when we

*Zach.*9.9.

vpon the Cxix. Pſalme.   57

we come to receiue the bread and wine in the Supper, our Lord Ieſus declareth vnto vs, that as hee once for all ſhed his moſt precious blood for our redemption, and ſaluation, that his body alſo is our meat and nurriture. Lo then, howe wee ought to be fully aſſured, that it is to vs which God ſpeaketh, and that he alſo offereth his mercie to vs in common. And ſee why Dauid alſo addeth, and ſayeth,

The ſame is my comfort in my trouble: for thy worde hath quickened me.

For this is the right and true vſe whereunto wee ought to applie the promiſes of God: to wit, that where it might ſeeme that wee were diſcomforted and caſt away, yet ſhould wee not but haue a firme courage, and an inuincible conſtancie. For els we ſhould greatly diſhonour God, ſince he hath tolde vs, that we ſhould not diſpaire, but that hee would be our ſauiour vnto the ende. Whereupon we muſt conclude, that ſo often as weé conceiue any diſtruſt in our aduerſities, ſo often do we blaſpheme his maieſtie. For we can not do greater iniurie and deſpite vnto God, then to accuſe him to be a lyer, & thinke him to be diſloyal or vnfaithfull. Now if we thinke God to bee true and faithfull, we muſt holde it for a full concluſion, that heé will neuer ſuffer vs to be fruſtrate, ſo long as we put our truſt in him. Now by this meane we ſhall liue euen in death.

Let vs therefore throughly conſider of this ſentence which Dauid hath here couched, that God hauing promiſed him to be his ſauiour, hath quickened him in this, yea in the middeſt of his afflictions, as if he had ſaide, O Lorde, ſince it is ſo, that I haue a teſtimonie of thy good will and loue, I ought not to be diſcouraged, nor faint hearted, for whatſoeuer may come to paſſe. Now it followeth,

The wicked, or proud haue had me exceedingly in deriſion, yet haue I not declined from thy lawe.

Here Dauid ſheweth his conſtancie in reſiſting the temptations and combattes wherewith Satan aſſayled him. For beholde howe our faith ſhalbe rightly and duely

H   appro-

approued: to wit, when as we shalbe assailed, and when as the deuill shall thinke that he hath gotten the better of vs, yet must wee perseuer and still continue to trust in God: lo, I say, a good proufe of our faith. And this is it that Dauid meaneth to signifie in this place: for it is an easie matter, when as we shall haue no temptations to trouble vs, to take a tast of the promises of GOD, and to hope that hee will doe that which he hath spoken. But when as we shalbe tormented with afflictions, then the deuill commeth and putteth vs in minde of many irksomenesses, and fantasies, as if God were retired and gone farre from vs, and that the wicked and vngodly make a mocke at our simplicitie: when I saye, that wee are so assayled: then must our faith shewe it selfe, whether it be true or not. And if then wee shall constantly perseuer without beeing vanquished and ouercome, O see nowe a sure and certaine signe that wee haue beleeued in good earnest and not hypocritically, that wee haue not taken his worde in vayne, but it hath beene liuely rooted in our soules. Let vs then well note, that if wee will haue a true proufe of our faith, and learne too speake in truth, that we haue trusted in God, and his promises: it is meete that wee should feele very boysterous assaultes: and yet for all that, we haue not beene forsaken and left, vntill such time as we withdrawe our selues from God.

Moreouer Dauid speaking here of the wicked, calleth them the proud: neither doth hee so intitle them without cause: for it is the propertie of all those which trust not in God. For it can not be chosen, but that a man which putteth not his trust in God, must needes growe proude, and swell therewith like a toade. And why so? For when men do know them selues to bee such as in deede they are, they must needes be cast downe and humbled. And this common prouerbe which reigneth euen amongs the faithfulle, saith, he that knoweth him selfe, maketh very litle of his painted sheath. Now we will speake this with the mouth, but yet it is to our condemnation. Neuerthelesse, it is God his will

that

vpon the Cxix. Pſalme. 58

that all men ſhould know this, bicauſe there ſhould be no excuſe. In ſumme, this is very true, that if men knewe them ſelues, thy ſhould be hübled, and vtterly diſcomfited. Hereypon they would come to ſeeke God, and hide themſelues vnder the ſhadowe of his wings, they would haue recourſe to him, to be aided in all their neceſsities. Contrariwiſe (as I haue already touched) it muſt needes be that all the faithles be ful of arrogancie and preſumption, to lift themſelues vp againſt God, to promiſe wöders as of themſelues, wherein very deede they haue nothing, neither yet are any thing.

See now wherefore Dauid in this place ſpeaking of the faithleſſe and enemies of God, calleth them proude. And it is not onely here, but the holy ſcripture vſeth this ſpeache throughout. And hereypon alſo it is that the Prophet Abacuc ſaieth, *That a man ſhall liue by his faith*. And hee ſetteth downe to the contrary, that they which lift vp them ſelues, and in ſuch ſort ſome out their pride, ſhall neuer take hold: they may well make a faire ſhew, but it can not be but that they muſt needes fall downe hedlong. Wee ſee then, that the Prophet comparing the faithfull with the faithleſſe, giueth this title and qualitie to all thoſe which put not their truſt in God. That they are puffed vp, and preſume without meaſure. Euen ſo then, let vs note, that if wee will render a true teſtimonie of our faith, we muſt needes be daſht dowāe ih our ſelues, & be truely humbled. And contrariwiſe, if we feele, that pryde puffeth vs vp, let vs conclude, that we haue as yet profited very ſlenderly in the ſchoole of God, & that if faith reigned in our ſoules, that this pride ſhould there be corrected. See then, howe wee ought to put this leſſon in practiſe.

Moreouer, let vs alſo note, that they which ſo lifte them ſelues vp againſt God, condemne and deſpiſe their neighbours; that all they which preſume vpon their own power and ſtrength, knowing not, that their whole bleſſedneſſe lyeth in the mere grace of God, theſe men I ſaye, can not be but cruell: and will be fierſe and malicious againſt their neigh-

Abac. 2.

neighbours. And therfore, after that wee shall haue learned to humble our selues before God, let vs vse such curtesie and gentlenesse vnto men, as that we practise that which Saint Paul speaketh of: to wit, *That euery man esteeme of his brother better than of him selfe.* Let vs not study to go about to aduaunce and esteeme of our selues, in reiecting and naught setting by of others, but let vs acknowledge the benefites which God hath bestowed vppon euery one of vs, and confesse the infirmities & vices which be in our selues: to the ende we might be humbled, and rather commende and prayse others. Let vs nowe come to this complaint, and protestation which Dauid maketh:

Phil. 2. 3.

The proud haue had mee exceedingly in derision: yet haue I not shrinked from thy lawe.

Whenhe saieth, that the proude haue had him exceedingly in derision, there is no doubt, but that hee meaneth that they derided him for his simplicitie, bicause hee put his trust in God. Very well say they, he thinketh that God should dandle him in his lappe, but we nowe see what is become of him.

Loe the combattes wherewith Satan daily assaileth vs. When as the vngodly do see the childrē of God in any miserie and calamitie, they rushe euen vpon them at the first dashe and say, ha, ha, this man thinketh that God ought to watche ouer him, and that no sorowe nor grief shoulde come vpon him, and nowe we see what is become of him. And bicause hee hath heard him speake, hee thinketh that God should neuer forsake him. But we see now what commeth of it. It is very true, that the vngodly of their owne motion and inclination, will soone vomit out such blasphemies: but surely this commeth a great deale farther of, for it is Satan that putteth it into their mindes & pusheth them on thereto, to the ende to shake their faith, and vtterly to ouerthrowe it.

Nowe this is not the first time alone that Dauid hath beene thus assailed: for this was an ordinarie thing with him: as wee see throughout the whole two and twentieth

Psalme,

vpon the Cxix. Pſalme. 59

Pſalme, and ſince he hath put his truſt in God, ſay they, let him now ſaue him; and let vs ſee whether God will helpe him or not. And as Dauid was grieued with theſe torments, there is no doubt but that Ieſus Chriſte hath abidden the like conflictes.

And ſince that this appertained to the ſonne of God, we haue to note, that it can not bee choſen but that it muſt ſpread it ſelfe throughout his members, & that euery faithfull man muſt bee exerciſed with ſuch temptations. And therefore, if we ſee the wicked, and the enemies of God ieſt and ſcoffe at vs when as we are in affliction, taking occaſion thereby to lift vp their hornes, and to deride vs, let vs not yelde for all that: but let vs remaine firme and conſtant, ſince that Dauid hath ſhewed vs the way: and not onely he, but alſo our Lord Ieſus, vnto whome we muſt be like: and therefore we muſt be of a luſty courage to follow him. And thus much for the firſt point. For the ſecond, let vs note that we haue not warre with men, when as the vngodly do ſo riſe againſt vs, and vomitte out ſuch mockeries: the ſame ſay I, commeth not from them: but it is Satan that caſteth his dartes at vs, and meaneth mortally to wounde vs. And to put by theſe blowes, wee had neede to bee armed with the woorde of God, which is our ſword, with the buckler of faith, and the Helmet of hope: euen as Saint Paul exhorteth vs to doe. Marke well this point: we muſt not bee too too tyed vnto men, when as they ſhall thus grieue and vexe vs: but wee muſt looke a great way farther: to witte, vnto Satan, who by ſuch aſſaultes & cōbattes goeth about al hee can too ouerthrowe our fayth, if it were poſsible for him to doo. Now the proteſtation which he maketh, is well woorthy the noting: for after hee had complayned of theſe rebukes and mockeries of the vngodly, hee addeth, *yet haue I not ſhrinked from thy way, O Lorde.* Let vs then conclude, that ſince wee haue the word of God, that if al the world, ſhoulde conſpire againſt vs too turne vs from it, we ought too abyde ſtedfaſtly in it, and too bee faſt tyed thereto, and too cleaue ſo harde vntoo it, as that wee might neuer bee

Ephe. 6, 16. 17

The 7. *Sermon of* M.I.Cal.

pulled away from the same. To this ende ought this protestation to serue vs: to witte, to strengthen vs in constancie, that wee might knowe, that if Dauid was so stedfastly setled in the hope which he had: that the truthe of God is not at this day diminished or decreased.

It behoueth vs then to make the promises of God forcible, and to be so sure and certaine, as that wee be not shaken, nor moued, for all the scornes and mockes which the wicked can make at vs. Let vs also marke, that Dauid speaketh not here of one combat, or of a woorde cast out at random, as sometimes it may escape from the mouth of a Scoffer or Iester among the wicked: But it must needes bee that the holy Prophet was throughly sooked in them: as hee him selfe declareth, that they derided and scoffed at him, and that exceedingly. Let vs applie this too our selues, that we quaile not, nor faynt for one conflict, wherwith Satan shall assayle vs by his substitutes: but that wee perseuere in all conflictes, that when we shall haue made an ende with the first, to bee ready and prest to enter into another, neuer altering or chaunging our determination nor will; come there whatsoeuer shall come; that the scoffes & scornes of the wicked, yea and whatsoeuer Satan shall craftily inuent against vs, hinder vs not from stedfastly abiding and continuing in faith, without turning or writhing vs awaye from the lawe of God, after the example of Dauid, as here wee haue heard him make thereof protestation.

And if there were such constancie in Dauid, hauing the lawe onely, wee that haue the doctrine, which is giuen by him, and by the Prophetes after him, by our Lorde Iesus Christe, and his Apostles: wee then which haue a great many moe conuenient helpes, then Dauid had, should wee be shaken and crushed, when as the deuill, the wicked, and all the girnardes and firebrandes of hell, shall assayle our faith? There remaineth nowe no excuse for vs, seeing hee hath done thus. Let vs then learne too helpe our selues with the meanes which God hath giuen vs, and putteth

into.

in to our hande, so that his woorde bee not vayne and vnprofitable vnto vs, but that it serue vs in deede as it ought. Nowe hee addeth,

For I remembred thine euerlasting iudgement O Lorde: and haue receiued comfort.

Here Dauid declareth that hee is confirmed (ouer and beside the worde) in all the iudgementes of God, which is the thing that we must also do, after that we haue meditated vppon the promises of GOD, by which hee testifieth that hee is nere vnto all those which call vppon him, after that wee haue knowne that which hee declareth and pronounceth, to humble and ouerthrowe the wicked, in shewing them to be their iudge: that ouer and besides this, we would acknowledge as at all times we haue neede, how he hath holpen and sustained his, howe hee hath deliuered them out of all the miseries they were in: and besides, how he hath stretched foorth his arme against the wicked, and contempners of his iustice. See, I say, howe wee must linke together the woorkes of God with his word, for the more notable confirmation of our faith.

And this is it which Dauid meaneth in this place: for he speaketh not here of the iudgementes of God as hee hath done before, and as he will hereafter: to witte, for his statutes, and commaundementes: but hee meaneth the actes and deedes which GOD in all ages hath done, to shewe him selfe to be iudge ouer all men. It is very true, that such iudgements as God hath put in execution, are conteined in the Scripture. But by this which is here spoken of them, we are warned how we ought to reade such histories: that is, that God neuer forsaketh his faithfull: and although for a while he slacketh, yet will he not leaue the wicked vnpunished in the ende. Dauid then meditated on these iudgements: and exercised him selfe in them. And so we are to remember, that when we haue made the word of God forcible, to resist Satan, and al the assaultes wherewith he shal assaile vs, we must also know, that God hath not only spoke, but wee should ouerslippe it; but should haue our eyes open, and acknowledge these thinges as they are declared vnto vs, when as also wee shall feele any of GOD his grace towardes vs, that wee ought to imprint the same surely in our myndes. Loe howe wee must followe Dauid, in that which hee sayeth, *O Lord, I haue remembred thy iudgements.* Moreouer, when it is said, that hee hath called to mynde the iudgementes of GOD from the beginning of the worlde, I praye you, what excuse shall wee bee able too make, if wee ouerslippe that, which hee setteth before our eyes? For when as at this daye GOD shoulde holde him selfe as if hee laye hidden, that wee should haue no token nor proofe, that hee shoulde bee the iudge of the wicked and vngodly, for to confounde them, and the Sauiour of those which trust in him, and call vppon him, yet that which is conteined in the holy Scripture, and that which we reade too bee done before wee were borne, the same, I saye, might suffice. But nowe since God declareth him selfe vnto vs, and sheweth vnto vs his presence, and all this to bee cast vnder foote through our vnthankefulnesse, must not wee needes be more then culpable or blameworthy? In summe, let vs marke, that here the holy Ghost accuseth vs of negligence: for if wee were such as in deede wee should be, wee should applye our studie to reade the holy Scriptures, where God sheweth vs his iudgementes as it were in beautifull glasses, and all for our instruction and profit. See then, how we ought to linke together that which is written, with that which we daily see before our eyes, and to be confirmed throughout all the histories, in such sorte as that they might serue as it were to seale vp the woorde of GOD, that it might bee of

a great

vpon the Cxix. *Pſalme.*

a great deale more ſtrength and force, and too magnifie the ſame when neede ſhalbe.

Nowe haue we ſo remembred the iudgements of God, and are wee ſo exerciſed in them, yea euen in thoſe, I ſay, which were made before we were borne into this worlde? Whatſoeuer then that we ſhall now perceiue and marke, & whatſoeuer alſo ſhalbe declared vnto vs ſo long as we liue, we ought by a more forcible reaſon, ſo much the narrowlier to conſider, & to bee a great deale the more confirmed in them, and not to be like vnto brute beaſtes, when as god ſtretcheth foorth his hand, & giueth vs ſome teſtimonyes, that it is he alone which ſo helpeth vs: when as I ſay, God ſheweth vs this, wee muſt thinke on them in good earneſt, and ſo ſtay our ſelues in them: to wit, that we make not account of them as vaine ſpeculations: but too apply all the Iudgementes of God to our vſe, ſince it is to this ende and purpoſe, that he ſheweth vs them. For when wee ſhall reade that God reuealed himſelfe to Abraham, and that hee did helpe him in ſuch a neceſſitie: Let this bee our concluſion, Very wel, that which God did vnto his ſeruaunt Abraham, is to aſſure vs, that he will doe the like for vs, and therefore we muſt euen now runne vnto God for refuge and ſuccor. See howe all the teſtimonyes which God hath lefte vnto vs in the holy Scripture of all his woonderfull works, ought to ſerue euery of vs for aydes and helpes.   Nowe Dauid ſetteth downe ſoone after.

I am horribly afrayd for the vngodly which forſake thy lawe.

Heere Dauid proteſteth that hee hath reſiſted another temptation ouer and beſides that which wee haue already ſeene. This is already a very ſore and harde combate too abyde, when as the wicked mock and ſcorne vs, as if God had deceiued vs, as if we had bin too too ſimple & fooliſh to put our truſt in him. Loe heere a great trouble for miſerable and wretched weakelings, yea and that ſuch as it cannot be choſen, but that they muſt (at the leaſte) be mooued and aſtonyed. But this temptation which heere followeth is none of the leaſt to ouercome: as when wee ſee all the

H.5. whole

The 7. Sermon of M. Io. Cal.

whole world addicted and giuen to wickednesse, that whatsoeuer we doe, is as it were to conspire & to lay a platforme to prouoke God his wrath, to distrust him, to reiect all his graces, and to treade them cleane vnder foote. When then wee shall see men so estraunge them selues from God, euen to make open warre against him, it goeth very hardly, if we be not as it were vtterly ouercome. And yet neuerthelesse it is, as Dauid heere protesteth: that it is so farre of that he gaue him selfe wickedly, seeing the corruptions to bee such as they were all ouer, as that hee was horribly affrayde for the vngodly which so forsooke the law of God. Wherefore, let vs learne to be thus horribly affrayde, so often as we see men exceede in wickednesse: Let vs learne, I say, too haue recourse vnto God, and as it were in gathering our wittes vnto vs, that we might conceiue an horrour & feare, when as we see such monsters, and such things so committed against nature. If this hath beene alwayes a necessary doctrine, it is at this day moste necessary: for let vs a little beholde what a generall confusion there is, when as we shal see the order and doings of the Papistes, wee shall finde it to be a most hellish outrage. And emongest vs alas, where the woorde of God should be of greater power and force, yet wee see howe the more parte will not onely alter and chaunge the lawe of God, but desire nothing more then euen vtterly to abolishe it. What is to be doone then? It is not inough that we followe not the wicked and vngodly in their impietie, and not to linke in with thē as their companions, but wee must bee horribly afrayde, because wee know that they must perish as miserable & wretched creatures: & therfore we should be greeued and vexed: but yet a great deale the rather, when as they see them make open war against the maiestie of God. For these are matters too to monstrous, to see mortal men lift them selues vp against their creator, and in very good earnest to fight against him. Lo then, what is heere shewed vnto vs by the spirite of God vnder the example of Dauid. And in this let vs see, whether we ought to couer our selues: with such horrible, yea and
most

vpon the Cxix. Pſalme.

moſt deteſtable filthynes & vncleannes, when as any talke ſhall ariſe of the contēning of the maieſtie of God, & of the diſcrediting of his law or worde, whether we ought I ſay, to make countenaunce as if ſuch talke were nothing, whether we ought to ſupport & maintaine the ſame: and to paſſe it lightly ouer, as though we cared nothing at al for it, or that it no whit appertained vnto vs. Nowe if in this behalfe we ſhal doe ſo, it is a ſigne and token that there is neither zeale nor affection in vs: And heerin we ſhew our ſelues not worthy that God ſhould take vs for his childrē: For we muſt remember that which is written, *The zeale of thy houſe hath euen conſumed me: and the rebukes and ſlaunders which haue bin laide vpon thee. O Lorde, are come vpon me.* Whē then we ſhall ſee the name of God to be contemned & made no account off, and ſhall ſee the wicked to caſte him cleane without the doores, in ſuch ſort, as that they wil make no more reckoning of the law of God, without all queſtion wee muſt not diſſemble and holde our peace, & make account as though it were nothing: but if we be the ſeruaunts of God, it ſhall behoue vs not onely to be touched, but alſo to be horribly afrayd, & to be as it were forlorne men when as we ſee ſuch abhomination, that it ſhould in ſuch ſort fall out, as to haue the name of God to be ſo contēned by his creatures. Now for a concluſion Dauid ſaith, *Thy ſtatutes haue beene my ſongues in the houſe of my Pilgrimage.*

This was yet another great temptation to Dauid aſwel as the other, that it ſo fel out as that he was once driuen out of the countrie of Iudea & was far from the temple of God, & dwelt among the Pagans and Infidels. Nowe he ſayth, that notwithſtanding al this, that hee was not eſtraunged from God, nor yet from the knowledge of ſaluation: but contrariwiſe, that he was the rather ſtirred vp to ſing prayſes vnto God, and thoſe Pſalmes which God did put in his mouth, yea euen ſuch as were taken out of the law. For we haue to note, that Dauid made not the Pſalmes, as a newe doctrine ne yet as a doctrine ſeparate from the doctrine of the lawe: but drew them from it as out of a Fountaine.

So then

The 7. Sermon of M. Io. Cal.

So then it is not without cause that he protesteth heere that the Statutes of God serued him for Psalmes and for songes, yea in steade of his Pilgrimages, that is to say, in a strange Countrie in the middest of Infidels, when he was as it were banished from the Church, that he could not bee in the Temple to make confession of his faith, yet was he not for all this wickedly addicted. Nowe heere, they which are trauellers, are admonished of their duetie. For albeit they see a greate many of enormities committed in the worlde, neuerthelesse they are stedfastly purposed to holde themselues in the feare of God, and to walke in a pure and sound conscience, albeit they are mingled emongst the infidels. As beholde euen the very Christians which are in the Papacy, although they are there prisoners, hauing no doctrine preached vnto thē, without libertie to serue God publikely, and to make confession of their faith as they would: yet doe they not exceed and outrage with the rest in these villanyes which reigne amongest them: but confirme themselues the best they can to the worde of God, take all their delight and pleasure therein, and make the lawe of God their song, which maketh them to withdrawe themselues from all the vanities and corruptions which they commit, so that they keepe them selues within this compasse.

Moreouer, if they which are in a place where the worde of life is not taught, and doe so, yea euen greate store of offences wherewith they may take occasion too be drawne to wickednesse, and to be corrupt with the rest: these, I say, be inexcusable, but are commaunded to take their delighte and pleasure in God, and in his lawe, and too incourage themselues, taking the holy songs to exhorte them to well doing, what shall become of vs, when as wee are in a place where the Bell ringeth too call vs that we might bee admonished by the woorde of God, to be instructed too call vpon his name, and to make confession of our fayth? When GOD then calleth vs vnto his Schoole, and openeth his mouth to instruct vs, I pray you, are not we worthy of most horrible condemnation, when as wee shall doe altogither

prepostenously

preposterously in that, whereof Dauid heere maketh protestation. As we shall see very many, which can neuer bee mery, but when as they shall deafely hearken vnto God: & if they come to a Sermon, it is onely to heare their condemnation. For whatsoeuer is sayd vnto them, and layde before thē to bring them into the right way, they soone forget what hath beene saide. Must not these mindes then be violently carried with a merueylous fury? Yes, without all doubte. And therefore let vs keepe in minde the conclusion which Dauid heere maketh: *That hee remembred the lawe of God vnto the ende.* As if he had sayd, Beholde what is the cause that I beeing a miserable vacabond, cast out of the Temple, and driuen out of my countrie, did yet neuer but stay vpon thee. And after that, beeing assayled by the Infidels, haue perseuered in the consideration of thy lawe, and delighted my selfe therein. Euen so also must wee doe, For if we see many offences and many things which might withdrawe vs from the lawe of God, let vs ouercome all that in the vertue and power of the promises which God hath made vs, that by them we might be confirmed in his loue and bountie, to the ende we fall not into such a confusion, as wee see the wicked and vngodly fall, and dayly caste them selues.

And according too this doctrine, let vs prostrate our selues before the Maiestie of our good God in acknowledging of our offences: Beseeching him that it would please him to make vs better too feele, what taste wee ought too take in his holy promises, and to be exercised in them, that we might valiantly fighte against those vices which might hinder vs, to stay vpon his protection, and that by the power of his holy spirit we might ouercome all offences and griefes, to the ende that beeing fortifyed by his grace, wee might not haue any accesse to Satan, whereby hee might winne and get of vs: but that we constantly perseuering in the holy vocation of this good God, might followe our course vntill such time as he shall take vs out of this worlde,

The 8. Sermon of M. Io. Cal.

to bring vs vnto that heritage, which hee hath prepared for vs before the beginning of the worlde, and also which Iesus Chriſte hath purchaſed for vs with his moſte pretious bloode.

And that hee will not onely graunt vnto vs this grace, but alſo to all people and nations of the earth, &c.

The eight Sermon of the hundreth
and nineteenth Pſalme.

HETH.

Thou art my portion, O Lorde, I haue determined to keepe thy lawe.

I made mine humble petition in thy preſence with my whole hearte: O be mercifull to mee according too thy woord.

I haue conſidered mine owne wayes: and turned my feete vnto thy teſtimonyes.

I made haſte & prolonged not the time to keepe thy Commaundementes.

The handes of the vngodly haue robbed me: but I haue not forgotten thy lawe.

At midnight I will riſe too giue thankes vnto thee: becauſe of thy righteous Iudgementes.

I am a companion of all them that feare thee, and keepe thy commaundements.

The Earth, O Lord, is full of thy mercie: O teache mee thy ſtatutes.

vpon the Cxix. *Pſalme.* 64

Heſe eight verſes nexte before conteine none other thinge but the proteſtations which Dauid maketh in giuing himſelfe wholly too God, & ſticking vnto his law: except two requeſtes which he maketh in the ſecond verſe, & in the laſt. Now (in the firſt place) he ſaith that his ſoueraigne good, and chiefe felicitie was, in that he was reſolute to keepe the law of God. It is very true, that ſome doe expounde this thus, that Dauid calleth God, *his inheritance.* But when as the matter ſhalbe well wayed and conſidered, the meaning is this, that he ſetteth his whole felicitie in this, that hee is fully determined and reſolued (as already hath bin touched) to followe that which God had ſhewed and taught him. Nowe this worde *Portion* in the Scripture is taken for inheritaunce: and inheritaunce is taken for the chiefeſt and moſt deſired thing that man hath. And ſo, it is as much as if hee had ſayde, That euery man might deuide it as hee woulde and luſted. As wee ſee the deſires of men too bee ſundry and diuerſe, one draweth one way, a nother another. And in deede (ſayth hee) euery man wiſheth as hee fantaſieth, but as for my ſelfe, I deſire none other bleſſedneſſe nor felicitie, but to content my ſelfe with the lawe of God, and when I haue this, I haue gotten a good and an excellent inheritaunce.

And nowe we ſee the ſumme and effect of this firſt verſe, it remaineth that wee gather out thereof ſuch Doctrine as is therein conteined. For when wee heare Dauid ſpeake after this manner, there is no doubt of it, but that the ſpirit of God declareth vnto vs where it is, that euery of vs muſt fully and wholely aſſure himſelfe. And this to doe, we muſt haue regarde too the deſires wherewith wee are allured by nature, for one man is giuen too bee ambitious, another

to be

The 8. *Sermon of* M. Io. Cal.

to be couetous, another to be lecherous. In such sorte as that men are carryed away with their desires, as heere before we haue declared. It is meete therefore that wee retire our selues from all these vaine and peruerse desires & lustes and to fight against all whatsoeuer may hinder vs to come vnto God: and when wee haue thus repressed our passions and fleshly lustes, let vs then desire nothing else, but that God would drawe vs vnto him selfe, linke vs vnto him, and graunt vs the grace to keepe his Commaundements.

But wee are oftentimes too note, that Dauid speaketh heere of a conclusion, which he holdeth for moste certaine and of no light motion: as when we haue sometimes a desire to goe vnto God, yet it lasteth not long: for the fleshe also pricketh vs on the other side, and withdraweth vs from that good, whereunto we had willingly bent our selues. It is not inough then to haue a little desire, which soone waxeth cold, or rather, which waxeth euen dead through contrary temptations: But we must holde a sounde and stedfast conclusion, as Dauid heere speaketh, *I haue fully determined,* saith he. He putteth in the word, *to promise:* But the Hebrues doe take it to be fully resolued, to stand firme and constant in a matter, to the end not to varie or chaunge.

Nowe (in summe) let vs note, that so long as men giue them selues too worldly things, they doe nothing else but wander: they knowe not wherein their felicitie consisteth, but we must come to this conclusion heere set downe vnto vs, to keepe the Commaundementes of God : & then shall we neuer haue occasion to haue a desire to these miserable foolish worldly things, which flye about in the ayre, which suffer them selues too be carryed after their friuolous and vaine desires. For we shall be assured to chose a good portion, when as we shall be so vnited to God, by the bond of his word. Nowe as we haue already touched, the seconde verse conteineth a request which Dauid sayth he continually made:

I made my humble petitiõ in thy presence with my whole hart: be mercifull vnto me according to thy word.

Nowe

vpon the Cxix. Psalme. 65

Nowe in saying, that he continually prayed vnto God, heerein he sheweth vs what the manner is to pray well: that we should be constant to follow it, and not too be weary, not that God needeth to be importunately vrged, but it is to exercise our fayth, and the better to try vs, whether wee seeke all our felicitie in him or not. For it is so, that the holy scripture requireth constancy in our prayers, especially and aboue all other things, and not to pray vnto God this day, and quite forget him to morrowe, but wee must continue, if we will be hearde. And loe wherein we must shewe our selues to haue trusted in God, that is, that although it seemeth to vs that he hath stopped his eares, yet for all that we must not cease too goe continually vnto him, and pray vnto him an hundred times asmuch as we did before: knowing it to be no superfluous labour, when as wee haue thus prayed. Loe heere as touching the perseuerance whereof Dauid in this place speaketh: Nowe let vs see what the substaunce of his prayer is, *O Lorde* (sayth he) *be mercifull vnto me according to thy worde.*

The requeste is generall: But Dauid sheweth the very springhead of all the benefites which wee are to craue of God, and which also he lyberally bestoweth vppon vs, as well for our soules as for our bodyes: too witte, that hee is mercifull vnto vs. For God oweth vs nothing, neither can we bring any thing with vs whereby wee maybee able to say that wee can prouoke our selues to do well: But this is the whole summe, that he vseth it towards vs of his meere and free liberalitie. Let vs then marke that Dauid his meaning is to shewe, that when God reacheth foorth his hande, liberally to bestowe vppon vs so many benefites as we receiue of him: that the same proceedeth and commeth euen from his meere goodnesse. Loe why, he saith, *O Lorde be mercifull vnto mee.* Wherfore, whatsoeuer thinge wee desire of God we must alwayes come with this minde to trust in his goodnesse. As howe, we must desire God to pardon our offences, and to assiste vs with his holy spirite: wee must beseeche him that wee bee not ouercome with

I. temptati-

The 8. Sermon of M. Io. Cal.

temptations: that hee will giue vs his grace, whereof wee are emptie and naked: that hee will feede vs: that he will heale vs when wee are sicke, that hee will keepe vs out of daunger: or wee may make any other or particular prayers whatsoeuer. Al these requests must be drawne out of the Springheade: to witte, that he giueth vs this of his own goodnesse, and that wee knowe why it is that God giueth vs so many benefites, aswell for this present life, as also for the health of our soules: to witte, because hee hath pittie and compassion vppon vs, and that wee are miserable and poore Creatures, without he inclyned himselfe to be mercifull vnto vs.

To bee shorte, before wee enter into all the particular prayers which wee make vnto God, let vs beginne at this ende, and let it be the foundation whereon we must build: That God hath pittie and compassion vpon vs. Now because we should be assured in our prayers, Dauid addeth this which he already before sayde: to witte, *according too thy word*: For if we desire of God that which seemeth good in our owne eyes, and that wee haue not his promise, that hee will heare vs, this commeth of presumption: and therefore wee muste come humbly and soberly with our Prayers, and not after a wandering and carelesse manner, neither must wee come before God with a shamelesse face, and boldelyer then we woulde come before men: but too come vnto him in such modeste and sober manner, as that nothing escape our mouthes without good warrant, which thing wee are not able too doe, except wee bee assured that all our Prayers are according to his heartes desire, and that he alloweth, and ratifieth them. And how shall this be doone? When as he shall haue sayde, that wee shoulde not followe our owne braine, giuing the raines too our owne wittes: but that when God shal say, Loe what I would haue you to craue of mee, come vnto mee, and make your requestes in this sorte: O, according too those promises of God, we may assure our selues to come vnto him after the example of Dauid and say, *O Lorde bee mercifull vnto mee*

accor-

according to thy word. And this is an holy presumption, and such one, as God alloweth. Nowe wee ought the better to note this doctrine, when wee see that it hath not onely beene obscured and darkened in the worlde, but also vtterly made voyde: As at this day it is in Popery, for when they pray vnto God, they pray at all aduenture. And especially, this is one of the poyntes that the Papistes striue most about, that wee must not assure our selues (when wee pray vnto God) that hee heareth vs: but remaine in suspence. Forsooth, but the scripture telleth vs that it is not possible that the man which is thus floating, as the waues which are tossed with the winde and tempest, shoulde obtaine any thing. It telleth vs that when we come vnto God, that we must come with faith, hope and boldenesse.

And so then, (as I haue already touched) this is an holy and a commendable presumption, that when wee stay our selues vppon the worde of God, to set downe in summe that hee will accomplish that which hee hath promised vs: For we hold him as one bound vnto vs: not that he is any thing in our debte: but because that of his meere liberality, he stoupeth so lowe, as to declare vnto vs that hee woulde, that wee should haue this libertie and leaue to present our selues so before him, with such boldenesse, and assuraunce, as already I haue declared. And thus much for the second verse. In the thirde it followeth:

I haue considered myne owne wayes: and turned my feete vnto thy Testimonyes.

This protestation is woorth the noting: For wee are admonished, why it is that men so greatly flatter themselues in their own follyes and deuices, and make themselues beleue, that they will make their Prayers vnto God, albeit they rest not vpon him, trust not vnto him, neither yet followe that which hee hath commaunded them, but onely their owne imaginations.

I.2. And

The 8. Sermon of M. Io. Cal.

And that forsooth in such sorte, as that they thinke a man shoulde offer them great wrong, if hee sayd, that all is loste labour which they haue bestowed: & that they greatly tormented themselues to no purpose, except they did knowe that God hearde them. It is most true, that euery one will say, And howe so I beseech you? wherefore wil not God think wel of that which I doe, since it is my small intent to to serue him? no, no, God forceth not of all this. And what is the cause that men so arrogauntly striue and spurne againſt God? It is because they call not their wayes too remembraunce: For if they had this consideration and wisdome, to looke narrowly vnto their dooings, and to think thus with them selues. Howe shall I doe? In what case am I? I must not goe astray, but keepe a sure and certaine way and good meane: and to consider how to liue: and aboue all, I must do thus much, as that God be not disappoynted of the souerainᵗie which he hath ouer his.

So then, when as men looke well to their wayes, it is very certaine and sure, that they will wholely giue themselues to followe the woorde of God, and therein take all their delight. And this is it that he sayth on the contrary part, that he would turne his feete too the testimonyes of God. Wherein he sheweth too all men by his example, that they shoulde walke as God hath commaunded them, and not too be ruled after their owne head and brayne. For see from whence this madnesse cometh, which possessethas it were all the whole worlde, that euery man will serue God as he thinketh best: It is because we turne not our feete vnto his Testimonyes.

Nowe wee ought so much the more too practize this which is heere declared: to witte, to looke too our wayes: that wee shoulde knowe that seeing that God hath placed vs heere in this worlde, that he hath not doohe it too that ende that we should doe whatsoeuer our senses would lead vs vnto: But our life must be ordered & ruled. And whence must wee haue this rule? Euen from the woorde of God.

And

vpon the Cxix. *Pſalme.* 67

And when as wee ſhalbe ſo carefull as too order and rule our life, there remaineth no more for vs to doe, but to followe euen whether our God calleth vs. Loe the teſtimonyes of God, loe his trueth which hee hath declared vnto vs: Loe, there muſt we place and ſet our ſelues. Wee muſt neuer heereafter make any more queſtion too wander any longer, and to diſcourſe and ſay, why ſhoulde not this bee good and commendable? No forſooth, not ſo, let not vs followe our owne fantaſies, neither let vs bee wiſe in our owne conceits: but let vs conſider with our ſelues to heare our God, and obey him, loe then the effecte of this thirde verſe, where it is ſayde, That Dauid looked vnto his wayes, and that he turned his feete to the teſtimonyes of God: to witte, to the lawe, where God hath declared his will. Now hee addeth:

I made haſte and prolonged not the time: to keepe thy Commaundementes.

He continueth his purpoſe: but he ſheweth that this his affection was not ſlowe, *I made haſte* (ſayth he) *yea and that without delay.* Nowe it is not without cauſe, that Dauid putteth to this: for we ſee howe ſtraightly wee oughte too deale againſt our owne appetites: yea euen they I ſay, who are beſt affected to ſerue god, do yet com as it were halting, trayling either an arme or a leg after them, as wee cōmonly ſay. And what is the cauſe heereof? We carry about with vs ſuch a number of corruptions, as that the very weight of them maketh vs to goe exceding ſlowly ſo that we haue much to doe to go on. And we know, and haue too too greate experience, howe weake our nature is, when as wee intende to doe well.

Let vs then vnderſtand and knowe theſe twoo thinges, and we ſhall neuer thinke it ſtraunge, that wee are ſo ſlowe and ſlack to followe God as in deede we are: yea euen theſe two things (I ſay.) For behold, Satan wil neuer ceaſe craftily to go about to imagine whatſoeuer he poſſibly can to cauſe vs to drawe backe, he will ſet barres and pitch Hayes before vs, hee will lay Buſhes, Thornes and euill fauoured ſtum-

bling

The 8. Sermon of M. Io. Cal.

bling blockes whatsoeuer which any way may hinder and let vs: that if we meane to march on but onely three paces, we shalbe violently carryed away to turne on this side and on that, not knowing what shall become of vs. Againe, wee shal bee solicited and moued by our inordinate appetites, to drawe vs cleane awry. For if we will wholly put our trust in God, the Deuil will drawe vs too the contrary and make vs to giue our selues vp too this worldly pelfe, and so consequently to all the rest. Seeing then, that we are drawen and haled with so many Cart ropes, yea and are of our selues so feeble to doe good, euen burning after wickednesse: Alas, no maruell though wee be slowe too followe God, but yet for all that we must needes fight. It is no question but that we flatter our selues, when as wee see such slacknesse in our selues, and say, in deed it is very true such is the state & condition of our nature, and againe our infirmities are so great as that it is an impossible thing for any man too discharge himselfe as he ought. O deere brethren, let vs not build vpon such a foundation, but let vs fight against our vices, and take and get vnto vs strength and courage, against all the stumbling blocks and ambusshes which Satan shall lay against vs, that we may breake all the bandes and Cordes wherewith hee holdeth vs bound. See I say howe we ought to doe in this case. For, let vs not thinke but that Dauid was a man, passionate as we are, and felt in himselfe greate infirmities: neither made he protestation of this in vaine, when he sayth, that he hasted and made no delay to doe the Commaundementes of God. And so let vs haste, after his example, when God speaketh, and let vs bowe downe our eares to heare him, and lift vp our foote to obey that which he shall say vnto vs.

Loe then what Dauid meaneth to declare vnto vs in this place: to witte, what readynesse ought to be in all the children of God, to heare his worde, and to receiue it, and not to deferre from day to day: For wee knowe not what time God will giue vs the grace to offer his woord vnto vs. They

which

which in such sorte delay the time, doe make their account that God is greatly bound and beholden too attend vpon them. Now we see how he scorneth such our arrogacy, when aswee pray vnto him with such tearmes and conditions. Wherefore, we ought a greate deale the more too force our selues, to the ende to attaine to that perfection, after the example which is heere set downe vnto vs, too runne without delay so often as God shall haue mercy vppon vs. It followeth soone after, that Dauid was not giuen too doe wickedly notwithstāding all the wrongs which the wicked had done vnto him, and had persecuted him with all the greefes and conflictes which he had sustained.

Albeit (sayth he) that the hands of the vngodly haue robbed me: yet haue not I forgotten thy law.

This is not heere put to without a cause. For wee shall heerein see very many which are peaceable and moderate inough, when as they be not greeued, but suffred to runne their owne course: But if any trouble ouertake them, and that they be molested, beholde then are they giuen to doe wickedly, then alter they their determination and purpose, and chaunge their coppy. So then, because men are so easy to be drawne to euill, although before they followed the thing that was good: see wherefore we ought diligently to note this place, which Dauid heere addeth. For it is as it were to ratifie that which he hath before spoken of the readynesse to followe the woorde: because that that had not beene inough, without he had beene so confirmed in it. For although the Deuill had so lyen vpon him, euen too haue discouraged him, yet was he not without hope, continually to make his parte good against him.

And so muste wee also doo in this case. When our Lorde then shall sette vs in the way, and shall giue vs some good motions: let vs beseech him so to confirme vs in the same, as that when the Deuill shall goe aboute for too assayle vs, wee might repulse and ouercome all the assaultes wherewith hee shall assayle vs : and alwayes too continue

I.4. and

The 8. Sermon of M. Io. Cal.

and remaine in our determination and purpose without chaunge. Loe the thinge which is heere declared vnto vs.

And we are also to note that there are two temptations, which we must resist, when as wee shall be greeued and iniuried. The first temptation is, that when we are iniuried, we are by and by mooued too render the like: Marke I beeseech you the state and condicion of our nature. Nowe since God commaundeth vs to flye that which is naught, &c. to doe that which is good, euen to loue our enemyes, wee had neede to bee very well armed and furnished with these textes of the Scriptures. For wee shall neuer bee able to attaine to the ende to ouercome any such temptation nor desire of reuenge, excepte God putteth to his helping hande. We think it also lawfull to doe euill, when we see our selues compassed with nothing else but euill, and wickednesse, if we looke into the order and gouernment of the world, wee shall see one man exceede in lechery, another to be an horrible blasphemer, one an extortioner & vsurer, and another a deceitfull bargainer, one in this thing another in that: & very many estranged from God, and become neere neighbours to Satan, violetly carried to this & that: Whē as then we are thus incompassed with euil and iniquitie, we thinke that we may take leaue to doe wickedly.

Loe how the children of God may be tempted, and how we see also an infinite number to be as it were dayly deceiued. And therefore let vs note, that if wee haue at any time beene boldely affected too come vnto God, and that hee hath reached foorth his hande for a season, to haue vs too come vnto him, that yet this is not inough: But wee must heerevpon indeuour our selues too gather vnto vs newe force and courage, to the ende the Deuill might not shake vs when as hee shall rayse vpp against vs troubles and vexations, and lay a great number of stoppes and stumbling blocks in our wayes. Wee muste therefore bee armed againste him, to the ende wee forget not the Lawe of God, whatsoeuer come of it.

And

vpon the (*xix. Pſalme.* 69

And here we are to note this circumſtance, that Dauid doth not onely ſaye, that he was greued by one man alone, ne yet by two or three, but he ſayeth, *The congregation of the wicked.* When he ſayeth, *The whole congregation*, this is very much: if there had beene but a ſmall number, it had beene enough: But he ſayeth, *The whole congregation*, ſignifying that he was aſſayled on euery ſide, that he was like a ſheepe amonge Wolues, Lyons, Beares, and other wilde beaſtes of rauyne: and yet for all that, that he alwayes put his truſt in the Lorde.

Now if we ſhall looke well into our ſelues, how few ſhall we ſee which haue not beene ouercome with the leaſt temtation that hath come vnto them? there ſhall neede but one man to oppoſe him ſelfe againſt vs, and loe we are by and by carried to do wickedly, now we knowe not that this cōmeth from God. To be ſhort, the leaſt flie which flieth before our eyes (as we ſaye) is euen enough to turne vs quite out of the right way. And ſurely we may be greatly aſhamed ſo ſuddainly to change our copie: where before wee made great ſhowe of following of God, and by and by to goe cleane againſt the haire. And we thinke this may be a moſt lawefull excuſe, when as we can handle the matter thus, to ſay, that we were carried to doe wickedly through ſome tētation. It is ſo farre of that this excuſe ſhould goe for payement, as that it is neither worth ware nor money. But wee muſt ſaye with Dauid, yea and that truely as he hath done, That whenſoeuer the whole congregation of the wicked ſhall aſſaile vs, let vs not ceaſe to perſeuer and cōtinue in the lawe of God. And namely he ſayeth, *That they haue robbed him*, which is yet the moſt grieuous and ſharpe thing that can come to a man, and which might ſooneſt make him to quaile. For it may be that the wicked will go about to moleſt vs, and yet come not to the ende of their enterpriſe: but Dauid ſaith, that he was put out for a pray, that he was as a wretched forlorne creature, and aſſayled on euery ſide: and yet that he forgot not the lawe of God. And in ſo ſaying, it is as if he ſhould haue proteſted and ſayde, that hee had al-

I 5 wayes

The 8. Sermon of M. I. Cal.

wayes one selfe and the same affection to followe the lawe of God.

Now let vs returne vnto that which we haue before touched. For this is no small temptation, that God suffereth vs to be so molested, greeued, and tormented. When GOD suffereth Satan and his suppostes too take this course, this should as it were discourage vs an hundreth thousand times. And in very deede this is Satan his policie, as we see in Iob. For when Satan ment to shewe, that it was an easie matter for Iob to serue God, O, saieth he, *he is wel at libertie, and liueth quietly, he is rich, and therefore it is a very easy matter for him, to prayse God: but whensoeuer he shall haue lost all that hee hath, all his substance, and be vexed with many anoyaunces and tormentes, we shall then see whether he will blesse God yea or no.* Loe then howe God proueth vs, when he suffereth the wicked to molest and trouble vs, that they are euen come to this point to set their foote vpon the very throat of vs. By that he meaneth to proue vs whether we loue him in good earnest or not. And therefore wee are the rather to marke this doctrine. For it is impossible for vs to serue God as we ought, without wee haue this constancie whereof Dauid here speaketh: to wit, that when we shalbe afflicted in any sort whatsoeuer, wee must not cease to praye alwayes vnto God, that we may be able to yeld our selues wholy to him. Loe what is the summe and effect hereof. And by this wee are taught, that neither afflictions nor any such other like things ought to stay vs from praying vnto God, to the end we might alwayes walke in his obedience. For if he permit vs to be afflicted in our flesh, we must not therefore say that his loue is diminished towardes vs, neither that hee hath litle care of our saluation: let vs onely attend and wayte to see the ende and issue of our afflictions, and in the meane while continue to walke according to his word, and neuer forget his lawe, howsoeuer Satan soliciteth vs to the contrary. Nowe it followeth by and by after,

At midnight will I rise to giue thankes vnto thee: bicause of thy righteous iudgements.

vpon the C*xix.* P*falme.* 70

Loe here an excellent proteſtation, which alſo hangeth vppon that, whereof wee haue already treated in the firſt verſe. For there Dauid proteſteth that this is our true and very perfect felicitie, when as wee giue our ſelues to GOD and too his woorde.

Nowe hee ſayeth heere, that *hee roſe at midnight too giue thankes vntoo God, euen bycauſe of his rightuous Iudgementes.* As if hee ſhoulde haue ſaide, I haue already declared, O Lorde, that my portion is too haue thy woorde, and too haue poſſeſsion thereof: which if I haue, I am bleſſed, and moſt bleſſed: And nowe, O Lorde, ſuffer mee not to be vnthankeful for ſuch a benefite, and priuiledge, whiche thou haſt giuen mee. He alledgeth alſo vntoo him his rightuous Iudgements. We haue here before declared what the meaning of theſe wordes importe: too wit, *the Statutes of Gods* which are to gouerne vs in ſuch ſoundnes as that oure life ſhal bee playne and honeſt. Dauid then, ſaying *that he prayſed God bicauſe of his rightuous Iudgementes,* ſignifieth, that hee thanketh him for that, that he was taught in his word, knowing it too bee a ſingular benefite. Wee are nowe too note this ſaying: For wee ſee what our vnthankefulneſſe is, not onely for al the benefites of GOD, but principally and chiefely for this, that God hath ſo declared himſelf vnto vs by his lawe, Prophetes and Goſpel, and yet wee neuer thinke of al this: and that which is worſe, that although he meaneth too ouercome our malice through his goodneſſe, and offereth himſelf vnto vs as a father and Sauiour, yet do wee fly as farre from him as wee poſsibly can. It is very true that we will make ſemblāce to ſeeke him, as it were for our diſcharge, yea and that ſhal bee too, when as wee ſhal bee theretoo forced: But yet if wee were at oure owne libertie and choyſe, wee woulde come as farre aloofe as were poſsible.

Nowe when wee ſeeke God in this wyſe, it is not too come directly vntoo him, but onely too ſay, Loe I am well affected vntoo GOD, I am one of thoſe which ſeeke him.

And

The 8. Sermon of M. I. Cal.

And in deede, when God goeth about to drawe vs vnto him by his worde, how may we be able sufficiently enough to vnderstand so notable a benefite? Wherefore let this doctrine be well marked, seeing it is so very necessarie to correct and amend our so great villainous malice and vnthākfulnesse? and that wee might hereafter learne to praise God, bicause it hath pleased him to make vs partakers of this Inestimable treasure, to wit, the doctrine of saluation: that his meaning is to rule & order our life, that we might not be like wretched strayed sheepe, to be cast downe hedlong into the bottomlesse pitte of hell. Here is likewise an ardent affection expressed in this saying, *That Dauid arose at midnight.* As if he should haue said, that the daye was not sufficient enough for him, but that in the time of his quiet rest, he lifted vp his minde into heauen to giue thankes vnto God. In this he signifieth that he continued prayfing of God without weerifomnesse.

Nowe then, if wee will rightly followe the example of Dauid, we must not giue GOD thankes when wee thinke good, and when we shall haue remembred him ones in fiftene dayes, or I knowe not when: or els when as it shalbe for fashions sake, as when the Bell ringeth to cause vs too come to the Sermon. But it must be alwayes, for wee must both in the euening, and morning, and also at midnight, haue our minees waking to giue him thankes. He addeth, *I am a compaignion of all them that feare thee: and keepe thy Commaundementes.*

By which hee signifieth, that hee hath sought all the meanes possible too giue himselfe to walke in the feare of God. We haue here to note, that Dauid was an excellent man, euen like an Angell amonges mortall creatures: and yet for all that, it was needeful for him to accompanie him self with faithfull men, men of good example, and pure, and holy in life and conuersation. And why so? To the ende he might be alwayes the better confirmed in his vocation and calling, and not to be withdrawne from the same by euill example. Nowe (as I haue already touched) if Dauid had

neede

vpon the Cxix. *Psalme.* 71

neede hereof, what shall become of vs, who are so inconstant and mutable in al our doings? Lo then the first point which we haue to note in this place; to wit, that Dauid protesteth, that although the holy Ghost assisted him, and that he felt him selfe confirmed, as wee haue seene, neuerthelesse, he yet sought other helpes to cōtinue and hold him in the feare of God: as the companies which were most meete for him, to cause him to followe his vocation, and not to withdrawe him from it, seeing there must be nothing that must pull vs aside from the right way. Now he meaneth to signifie further, that he ioyned him selfe with men that feared God, to the ende also that hee might serue him as hee ought. For we are bound to stirre vp one another through mutual exhortations and good ensamples. It is meete then that we haue these twoo considerations: in the first place we are to consider to followe those which can aduaunce & further vs in the right waye, who can profite vs more and more in the feare of God, and after that, wee must also labour to profite those with whome wee shalbe likewise conuersant, inciting them by all meanes possible, to followe the right trade, wherein God shall haue set them; to the ende he may be honoured with one accord: and that euery of vs might say, come let vs goe, and let vs trauell and take paines to cause others to goe with vs, that wee may altogether honour the Lord our God. Now the conclusion of the eight verse, is the second request.

The ixth, O Lord, is full of thy mercie? O teach mee thy statutes.

Here we see howe necessarie a thing it is for vs to bee alwayes praying to God, beseeching him more amply to instruct vs, that we may acknowledge him better then heretofore we haue done: yea, and that specially, when as wee thinke we knowe al that is to be knowne, that we throughly consider, that wee haue yet great neede to profite continually more and more. For, which of vs, I pray you, dareth be so bolde as to compare with Dauid? Loe so excellent a Prophet, as that he is like vnto an Angel of God: wee see

also

The 9. Sermon of M. Fo. Cal.

also how God hath reueled vnto him his secrets, as if he had bin taken vp into the heauenly kingdom: & yet he hauing such excellent gifts as we know, desireth notwithstanding to be instructed in the statutes of God. And which is hee amongs vs that hath not greater neede of thē? So then whē as we shalbe greatly learned in the word of God, not onely for our selues, but also to instruct our neighbours: let vs for al that be coueted to yeld our selues to be taught of him, to beseech him to grant vs his grace, that we may daily profit more & more. And therefore we ought the better to note the reason, which Dauid setteth first down, *For the earth, O Lord is ful of thy mercie*. As if he should haue saide, thou O Lorde spreadest abrode, thy fatherly goodnes ouer all creatures: we se how of thy mercy thou feedest the beasts of the field, we se the trees florish, the earth bring forth her increase, thy goodnes spreadeth through heauē & earth, & how is it then possible, that thou shuldst not do good vnto thy children? I am one of that nūber which call on thee, & that put their trust in thee: Seing thou art so louing & mercifull to al creatures, thou shalt not forsake me. The reason, here set down, serueth Dauid for a confirmation, that he should not dout to obtaine the request which he had made. And so as oft as we desire God to instruct vs in his statuts, the goodnes, wherwith he ouerspreadeth al his creatures serueth vs as a foundation, wheron to build al our petitiōs, And since that God hath giuen vs this grace to allow vs in the nūber of his children, and to shew him self to be our father, let vs be sure that he wil not refuse to giue vs those things which he hath promised. And according to this holy doctrine, let vs prostrate our selues before the Maiestie, &c.

The nienth Sermon of the hundreth and nineteenth Psalme.

TETH.

O Lorde, thou hast dealte gratiously with thy seruant, according to thy woorde. O teach me good iudgement and knowledge: for I haue beleeued thy commaundementes.

Before I was troubled I went wrong: but nowe I keepe thy worde.

Thou art good and gracious: teach me thy statutes.

The proud haue imagined a lie against me: but I wil keepe thy comandements with my whole heart.

Their hart is as fat as grece: but my delite is in thy law

It is good for me that I haue beene in trouble: that I may learne thy statutes.

The law of thy mouth is better vnto me: then thousandes of gold and siluer.

IF we be oftetimes foolish & vnaduised in a great many causes, it may chiefly appeere whē we meane to pray to God: for thē if there be but one drop of wit or reason in vs, it wil shew it selfe: but we discouer our owne folly in that behalf, more then in al the rest of our actions: And what is the reason? Forsooth we wil behaue our selues more modestly, whensoeuer wee shall craue any thing at the handes of men, then when we come before the maiestie of God: for we go on hedlong thereto, not knowing what we ought to desire of him: but euen powre out at all aduenture whatsoeuer shall come into our mouthes. And we should then the rather call to minde our lesson, to the end we might know the order rightly how to pray. For we profane the name of god, & shew our selues too much to contēne his maiestie, if we beg at his hands any other thing thē that, which he hath declared vnto vs to haue liking off, in such sort, as that his will, be alwayes preferred, and our desires thereby chiefly ruled. Now we are heere aduertised, that aboue all thinges we ought to pray vnto God that he wil teach vs, & cause vs to vnderstand his wil, accordingly as he hath declared vnto vs in his worde: & to open our eies that we may doe it, so that wee might vnderstand that which is comprehended therin. And

The 9. Sermon of M. Jo. Cal.

And this is the summe and effect of these eight verses, which here we haue nowe to handle. For Dauid demaundeth of God none other thing but to knowe the contents of the lawe, and the doctrine thereof, that he might be ruled thereby, and his whole life framed thereafter.

But in the first place he remembreth God of all the benefites which he had already receiued from him. For that is it which must giue vs trust and confidence, when as wee come to make any prayer vnto God. And in deede there is nothing in the world which giueth vs a better accesse, nor that doth more readily assure vs to be heard, then when we beholde his benefites bestowed vpon vs. And howe must that bee? Thus must euery man consider with him selfe and say, I haue found heretofore by experience the bountie of my God: yea, I haue had as great proufe hereof, as is possible. And therefore it were vnreasonable that I shoulde mistrust him, and stande in any doubt that he would not now graunt me that which I desire of him: considering that I haue so good a proufe of his loue, that he is alwayes ready, liberally to bestowe vpon mee his benefites. When then I shall haue receiued so many benefites of him, should I now thinke with my selfe, howe is it possible that this thing should come to passe? to witte, that I should obtaine that which I am about to praye for? If wee shall stande in this doubt, we shall do God great wrong, and shewe our great vnthankefulnesse vnto him: for he neuer doth vs any good, but it is to this ende and purpose, that we should be partakers of his mercie and grace, which hee will continue vnto vs euen to the ende: for he is neuer wearie in liberally bestowing his benefits vpon vs, as mē are wont when as they bestow bountifully of any, and by & by plucke their heads againe quite out of the coller. But God is no such maner of one, he is a well that can neuer be drawne drie. Loe then whereunto this tendeth which is here spoken in the first verse: *O Lorde, thou hast dealt gratiously with thy seruant*. Dauid spake not this to the ende to measure him selfe, that he would haue God neuer hereafter to bestowe any moe benefites

vpon the Cxix. Psalme.

benefites vpon him: But cleane cōtrarie, that bicause he had had already so great experience of the grace of God, he was fully resolued, that hee shoulde also feele his benefites too come. For God is no chaungling: and as I haue already saide, his grace is neuer lessened, but hee will alwayes encrease it towardes vs. And so let vs learne after the example of Dauid, that as often as we are to praye vnto God, to consider with our selues, and call to minde, the benefites which we haue receiued from his hād, that the same might be as it were an entrance for vs vnto prayer, and therevpon to conclude, that seeing God hath shewed him selfe heretofore liberall: wee should feele him also to bee the same, euer hereafter vnto the ende.

Now namely Dauid addeth, *According to thy word*: And not without cause: for this is not al that we ought to know, that God hath done vs good, and that al that we haue, proceadeth from him: but wee must put this confidence vnto it: to wit, that he hath done it according to his word. For like as meate, although it be good and sweete, hath no sauour nor taste, but is altogether vnsauery without salt: euen so likewise the benefites of God, will haue no perfect taste, that we might sauour them as appertaineth, if it bee not, that they bee salted and seasoned with faithe and beliefe, and too knowe that the graces and benefites which GOD hath bestowed vppon vs, haue beene according to his worde & promise. And why so I pray you? For if we shal not haue the worde of God and his promises: yea and although (as I haue already saide) wee might very well make our petitions vnto him, and come before him, in building our selues vpon this, that hee hath already ayded vs of his meere fauour and goodnesse: yet should we not for al that, be assured that hee will alwaies doe the like, ñe yet abide constant therein, that when hee hath begunne, that he will finishe it, wee can neuer bee able, I saye, too haue any such certaintie without his woorde. And why so? when God sayeth vnto vs, goe to nowe, and hearken vnto me, I wilbe

K your

your father, and shewe my selfe a sauiour towardes you, and you shall finde me to be such one for euer: after that we haue felt the proufe and effect of these promises: wee maye then very well applie his benefites to that vse whereof I haue already spoken: hath God done mee good but for a fit? hath he done this onely, but by the waye of talke? and will he not now hold and continue it? no, not so: but hee hath done it according to his word. Doth the word of God stand but for a day or for a moneth? No, it remaineth and abideth both in life and death. Let vs then conclude, that the benefites of God are euerlasting, and that he wil continue them vnto all those that are not vnthankefull. Loe this sentence which Dauid addeth is not superfluous, but of great waite, when he saieth, *O Lord, thou hast dealt gratiously with me, according to thy word.* If we will then be confirmed by the benefites of God, which wee haue heretofore receiued: and when wee shall make our requestes, that wee would haue him to heare vs, wee must ioyne his benefites with his word, and euen to speake properly, like vnto confectes closely wrapped vp together in sauory salt, for otherwise we shal neuer be able to feele any such taste of them, as to applie them to such an vse, to builde a true certaintie of faith in him. Now Dauid hauing vsed such a preface, addeth,

O teach me good iudgement and knowledge: for I haue beleeued thy commaundements.

Here Dauid desireth God to giue him true wisedome, that he might knowe what he had to do. And why doth he so? he setteth downe the reason which is that, that we haue already seene, *for I haue beleeued,* saith he, *thy worde.* Nowe it seemeth to implie, that they which haue beleeued, are sufficiently instructed, that they haue, I saye, true vnderstanding, and so great wisedome, as they neede not to pray vnto God, to inlighten them any more. Wherein consisteth and standeth all our wisedome but in faith? when as wee receiue the wordes of God, and being taught by it doo rest

vs in

vs in that which he saieth vnto vs? Loe this is our full and whole perfection. Nowe Dauid protesteth, *That hee hath beleeued the word of God*: wherefore then desireth he to bee taught, as if hee were without knowledge and ignorant? Nowe here wee are to note (as we haue touched this morning) that we beleeue the worde of God twoo wayes: to wit, our faith must be distinguished in twoo partes: not that wee meane to deuide, and dismember the same, but to make a distinction of it, as is comprised in her owne natures kind. From whence then taketh faith her beginning? Forsooth, she must despise her selfe to receiue whatsoeuer God shall say, wee must suffer him to be maister, and to acknowledge whatsoeuer cometh from him, to be good, holy, and iust: that before hee hath spokē vnto vs, we be already prepared and disposed to obey him: and albeit we knowe not yet his will, neuertheleffe to haue this resolution with our selues, dooth God speake? Well then, wee must not onely giue our eare and attention: but also receiue without contradiction, whatsoeuer shall proceede out of his holy mouth.

Loe here what is the first part and condition of faith. Now there is a second part & condition: to wit, the instruction which God giueth vs, after that we are come vnto him with that reuerence that Schollers ought to come to their maister: for we are more fullie and soundly taught of him. This is it that Dauid desireth. He protesteth *That hee hath beleeued the woorde of God*: that is to say, to haue knowne the maiestie conteined therein, to haue obeyed it, and to haue yelded himselfe subiect vnto the same. When hee had made this protestation, O Lorde, sayeth he, now that I haue felt the power and vertue of thy woorde, and haue chiefly beene desirous thereof, graunt mee this grace that I may comprehende it.

Loe here a notable place and worthy the noting. For in the first place, we are aduertised, that wee shall neuer profit our selues either in the Gospel, or yet in any parte of the holy Scripture, if wee haue not this modestie with vs,

The 9. Sermon of M. Jo. Cal.

as too yeelde our selues too God: with this persuasion, that the same which wee accompt too bee good and faythfull with vs is nothing in respect of that which he meaneth too doo therein on his behalfe: considering that hee hath shewed it vntoo vs: For wee are simple and ignorant, and cannot conceiue the thinges which are necessary for our saluation, vntil such time as we haue yeelded our mindes to this reason. And loe wherefore there are so fewe schollers of God at this day in this poynt, For howe many shal we find at this day, which haue their mind so humbled as it ought? But the greater parte are arrogant fooles, wee shall find very many in this behalfe, that wil make no more accompte of the woorde of God, then if a mortall and seelie man had spoken. Forsomuch then as men come thus too God with such a pryde, let vs not woonder although hee leaneth them without wit or reason: and although the Sunne shyneth bright before their eyes, yet remaine they continually blinde, and groape about, as it were in the darke, and wander about euen too the hazarde of their necke breaking. We must not be abashed at this, although God depriueth them of his grace, since they wil not submitte themselues vntoo his woorde. Euen so, when as this shalbe in vs to attribute vnto God the authoritie and honour which he is worthy off, wee may after the example of Dauid, hope that he will instruct vs more and more: and also make this request vnto him. For this is the first degree and steppe of all Christian wisedome: to witte, to humble them selues in such sorte, as that they be euer ready to receiue whatsoeuer God shall say vnto them. When as they shalbe thus prepared, they can not do amisse, nor yet feare that God wil euer forsake thē: but that he will spred furth his power to mainteine thē, as he hath therein promised thē to doe. And thus much as touching these two verses. Now it followeth,

Before I was troubled I went wrong: but nowe I keepe thy worde.

Here Dauid signifieth that he was more daunted, then euer he was; bicause God corrected him: As if hee had sayd, In very

vpon the Cxix. Pſalme.　75

very deede, O Lorde, amonges all the reſt of the benefites which I haue already alleaged, this is one, that thou haſt made me to know my ſelfe through affliction: loe, it maketh me to keepe thy commaundements. Nowe when wee tell God thus of the graces which hee hath beſtowed vpon vs that we might bee prepared to ſerue him, it is for this cauſe that he might encreaſe and augment them more and more in vs, vntill ſuch time as he hath brought thē to their perfect end. Now we haue to note in this matter, the order which Dauid keepeth, O Lorde, ſaieth hee, *I confeſſe that I haue erred.* The firſt point, is this confeſsion which he maketh: for when God findeth vs to be vntamed and hard to be kept in aray, it is meete that this our ſtubburneſſe ſhould be pulled downe, and hee to ſhewe his authoritie ouer vs, to the ende we might ſoone after feele his clemencie. And therefore, Dauid knowing that hee was once very wylde and vntamed, and had not walked in ſuch feare of God as became him, confeſſeth, that although hee had beene taught, yet that it was needefull for God to ſet him in aray, and to keepe him in good order. *O Lorde ſaith hee, I confeſſe that I haue erred, yea and that was before thou haddeſt chaſtiſed me: but now I keepe thy commaundementes.* By this hee ſignifieth in effect, that which I haue touched: to wit, that he was already prepared in this wiſedome of the knowledge of God: yet he alwayes prayed that hee would augment this grace in him, and confirme him therein vntill ſuch time as he were throughly made perfect. In the meane while we haue to note, that Dauid was not a man altogether wickedly bent, ne yet ſo vntamed as a great number of the contempners of God are: It is very true that hee committed very grieuous and extreeme offences, were it but this adulterie which hee committed with Bethſabe Vrie his wife, which was ſo horrible an acte, as that he deſerued euen for that to be vtterly forſaken of God. And after that, he became ſo proude when he woulde haue muſtred the people, as that he was violently carried with a vayne

K 3　　　　　　　　　and

The 9. Sermon of M. I. Cal.

and foolish arrogancie, cleane forgetting who it was that had aduaunced him vnto this royall seate: and in steade of dooing homage vnto God for such a notable benefite, hee determined with him selfe to haue escaped away on horsebacke. Loe what grieuous and shamefull faultes these are. But if we looke into the course of his life, wee shall finde that he was a man of a continuall singlenesse very teacheable and full of curtesie, following the vocation of God, and wholy giuen thereto. Nowe herein appeareth a great difference betweene a man which outrageth all the dayes of his life, and him which committeth some particular euill, shewing neuerthelesse in all the rest of his life a feare of God: As it may happen, that a man shall serue God all his life, and yet in the meane while may somewhat fall, and perhappes very grieuously: as we see to haue come to passe in Dauid. Nowe wee shall see others to be very wicked, and to despise God all their life long, delighting altogether in wickednesse. But Dauid neuer was such one: and yet for all that he confessed that hee had erred, before such time as God had visited him with afflictions: And if this came so to passe in Dauid, alas what shall become of vs poore wretches? So then, let vs vnderstand that afflictions, are more necessarie for vs, then bread and drinke.

We craue of God that he will feede and nourishe vs. It is very true, and hee giueth vs leaue for to make such request: but yet we must not leaue out the principall point: to wit, we must beseech him not to make vs so fatte, as we, make pampered and restife Iades, too wynse and kicke at him, but that being gouerned through his bountiful goodnesse, we might be easie and tractable to bee guided according to his will. So it is (as already I haue sayde) that wee ought in deede, to be tamed through afflictions: or els wee should alwaies become like vnto sauage and wild beastes.

And too proue that it is so, wee see our nature so rebellious, as is most pitifull: and our affections such terrible beastes, as that we are not able to holde them in any good order

order: in so much that if God slack the reynes, and laye the brydle in our necke, it is out of all question that wee will be very stubborne and rebellious against him: and in such sort outrage, that wee will desire nothing els but clearely to ouerthrowe all iustice, equitie, and right. To be short, it wilbe out of all doubt, that wee will euen iustle and spurne against God, when as we shall liue at our owne pleasure, and in great prosperitie.

Nowe there is none other remedie to helpe this matter, but to haue God to afflict vs, for this is the only meane, by which he keepeth vs in subiection and in awe, otherwise, if he leaue vs in rest and at quiet, it were vnpossible but that our nature should stubburnly rebell against him. If wee carrie away this lesson well, wee should neuer be so grieued with the afflictions which he layeth vpon vs as wee are: but wee should take another maner of consolation in all our miseries and aduersities then wee doo: knowing that although they be bitter medicines vnto vs, yet that they shal turne to our health: Let vs chose whether wee wilbe like wilde and madde beastes, straying from the waye of saluation, yea euen like very frantique men to lifte vp our selues against God, rather then to be chastised with his roddes, and to be so coquered as that by the same meane he might order vs to liue in his obedience.

Since then we be so profited through afflictions, as that the gaine which we get thereby is not heauy and grieuous to beare, let vs comfort our selues therewith, attending the issue which God shal giue vnto vs. Moreouer, let vs also haue in memorie, that wee must not bee incorrigible, after that God hath lifte vp his hand to chastise vs, and hath rebated out foolish and inordinate appetites, neither moyle and groyne as we are wonted, as if he did vs great wrong: but let vs suffer our selues to be chastised and afflicted after the example of Dauid. Loe, the very sauage and fierce beastes, yet for al that at last they may be made tame, whē as a painfull and industrious man shall take them in hande, which can tell howe to rule them.

K 4   Behold

Beholde the vntamed horse, of nature fierce and stout, and yet for all that he suffereth him selfe to be handled and led, turneth with the bit, when he shall haue a man vppon his backe which knoweth howe too ride and tame him. I beseeche you, ought not wee to be greatly ashamed, when as our God shal employe him selfe to order vs, and winne vs vnto him selfe, and yet cannot compasse it? So then, let vs after the example of Dauid, striue to profite our selues vnder the rodde of God, to the ende wee might keepe his lawes, after that hee hath scourged vs. Nowe it followeth soone after.

...Thou art good and gratious: teach me thy statutes.

Dauid here repeateth againe the same petition which we haue heard. And it is the very same which I haue already touched: to wit, that amongs all the praiers which we must make vnto God, this is one of the most principall, to desire him to instruct vs in his woorde: that wee be not giuen in such sort to that which concerneth this present life, and our bodies, as that wee thinke no whit of the glasse of our soules. Nowe this glasse is it which consisteth in the worde of God.

So then, let vs not forget this so great a benefite, when as we are about to praye vnto God, that wee haue this in a most especiall remembrance, that wee may be instructed in his statutes. Nowe ouer and beside this request, Dauid vseth the same reason which hee hath set downe in the first verse: that is when he sayeth, *That God is good and gratious.*

It is very true, that they are twoo sundrie sentences: but yet they proceede from one selfe same springhed, and the meaning also tendeth to one and the selfe same ende. Hee hath saide, thou hast dealt liberally with thy seruant: and here, thou art good and gratious. There hee hath sayde, euen according too thy woorde: and here hee hath put them in both: so that wee may see, that this verse is but a confirmation of that which wee haue seene in the twoo first: that Dauid alledging to GOD, his bountie, which hee vsed towardes his, euen according to his nature,

beseecheth

vpon the Cxix. Psalme.

beseecheth him that hee woulde teache him his Statutes. Nowe he addeth,

The proude haue imagined a lye against me: but I will keepe thy Commaundementes vvith my vvhole hart.

This is alledged for two reasons: the one is, that by it Dauid sheweth the neede which he hath of God his helpe, and to be confirmed in his worde, yea and to be instructed in the same. And why so? Forsooth to withstand temptations. As if he had sayd, Alas my God, if thou instruct mee not, and guidest mee by thy holy spirite, what shall I doe? For I am not without temptations, when as I shall haue but mine owne will which euer striueth against thee: But I haue also enemyes without, which oppresse and greeue me: Wherfore I haue very great neede to be guided and gouerned by thy hand. Dauid then considered that it was needefull for him to bee chastised of God: to the ende he might a great deale the easelyer obtaine his request.

Nowe in the meane while hee meaneth too shewe that he made his prayer without hypocrisie: that he came too GOD in very good earneste, and with a pure and sincere affection: as if he had sayd, O Lord I desire not to be instructed in thy lawe and Statutes for fashions sake: but because I esteeme of this good that is in it, and for that I knowe this to be the moste soueraigne felicitie that we can haue. And to proue that it is so, although the wicked haue assayled me, and taken great paines to drawe mee too doe wickedly, and haue bent all all their force and power thereto: yet haue I kept thy commaundements, By this hee hath made good proofe howe greatly hee loued the woorde of God, when as hee lothed it not whatsoeuer they craftely and malitiously practized against him.

See then the two reasons which vve haue heere to note. Now (in the first place) when Dauid speaketh heere of the proude, let vs remember that it is the title which the Scripture comonly attributeth to all Infidels & contemners of God. For from whence commeth this villanous and beastly

K.5. impietie

The 9. Sermon of M. Io. Cal.

impietie, that men will not bowe them selues vnder the hand of GOD, but are hardened, and lifte them selues vpp against him? It cannot bee chosen but that this muste needes be an horrible pride. Euen so then this infidelitie is it that giueth too man as it were Hornes which he so naturally esteemeth (although in deede it bee lesse then nothing) and thinketh the same to be wonderfull. And contrariwise, let vs marke that it is onely Fayth that muste induce vs to humilitie, and which frameth and fashioneth vs therein, considering this swelling of our hearts, our growing in presumption, like vnto swelling Toades. There is nothing I say, that can amende this vice, but Fayth alone. The reason is, becaufe that Fayth bringeth vs vntoo God.

Nowe when as wee knowe what the righteousnesse of God is, Let vs then come vnto our selues, and wee shall finde in vs nothing else but iniquitie: when wee shall consider of the Wisedome of God, we shall see that all whatsoeuer we thought too be good reason, to be nothing else but vanitie and follie. So then, when men doe wonder and looke at the brightnesse of God, they then learne that they are no better but doung and filthy stench, are euen angry and displeased with them selues, and greately ashamed of their owne filthynesse. See then, that humilitie proceedeth from faith. And therefore Dauid sayth, *that the proude*, to witte, the wicked and Infidels *imagined a lye against him*. Let vs then knowe, that pryde is ingendred of men, and that they bringe it with them into the worlde so soone as they are borne, that it groweth and increaseth vnto ful age, vntill such time as God correcteth it by his holy spirit and by Fayth. And so when as wee shall see the contemners of God, and the wicked who knowe not what it is too be ordered by GOD, when wee shall see them, I say, thus outrage: let vs not think it straunge, seeing it is the course of nature.

Moreouer, let vs well note that Dauid speaking of the neede

neede which hee had of God, sheweth vs by his example, that the more wee are vexed with temptations, that so much the more bolde wee ought too be, too beseech him of his ayde, that he will reach out his hand too vpholde vs, and not to suffer vs to be ouercome. And this is specially too be noted: for when wee are greeued with any temptation, we knowe not that the same is to make vs runne too God, who is the onely remedie by which wee must be deliuered.

And so the Diuell may very easily enter into vs too ouerthrowe our faith, since it is as it were put out there vnto him as a pray, and besides we vouchsafe not once too receiue the remedy which is offered vs for our helpe. So then, let vs keepe the order which Dauid heere setteth downe: to witte, that if we be assayled with great and very strong temptations, that then it is high time for vs to haue recourse vnto God, beseeching him to saue vs, and too remedy our faultes, which else would leade vs too euerlasting destruction. And thus much for this.

Nowe wee haue soone after too note: that we shall make good proofe of our well willing to serue God, if wee resist the temptations. If the wicked goe about too drawe vs vnto wickednesse, and yet wee stand fast and sure, then is our Fayth and constancy well approued. And this is spoken, to the ende that no man shoulde flatter himselfe, for wee thinke this to be a sufficient excuse, and that God should also bee well contented therewith, too say, that wee were drawne to doe wickedly by the meane of some other. See I pray you, will euery one say, I was once in a very good forwardenesse, and desired to liue according too the will of God. But when I see the worlde so peruerse and wicked, and that all men were giuen to so many vices, it was impossible for mee too escape, but that I muste doo as other men did. When wee shall alledge for our selues such excuses, wee thinke that God shoulde holde himselfe well contented therewith.

But

The 9. Sermon of M. Io. Cal.

But contrarywife, we fee heere that the faithful neuer ceafe for all that to ferue God: when all the whole worlde goe about to hinder and let them: that although the wicked inuent neuer fo many lyes, & lay neuer fo many ftumbling blockes in their way to caufe them too turne and decline from the right way, yet doe they ftill ftande firme and fure. And fee alfo how we muft be faine too doe, that if wee will faithfully ferue our good God, wee muft not ceafe too purfue our vocation, yea although the wicked bente all the force they were poffibly able to make againft vs, too turne vs cleane from the way of faluation.

Nowe if this admonition hath beene alwaies neceffary, it is more needefull at this day then euer it was. For wee fee that the worlde is growne too a monftrous heape of all iniquitie, that we are not able too ftep foorth one ftep, but that we fhall meete with great ftore of euil and daungerous incounters, which might weary and withdrawe vs, and carry vs to doe wickedly in all kinde of thinges. Therefore we ought fo much the rather to practife this doctrine, That the wicked haue imagined lyes againft vs: but yet that wee haue kept the lawe of God. For the lyes which the proude and the enemyes of God doe imagine againft vs, are not of one kinde. For fometimes they wil feduce vs vnder the colour of Friendfhip, fometimes they will charge vs with a great many of thinges to make vs faint harted, fometimes they will make fuch a confufion of all, that we fhall not be able to difcerne betweene white and black. We muft then be fo much the more well aduifed, and ftand the furer vpon our garde. And although the deuill transforme himfelfe fo into diuerfe manners, let not vs leaue to keepe the lawe of God, yea and that with our whole hearte: which is a thing that we ought diligently to mark. For if we haue but only fome little and feeble affection too followe God, wee fhall foone be very weary thereof. Our heart therfore muft be wholy addicted thereto, for els we fhall neuer be able to make our parte good againfte Satan. Nowe it is fayde a little after,

Their

vpon the Cxix. Pſalme. 79

Their hearte is as fatte as greace: but my delight is in thy lawe.

Heere Dauid maketh a compariſon betweene the contemners of God, and thoſe which deſire to ſerue him. And why doth he ſo? He ſheweth, that the cauſe which ſo induceth the Infidels too contemne G O D, is the diſſolute and brutiſhe life which they leade: becauſe they are as fatte as an Hogge in his ſtye, that hath beene fed with Accornes and Barley, and that lyeth wallowing on an heape in his owne greace. Hee is ſo very fatte and heauy that hee is not able to get vp: and although hee bee already a meruelous fatte and heauy beaſt, which deſireth nothing elſe but draffe and ſwill, yet will hee bee farre fatter and heauyer, when as he ſhall be ſtyed vpp and ſo fatted. Euen ſo fareth it with theſe curſed conteners of God, which haue no regarde vnto euerlaſting life, but are wholely giuen vpp too their God the belly. They wallowe them ſelues in their owne greace, as a Swine which hath his groine alwayes in the trough. Nowe contrariwiſe Dauid ſayth, that all his delight hath beene in the woorde of God. Whereby hee doth vs to witte, that although God had made him fatte, yet that he wallowed not for all that in his owne greace, but delighted in that ſpirituall gifte which was giuen him, becauſe that God had taught it him in his Schoole.

Loe then what we haue to gather out of this place: that although wee ſee the greater parte of the worlde contemne God, yet muſt we not be abaſhed thereat. And why ſo? Let vs well conſider wherein men doe put their chiefe felicitie: and wee ſhall finde them too be lyke vnto Oxen, and Swine, deſiring naught but to liue heere in this world, without lookihg any farther. Nowe wee muſt haue a farther regarde, if we will ſerue God as too him appertayneth: to witte, that wee take ſuch pleaſure and delight in the worde of God, that wee bee no more giuen too the worlde, as we are ouermuch. And although God giueth vs aboundaunce, yet that wee haue our eaſe and commo-

dities

dities in this worlde, let vs not settle our mindes on them, but knowe that all these are but pety small meanes and necessaryes: but let vs labour to goe too the principall, and acknowledge him too be our Father and Sauiour: And when we knowe him too be so, then let vs clime vpp vnto him, and too that euerlasting life, wherevnto hee inuyteth and calleth vs. Loe I say, what wee haue heere too retaine.

Moreouer if God tameth vs by affliction, Let vs come to that which Dauid addeth, to witte, *That it was good for him that he had beene in trouble.* Although then that God pulleth back his hand, and that in steade of gently intreating vs, hee handleth vs roughly, in steade of sending vs plentie of wealth, he causeth vs to suffer hunger and thirst, in steade of giuing vs health, hee greeueth vs with diseases: that beeing vexed with many anguishes and tormentes, so that wee knowe not what too doe: yet must wee alwayes looke to the ende, to be comforted with Dauid, in saying, It is a good turne for mee O Lorde, that I haue beene in trouble, *That I may learne thy Statutes.*

Nowe since it hath so fallen out, that Dauid was afflicted, to the ende he might be the better disposed too learne the ordinaunces of God, what shall become of vs, which are full of worldely vanities ? Let vs then knowe that wee had neede to be corrected by the hand of God, and to be tyed short, if we will profite in the doctrine of saluation. Loe then, how we must practice the admonition of Dauid. And when we shall haue so done, we may conclude and say with that which is set downe in the laste verse, to wit : *That the lawe of God is more deere vnto vs then Golde or Siluer.* And this is it that we must doe in this point, wee must esteeme and make much of the worde of God, as it is woorthy and not to stay our selues on the thinges of this worlde, but to looke alwayes farther off : to wit, vnto heauen. When then wee shall haue profited our selues thus by the afflictions which God shall send vs, hee will bestowe his grace vpon vs

by

by little & little, that we shal so esteeme of his word, as that we shall wholy stick to it. And let vs beseech him, that it would please him too dispoyle vs of all our wicked fleshly desires and affections, & to cause vs to craue none other thing but that he wil reigne and liue in vs.

According too this holy doctrine, let vs prostrate our selues before the maiestie of our good God, in acknowledging our offences: Beseeching him that it woulde please him too take from vs the wicked affections whiche might turne vs away from him, and from his seruice: and that wee might forget all whatsoeuer might turne vs from the right way of saluation, that we desire nothing but that wee may attaine too that euerlasting life, which we looke for in heauen. That it would please him not too suffer vs to liue heere like brute beastes, not knowing to what end we were created in this world: but that we might acknowledge him to be our Creator, our Father and Sauiour, that wee might subiect our selues vnto him as his creatures, and obey him as true and faithfull Children, vntill such time as hee shall take vs out of this world to make vs partakers of that euerlasting blisse, & immortall inheritance, which he hath prepared in Heauen, and which is purchased for vs by our Lorde Iesus Christe. That hee will not onely graunt vs this grace, but also vnto all people and nations in the worlde, &c.

The

The tenth Sermon of the hundreth and nineteenth Psalme.

IOD.

Thine hands haue made and fashioned mee: O giue me therefore vnderstanding that I may learne thy Commaundements.
So they that feare thee, when they see mee shall reioyce: because I haue put my trust in thy word.
I knowe, O Lorde that thy Iudgementes are right: and that thou hast afflicted me iustly.
I pray thee that thy mercie may comfort me: according to thy promise vnto thy Seruant.
Let thy tender mercies come vnto mee, that I may liue: for thy lawe is my delight.
Let the proude be confounded, for they haue dealte wickedly and falsely with mee: but I meditate in thy Commaundements.
Let such as feare thee, and know thy Testimonyes: turne vnto mee.
Let my heart bee vpright in thy Statutes: that I bee not ashamed.

WE E ought to holde and keepe this rule and order in our praiers to God, not too measure his affection and loue after our own imaginations & thoughts but to acknowledge him to be such one as in deede he is, & as he sheweth himselfe vnto vs to be. And loe why he saith by his Prophet Esaiah, after he had declared, that he would haue compassion to saue his church.

Thinke

Thinke not (fayth he,) *that I am like vnto you, for there is as great diftance betweene my thoughtes and yours, as is betweene Heauen and Earth.* Let vs then meafure the goodneffe of God, after our vaine imaginations: But (as I haue already fayd) let vs knowe that it is not in vaine, which he declareth and teftifieth vnto vs, that the good will and loue which he beareth vs, are infinite thinges which wee muft beholde by faith onely. And it is to the ende that we fhould come vnto him with greater boldeneffe too call vpon him, not doubting but that we fhall obtaine whatfoeuer wee craue at his hands, yea euen afmuch as fhall be expedient for our faluation. And according to this, Dauid heere fetteth downe, that God had made him. As if he had faid, I come not vnto thee, O Lord, as we commonly come vnto men. I fet not downe any merite or worthyneffe, whereby I haue bounde thee vnto me: For thou art beholden nothing at all to me: but I talke of thy benefites which I haue already felte, too the ende I would haue thee to continue them vnto me. For beholde the true and very perfect nature of God: to wit, his nature is alwayes to fpread vpon vs his graces without ceafing: as hee is a fountaine, which neuer can bee drawen dry: euen fo muft we not feare that he diminifheth or leffeneth them, neither yet is fparing of his benefites, for hee hath plentie inough to continue them without end or ceafing. Let vs then throughly confider this argument which Dauid heere vfeth: to wit that he telleth God that he is his Creature, to the ende he might teache him, yea euen to vnderftand his law. We haue heere then to note, that Dauid putteth not in himfelfe heere, fimply in the ranke with all the reft of his creatures: but commeth before God, as a man fafhioned after his own image and likeneffe: *Thy hands* (fayth he) *haue made me and fafhioned me*: that is to fay, Thou haft graunted me O Lord to be an inhabiter in this world, yea, and haft made me a reafonable Creature. Since then it is fo, O Lorde, that thou hafte already begun fo gently too intreate mee, I befeech thee that thou wilte continue it.

Nowe we fee what a kinde or vaine of fpeaking we muft vfe

The 10. Sermon of M. Io. Cal.

vse, to be assured that God will heare our requestes: to wit, that we must lay before him his graces, which we haue already receiued of him. For that ought to make vs to hope that like as hee hath begunne, so likewise will hee goe through with it, vntill such time as hee hath brought his work to perfect end. Now, if we desire god to giue vs vnderstanding to comprehēd his law, inasmuch as he hath made vs mortal men we haue so much the better occasiō to do it, in telling him that he hath adopted vs to be his children, & taketh vs to be as of his housholde. Now, when as we haue this aduantage and priuiledge, our confidence ought to be so much the more certain, that we shuld not dout but that hee would augment those graces which he before had bestowed vpon vs. And so, to the end we might profite by this place, we haue to gather briefely three poyntes: The firste and principall which we are to wishe is this, that God will instruct vs in his lawe, that we be not so giuen either to the goods of this worlde, or else to the pleasures of the body, and to all the reste, but that we might alwayes haue regard to our spirituall health.

As touching the first, wee are to desire that this affection may reigne in vs, to the end to keepe all the rest in good order, which violently might carry vs away: to witte, that we should desire to be the right Scholers of God. And thus much for this. Now immediatly after followeth the meane to beseech him, that he will bestowe vppon vs his grace to be taught in his lawe: to wit, because he hath made vs too this end, and not like vnto Oxen, Asses, nor Dogges, which are brute beastes, and nothing but corruption: but that he hath imprinted in vs his image, and ordayned vs too euerlasting life. Seeing then that he hath created vs after this manner, let vs trust in him, and beseech him, that hee will continue and make perfect that, which hee hath begun in vs. But we shall haue the greater courage too make this request vnto him, when as we shall bee brought vnto him in the seconde place, that ouer and besides that hee hath made vs men, he hath chosen ys also to be his childrē, hath

made

upon the Cxix. Pſalme. 82

made vs partakers of this diuine wiſdome, which is contained in the Goſpell, hath ſhewed him ſelfe to be our father, and called vs into the company and fellowſhipp of his Sonne Chriſte Ieſus, that wee might bee members of his body. When as then wee may charge God with this. Loe this is a farre greater approbation of our Faith: and wee ought to beſeech him with much more certaintie and aſſuraunce, without doubting that it woulde pleaſe him too heare vs. And thus much for the ſeconde poynte.

The third is, that although God hath taught vs, wee muſt not by and by thinke that wee are ſuch great Clarkes, and ſo well learned, as that we neede not to deſire him too confirme vs more and more in his knowledge, and too bee alwayes like vnto prentiſes & yong nouices. As in very deed they which haue moſte profited, ſhoulde alwayes bee thus humbled, not to think that they had attayned to the greateſt abundaunce of knowledge: But that they had onely ſome little taſte and ſmattering of the wiſedome of God, that they had neede too haue him to increaſe it alwayes in them more and more.

Nowe if Dauid made this requeſt, yea and that in trueth knowing that he had great neede to be inſtructed of God: I pray you what arrogancie ſhall this be in vs, when as wee ſhall preſume to haue our braine ſo full ſtuffed, as that wee needed no more inſtruction? that wee ſhoulde content our ſelues with that which he had learned: ought it not to bee ſayd that we are moſt arrogaunt? And ſo, let vs after the example of Dauid, all the dayes of our life pray vnto God to teach vs, and that we be neuer weary of beeing taught of him, vntill ſuch time as he hath deſpoyled vs of this mortall body: For ſo long as we ſhall remaine in this body, wee muſt needes be compaſſed aboute with blacke and thicke cloudes of ignoraunce, from which hee will then deliuer vs, through the brightneſſe of his comming. Nowe it followeth ſoone after,

So they that feare thee ſha'l reioyce to ſee me: becauſe I haue put my truſt in thy word.

L 2. Dauid

The 10. *Sermon of M. Io. Cal.*

Dauid bringeth in heere yet another reason, for the obtayning of his request: to witte, that the faythfull will bee glad seeing that God hath hearde him. And this is a place greatly woorth the marking: For we are let to vnderstand by these woordes, that when God bestoweth any benefites vpon any one of our Brethren and neighboures, we ought not onely to acknowledge this goodnesse in this acte simply, but wholy apply it too our owne vse, that it may serue vs for our better confirmation: that we might vnderstand, that we shall be no more refused, then he which hath already obtayned his desire. And why so? For God is equall and iust to all those which call vpon him vnfaignedly. He sayth not, that hee will doe good too one and not too another: but we haue a generall promise which extendeth it selfe too all without exception: to witte, that if wee come vnto him for succoure, and that in trueth, that hee will bee very ready to receiue vs: yea, that before we shall open our mouthes hee will stretch foorth his hand too giue vs whatsoeuer he knoweth to be good and profitable for our saluation. Since then that this promise is generall, if wee be not too too vnthankfull, we must needes beleeue that God will heare vs aswell as those whome wee haue already seene him to haue hearde heeretofore: and wee muste take their example for our better cōfirmation of the promises which he hath made vnto vs. See heere, why Dauid sayth, That they which feare God, shal see him, and in seeing him, will be glad of it: yea, and wee are throughly too consider of that which followeth: *for I haue put my trust in thy Commaundements.* As if he had said, They shal find nothing in me why thou haste shewed thy selfe so louing and liberall, when as thou hast taught me by thy holy spirit, but becauseI haue put my trust in thy word. Now thy woorde, is come too all those which feare thee. So then, let them knowe that the same which thou hast doone too my person, appertayneth too them also, and may applye it too their owne vse. This is said for a better cōfirmatiō of that which I haue already spoken: to witte, that if God hath gently dealte

with

vpon the Cxix. Psalme.

with any of our neighbours, that he hath had compassion vpon him: we are to conclude, that we shall feele him too doe the like vnto vs And why so? Because he hath giuen vs his woorde: which is true and will neuer deceiue vs. Let vs then put our trust in him, and we shall feele the like of that which wee haue seene in others that haue gone before vs, and shewed vs the way, and haue giuen vs an example too repose all our trust in the goodnesse of God, hauing the promises which he hath offred vs. Loe heere the meaning of Dauid in this verse. Now it followeth,

I knowe O Lord, that thy iudgementes are right: and that thou haste afflicted me iustly.

Dauid thinketh good to speake heere a common thing, That he knoweth the statutes of God to be right. For what is he that is so accursed, which will not confesse that? Yea, euen they which dare blaspheme and speake euill against God, when they shall be pressed thus farre, yet will say, that the holy scripture is a doctrine that cannot bee amended, and that the lawe of God is the rule of all equitie. The very wicked then, will speake thus wel of it: but yet there are very few which haue this consideration imprinted in their harts: to wit, to make this estimation of the lawe of God, as too say, that what soeuer is conteined therein is iust. And why so? That is first, by reason of the cotrarietie that is betwene our wit and the wisedome of God. And next, by reason of the contrarietie of our wicked lustes, and affections, with the bridle which he holdeth vs, too rule vs according too his pleasure, and in his obedience, when as men will take councell of their owne head, that they thinke to controle thereby, whatsoeuer God speaketh in his woorde: wee then agree euen like fire and water. For all our wisdome is but vanitie and leasing, when as wee shall appose and set our selues againste the holy Scriptures, the doctrine of the Lawe, and whatsoeuer is contayned in the Prophetes and the Gospell. As we see at this day, the worlde will in no wise subiect it selfe thereto. From whence come all these contro-

controuersies and diss̃entions throughout al chriſtendom? Forſooth it is becauſe that men ꞇwill be ouerwiſe, and will neuer honor God in ſuch ſort, as to ſay, Although O Lord our ownwittes lead vs altogither prepoſterouſly, yet muſt wee needes be ruled by thee. And becauſe that wee are not able to attaine to this reaſon, it cannot bee choſen but that the tyle ſhardes muſt needes flye about and the worlde bee infected. See then, what is the cauſe that letteth the bigger number too confeſſe bothe with hearte and mouthe, that the iudgementes of God are right: to wit, that all perfection of wiſedome is in his lawe, in his Prophetes, and in his Goſpell: that it muſt needes fall out, that we ought to doe him homage in all this, knowing that it is impoſſible too finde any one iot therein contayned, to be amended. For although wee very well knowe, that the iudgementes of God are right, to wit, in ſuch ſorte as that our wittes and mindes might thereby be confirmed, that we might iudge it to be ſo: yet it ſo ſtandeth neuertheleſſe, that beholde our luſtes and paſſions, doe violently withſtand God, and are euer againſt him. As howe? An whoremonger ſhall be vanquiſhed that his whoredome is wicked and abhominable. A drunkarde ſhall condemne his drunkenneſſe: and ſhal neuer be able to ſay, that the vice whereunto he is giuen is a vertue. And ſo much may bee ſayde of the ſwearer and theefe. But yet it is ſo, that ſuch kinde of people cannot giue God the glory, ſaying, that his lawe is right: For they murmure againſt him and are very angry, that they haue not the raynes of the bridle layde in their neck, and giueth them not all the lybertie that may bee too doe what them ſelues liſt. No doubt of it, if it lay in their power, they would plucke G O D out of his ſeate, that hee might haue no authoritie ouer them. Loe what mens affections and deſires are. So then, we ſhall finde a very ſmall number of people to be like vnto Dauid, which wil ſay in trueth and without hypocriſie, I knowe O Lorde that thy iudgementes are right, When hee ſayth, that he hath knowen, he meaneth

that

that hee hath gotten newe vnderstanding which hee neuer had before, as if hee had sayde, I haue O Lorde profited so much, that I haue cleane giuen ouer mine owne witte and reason. For I knowe it to be blinde, becaufe that men will alwayes lifte vpp them felues aboue meafure. But nowe O Lorde, thou haft brought me to this poynt, that I will no longer bee gouerned by mine owne heade and fantafie: I will not truft to my felfe to knowe whether the matter fhall be good or not, but I will reft me on that which thou fayeft vnto me. And thus much for the firft poynte.

And a litle after he fayth, Although mine affections are cleane againft thy law, that they are ready to caft mee quite out at the Cartes arfe, as we fay, yet for all that O Lorde, I haue bridled all my paffions, yea and that through thy mightie power befeeching thee to continue and holdthem as pryfoners, vntill fuch time as thou fhalte fully haue deliuered me from them. Loe how Dauid practifed this knowledge which he fayd he had of God by his worde. And let vs after his example continually recorde this leffon: Let vs beftowe all our ftudy both euening and morning vpon it, to the end we may fay that we haue knowne, that it is that, which G O D hath commaunded vs, yea too followe it. But Dauid dooth not heere fet downe this fimple knowledge of the woorde of God: but goeth on farther: too witte, that God of very faythfulneffe, *had caufed him to bee troubled.* Nowe is this farre harder then the firfte.

It is very true, that we fhall haue great conflictes before wee can be able to fubmit our felues to God, in fuch humilitie, as for to knowe & fay, that he is onely wife: But yet, they which knowe this, think not his chatifements too be gentle and gratious', but are impacient, and conceiue fome griefe, that maketh them too grinde their teeth. Nowe Dauid ioyned thefe twoo togither, to wit, that he did not onely make much of the word of God, but alfo of the punifhment which he fente him: as if hee had faide, O Lord, I do not only fuffer my felf to be taught by thy word, but to bee chaftifed alfo with thy hand: and I befeech thee to scourge and beate mee with thy rodes, so often as thou seest mee too doe amisse, and too cause mee too amende, shewing thy selfe a moste louing and pittifull Father towardes mee.

Wee haue heere nowe a very good admonition: to wit, that first we must learne to be ruled after the will of God, to receiue his woorde without contradiction, that wee reply not according as it pleaseth our owne wittes and affections, neither too make any noyse when wee heare God speake: But let him haue such authoritie ouer vs, to make vs so silent, as that wee may knowe that whatsoeuer hee sayth vnto vs is iuste and true. And thus too doe, let vs learne not to be so sleepy and sluggish, as wee are by nature in our vices and sinnes, and specially in this vice of ambition, hauing alwayes a greedy desire to be aduaunced.

Let vs rather knowe that God is the Mayster of the humble and lowely: and let vs therfore humble our selues, & not looke so bigge and bee so foolish hautie, which doth nothing else but cast vs hedlong into destruction, when as wee aduaunce our selues higher then becommeth vs. Let vs rather be aduised to bridle all our Lustes and that which holdeth vs as it were captiues as Saint Paul sayth. For what is the cause that so many people at this day doe set themselues against the Gospell? It is not, becaufe they know not this doctrine too be good, and that they iudge not so of it: But yet are they not therein thorowly perswaded too say, Loe howe we must liue! Euery man will doe whatsoeuer himselfe thinketh to be good. We must then needes confesse that the iudgements of God are right, that wee learne to holde all our passions in bondage: that we suffer our selues to be condemned by him, and to be rebuked for all our vices and imperfections as becommeth vs. Now can we doe this? to wit, are we become subiect & obedient to the word of God? We must also submit our selues vnder his hand, to strike vs when it shall please him, and liuely to vnderstande that wee haue doone amisse, confessing that he hath iustly chastised vs, or as heere it is sayde, of very faithfulnesse.

This

vpon the Cxix. Pſalme.

This is the ſumme and effect, that he is iuſt in puniſhing of vs, as he is wiſe in teaching of vs: the one hāgeth on the other, that is to ſay, the ſecond hangeth vpon the firſt. For whoſoeuer ſhal come to this humilitie that Dauid ſpeaketh off, to knowe, that in the worde of God there is but one holy doctrine, one infallible truth, one ſo perfect equitie, as can be no perfecter: hee that ſhall haue knowne this, ſhall by little and little haue wherewith too bee fortified too receiue the corrections with a meke ſpirite, and not to bee grieued, and to kicke againſt the pricke, as wee are wonted to doe. Let vs nowe then ſuffer God to rebuke vs, yea and to correct vs, ſeeing hee doeth all this for our profit and health. And this is the ſumme and effect of this verſe. It followeth next after,

I praye thee that thy mercie may comfort me: according vnto thy promiſe vnto thy ſeruant.

Here Dauid maketh a more generall requeſt, then that which before we haue ſeene. Hee deſireth God to inſtruct him: and now he addeth, O let thy mercifull kindnes bee my comfort. As if he had ſaid, O Lord I haue beſought thee for a ſpeciall and particular thing, but I adde nowe, that thou wilt be mercifull vnto me in all and through all, that thy mercie bee extended vpon me, that I faile in nothing. Thou knoweſt what is neceſſarie and profitable for me: O Lord let mee feele thee to bee grations and pitifull all maner of wayes. Loe what difference there is betweene the firſt requeſt which we haue already ſeene, and this ſecond. Now this is a point worth the noting. For(as wee haue before ſaid) ſee the firſt which we ought to haue in a ſingular recommendation, and that is, that wee may bee taught by God, and not to be taught onely by wordes, but that hee will alſo lighten vs with his holy ſpirite, to make vs knowe, that it is his worde which guideth vs. See here, I ſay, the very right way to ſaluation. Nowe haue wee made this requeſt? we may craue of God that hee will not let vs fall in any thing whatſoeuer, that his mercy may comfort vs. But yet here we ſe how that Dauid was not comforted nor yet

L 5 reioyced

The 10. Sermon of M.I.Cal.

reioyced but onely in God, knowing that all the ioye that we haue here bilowe shalbe accursed, when as wee haue no regarde vnto our Creator. And yet for all this, se how commonly wee are wonted to reioyce and comfort our selues, that is, euen to forget God, & to turne our backs vpō him. Now accursed be such ioy, for the issue thereof can be none other, but as our Lord Christ Iesus sayeth, That it shall bee turned into weeping and gnashing of teeth. Howbeit, the worlde is waxen dronke, for whatsoeuer is saide vnto it, it maketh no reckoning thereof, but vtterly refuseth al good & sound doctrine. Indeede this is true, that this same was not written in vaine: but that we shalbe so much the more inexcusable, when as we shall haue the example of Dauid, except we folowe it. See then for this first point, that after Dauid had compassed the whole worlde both aboue and beneath, he founde no rest to comfort his spirite and soule, but at such time as he made his repaire vnto God. And there I say, he found wherwith to reioyce and comfort him selfe: finding nothing els but vnquietnesse in all liuing creatures. Now he soone after setteth downe, how we ought to reioyce and to be comforted in God: to wit, through his mercie: for if God shoulde deale with vs according to our desertes, we should haue no cause wherefore to reioyce, but rather be confounded with very horrour and feare. When as God shal declare him selfe to be our iudge, alas, which way shall wee be able to turne vs? Must wee not needes bee cast headlong into the deepe pit? If it be said that wee must appeare before the maiestie of our God, what shall become of vs which sucke vp iniquitie euen as the fishe sucketh in water, as it is written in the booke of Iob? Wherefore, let vs know that if we will rightly reioyce, and finde sure rest in our consciences, wee must betake our selues to this free mercie of our God, that he declareth him selfe pitifull vnto vs in that he seeth vs to be miserable & wretched creatures, and to put foorth our hand vnto him to receiue his mercie. Nowe Dauid in the ende sheweth whereuppon he buil-

deth

vpon the Cxix. Psalme. 86

deth him selfe, in making such a request:

According vnto thy worde, made vnto thy seruant.

Loe whereupon we must builde and settle our selues, when as we will come vnto God, to be heard of him: to wit, vpon his meere mercie, as we haue here aboue said. But are wee already come thus farre furth? And if wee be, yet is there an other point farther required: to wit, wee must assure our selues that the graces of God shall adorne and garnishe vs, so we seeke them according to his word. And to proue it to be so, marke I beseeche you, for it were maruerlous great presumption in vs, to come vnto God, without we had his promises for it, and to desire of him any thing, and say, O Lord, I haue neede of this and that. Go to now, here is already some occasion which causeth vs to come vnto God. And againe, O Lord, thou art good and gracious: loe this is an other thing also which augmenteth our courage and boldnes. But bicause we are so farre from God, that we are not able to come nere his maiestie, without he come down vnto vs: we must then, before wee can haue any accesse to make our prayers vnto him, lay this foundation which is here set before vs: that is to say, the word of God, when as thereby God witnesseth vnto vs, that his mercie is alwayes readie, that he there laieth it before vs, and offereth the same there vnto vs. There remaineth now nothing els, but that wee receiue it by faith, and that there wee declare our faith through our calling vpon him. So then we see, the order which Dauid here setteth downe, that is, that hee bringeth vs to God, to the ende we might take our whole contentation, repose, and reioysing in his meere goodnesse. And since, that he hath receiued vs through his mercie, let vs beseeche him that he would looke vnto vs with his eyes of pitie. For the third point, he sheweth vs how we ought to make such our petitions, that is, bicause God hath bounde him selfe vnto vs of his own good will, and hath witnessed vnto vs that he wil be neare vs. When then we shal come vnto him in this sort, let vs not doubt but that he wil heare vs & graunt whatsoeuer we shall desire according to his will.

And

The 10. Sermon of M.I.Cal.

And namely he sayeth, thy woorde made vnto thy seruant, to thende he would declare to euery of vs that euery man should apply the promises of God particularly vnto him selfe. And not to vse the maner of the Papistes, to saye, It is very true that God hath promised this and that, but we know not whether the same belongeth vnto vs or not. And these are no fooles, which say thus, but this is the doctrine which they teache in all their Satanicall and deuelish Schooles and Synagogues. Loe here the very doctrine of popish doctors, that the promises of God are vncertaine, & that we must receiue thē as things hanging in the ayre, not to take them generally, to say, I doubt not but that G O D speaketh the same vnto me. But contrariwise, we must conclude as Dauid here doth, and say O Lord let it be done vnto thy seruant according to thy word. He saith not, according to thy word, I knowe not to whom, nor vnto such mē of which number I am not, so that I can not builde vppon it: but he saith, according to thy promise O Lord, made vnto me. Let vs then learne by his example, that when we desire the Lord God to assiste vs, to charge him with his promises, yea & let vs apply them vnto our selues, and beleeue that they are also spoken to euery of vs in particular, and generally vnto all: I meane vnto all the faithfull. When as the Lord our God saieth, I receiue all sinners to mercy: let euery one saye, O Lorde, I am one of those miserable and wretched creatures, and therefore I come vnto thee, charging thee with thy promise made vnto me. Loe howe wee must behaue our selues herein: for els, we shall but wander in the holy scripture all the daies of our life. It followeth immediatly after,

Let thy tender mercies come vnto me that I may liue: for thy lawe is my delight.

In this verse we may very well see, that Dauid was as it were estranged from the mercie of God. Now this is a very notable point to be considered off: for what is the cause of our distrust, yea euen to close vp the gate againſt God for that we would not come vnto him, but onely bicause wee thinke

thinke that God hath eſtraunged him ſelfe from vs, and that we ſhould be thereby confounded. It is very true that he will ſometimes cauſe vs to feele them, as if he had cleane turned him ſelfe away from vs, and all bicauſe we firſt forſooke him: but yet we muſt notwithſtanding returne vnto him, and not be diſcouraged, but followe the example of Dauid, that although the mercies of God to the outwarde apparance and in our iudgement bee farre from vs, and in ſuch ſort, as that we may well perceiue it: yet muſt we neuer ceaſe to ſay, O Lord, let thy louing mercies come vnto me: ſurely to the outrward ſhew, & ſo farre as I can iudge, they are farre of me: but yet O Lorde, I knowe that thou wilt in the ende make me to attaine vnto them: yea and although thou manifeſtly ſheweſt me them not, yet notwithſtanding I will wayte and ſurely looke for them, with an aſſured faith and hope. Moreouer, when he ſayeth, that I may liue: that is to ſignifie vnto vs the ſame which I haue already ſaid, to wit, that although his wit and ſpirite, ſtayed it ſelfe vpon creatures, yet that he was but as a dead man, & whiles he thought God not to be neare him, hee ſuppoſed him ſelf to be but as a forlorne man. And in deede although we had all the world on our ſide, and had GOD againſt vs, and were ſure that he neither loued nor fauoured vs, all the reſt would turne but to our ruyne and deſtruction. And if wee eſteeme not thus of him, muſt it not needes be but that we muſt bee bewitched by Satan, and caried violently away, when we ſhall content vs onely with theſe worldly things, and neuer haue regard vnto the ſpring head and fountaine of all goodneſſe: to wit, the bounty of God? But in the meane while let vs note this, that although we bee dead for a time, after the example of Dauid, yet ſhall wee be quickened, ſo that we come to God, beſeeching him not to holde backe his mercies farre from vs. Now he ſaieth in the ende, *For thy lawe is my delight.* By this we are admoniſhed what it is that we muſt craue at the handes of God in good earneſt, forſooth that his mercies may remaine with vs: to wit, when as we are conformable to him and to his woorde.

Let it

The 10. Sermon of M. Jo. Cal.

Let it not now abash vs although wee feele so little taste of God his mercies. And why so? For what is he that will acknowledge it? Wee are so beguiled with these false deceiptes of the worlde, that we thinke we may triumphe by them, that wee shall bee exceedingly blessed when as wee shall haue all thinges after our owne heartes desire. But in thus doing we can contemne God and his grace. We must not then be abashed if we be set besides that which apperteineth to our saluation, and that God suffereth vs to languishe in wretchednesse and miserie. And so let vs learne after the example of Dauid, to bee as it were reiected of the worde of God, and to bee as it were estraunged from it to craue in good earnest, to cause his mercies to retourne vnto vs: to wit, that he would graunt vs this grace, to let vs in such sort vnderstand what neede we haue of his fauour and aide, that notwithstanding that we haue declined from his commandements, yet that he would graunt vs for all that, to feele his mercie, although he hath held the same from vs for a season. Now it followeth,

Let the proude be confounded, for they haue delt wickedly and falsely with me: but I meditate in thy commaundementes.

Here Dauid setteth downe another reason, to confirme him self continually more and more, that hee shall obtaine that which he praieth vnto God for: to wit, bicause the wicked do persecute him: whom he calleth the proud. And this is the sentence which wee haue already heretofore treated off, neither will the time suffer vs to stay any lenger vpon it. It shall therefore suffice vs for this time, that faith onely is the thing which bringeth vs within the compasse of humilitie, when as we know that there is nothing in vs but wickednesse, and that wee are thereto tied, by the iust iudgementes of God. When I say, that the faithfull knowe this, it pulleth downe their high mindes, they are no more arrogant nor presumptious, to lifte them selues vp against God, and their neighbours. Contrariwyse the wicked and enemies of GOD are called proude: for the pride which they vse against GOD, engendreth also crueltie against

their

their neighbours.

As many as will humble them selues before God, will also bee very gentle too their neighbours: but they which haue a fierse and high mynde to stande against God, must needes likewise cast their poyson against their neighbours. And for this cause Dauid sayeth, let the proud O Lord be confounded, for they go wickedly about to confound me. Whereby wee are admonished, that although the wicked vexe and grieue vs neuer so iniuriously, and without cause, yet we are thereby taught to haue the rather a great deale more trust that God wil haue mercie vpon vs. And why so? bicause it is he which graunteth our request: and when as we shall make it vnto him, it shall not come of our selues, but he shalbe authour thereof. So then, when as we shall be grieued and iniuried by malitious and cruell men, let vs go boldly vnto God, and beseeche him to haue pitie and compassion vpon vs. Nowe he addeth, that he neuer ceased to meditate vpon the testimonies of God, although he was so afflicted. And this is an excellent admonition for vs, that when wee are tormented both from heauen, and on the earth, that God on the one side, to the outwarde shewe, estraungeth him selfe from vs: and we on the other side are so forsaken, that wee are troden vnder mens feete, besides a thousand other villaines done vnto vs: when as, I say, wee shall be so vexed and grieued. We must learne after the example of Dauid to meditate of the testimonies of God, and there to seeke our whole comfort, for that is the very meane by which God meaneth to plucke vs out of all our anguishes and griefes which might any way trouble vs.

That now which foloweth, hath beene already handled: to wit, that men which feare God doe turne vnto him: to say, that they will keepe him companie. And in the ende he setteth downe this conclusion:

Let my heart bee vpright in thy statutes: that I bee not ashamed.

Now like as in the first verse hee desireth GOD to giue him vnderstanding that hee might learne his Lawe, here

he

The 10. Sermon of M. Jo. Cal.

he desireth that he would graunt him affection. Whereby we may see, that this proceedeth from vs & from our nature: to wit, to be very poore blynd soules, vntill such time as God openeth our eies.

And thus much for the first point. But yet vnderstanding onely shall not serue. God must make our heartes pliant vnto his obedience, and place vs so with him selfe, as that we haue none other desire but to serue him. Let vs thē learne to pray vnto him as Dauid here hath done: for after he had desired him to giue him vnderstanding of his law, he desireth him also to giue him a pure and a sound heart: yea and that we should also doe the same in veritie & truth, not doubting but that when God hath bestowed vpon vs some graces, that he will also encrease them more & more, and haue compassion vpon vs, so that we be obedient vnto him in our behalfe, and yelde him the homage and authoritie which vnto him belongeth.

And according vnto this doctrine, let vs in all humilitie prostrate our selues before the maiestie of our good God, in acknowledging our offences, beseeching him so to touch vs, as that wee might learne after the example of his Prophet, how to make and present our requestes vnto him, & to bereaue vs of all our earthly affections, which we feele to be most violent against vs, to the ende that our minde bee not withdrawne through them from his righteousnes, but that wee submit our selues wholy vnto his holy will, desiring nothing els but to haue him to gouerne vs: to the end that being fortified by his holy spirite, we might perseuere vnto the end to resist those temptations which shal grieue vs, to obteine the victory abouesaid, and come to the triūphe which is prepared for vs in heauen aboue. That he wil not onely graunt vs, this grace, but also vnto all people and nations of the earth, &c.

The

The eleuenth Sermon of the hundreth and nineteenth Psalme.

CAPH.

My soule fainteth for thy saluation: yet I wayte for thy worde.
Mine eyes faile for thy promisse: saying, when wilt thou comfort me?
For I am like a bottle in the smoke: yet do I not forget thy statutes.
How many are the dayes of thy seruant? when wilt thou be auenged of them that persecute me?
The proude haue digged pittes for mee: which are not after thy lawe.
All thy commandementes are true: they persecute me falsely: be thou my helpe.
They had almost made an end vpō me on the earth: but I forsooke not thy commaundements.
Quicken me according to thy louing kindnesse: so shall I keepe the testimonies of thy mouth.

If we could rightly call to our remembraunce the promises of God in our afflictions and miseries, it were sufficient enough too make vs pacient. And by this meane we should render a true proufe of our fayth: but so soone as we are grieued with any affliction, we by and by waxe fainte hearted, bicause we forget all the promises of God: which to our
M   seeming,

seeming, we had long before very well vnderstand and learned: Now we should not at the least be forgetfull of them, when neede requireth, yea, and that when wee are thereby enforced. And for that cause wee haue here a very excellent lesson for the purpose, & worthy the noting: for Dauid doth not only teach vs as a Prophet of God, what our dutie is, & what the power and vertue of our faith ought too bee: but sheweth vs also the way by his example, howe wee must bee pacient in all our aduersities, and howe we ought not to fal from that: to wit, that we alwayes haue our eye fixed vpon the promises of God. For that shal be enough to entertaine and keepe vs, in such sort as that we should paciently waite for his sauing health, yea, euen in calling vpon him. But that we might the better profite by this doctrine, wee are here to note, that the twoo first verses are both of one and selfesame substance, saue that the order of the wordes are changed. Hee saieth in the first place, *My soule fainteth for thy saluation,* That is to say, O Lorde, I haue longed, albeit the afflictions and miseries which I haue abidden, were very great: and lasted long, and that I see neither ende nor issue of them, yet neuerthelesse I rested altogether hereon, that I alwayes trusted, that thou wouldest bee my supporter and aider. Nowe hee addeth the reason howe hee coulde so faint: to wit, bicause he trusted vnto the promises of God. In the second verse he saieth, *That he hath stayed for the promise of God, yea euen looking for this promise,* and that he hath said, *When wilt thou comfort me?* And in the third he handleth that which before hee had spoken of: to wit, that although he had beeene as it were parched and dried, *euen as a skinne bottle in the smoke,* so that there remained neither moysture nor substance in him, but dried vp with verie miseries, *yet that he had not forgotten the testimonies of God.*

We see then nowe what the summe and effect of this is, which is here shewed vnto vs: to wit, that there is but one onely meane too cause vs to bee constant and pacient, when as we are afflicted, and that our aduersities doe euer long last as wee imagine: that is, too bee mindefull of the
promi-

promises of God, and to haue them depely imprinted in our hartes. For if that bee so, it wil not cost vs much to be patient: and although it bee an harde matter, yet wee shall at the last come too the ende of it. Let vs then now marke, from whence our impatience springeth, and what the reason is why wee are so oftentimes ouercome with temptations: or else, when as wee shal haue for a tyme resisted them, yet in the ende wee are confounded and faintharted, Truely, it is bicause wee forget the testimonies of GOD, and turne away from his woorde. In very deede, this at the first sight may seeme too bee a common matter with vs. And to say the truthe, euery man wil say, that we ought to remember them, and that it is the onely remedy too comforte vs. But wee shal the oftener doo it, when as wee shal haue learned this lesson which is heere set downe vntoo vs, and that wee recorde it al the dayes of our life: For this is one of the principallest pointes that is too bee required in al Christians, that when they perceiue that God hath laide his hand on them, that they bee as it were almost cast downe: yet that they might comfort themselues, in staying of the promises of saluation which God hath promised them. But yet, let vs throughly consider the worde which Dauid here vseth: *I haue longed* (sayeth hee) *after the saluation, and I haue hoped*, or after that I had hoped, *bicause of thy woorde*.

The seconde parte of this verse, is as it were the foundation whereon Dauid buildeth. Let vs vnderstande then this hope which wee ought to haue in the worde of God, as Dauid had: For without that, it is impossible but that wee must bee confounded. For although it seeme in the iudgement of menne, that there is in vs some vertue and soundnesse too indure and suffer patiently, yet shal it not be such a true patience as GOD alloweth. And why so? For wee shal neuer beare him that affection too obey him, without wee comforte our selues that hee loueth vs, and that we trust to his bountie,

M 2   A man,

The 11. Sermon of M. Io. Cal.

A man, I say, shall neuer be disposed to obey God, and to glorifie him in afflictions, except hee haue a taste of the bountie, and fatherly loue, which he beareth vs. Now how can it be that wee should bee fully perswaded that God loueth vs, and procureth our wealth and health, when as he afflicteth vs, without we be armed with his promises? For it is impossible for vs to knowe the truth of God, except he declare the same vnto vs in his word. Let vs learne then, as I haue already said, that the pacience of the faithfull can not be built, but vpon faith and hope in the promises of God. Loe then what we haue to note in this place.

Now Dauid hauing laid such a foundation, buildeth thereon, saying, that his soule longed after the saluation of God: when he saieth that his soule longed, he meaneth not that he was so forlorne, as that hee had in the ende giuen him cleane ouer: ne yet that Satan had gotten any aduauntage of him: but that worde, *to long*, is taken in the scripture, for that which notwithstanding is conioyned with such obedience as we ought to yelde vnto God, staying and setling our selues vpon him. As howe? Saint Paul sayeth, *That we ought to hope beyond all hope as Abraham did*: to wit, we must surmount all our wittes and imaginations, when there is any question of our beliefe in God. For if wee will measure the promises of God by our owne wittes, what shall become of it? our faith then must exceede and goe beyond all the wisedome of men, as here it is sayde, *That his soule hath longed*: which is as much as if Dauid had said, it is true O Lorde, that according to mans reason, I was vtterly forlorne: yea I was so oppressed with miseries, as that I could beare no moe: but when I was in the middes of death, I ceased not for all that vntill I was arriued at a sure hauen: to wit, thy ayde and helpe. Now he namely speaketh of Gods succour, bicause it shall goe very hard, but that we wil wander, looke aboue, and beneath, both before and behinde, to see if wee can finde readie helpe.

But if the trouble last long & we see not which way to get

out

out of it, but that it is like a bottomles pitte: although before we somewhat trusted and hoped vpon God, yet for all that wee shall then bee driuen and egged, to seeke for aide here and there, we know not where. And howe so? Is it not possible for me to finde remedie? Bicause, I saye, wee are so dull, and the hope which we haue in God, passeth so lightly away from vs, and melteth, and runneth about; this way and that way: Dauid for this reason sayeth, *That hee hoped for the saluation of God.* Hereby then hee sheweth, that although this occasion was offered him to seeke after other helpes, and to cast his eyes vppon creatures, and to forsake God: yet that the temptations had not so wonne vpō him, but that he alwayes remained constant in this resolution, that it was God which must relieue his neede. Nowe hereypon he addeth,

Mine eyes faile for thy promise, saying: when wilt thou comfort me?

I haue already said that this verse conteineth no new or strange thing, but Dauid chaungeth onely the order of the wordes. For when he saieth, *That his eyes sore longed after the word of God*, he meaneth none other thing but this, that although all his wittes were troubled, and that hee was as it were blinded with the multitude of afflictiōs which he endured, yet that hee alwayes stayed him selfe vpyon this word of God, and neuer ceased calling vpon him, saying: *O when wilt thou comfort me?* By this hee sheweth vs, that if we haue a true faith setled vppon the promises of GOD made vnto vs, when as it shall please him soone after to afflict vs, we must not by and by bee angry, biting the bit as Mules do: but let vs yelde him true obedience, saying: *O Lord, when wilt thou comfort me?* Wee must then suffer and abide thus to do: to wit, that when we beseech and require God, to helpe vs according to his promise, wee must also desire him, to shewe it vs by the effect: and wee must remaine firme and constant, vntill such time as he causeth vs to perceiue it: for although hee delayeth his aide, and holdeth it as it were in suspence, yet must we be fully persuaded

M 3   that

that he hath not forgotten his office, which is, to comfort vs. By this meane we shall finde in the ende the fruite of our prayers. Nowe he fully and wholy explaneth in the third verse following, when as hee sheweth it to be no small matter to be thus cast downe, had not the woorde of God sustained, and vpheld him, but that there was great reason in it. I am, saith he, like vnto a Goates skinne, wherein oyle, or wyne is put, hanging in the smoke, and so dried and parched, as that there was neither substance nor moisture left in him. Dauid vseth this similitude, to shewe that his afflictions were so great and excessiue, as that hee was without all strength, and without hope of life. Now he addeth notwithstanding, *That he did not yet forget the statutes of God.* For an example: which wee ought too followe, neither must we alledge here our infirmitie: for Dauid was a passionate man as we are: he might very well haue fainted, if God had not strengthened him. And how so? Hauing the promises, he hoped vpon them: knowing that God continueth his benefites towardes his children, bicause they should haue recourse vnto him: hee called vpon him, for that hee had already founde mercie and succour of him: God so holpe him through his holy spirite. Nowe, haue not wee at this daye the same promises which Dauid had? Yea, haue wee not more large and ample promises? Haue not wee a great deale more familiar accesse then Dauid had, bicause that Iesus Christe is declared too bee a mediatour more manifestly, then he was vnder the lawe? When God then rendreth vs such a testimonie of his good will, that wee may freely come before him to praye vnto him, to the ende hee might helpe our necessities: I praye you what excuse shall wee make, if wee come not boldely vnto him as Dauid did, and be constant to perseuere in the same purpose, seeing that God offereth the selfe same meanes, to fight against whatsoeuer may turne vs awaye from it. Moreouer, is the power of God lessened since that time? Doth he not at this day helpe all his faithfull with his holy spirite

spirite, as he did vnder the lawe? Yea, doth not he saye that he will encrease the kingdome of our Lorde Iesus Christe, more then euer he did at that time?

There is nothing then but our vnthankefulnesse which hath shut the gate against God, so that his graces can haue no accesse nor entraunce into vs. It is very true, that he will say enough vnto vs, but we will stope our eares: he wil make vs fayre promises enough, but we will soone forget them: or els if we keepe them in minde, it shalbe but a raunging imagination, neither shall it haue any deepe print, or yet liuely roote in vs. Bicause therefore, that wee esteeme not of the promises of God, loe the reason why wee are so suddenly cast downe, euen with the least temptation that may come. Howe exercise we our faith in prayers? what readinesse and zeale is there at this daye amongst Christians in calling vpon the name of God? Alas it is so colde and feeble as it can not be more. And so see why God hath pluckt backe his hand from vs, bicause of our infidelitie, so that we feele not his helpe as we should. The more deepely therefore ought we to consider of this sentence here, when Dauid declareth *that he was cleane dryed vp, and yet for all that forgot not the promises of God.*

Let vs now goe and vaunt our selues to bee good Christians, that we haue greatly profited in the Gospel, and yet when as wee shalbe touched with any little, yea, and that with a very light affliction, wee shall bee so amased as it is woonder. Alas what should become of vs, if wee should be as Dauid protesteth hee was? that God threatned vs through stitche, that there were but one droppe of substance of life, and that it should seeme that we were euen as it were dead. If then there were such a kinde of parched drynesse in vs, what should become of it? But what therein resteth the faulte, that every man flattereth him selfe, and wee also thinke that GOD shoulde submitte him selfe to our flatteries.

M.4　　　　But

But it is not in vaine that this example is here set before vs. Let vs exercise our selues then better then we haue heretofore done, and call to minde the testimonies of God. When as we shal bee parched, and so dried, as that it might seeme wee had not one droppe of life, let vs notwithstanding, meditate yet more then euer before we did of the promises of God, to the ende we might get vs newe force and strength. Now when Dauid had thus spoken, he addeth,

How many are the daies of thy seruant? when wilt thou be auenged of them that persecute me?

The proud haue digged pittes for me: which are not after thy lawe.

Here Dauid pursuing his purpose maketh metion of the griefes which he endured, that is, the wicked and vngodly persecuted him wrongfully, and that hee beeing retired to God, as to his saulfegarde, found no succour of him at the first dash, but that God held him at a bay, as a forlorne ma. Now hereupon hee rightly sheweth that his faith was not cleerely quenched, no yet lessoned, but that he stil continued in praier. And in the ende concludeth, that he will yet better remember the word of God, when as he shall bee so restored by him, and raised vp againe as it were from death. Let vs then note, that Dauid here setteth downe a certaine maner and order to shewe vs, that when God, to the outward shewe shall seeme to estraunge him selfe, yet we must take hede that the same keepe vs not from hauing recourse vnto him. Now it may very wel seeme, that God sometimes thinketh not of vs, but specially, when hee shall suffer the wicked to runne whether they list, and let them doe whatsoeuer they desire.

Now this is a terrible temptation. And why? For on the one side we looke, that if God tooke vs for his children, & loued vs as he testifieth, should he not by and by haue compassion of our miseries? should he not put forth his hande to helpe vs? When then he suffereth vs to be thus vniustly troden vnder foote, it is a signe that hee hath forsaken vs, and that he hath no care of vs, nor of our health,

Loe

vpon the Cxix. Pſalme. 93

Loe heere a very hard and greeuous temptation. And the ſecond is, that it ſhould ſeeme that God doth not his office, How is that? Beholde how the vngodly fall out with him ſo that it ſeemeth they would giue him open defiaunce. For is not this to make warre againſt him, when as they giue them ſelues licence to doe wickedly: that whatſoeuer can be ſayd vnto them, they can neuer bee brought too goodneſſe? And yet God maketh ſemblaunce as though he had no care of their wicked dealing. Theſe we ſee are two maruelous daungerous temptations. And this is the cauſe namely why Dauid hath heere recited his perſecutions, which he abode at the handes of the wicked. Now it is ſo, that he beeing in ſuch conflictes, hauing to fight againſt theſe two temptations, which I haue noted ſheweth right wel that he remained ſtil conquerour. And ſee why he ſayth, *How many are the dayes of thy ſeruant? when wilt thou be auenged of thē that perſecute me?* Dauid ſignifieth that he made not this requeſt vntill ſuch time as hee was driuen too this extremitie, that he was no longer able to abide it. As if he ſhould haue ſayde, Alas, my good God, wilt thou helpe me after I am deade? For thou ſeeſt that I haue alreadyabidden ſo much, as it is not poſſible to indure more: thou ſeeſt me euen at the graues brinke: It is now time, or elſe neuer to helpe. But yet I perceiue no ſuccour comming from thee. And what is the cauſe? When wilt thou doe it? It cannot bee choſen but that Dauid had as it were an intollerable affliction, when he called vpon God in this manner. Wherefore we are ſo much the rather to meditate on this place. For although God ſuffereth vs to be afflicted but for a little while: yet the ſame laſteth ſo with vs, as that we beeing vexed euen to the vttermoſte, will ſay, I knowe not where I am, nor what to doe heerein. What is the cauſe why God deferreth his ayde ſo long? For in ſteade too call vpon him, it is out of doubt rather that we murmure, yea and moyte as it were ſecretly againſt him. Nowe the right remedy to ouercome theſe temptations, & not ſo to murmur againſt God in our afflictions, is this, to call vpon him

M.5. with

with full assuraunce, beseeching him to graunt vs his grace, that notwithstanding al the afflictions which he layeth vpon vs, yet that he leaue vs not for all that too hope after that which hee hath promised vs. And this is it which Dauid declareth yet more fully, when after he had sayde, that the vngodly had gone aboute to digge pittes for him, which is not after his lawe, hee addeth, and sayth,

All thy Commaundements are true, they persecute me falsely, be thou my helpe.

Heere he expresseth what the iniuryes & outrages were which they had done him, *They haue* (saith he) *digged pittes for mee,* yea and he protesteth that they did it vniustly, that he neuer gaue the wicked occasion to hurt him: but that he had walked in a good and pure conscience. Yet saith hee, *They haue gone about to circumuent and compasse mee rounde about.* Wee see then that Dauid had no small assaultes, but such as were euen deadly, that it was without all question that he must be vtterly confounded: yea & although he neuer hurt any of them, that it might be sayd, that he had iniuriously persecuted them, yet had he alwayes his recourse vnto God. So then, we may now bee better confirmed in the doctrine which we haue heeretofore handled: to wit, that to whatsoeuer extremititie we are driuen vnto in our afflictions, we shall bring them to a very good end, when as we being fenced with the power of the spirit of God, do looke vnto his promisses. Now let vs see why he addeth and sayth, *Thy Commaundementes are true, they persecute me falsely, O help me.* Dauid setteth downe heere three poyntes, The one is that God is true: & after he addeth a protestation of his good conduct and guydance, and of the malice of his aduersaryes: Thirdly, he calleth vppon God in his afflictions. Now as concerning the first, hee sheweth vs, that although Satan to shake vs, and in the ende vtterly too carry vs away subtilly and cunningly goeth about to deceiue vs, we must, to the contrary, learne how to knowe his ambushes, and to

keepe

keepe vs from out of them. So often then as wee are greeued with aduersitie and affliction, where must we beginne? See Satan howe he pitcheth his nettes, and layeth his ambushes to induce and perswade vs to come into them, what sayth he, doost thou not see thy selfe forsaken of thy God? where are the promises wherevnto thou diddest trust? Now heere thou seest thy selfe to be a wretched forlorne creature. So then, thou right well seest that God hath deceiued thee, and that the promises wherevnto thou trustedst, appertaine nothing at all vnto thee. See heere the subtlety of Satan. What is nowe to be doone? We are to conclude with Dauid and saye, yet God is true and faithfull: Let vs I say keepe in minde the trueth of God as a sheelde too beate back whatsoeuer Satan is able to lay vnto our charge, when as he shall goe about to cause vs to deny our Fayth, when as also he shall lye about vs too make vs beleeue that God thinketh no more of vs, or else, that it is in vaine for vs too trust vnto his promises. But let vs khowe cleane contrary, that it is very plaine and sounde trueth which GOD sayth vnto vs. Although Satan casteth at vs neuer so many dartes, although he haue neuer so exceeding many deuises against vs, although nowe and then by violenve, sometimes with subtiltie and cunning, it seemeth in very deede too vs, that he should ouercome vs: Neuertheleffe, he shall neuer bring it to passe, but that wee shall haue the trueth of God, to be sure and certaine in our heartes. And thus much for the first.

The protestation which Dauid maketh, ought too stirre vs vpp too walke in such sorte with our neighboures, as that wee giue them no occasion too hurte vs. But too liue plainely and simply one by an other. The wicked may very well hurte one another, yea and euen destroy them selues: but in the meane time, the Children of God muste haue this testimony alwayes with them, that they will neither doe nor yet procure them any hurte: but are greeued and sorrowfull too see them runne headlong into destruction.

When

The 11. *Sermon of* M. Io. Cal.

When this mind shalbe in vs, then shal we haue an excellent entraunce to call vpon God: but contrariwise, if we render euill for euill, beeing molested by our enemyes, and inforce our selues to doo the like, and cry quittance (as we say) with them, our cause wil quite bee ouerthrowne. And why so? For if we shall be so vengefull, it is impossible for vs to trust and beleeue that God wil helpe vs. Yea euen then I say, when we shall haue a good and iust quarrell. For God will discharge vs if wee shall not haue a good conscience: and although some there, are which would both wish and doe vs hurt: We must say, O Lord, this is iniuriously and falsely doone. But (as I haue already touched) let vs haue such a testimonie in our heartes, that although they which persecute vs are the instrumentes and limmes of Satan, and do it of meere malice: Let vs not cleane contrary purchase them any hurte or displeasure. Then may wee call vppon God with Dauid, knowing that hee will neuer faile those which are wrongfully persecuted. Loe then the meaning of these three poyntes which are heere touched. Now after that Dauid had thus spoken, he addeth,

They had almost made an ende of me vpon the Earth: But I forsake not thy comaundements.

See heere a sentence worthy to bee well weyed. It is very true that Dauid expresseth that which he had before spoken, *I haue not* (sayth he) *forsaken thy commaundementes O Lord, although I was as one clearely dryed vp, and as a man vtterly forlorne, yet for all that haue I not forsaken thy Commandementes.* Nowe it must needes be that Dauid resisted two temptations in continuing so firme and constant in the obedience of God. The first was, that he might haue beene brought into some distresse. The second, that he might haue bin bent to haue done wickedly. And why so? seing that the wicked had vniustly persecuted him, hee might haue beene reuenged of them. Loe the two assaultes which was meete and conuenient for him to sustaine and keepe of: Euen so must we followe his example: For when men shall vniustly molest and greeue vs, and that they shall not onely doe vs

one

vpon the Cxix. Psalme. 95

one iniury, yea two or three. but that our trouble shal continue without ende and without ceasing, let vs yet learne to be pacient. And chiefely, when as there shall be no question of abiding a little damage, or small greefe. But that we shall be mortally persecuted, and our life too be as it were desperate, to be already as it were in the very throte of the Woulfe, yea to bee already euen as men swallowed vp and deuoured. When as we shalbe brought euen to such a passe, yet let vs not cease to say with Dauid, *I haue not forsaken thy commaundements.*

And so that wee might the better practise this doctrine, and apply it to our owne vse and profite, let vs learne too haue recourse vnto God in all our afflictions, calling vpon him to be our warraunt and safegarde. And in the meane while, although we be wrongfully molested, let vs beseech him to graunt vs his grace too yeelde our selues vnto that which he hath commaunded vs: to witte, too loue our enemyes, to doe good vnto them which seeke to doe vs all the hurt they can, to pray for those which slaunder and wishe vs asmuch euill as is possible. Loe heere wee must meditate vpon the Commaundements of God, although wee be as it were consumed on the earth.

Now heere we are to note, that it was not without cause, that Dauid sayth, *that he was almoste consumed.* For this shall euen so come to passe in vs, when men shall iudge and condemne vs, and that wee haue already receiued sentence of death in our selues: as S. Paule sayth in the seconde too the Corinthes. Euen so Dauid beeing as one condemned too death, and seeing no likelyhoode too be deliuered, ceased 2. Cor. not for all that to call vpon God. So likewise must we doe, knowing that hee will neuer forsake vs: for see what the cause is, that God oftentimes keepeth backe his helping hand from vs, but euen when we preuent him by meane of our owne lightnesse and inconstancy. For so soone as wee are greued somwhat more then we are wonted: we straight wayes conclude and say, O, all is naught: we are cleane vndoone: it is past all hope. When we after this sorte preuent
him

The 11. *Sermon of M. Jo. Cal.*

him, it is like vnto a man that would cast himselfe into his graue before he is deade, and so smooth her himselfe. After this manner, say I, doe we, preuenting by this meane that ayde, which God hath deferred to giue vs, vntil the time be come, which he knoweth to be moste meete. Let vs then well consider, that when God shall deferre the ayde which he meaneth to giue vs, although wee seeme as deade men, and our life desperate, yet that hee can restore vs againe in the minute of an houre, although in the sight of men wee were euen as the pictures of death, yet that hee leaueth vs not without life inwardly. For as wee see in Winter the trees to be as it were deade, that wee can perceiue neither sappe, leafe, nor nothing else: yet there is life hid in them. Euen so fareth it with vs: For when we shall be still & quiet attending for ayde at the handes of God, wee are sure that when Winter is past: to witte, the time of our afflictions, that God will giue vs life, which was before as it were hidden. Now to conclude the Psalme he sayth,

Quicken me according to thy louing kindenesse: so shall I keepe the testimonyes of thy mouth.

We see heere, that Dauid speaketh as one that were dead, when he sayth, *O quicken me*, he sheweth then that hee was not beaten softely with the rodde, or with a meane affliction: but was punished euen too the vttermoste. For hee was so dryed vp, as before we haue saide, that there was no substaunce at all lefte in him. Loe what was the cause why Dauid after this manner made his petition.

Let vs learne then, not too flatter our selues, when as the Lorde our God shall visite vs with any little affliction, that wee thinke too haue doone euen sufficiently, if wee call vppon him: But if wee shall haue doone so an hundreth thousande times more, yet that wee muste not giue ouer praying and calling vppon him. And heerein may bee seene the hypocriticall dealing of men: For they are so womannishely minded and tender hearted, that they thinke themselues too haue wrought a million of miracles, when as they haue sustained neuer so little aduersitie, no

not

vpon the Cxix. Pfalme.   96

not woorth the value of an houre.

Moreouer if they be ouer loden with any aduerfity they may be bolde, as they thinke, cleerely too forget both God and his woorde. But our good God wil not haue vs to proceede in this forte: For he fetteth before vs heere, the exa̅ple of Dauid for our inftruction, but yet hee hath fet it forth vntoo vs for this ende and purpofe, that wee fhoulde not ceafe to continue too cal vpon him in our aduerfities : yea were our afflictions neuer fo great, & lafted neuer f. long, yet that we fhoulde notwithftanding continually perfeuere in prayer.

To be fhorte, let vs vnderftande, that Dauid made this prayer at fuch tyme as hee thought not too haue liued any longer, but that hee was as a dead man, when hee fayeth, *O quicken mee.*

Moreouer we may fee, that his conftancy was not lyke a puft of winde, but that he perfeuered therein. For although his troubles conteined, that he was as it were in a very depe pit, whereout he was not able too get: yet ceafed hee neuer but to truft that god would deliuer him out of it: and there vpon called on him, and receiued greate courage. Namely, he defireth *too bee quickened* according to the louing kindnes of God For wee muft alfo bee at that point, if we will bee hearde, to knowe that God is bounde vntoo vs of his meere grace and fauour : and that wee alfo muft haue recourfe vnto him, if wee wil haue him too accomplifhe his promifes vnto vs. Men muft not then abufe themfelues, too looke vntoo their owne dooinges, ne yet too haue regarde vntoo worldly meanes: But that they feeke for the fame in G O D, and in his meere goodneffe and free gifte, for the which he wil heare them, and receiue them alfo vntoo himfelfe. In the ende Dauid protefteth, *that he wil kepe the teftimonies of the mouth of God.* Now let vs not vnderfta̅d hereby, that hee had not kept them before For wee haue feene the cleane co̅trary. But this is to fignifie, That feing in the midft of the afflictio̅s which I haue fufteined, thou haft alway giue me the grace to perfeuere in faith, & that I haue continually
                                    called vpon

vpon thee, Satan hath not shaken me, to cause me too doe wickedly, since then, O Lorde, thou haste giuen mee such constancy at the time that thou wast estraunged from me: by a more strong reason, when thou shalt be mine ayde and succour, & shalt restore me, I shall haue a farre greater constancy, to keepe the testimonyes of thy mouth. See then, howe that in the middest of all our afflictions wee must glorifie God, not doubting of his faithfull dealing, that he will performe whatsoeuer hee hath promised, haue pittie on vs in the end, and confirme vs more and more too keepe the testimonyes of his mouth: knowing that hee wil continue to doe that vnto vs, which he hath already once shewed vs.

And according to this doctrin, let vs prostrate our selues in the presence of our good God, in acknowledging our offences: Beseeching him that it would please him to open our eyes better that we may beholde the power and vertue of his worde, and thereon to stay vs: in bereauing vs of all the lightnesse and inconstancy, which might turne vs away from it, desiring him also not to suffer vs too wander this way and that way, as commonly we are woonted, to turne vs from the right way, as we are by nature ouermuch inclyned therto: but beeing fully resolued, that it is not in vaine which he hath declared vnto vs, that hee will assist vs in all our necessities, which wee shall craue of him in true fayth: yea not onely in our small and meane afflictions: but euen when as he thinketh wee shoulde be vtterly ouerthrowne: knowing that he will accomplish for our profite & health, whatsoeuer we may hope after, and beholde with the eyes of fayth. Let vs beseech him that hee will not onely graunte vs this grace, but also vnto all people and nations of the Earth, &c.

The

The twelfth Sermon vpon the hundreth and nineteenth Psalme.

LAMED.

O Lorde, thy woorde indureth for euer in Heauen.

Thy trueth is from one generation to another: thou haste layed the foundation of the Earth and it abideth.

They continue euen to this day, according too thy ordinaunce: for all are thy seruauntes.

Except the Lorde had beene my delighte: I shoulde nowe haue perished in my trouble.

I will neuer forget thy Commandements: For by them thou hast quickened me.

I am thine, saue me: for I haue sought thy Commandementes.

The vngoodly layd waite for mee: but I will consider thy testimonyes.

I haue seene an ende of all perfection: but thy commaundement is exceeding large.

WEE see howe chaungeable men are. It is very true that when wee shall talke of the shadowe, wee may say that it remooueth and chaungeth euery minute of an houre, so that it resteth not: but if wee looke well and thorowlye search out that which is in the minde of man: wee shall see there a

The 13. Sermon of M. Io. Cal.

there is great deale more vanitie and chaunge, then is too be seene in the very shadowe. And that which is more, Dauid sayth in an other place, that if man were laide in one schole, & vanitie in an other, that vanitie which is nothing, would way downe man greately. And wee shall not neede too stande longe disputing of this: For euery man by his owne experience can testifie what it is, and what it can do, albeit there were nothing written nor yet any thing thereof conteined in the Scripture. What resteth there then for vs to doe, Forsooth wee must seeke for our constancy else where then in our selues.

Nowe God giueth vs a very good meane if we will take it, which is, to builde and settle our selues vpon his word. And for this cause it is, that the Prophet Esaiah sayth, *That the worde of God indureth for euer*: Hee had spoken before of the frailtie and ficklenesse of men, as that nothing could be more: & although it might seeme that there was some strength in them, it is yet incontinent cleane parched and dryed vpp, that it vanisheth away into lesse then nothing: But he concludeth and sayth, *That the Woorde of God abideth for euer*. So then, see the meane, howe that men (although they be transitory, and haue no constancie at all in them) shall notwithstanding haue a perfect constancy, and sure estate: to witte, when as they shall stay themselues vpon the trueth of God and his worde. According to this, it is heere sayd, *Thy worde O Lorde abideth for euer in heauer*. Some expounde this, as if it had beene sayde, That because the heauens haue continued long, they render a good testimony of the trueth of God. But heere Dauid namely speaketh of the heaues, because we see by them a more manifest signe of the Maiestie of God then we see here belowe on earth. And in deede in that we are rude and earthly, we had neede to haue God to guide vs, and too lifte vpp our mindes when that he would haue vs to thinke on him: too the ende we might forget the world, & all the corruptible things heere beneath. See the the reason why Dauid in this place.

Isai 40. 8.

maketh the seate and house of the word of God in heauen: because we had nede to looke a great deale more hyer then into our owne senses, when wee would comprehend howe God is true and faithfull. When wee woulde feele the certaintie and assuraunce of his woorde, we must enter into a more deepe consideration, then our sense is able too beare, and not looke so into the visible thing, or into that which we conceiue on earth.

Hee addeth, *That the trueth of God is from generation to generation.* As if hee shoulde haue sayde, It is true, O Lord, that men are heere very circumspect and aduised: and we see also howe thinges haue their alterations, so that there is nothing which is not wauering and inconstant: wee are as it were in the whirlewindes and tempests: and if at some times thinges bee in peace and at quiet, it lasteth not longe: and although the creatures bee peaceable and at quiet, yet are the men neuer at rest, but are continually chafed and troubled. But thy trueth, O Lorde, is sure and certaine, which can neuer be shaken through the alterations and chaunges which heere we see, no otherwise but by the lightnesse and inconstancy of men, when as they doe nothing else but wander heere and there. True it is, O Lorde, that all this impayreth no whit the certaintie of thy trueth and woorde.

Loe heere in summe, the meaning of Dauid in this place. Nowe hee bringeth in a proofe of this sentence, too witte, That *God hath layd the foundation of the earth, and it abydeth:* that is to say, That the order of nature hath her course, and so continueth without ende. And why so? *Forsomuch as God hath appoynted them:* because that hee hath so declared it; and that al creatures are subiect vnto him. This disposing & ordering must needs continue in his estate. And although wee see all things to turne on this side and on that, yet God alwayes giueth vs some visible signe, too shewe vs that hee neuer altereth nor chaungeth his purpose. And chiefely, that his trueth is neuer subiecte too any chaunge.

We see nowe in summe what the substaunce is that is contayned in these three verses.

Nowe that wee may apply all this too our vse, and too make our profite heereof, let vs learne too haue recourse vnto the woorde of God, so often as wee shall bee astonyshied, and knowe not what shall become of vs: too witte, all the dayes of our life: For there passeth not one quiet day ouer our heads, wherein wee are not mooued too thinke either of this thing or of that. Sometimes the temptations are easie too ouercome: but after, wee shall see some apparaunce of daunger, that shall trouble vs a great deale more, yea and some one threate or other we shall haue that shall euen abashe vs. And if that were not so, yet shoulde wee haue occasions enough in our heads too make vs vnquiet, that we should not nede to be otherwise troubled: but euery one of vs hath in himself store of tempests & stormes, so that if there were nothing else but our owne very fantasyes, they would be so many whyrlewindes, too make vs neuer to haue quiet mindes. Nowe see then a good remedy, that is, Let vs knowe, that although wee are enuironed with a great number of daungers, although there bee no certayntie in our life; although there is alwayes an hundreth deathes before our eyes, yea that we thought the deuill shoulde swallowe vs vpp euery minute of an houre: yet must we be peaceable, and holde our selues quiet and stil, because that God hath layde the foundation of our saluation in his woord: and that he hath promised to keepe our life. When then, wee shall haue the worde of God, to certifie vs, that he hath care both of our soules and bodyes, let vs knowe and be certainly assured that heerein consisteth all our constancy.

So then, let vs rightly applye this doctrine for our instruction, that when it is sayde, that the worde of GOD is permanent in Heauen, that his truethe sheweth it selfe from age to age, & so continueth, that it is namely spoken, to the ende that we should be patient in the middest of all

the

the troubles, giefes, and anguishes, which wee may haue, beeing shaken amidst so many daungers: and also, seeing the endlesse and incessaunt chaunges which are heere beneth, and nothing else but all vnquietnesse. Let vs then see, what is heere to be considered for the first point: wee must not seeke to take our rest in this worlde, for wee shall neuer haue it heere: But let vs alwaies haue our recourse too the ttueth of God.

Moreouer, let vs see if we can rightly practise this doctrine, that nothing hinder vs, but that wee may liue in peace and tranquilitie in the middest of the most great and dangerous confusions which may light vpon vs. Let vs also see, that whether the windes blow in this corner or in that, that there be garboyles of war, that there bee pestilence & famine, and such like, that it seemed wee should perishe a thousand manner of wayes: yet all they which settle them selues vpon the woorde of God, wil neuer be but certaine: For they shall feele bothe in life and death, that they are in his hande and protection. And hauing this confidence with themselues, they will make no reckoning of all whatsoeuer shall come vnto them: as wee see Saint Paule commaundeth vs too exalte our selues against all thinges present and too come, so that wee be fully resolued, that God loueth vs. When this shall be in vs, and we shall haue heereof a good testimonie in our owne consciences, through Fayth and the woorde of God: Loe howe wee may assure our selues, and solace our selues in the middest of all our troubles and confusions which heere wee see: and by that meanes be neuer at peace and reste, and not too be greatly turmoyled for any thinge that may come vnto vs the next day. And why so? For hath God, who hath declared him selfe vnto vs too be our Father, spoken it but for a day onely? where as hee hath testifyed vnto vs, that hee will haue our saluation in his hand? is heere any time lymitted?

Rom, 8. 38. 39.

Nowe we see too the contrary, that God sayeth, That hee

hee will neuer forsake vs. Our hope then must stretch it self cleane beyonde the worlde, and so we shall not bee tossed with the windes and tempestes which shall blow against vs, to make vs turne back, when as we shal haue a sure foundation vpon the word of God. And as concerning this proofe which Dauid addeth, saying, *That God hath layd the foundation of the earth*, the same is but a little tast which he giueth vs of the trueth of God. Nowe it is not enough for vs to haue this taste onely, to knowe whether God be faythfull and that his trueth is euerlasting. For to proue it to bee so, we see that neither heauen nor earth, but are subiect too corruption, and that all muste passe, onely the woorde of God is said too last for euer. And it must needes bee so: for else what shoulde become of our saluation? It shoulde be corrupt very soone.

Let vs not once thinke then, that Dauid his meaning heere is too make a comparison, and an equall proportion, of the continuance of this worlde, and the constancye which wee see in the order of nature, with the trueth of God. But he sheweth vnto vs that euen in these corruptible thinges, wee might the better perceiue howe faythfull GOD is: and if hee bee true in these thinges on the earth, what shall hee him selfe then bee? I beseech you tell mee, from whence hath the earth her foundation? It is founded bothe vpon the water and also vpon the ayre: Loe her foundation. Wee can not possibly build a house fifteene foote hight vpon the firme grounde but that wee muste lay a foundation. See all the whole earth is founded onely wauering, and as it were hanging, yea, and vppon so bottomlesse deapthes, as that it might be turned vpsidedowne in the minute of an houre, and the whole substaunce of it vtterly ouerthrowne. It must needes then be, that there is a wonderful power of God shewed in the conseruing of it, in the same sort it stādeth. And that is it which is here shewed vnto vs: to witte because that God hath sayde, That the earth was in the middest of the worlde, and that it was so

layde

vpon the Cxix. *Pſalme.*

layde as it is : heereby we knowe what the certaintie of his trueth is. But wee muſt heere forſooth compare the leſſe thinges with the greater, as we ſay. How from the leſſer to the greater? I wil ſhew you by example, If I ſay we did ſe ſuch excellēcie in the body of a man, as that it might bethought to be euen the very image of God: wherby we knowe the thing that is writtē, that God hath ordayned man to be the chiefe of all his creatures, and giuen him greate dignitie, nobleneſſe, and power ouer all liuing creatures. Euen ſo alſo, in prayſing that which is in man, we may deſcende from the body to the ſoule: and this is from the hyeſt too the loweſt, and from the leſſe to the more: So likewiſe is it in this place, when Dauid ſetteth before our eyes the order of nature: This is not (as I haue already ſayde) to meaſure and compare the trueth of God, with ſuch a meaſure: But to the ende wee might reaſon and ſay, If in theſe frayle and tranſitory thinges which are ſubiect to corruption, wee ſee ſuch a conſtancy becauſe it is God his will it ſhoulde be ſo: What ſhall we then ſay of his trueth, which ſurpaſſeth all the worlde? When then we ſhall make ſuch a compariſon, betweene the ſtate of the worlde, and the trueth of God, we may certainly conclude, that God ſufficiently graunteth vs wherewith too ſettle our ſelues vpon his woorde, we muſte not bee ſo inconſtant as too let our Fayth bee ſhaken, ſo often as wee ſhall ſee the worlde toſſed with any troubles, but rather too take this place which is heere ſhewed vnto vs by Dauid for our refuge. And this is the ſumme of this place. Nowe it followeth afterwarde,

Pſal. 8. 6.

Except the Lorde had beene my delight: I ſhoulde nowe haue periſhed in my trouble.

Dauid heere ſpeaketh this of his owne proper experyence and knowledge before hee ſpake of the trueth and excellencye of GOD in generall, and ſayth that it was in

The 12. Sermon of M. Io. Cal.

heauen: and afterwarde he prooueth it by visible thinges, which is very manifest vnto vs, and which God poynteth out vnto vs, as it were with his finger. In the third place hee sayth that he speaketh not of vnknowen thinges, that hee might dispute of them at randon, but that hee had rightly practized that which he had spoken, becaufe that hee was preserued by the woord of God. And therefore hee nowe sheweth vs, where we ought to seeke for this worde, whereof hee had generally spoken heeretofore. For wee may vse this name of the woorde of God, and yet it may be hidden in the ayre, or emongst the Cloudes: But becaufe hee hath giuen vnto vs his word familyarly, and communicateth the fame with vs dayly, euen in the holy scripture: Let vs consider, that in giuing honor vnto the worde of God. Wee say that it is infallible, Let vs not imagine it to be an vnknowen word, but let vs goe vnto that, which God at all times hath giuen to his seruaunts: and that is it which is contayned in the law. See then, how God hath first declared his woorde vnto vs, wherein our saluation is altogither certaine.

Nowe heere wee haue to note in this streine, that Dauid hauing had such experience, deserueth wel to be heard, and that they are no vayne woordes which hee heere setteth downe before hand: But that God also woulde haue it so, too the ende wee should giue the more credite vnto it, and that wee shoulde no whitte doubt of any thinge that hee teacheth vs, when as hee him selfe hath made proofe of all that which he before had spoken. And thus much for the firste poynte. The experience then whereof Dauid speaketh shoulde very well serue vs in steade of our Seale, by which GOD meaneth too make the Doctrine of his Prophet to be of so much the more antiquitie. And thus much for this.

Moreouer, let vs learne rightly too vnderstande, howe sure wee ought too bee of the woorde of GOD, not too seeke for the certaintie thereof without our selues, but rather in our owne Consciences. It is true, that wee ought

vpon the Cxix. *Pſalme.*

ought throughly too looke bothe aboue and beneath, too make the teſtimonies which GOD giueth vs too ſerue our faith, too the ende wee might bee certified of the trueth of his word, as already wee haue heard: but yet the principall point is this, for euery man to enter into himſelf, and make ſuch accompt of this certaintie of the woorde of God, that it may take ſuch roote in our ſoules, as that wee may there feele it to be ſuch as here it is ſaid: to wit, that it neuer be ſhaken, although the whole world ſhould be confounded, and that it is the ſame which muſt giue vs peace and reſt, notwithſtanding it ſeemed, that all were vtterly ouerthrowne. We muſt then acknowledge the effect and accompliſhment of this certaintie, which the Prophet here attributeth vnto the word of God. In ſumme, it is aſmuch as if he had ſaide, that no man is able rightly to feele howe God is faithfull, and his worde certaine and ſure, without he hath a true faith and beliefe thereof within his heart, & the ſame to bee diſcharged of whatſoeuer is contrary to his ſaluation. As namely he ſaieth, *that he ſhould haue periſhed in his trouble, if he had not delighted in the word of God*. Dauid here ſheweth what experience he had: to wit, that he was ſo afflicted, that he was as it were euen in the gulfe of death.

Now if the worde of God bringeth vs out of the graue, quickeneth vs in death, & preſerueth our health, notwithſtanding that it ſeemeth to be ſwallowed vp in the gulfe, do we not ſee a good proufe giuen vs from God, how firme & ſound it is? So then, let vs well conſider (as we haue already ſaid) that ſince we haue knowen the power of the worde of God, to be ſuch as it is here ſhewed vs, wee may in ſuch ſort reſiſt all the greateſt temptations which the deuill is able craftely to worke againſt vs, ſo that we ſhalbe able to eſcape as it were both from death and the graue. And thus much for this.

Now for the ſecond point, Dauid ſheweth vs howe it is that we are preſerued in all our afflictions by the worde of God, how our life ſhalbe ſaulfe, & our health aſſured thereby. And that is, if we delight therein: to wit, that wee bee ſo comfor-

The 12. Sermon of M. Io. Cal.

comforted with the loue which GOD there sheweth vs and wherewith he certifieth vs, that since he hath adopted vs for his children, he will therefore alwayes shewe him self to be our father. Wherefore we may boldely recommende our soules vnto him, and he will receiue them, so that wee shall not perishe, hauing all our refuge so vnto him. If wee then content our selues so, the worde of God will giue vs life in the middest of an hudreth thousand deaths. But if we heare it without hauing any such affectiō, that we taste not of the promisses of God; or els that wee alwayes somwhat distrust and doubt, to reason how it goeth, and afterwarde wander after creatures, or els builde vpon our selues, if wee bee so changeable, wee shall neuer feele any vertue of the worde of GOD, but may bee ouerthrowne an hundreth times: the least affliction in the world, shalbe as a gulfe to swallowe vs vp: that we shall not neede the mayne sea; but euen a finger depth of water too smouther and drowne vs, if it were not that we had learned of Dauid, to bee assured of the loue which God beareth vs: and that by his worde.

So then, let vs vnderstand what the true delight of the faithfull is, and that which preserueth them from death, & quickeneth them: that is, when they are contented with the loue of God, to set their whole felicitie there, to haue him to be mercifull and fauourable, to haue this priuiledge to haue recourse vnto him, being assured that he will heare them. See, I say, how we should be quickened by the worde of God. Nowe when that Dauid hath declared the profit which he receiued by the consideration of the lawe, he addeth, *That he will neuer forget it.* Wherein hee protesteth that he will not bee vnthankefull to GOD, as wee are accustomed.

Now although wee are not without a great number of vices, yet is this one of the greatest, that we doe not onely so oftentimes suffer the benefites of God to escape out of our mindes, but we are also so wicked, as that we desire nothing more then for to burie thē: we thinke we should haue

neuer

neuer time enough vtterly to forget them. See, I faye, the ſtate and condition of our vile and corrupt nature. And therefore, Dauid in this place proteſteth, that *he will neuer forget the commaundementes of God, bicauſe he hath bin quickned by them.* And moreouer, he ſpeaketh it not only for him ſelf, but ſheweth vnto vs by his example, what our office & dutie is. When God then ſhall haue thus aided vs in our afflictions, that he ſhall haue raiſed vs vp euen from the graue through the might and power of his worde, and that wee ſhall feele ſuch a benefite, let vs neuer forget it, but be alwaies mindfull thereof. And yet Dauid meaneth to ſhewe vnto vs a farther point: to wit, that bicauſe the woorde of God hath already profited him, that hee will eſteeme of it and haue it in great price for the time to come. Knowing that it is is not for a time onely, that we muſt bee preſerued and comforted by the word of God, but for euer and euer. This might ſeeme for vs to be very obſcure, were it not declared vnto vs more at large. See now then what Dauid his meaning is. If a man be as it were caſt downe, not taſting of the promiſes of God, and when it ſhall be laide before him, that although God afflict his childrē, yet that he doth it not vtterly to querthrow & deſtroy thē: but to the end to calthē to repentance, that afterward they might feele his mercifull goodneſſe. If a man then be thus admoniſhed by the word of God, it may be, that this admonition will ſerue him to no purpoſe, bicauſe he him ſelfe ſeeketh not after the remedy which is ſet before him, and ſo is made voyde of this cōfort which is here touched, and by that meane the power of the woorde of God turneth into all euill to himward. What is thē to be done? Let vs marke wel that which Dauid here ſpeaketh, that he wil neuer forget the cōmandements of God, bicauſe he hath bin quickened by them. As if he ſhould haue ſaid, when as thou haſt once preſerued me by meane of thy word, that thou haſt giuē vnto it this power & property that I being as one dead & out of the world, haue bin therby fully reſtored to helth, thē haſt thou taught me what I ought to doe all the daies of my life: that is, I muſt

meditate

The 12. Sermon of M. Io. Cal.

meditate vpon thy worde, I must exercise my selfe therein, and I must continually study to thinke vppon the testimonies, which thou of thy fatherly loue hast bestowed vppon me: to the ende I might hold mee contented, and bee sure that thou wilt neuer forsake me. The vse, O Lord, then that I feele by thy worde, hath caused mee to applie the same to my profite all the dayes of my life: to the ende I might bee able to resiste whatsoeuer Satan shall craftely goe about to worke against mee, and too perseuer in thy feare and loue, whensoeuer the wicked and vngodly shall make warre against me. Thou then, O Lorde, haste shewed mee that thy worde ought alwayes to be before mee. For that neuer loseth his power and strēgth: neither is it a thing that is consumed and worne by much wearing. A man may soone make an ende of a loafe in eating it: but when hee hath so done, he must looke for more bread. And in continuall drinking of wyne, the hoggeshead wil be empty: but when as the woorde of God hath serued to quicken vs, it still remaineth sound and whole, without diminishing any whit at al. So then, let vs learne after the example of Dauid, too make estimation of the vertue and power which God hath giuen to his worde, and neuer forget it. Nowe hee addeth by and by after,

I am thine, saue me : for I haue sought thy commandements. The vngodly layde wayte for me to destroye me: but I will consider thy testimonies.

After that Dauid had made such protestation, hee committeth him selfe to GOD, euen declaring that hee hath sought his commaundementes. And so hee speaketh not only of the time past, but remaineth alwaies cōstant in this purpose. Now we haue here to cōsider of three points: the one is, the request which Dauid maketh to God, *O saue me*: The second is, the reason why he desireth God to saue him, *Bicause* saith he, *I am thine*. And afterward he sheweth how he is gods, that is, *for I*, saieth he, *haue sought thy commandements*. And thus we see in the first place, how God offereth himselfe vnto vs, and that hee desireth nothing els but to

holde

holde vs in his protection, to haue care of our saluation, yea so that we come vnto him after the example of Dauid.

And I beseeche you, what priuiledge is this, that we haue such libertie to come vnto God, and to commit our selues into his handes? whether we wake, or sleepe, whether wee labour either in the towne, or in the fieldes, that God is as it were a watchman ouer vs, to keepe vs? Yea, and that he hath not care ouer our soules, to keepe them from the ambushes of Satan, but also that his fatherly prouidence and loue extendeth it selfe euen to our bodies? When God thē, I say, giueth vs the libertie, that we may make such request vnto him, I pray you tell me, is not this an inestimable priuiledge? But we neuer a whit thinke of this: as may well be seene by our slackenesse and wearinesse in prayer to God at this daye. And yet for all that, it is not without cause that Dauid setteth downe here this request: but to the end that we should knowe, that in praying to God, he will graunt vs the grace to commēd our selues wholy vnto him, no more also should wee haue too too great a care ouer our life: for we being assured of his loue, should bee contented with all the rest whatsoeuer. And thus much for the first point.

Now for the second we are rightly to consider, that if we will haue God to be our warrant, and to be vnder his protection, we must needes be his, and may say truly, as Dauid here doth.

It is very true that God keepeth his creatures, who are not worthy thereof, as hee also causeth the Sunne to shine as well vppon the good as on the bad, and that it is of his owne goodnesse and mercie that the wicked doe liue: but yet to their vtter destruction. And when it is here said, *to be kept by God*: It is such a keeping and preseruation, as that the issue thereof is both good and healthfull. And this is not done saue onely to such as are truely the possesion and inheritance of God, and his true housholde seruantes and children. Will we haue God then to receiue vs into his protection, and to be our protector? Wil we haue him to take care and charge both of our soules and bodies? Let vs first
be his.

The 12. Sermon of M. Io. Cal.

be his. And howe shall we be his? Forsooth, we must come to the third point: to wit, to seeke his testimonies. Loe then how God will take vs for his possession: for hee euen then alloweth vs for his children, when as wee put our whole trust in him, seing that he hath so familiarly called and bidden vs, and hath certified vs by his word, that he will neuer forsake vs. If then we so seeke the testimonies of God, and sticke vnto them with a sure faith, let vs neuer doubt but that he wil allowe vs for his houshold meiny and children, And then we may well say with Dauid, saue me O Lord See I say, in what maner we ought to come vnto God, if we will be sure to haue him to protect vs. Now Dauid addeth,

The vngodly haue laid wayte for me, to destroy me: but I wil consider thy testimonies.

Whereby he doth vs to wit, that although God is stedfastly purposed to be the protector of the faithfull, yet that they are not without a great number of griefes and troubles, subiect to many sorrowes: and bee maruelously, entrapped and thereby thinke, that they can not chose but to fall into the snares of the vngodly. And besides, the subtelties of Satan are great: and againe, all the vngodly which serue Satan, and are lead by his spirite, cease not to inuent subtelties and deceiptes, to entrappe the childrē of God, by lying in wayte for them. Dauid his meaning then here, is to declare vnto vs, that although God preserueth vs, it is not therefore to be said, that we are without molestations, and temptations. But what? So it is that the woorde of God ought to suffise vs, as he saieth, *I will consider thy testimonies.* As if he should haue saide. O Lorde, I haue made this my buckler and fortresse, which is, that thou hast promised to be my sauiour: and hereupon haue not forced for all the treasons, that all the vngodly can conspire against mee. It is very true that they haue layde a platforme to betray me, yea, and it seemeth that I am already within their clawes and teeth, ready to be denoured: but thy testimonies, O Lorde, haue so strengthened me, as that I haue not fainted. Let vs learne then to fight in this sort against all the subtelties of ties of Satan, and malices of men, and notwithstanding that they shall goe about to destroye vs, yet let vs fasten our eyes vpon the worde of God, attende vpon it, and therein perseuer vnto the end. Nowe for cōclusion Dauid addeth, *I haue seene an ende of all perfection: but thy commaundement is exceeding broade, or large.*

The word then which Dauid vseth, signifieth sometimes perfection, and sometimes accomplishment: bicause that the things which are come to a perfection, haue an ende. Now he saith in summe, that when he hath throughly considered of all things, that there is nothing in this worlde which hath not an end, and that is not consumed by continuance: but that the word of God is plentiful: that is, it extendeth it selfe vnto all the creatures of God, and ouer all whatsoeuer wee are able to see. See here a sentence very like vnto that which we haue seene in the first verse. Dauid then by this conclusion confirmeth the saying which before hee held, to wit, that *the word of God is euerlasting*. Although that we here see maruelous alteratiōs, that we se the world tossed with so tempestuous whirlewindes, as that there is nother end nor measure of thē, yet shal we haue in the midst of al these troubles an euerlasting aboade in the worde of God, which will assure vs of all together.

Let vs not then measure our saluation by the present estate of the world, and as it seemeth now in our eyes, wherby we may well perceiue and discerne the same. And why so? Bicause that all things here belowe haue an ende, as wee haue said, that heauen and earth shall perish: but God hath giuen to vs his truth, which is of such an euerlastingnesse, as that it surpasseth both heauen and earth. It behoueth vs then to bee lifted vp and rapt with this eternitie of the kingdome of God, so often as his word shall be spoken vnto vs, wherein consisteth all our saluation.

And according to this holy doctrine let vs prostrate our selues before the maiestie of our good God, with acknowledging our innumerable offences, by which wee cease not daily to prouoke his heauy wrath & indignation against vs:

Beseeching

The 12. Sermon of M. Jo. Cal.

Beseeching him that it would please him to cause vs to feele our wretchednesse more then heretofore wee haue done, to the ende we might be displeased with our sinnes, & seeke for remedie, where it is shewed vs: to wit, that seing there is nothing els in vs and in all creatures, but vanitie, that we beseeche the same good God to confirme vs in his promisses: that all our studie be wholy there: knowing that all our life resteth in them, to the ende wee searche no other where but there where hee hath promised wee shall finde it, that is, in his worde. That it would please him so to make vs taste and sauoure the power and strength thereof, as that we may be wholy giuen to serue him, and that receiuing vs into his holy protection and conduct, he wil not impute vnto vs so many vices and imperfections as are in vs: but that he will supporte them through his goodnesse, vntil such time as he hath despoyled vs of al together. And that it would please him also, too vse the like grace and fauoure towardes all people and nations of the earth. &c.

The thirteenth Sermon vpon the hundreth and nineteene Psalme.

MEM.

O Lord what loue haue I vnto thy lawe? al the day long is my study in it.

Thou through thy commaundements hast made me wiser then mine enemies: for they are euer with mee.

I haue had more vnderstanding then al my teachers: for thy testimonies are my studie.

I vnderstode more then the aged: bicause I keepe thy commaundements.

I haue

vpon the Cxix. Pſalme. 105

I haue refrained my feete from euery euill way: that I might keepe thy worde.
I haue not declined from thy iudgementes: for thou diddeſt teach me.
How ſweete are thy woordes vnto my throat: yea, ſweeter then hony vnto my mouth.
Through thy commandementes I get vnderſtanding: therefore I hate all the wayes of falſehood.

We ſhall ſee in this behalf a great many which will not ſticke to bragge, and ſay, that they haue greatly profited in the woorde of God: but yet if we looke into their liues, wee ſhall ſee and finde that they haue profited as much, as if they had neuer read, nor heard, one worde of the holy ſcripture. Moreouer, all the goodly and gay proteſtations which they ſhal make, tende to none other end but to get them ſelues eſtimation and credit: there is noone other thing in them, but a fooliſh and vaine glorious ſhewe, that is, they deſire to bee commended and prayſed, as though they were the moſt able and worthy people of all others. Nowe when we will ſaye that we haue profited in the ſchoole of God, firſt of all we ought to ſhewe by our life and conuerſation whether it bee ſo or no. For this is the true teſtimonie whereunto wee muſt holde vs. God teacheth vs not to the ende we ſhould do nothing els but prattle and babble: but he inſtructeth vs in what maner we ought to liue. Hee then which ſhall leade a diſſolute and wanton life, declareth manifeſtly, that he neuer knew either God or his truthe. Moreouer, the meaning is not that we ſhould ſet foorth our ſelues, to bee had in eſtimation of men, or to get vs reputation and cre-

O   ditibut

dit: but we ought rather to glorifie God, knowing that we are so much the more beholden and bounde vnto him, in that it hath pleased him too bestowe such his grace and fauour vpon vs, as that we surmount others in learning, for that commeth not vnto vs by reason that wee are sharper witted, or that we haue gotten it through our owne industrie: to know, I say, the way of saluation, but it is a free gift which commeth vnto vs from aboue. Furthermore, when wee shall acknowledge this too come from God, it is then great reason that we should drawe our neighbours with vs, and like as we are in a good way, euen so ought wee to bee desirous to haue euery one to followe vs.

Loe to what intent Dauid declareth in this place, that he hath loued the worde of God aboue all, and that by it he hath beene so well taught, as that hee surpassed his maisters, and enemies, and all those which were in great reputation and credit. Very certaine it is, that Dauid is not here led by an ambitious or high minded spirite, meaning to be coyed and clawed, and looking to bee thought to haue greater vnderstanding then others: but desireth none other thing, saue that the profite which he had receiued by the lawe of God, might be throughly engraffed in all men, and that it might be a thing common vnto euery one. In very deede, since that we are all members of one body: wee ought continually to labour and trauell for the vpholding and mainteining of it one with another: neither ought any of vs to serue him selfe, and his owne particular profit, but we ought rather to desire to haue the graces of God to abound in all our neighbours, that euery of them might haue a feeling of them, and that when as wee shall haue enioyed this common saluation, that we might all with one accorde, and as it were with one mouth, glorifie him. And besides, Dauid sheweth soone after, that hee was no babbling scholler, to shewe it onely in mouth, too haue many times turned ouer the leaues of the lawe of God, and to haue very well vnderstood it: but sheweth his life to bee agreing to his speeche: and that God hath giuē him grace to

walke

walke according to his will. A great deale the rather ought we then throughly to consider of the order that is here set downe in the first verse: he saith, *O Lord, what loue haue I vnto thy lawe: all the day long is my study in it.* The saying which Dauid here vseth, signifieth *speach and meditation*. And the verbe whereof it commeth, signifieth, *to speake, to deuise, to talke, or rather to applie his minde to any thing, to be therein exercised, and studied.* Now there is no doubt, but that Dauid spake here of a matter which is conioyned with meditatiō. For (as before we haue said) it is not meant by them which make some certaine shew at their tongues ende, and yet to haue nothing to be found in their life and conuersation of the thing whereof they babble. Hee then was exercised in the word of God, and that not onely for his owne particular vse, but to thende also to instruct his neighbours, and to communicate to them the matter which he had heard and learned. Now we see the summe and effect of this first verse. He protesteth that he hath loued the word of God, & that not after a common manner, but with a vehement zeale, in such sort as that it hath beene his whole purpose and drift: as when we haue liking of any one thing, we cannot holde from talking thereof, & continually to be thinking of it. As we shall see a miserable couetous man, neuer but hunting after his wealth: occupied about his lands, possessions, marchandise, & cattle: & must make prouisiō for this and that, In like sort also is it with the whoremonger, and the glutton: and accordingly as euery mans desire leadeth him, so must the tongue speake, & euery one apply him self wholy to that. Se wherefore Dauid addeth, that *he was continually exercised in the word of God:* meaning thereby to shew, howe greatly he hath loued it, as he hath in deede said. And nowe we see what thexample is which is here set down before vs: for Dauid speaketh not this for himself, but telleth vs what we ought to be, if we will haue God to instruct vs, and too haue him to make vs partakers of his truth, wherein consisteth our whole felicitie and welfare: for if wee wax colde, & make no accōpt of the word of God, we are not worthy that he should giue vs the least taste thereof. And for this

cause,

cause, we must not maruelle much, though so small a number at this daye haue profited in the scripture. Although euery man desireth to be praised and esteemed amongest men to bee very able and sufficient, yet for all that wee see what ignoraunce is in the greater number. And therefore it is good reason that God should shut the gate vpon vs, so that we might not haue so much as the least entraunce into his woorde. And why so? For where is the loue and desire that Dauid here maketh mention of? Nowe when we shall know such a vice to be within vs, we ought by and by to seeke to amende it, and beseeche God to put this coldnesse from out of our heartes, and that it would please him to enflame vs in such sort, as that wee might learne to preferre his worde before all our fleshly desires: that we be no more so much giuen to all these vayne follies of the world, but that we may looke vnto the principal thing. Let vs now come to that which followeth. He sayeth,

Thou through thy commaundementes hast made mee wiser then mine enemies, teachers, and auncientos.

He setteth down here three sortes of people, with whom he compareth him selfe, and saith, that God hath bestowed this grace vpon him to surpasse them all. Now here Dauid sheweth vnto vs, what profit shall redounde vnto vs, when as we shal reade the word of God, after his example: to wit, that we shall get thereby such wisedome as shall defende vs from our enemies to be better learned then our teachers, and those which otherwise should haue byn in stead of our instructours. To be short, that all the men of the world shal not haue that which wee shall finde there, and that all the wisedome which is in al the creatures of God, deserueth not to bee egall and comparable too it. Loe here in effect, that which he meaneth. Now we ought alwaies to cal to minde that which we haue already touched. When as Dauid here setteth downe him selfe in the first ranke, and sayeth, that hee hath surpassed his enemies, teachers, and those which were the moste wyse, and of greatest vnderstanding, that this is not too attribute anye thing vntoo him selfe, and

and to his owne persone: but to the ende that God might be glorified in him: and that we might knowe what profit shall redound vnto vs by the word of God, when as we shal giue our selues vnto it. We see then that Dauid had no regarde to him self, but meaneth rather to giue vs occasion to glorifie God. And besides his purpose is to stirre vs vp to the loue, as we haue already touched, which hee had to the word of God: knowing the same to be so profitable for vs. For what is the cause that wee are so very negligent, as in deede wee are, in giuing our selues to the study of the holy scripture: that we thinke it to be euen labour and time lost if we onely spend but one houre of the day therein? What is the cause of such contempt? Verely bicause we know not the profit that might come vnto vs thereby: for if we were thus persuaded that all our wisedome is and consisteth in the worde of GOD, and that without it we are like vnto miserable beastes: so that Satan hath caught and holdeth vs fast bound in his grinnes and snares, and that we cannot erre in all the whole course of our life if we know this: and againe, that it is sufficient that God hath taught vs, and so haue thereby such a cleare light, as that will neuer faile vs, that we be fenced against all the ambushes of Satan, and against all the villanies and deceiptes of the world: if then we were thus throughly persuaded that the worde of God were sufficient against all this, it is most certaine that wee should be a great deale more in loue without all comparison with the studie thereof, then now we are.

And therefore, let vs well recorde this lesson, which is here set downe vnto vs by Dauid: to wit, that in the first place, wee shall be wyser then all our enemies, if that wee haue the woorde of God alwayes remayning with vs.

Nowe when he sayeth, that *hee was made wyser and had more vnderstanding then his enemies*, hee meaneth that hee had so excellēt a knowledge, as that God would not suffer him to fall into the ambushes & priuie engines which the vngodly had layde for him, suddenly to bee entrapped & caught

caught by their subtill traines and pollicies. Loe already a wonderfull profit which we receiue by the worde of God, that although wee be encompassed with the wicked which seeke nothing but our destruction, when as wee doe thinke that we should perishe euery minute of an houre, yet that we shall bee guarded from all whatsoeuer, that they may any way attempt and prinily laye in wayte against vs, so that we be instructed in the worde of God.

Lo, say I, an inestimable treasure: but we must cõsider who they be that are our enemies. For we haue not onely to do with men which seeke our hurt, dishonour, or that which might grieue vs as touching this present life: but wee haue Satan, and all his fauourers and mainteiners, which are deadly enemies too our soules, who seeke nothing els but our destruction: yea, not onely as concerning the worlde, but to withdrawe vs cleane awaye from the kingdome of God. Nowe it is very sure, that when the worde of God shall remaine and continue with vs, that wee shall haue wisdome enough too defende and keepe vs from all such enemies. We are then throughly too waye this saying: too wit, that if wee applie the worde of God to our owne vse, after that we haue bene instructed therin, we may be sure to walke in sauftie and without daunger. And how so? Bicause God will preserue vs against all our enemies: for although Satan pitcheth his nettes to take vs, notwithstanding all the marueilous pollicies of men, yea notwithstanding all our owne craftes and deceites whereunto we are sufficiently enough inclined of our selues, yet cannot we be assayled nor shaken, either on the one side or on the other: but shall be well fenced, when as God shall hold vs with his hande, and that we suffer our selues to bee gouerned by him. And besides our soules shall not onely bee preserued, but also whatsoeuer we haue to do in this world: neither shall our enemies be euer able to hurt vs, when as we shall haue beene throughly instructed. It is very true, it shall not bee otherwise, but that they will molest vs: as we see the faithful to be greatly troubled and vexed through the wicked and vngodly:

godly: but what commeth of it? We se that God in thende turneth all to their profit, and too the confusion of those which persecute them. Moreouer, let vs marke, when Dauid saith, that he was made wiser thē all his enemies, he very wel sheweth that there were a great many of people, which sought nothing els but to destroy him: neuertheles he speaketh not so much for him selfe, as he seeketh to shewe a cōmon example appertaining to all the faithfull. And this ought the more to encrease our courage, to be more carefull to profite in the word of God, And why so? we had need to be very wel aduised, and of good vnderstanding, bicause we are cōtinually to fight against Satā, & his cōpaignions, which will neuer ceasse to lie in priuie waite for vs, And since we see that the wicked are as hungre staruen dogges, & rauening wolues against vs, their crueltie is insatiable.

Seing then we see by experience, that the childrē of God must needes be compassed with enemies, & that there are many ambushes layde, and many wicked trecheries practized against them: so much the more ought we to haue our refuge to this worde, which can only keepe and defend vs, in such sort as that our enemies can do nothing against vs, but that we may be assured, as Dauid here maketh mētion. But we must note that which he saith, that he hath had the word of God continually with him: for so he vseth to saye, And that is to signifie vnto vs that wee ought neuer to depart from that which God hath once declared vnto vs, and not to be so fitching, as the more part of vs is accustomed to be. And there is not that he amongst vs, which is not infected with such a vice: that although the worde of God hath taken roote in vs, yet can we not hold our selues from howling as the wolues do (as we commonly saye) when as we shalbe vexed with any temptation. But see howe Dauid sheweth vs, that he abode stedfast & constant, whatsoeuer came of it, although hee had a number of enemies which sought nothing els but to oppresse & assault him with horrible temptations, he notwithstanding helde the worde of God for euer: and whatsoeuer vexing and turmoiling hee sawe on thother side, he stil held him to it. It followeth,

That

The 12. Sermon of M. Jo. Cal.

That hee was wyſer then his teachers: yea bicauſe, ſaieth hee, *that vpon that was my whole talke,* or, meditation, *as the teſtimonies of God.* In this, and in the verſe following, Dauid meaneth, that there is no worldly wiſedome, nor doctrine, which is worthy to be cōpared with that which wee learne in the ſchoole of God. It is very true that we may wel ſtudy the doctrines of men, and attaine therby vnto ſome iudgement, as ye knowe that learning doth fine a naturall mans wit: but what ſhall it be, if wee were the moſt perfect that is poſsible to be ſpoken of in all ſuch knowledge: to wit, in whatſoeuer man can teach vs? It is al but an A. B. C. For we come neuer a whit the ſooner to heauē by it, but it abideth ſtill in this preſent life. So that, as our life is tranſitorie, and leſſe then nothing: euen ſo alſo muſt we confeſſe, that al the ſciences which men teach vs, are no better then ſmoke: it is a tranſitorie thing which is ſoone vaniſhed. And as there is nothing euerlaſting but the kingdome of God, ſo alſo is there but one onely truth which is a wiſedome euerlaſting, and hath a ſure and euer continuing foundation. See then what Dauid his meaning is here to ſhewe vs, that men may very well teach vs, yea, but that ſhalbe but as an A. B. C. vntill ſuch time as wee are come to the ſchoole of God.

It can not be denied, but that God teacheth vs very wel by the meane of men, as in deede it commeth from him which wee learne, when as men make playne vnto vs his truth, and leade vs in the right waye of the Scripture: but here, Dauid ſpeaketh of that, which might bee taught him, without this doctrine which hee hath learned of G O D, when as hee hath beene inlightened by the holy Ghoſt, and hath knowne what the ſecretes of the lawe are. When then hee hath had this ſpirituall knowledge, hee ſayeth that all whatſoeuer hee had learned of men, was nothing in compariſon. Nowe hee addeth for confirmation,

That he was wiſer then his enemies.

Here, hee doth not onely declare, that the word of God inſtructeth vs more perfectly, then all the Sciences in the worlde

upon the Cxix. Psalme.   109

worlde are able to doe, but also scorneth the vsage, experience, and subtletie of all whatsoeuer that may any way come frō men, saying that it is all nothing in respect of this wisdome which we learne in the schoole of God.

Loe heere a place right worthy to be noted and imprinted in our memoryes. For we see how men extoll and magnifie them selues, when they haue attayned too any knowledge, to get them selues credite and estimation. For if a man be eloquent, and can speake gallantly, and write excellently, or that hee hath some other especiall science or knowledge, he thinketh him selfe a meruelous man, & able to catch the Moone with his teeth, as we say. Seeing then it is so, that men are so rash and hedstrong, that they persuade themselues to be woonderfull men, if they haue once gotten neuer so little knowledge in humanitie, whiche passeth no farther then the outwarde elementes of the worlde: by this wee are so much the more too be admonished, too esteeme this heauenly knowledge which is cōtayned in the holy Scripture, which we can neuer be able to attaine vnto without it please God to instruct vs: to the ende that in the firste place, none of vs all shoulde bee proude of our good wittes, ne yet of our other excellent aydes, nor too be hautie in that wee haue greatly profited at Schole, haue vnderstood all the liberal sciences, and to be men of greate experience. When then a man shall be the moste perfect in science, and knowledge, that it is posibly to be imagined, yet ought we to learne to humble our selues, and to cast all our pride cleane vnder fote that the worldly knowledge which God hath giuen vnto vs to serue him, bee subiect vnto his worde. Shall we finde a man that shall be moste eloquent, most cunning and most excelling in euery condition all others? That man I say, ought to doe homage vnto God for that which he hath receiued frō him knowing that no worldly science or knowledge ought to shadowe or darken him who farre surpasseth the same, becaufe the Heauens are farre aboue the earth. In very deede both two proceed from the meere goodnesse of God. But to this point must

O 5   it be

it be brought, That whatsoeuer he be that shall attayne to the true and heauenly light, must say, I am nothing O Lord: For all that which thou hast giuen me commeth also from thee, receiue thou then the same as the most speciall thinge aboue the rest. And since thou haste shewed mee that grace and fauour to be instructed by thy worde, worke so in mee I beseech thee, that all the rest yeelde suche honor and homage as appertaineth to this wonderful knowledge which I haue learned in thy schoole.

See then, what it is that Dauid meaneth to learne vs by his example. And besides, when he sayth, *That he is become wiser then his auncients*: It is to shewe vs, that wee ought too haue such a certaintie of our fayth, as that when there shall bee layde before vs whatsoeuer shall bee alleadged of this worlde, that it be sayde, And what I beseech you? muste not the auncient men bee wise? They lyued thus in the olde time. There are a great number of persons: And wee see a great many to be of the contrary opinion to this. If then they shall alleadge vnto vs men for their age, for their long experience and all their study, and whatsoeuer else that may bee sayde: What of all this? All that can bee sayd, is nothing in respect of this word of God. So then, wee see howe Dauid after he hath taught vs the way vnto humilitie, to the end we should present before God all the knowledge that is in vs, he sheweth againe that the word of God ought to be of that authoritie with vs, as that wee shoulde not feare too walke the way which hee hath taught vs, although we see all the rest of the world to go cleane cotrary. Whē as we shal heare that that may be said, And what I pray you? Is it possible that they which are helde and accounted to be so wise, should erre like poore and miserable beastes? yea, and that the same hath continued so many yeeres? wil any man say, that it hath no reason for it in all the whole worlde? Is it possible that this may be so? we ought not to trouble our selues for all these speeches. And why so? I answere: hath god spoken the word? Then, I say, let mans reason & wit stay there, let it humble & make it selfe nothing worth

vpon the Cxix. Psalme. 110

worth, and let vs confesse with Dauid, that there is one onely word of God, which ought to beare rule ouer all, & that this woorde hath such an excellent wisedom in it selfe, as that it shall consume all the knoweledge and wisedome whatsoeuer, that men thinke they haue. Nowe like as the faythfull ought to scorne that which men on their behalfe shall alledge, to the ende too diuert them from the obedience of God, and the certaintie which they haue in his woord: so also let vs learne, that the olde men ought not too bee opinatiue againſt God, vnder this shadowe that they haue seene much: that they haue seene many thinges euen before their eyes: as many of them there are which in this poynte vnder the shadowe of their age, would goe beyonde God, and remaine in their opinion stiffe, and obstinate saying, What I beseech you? I haue lyued thus longe and thus many yeeres, and would you haue mee nowe too chaunge my condition, and manner of dealing: It is for wilde headed young Gallants so to doe, which knewe not what it meaneth. But since I haue liued thus long: be it as be may, I will ende my life so. See then howe aged men will go beyond God. But in this place Dauid shewth vnto vs, that when as we shall be young as hee hath before treated, that although we haue hot boyling affections, & that our wittes are troubled with many hard matters, that wee be without all consideration: yet if we be ruled by the word God, no dout it wil make vs peaceable & quiet & cause our life to be rightly gouerned. And thus much for the younger sort. As touching the ageder, it is folish arrogancy in the, to build vpon that which they haue seene, and passed through their hands: but let them know that true wisdome which is, to be ordered by God, is common to all : & that therefore they ought to apply and giue them selues therto in all ages. And for this cause it is that S. Iohn in his Canouical Epistle, after that hee hath made a generall exhortation vntoo all men, sayeth *I speake vnto you fathers, to the ende you shoulde haue regard vnto him who is the Father of all the world, I speake vnto you yong men, to the end you should cal vppon your heauenly father*

1. Iohn. 2.
12. 13. 14.

The 13. Sermon of M. Io. Cal.

father. And you olde men, I sende you againe vnto him which is from the beginning.

To be shorte, Dauid sheweth vnto vs by this place, that the faithfull haue wherein too reioyce, when as they are taught in the worde of God: that they haue whereon too stay and assure them selues, knowing that they shall neuer want any thing: that they ought not to be drawen neither this way nor that way, becaufe they follow him of whome they helde the doctrine. So then, they beeing settled heerevpon, may be able too make their parte good without any great a doe: and when they shall see euery man goe aboute to withdrawe them, let them pray vnto God that hee will giue them the grace to holde them selues simply vnto him. Loe heere Dauid his meaning. Nowe hee addeth soone after.

I haue refrayned my feete from euery euill way: that I might keepe thy woorde.

Heere Dauid teacheth vs, that they which are desirous to serue God and to stick to his worde, are neuer without afflictions. But what is then to be doone? We must be of a good courage to withstand all the temptations which Satan can any way assayle vs with, to withdraw & turne vs frō that which is good. *I haue* sayth he *refrayned my feete from euery euill way.* And had Dauid neede of this? hee that was an holy Prophet, yea, and such a one as wee see the holy Scripture too haue reigned in, euen from his youth: Hee then hauing receiued so excellent graces of God, beeing a mirror of all perfection, was it needefull that hee shoulde keepe him selfe frō euery euill way? It should seeme that he was alredy vtterly past going any euil way: Yea, but becaufe he was a mortall man, he was not for all that without beeing incompassed with many vices and euill lustes againste which he was to fight. And in deede, we see how God suffred Dauid to fall once so greeuously, as that his fall ought to be an horrour vnto vs all.

Moreouer, let vs well confider, that if it was needefull for Dauid too fight againft the temptations which might

with-

vpon the Cxix. *Pſalme.*

withdrawe him from the right way, and that hee was with much to doe, turned away from euill wayes to ſerue God: euery of vs verily ought a great deale more too enforce our ſelues: For we are nothing ſo forwards as he was. For if hee hath gone on an hundreth paces, wee haue hardly gone on that way three or foure. So much the more then ought we rightly to practiſe this doctrine, when it is ſaide, that we ought to refraine our feete from euery euill way. And too doe this, let vs a little beholde howe naturally wee are inclyned to wickednesse. We neede neuer once too remoue our armes, legges, head, nor any thing elſe within vs to doe wickedly: For we are altogither giuen therto. And beſides, we are as it were vpon the yſe. I pray you tell mee, when a mā is not able to hold himſelf vp, that he ſhal haue neither feete, nor legges, but that all ſhall tremble and be afrayde, and ſhall be ſet vpon the yſe, and in a ſteepe place, howe is it poſſible for that man to hold him ſelf vp? In like ſorte is it with vs: for firſt & formoſt there is nothing in vs but debilitie and weakenes: & beſides, what is our life in this world? Haue we any firme or certaine place to holde or ſtay vs in? We are alwayes vpon the yſe, conſidering the temptations which aſſayle vs on euery ſide. And Dauid alſo vſeth this ſimilitude in another place: and yet this is not all, that wee are vpon the Yſe: but the place is alſo ſteepe too bring vs downewarde. The more therefore haue we neede too pray vnto God, that he will ſtrengthen vs, to the ende wee bee not ouercome of the euill: For otherwiſe, wee ſhall neuer come to that ende and perfection, conſtantly too abide by his worde.

Nowe when Dauid ſayth that *He kepte him ſelfe from euery euill way*, Hee meaneth not that hee was ſo throughly preſerued from all, but that he might be amended. For as we haue already ſaide, hee fell ſo horribly, as that the very thought thereof ſhould make the hayres of our heade too ſtand vpright. He meaneth not that his life was ſo perfect, as that he was able to ſay, that hee fayled not in ſome one pointe, and that he had wholely fulfilled the law of God.

That

The 13. Sermon of M. Io. Cal.

That is not the intent of Dauid. What is then his purpose? he meaneth simply, that for the holding of himselfe in the obedience of God, and keeping of his woerd, it was needeful for him too resiste a number of temptations: too stand vpon his guarde, and to be watchfull, or else that hee should be throwne downe hedlong an hundred thousande times. And hereby he admonisheth vs, that if we wil follow the way of saluation, and take good heede that wee be not turned therefro, that there is no question of bending, nor of leading vs heere and there, but that wee must remaine constant in the vocation of God, whē we are once brought into it by him. It followeth anon after:

I haue not declined from thy iudgementes: for thou haste taught mee.

Lo in summe what Dauid heere sayth, that because God hath instructed him, he hath not turned away frō his commaundements. When he saith, *That hee hath bene taught by God*, he meaneth not that he hath learned any such simple knowledge as is with vs, when God sheweth vs that fauor and grace, to haue his word faithfully handled amongst vs; his Gospel to be preached, or that wee haue Lectures reade vnto vs, which are requisite to our saluation. For we shall haue a great many hearers, which shall yet profite nothing at all, because it pearceth not their eares. Dauid therefore speaketh heere of such a manner of instruction as specially belongeth to Gods chosen, For this grace is not common to all: but God bestoweth it on them on whome it pleaseth him: neither must we say that we are giuen thereto as of our selues: But when as it shall please God to instruct vs, the same proceedeth from his meere good will and mercie. So then, Dauid saith not simply in this place that hee was taught, because he had a Booke of the lawe, and that it was made plaine vnto him: but his meaning is that hee was inlightened by the spirit of God. And for this cause declyned he not from the right way. Nowe he addeth in the end for a conclusion;

O sweete

O how sweete are thy woords vnto my throte: yea sweeter then hony vnto my mouth.

This sentence hath beene already handled, and therefore we will no longer stand vpon it. There are two thinges in the woorde of God which we ought rightly too keepe. The one is, the maiestie which God sheweth vnto vs therein, to the ende we should be brought to a reuerence, whereby euery one should humble himselfe, and say, It is meete O Lord, that we tremble and fall downe before thee. As also it is said by the Prophet Isaiah that the spirite of God shall rest vpon those which tremble at the woorde of God. The firste duetie then that wee owe vntoo the woorde of God, is this reuerence and feare. Becáuse, I say, that God sheweth there his maiestie vnto vs, that we might be thereby abased and humbled: to be short that we should haue it in great admiration. The seconde is, that it is sweete and amiable vnto vs. For we might in some sorte very well feare the worde of God: and yet for all that wee should not bee touched therewith as was meete. And in very deede, you shal se very many which wil not stick to say, Loe God, which speaketh, & therfore it is good reason that wee should lay our eares vnto him: But that they should bee subiecte vnto him, in all, and through all, they make thereof no noueltie, but caste that farre inough off, And that which is more, They woulde if it were possible, pluck him out of his Throne, and make voyde and caste of all instruction, to the end they would not be so straightly kept in: to be short, that they would neither be subiect to God, nor too what soeuer else might bee sayde vnto them. Nowe in the ende he sayth,

Through thy commaundements I get vnderstanding: therefore I hate all the wayes of falshoode.

Wherein hee signifieth vnto vs, that wee shall neuer hate that which is euill, vntill such time as wee know, what goodnesse is. It is very true that we shall somtimes see men to haue a great desire to doe good, forsooth as they thinkes

But

The 13. *Sermon of* M. Io. Cal.

But indeede that is nothing: all is but hypocrifie, vntil such time as God hath so taught vs, that wee might knowe and discerne in good earnest and say. Loe it is God that speaketh, and therefore let vs see what it is that hee sayeth vnto vs. And so after that we are fully resolued in his truth, then shall we beginne to hate all the wayes of wickednesse: For it cannot otherwise be, but whatsoeuer is against God wee must needs detest and abhorre. For howsoeuer Satan indeuoreth himselfe to carry vs to doe wickedly, we ought too haue this by and by in our mindes. What, shall we estrange our selues from our creator, whose we are? Shall the deuill beguile vs too make vs renounce him, who hath so dearely bought vs? And besides we also knowe, that the health of our soules, and all our felicitie consist in the obedience of our good God. Whē thē we shalbe thus taught by the word of God, we shall hate all wicked wayes. Without this, contrariwise, it must needs be that we should be wholy inclined thereto, and that the deceits of Sathan shall please vs: as we see it come to passe emongst the infidels, vnto whom we shal be very like, without God restraine vs with a bit. For if we walke after our owne nature and fantasie, what shall beecome of all our wicked wayes? And so let vs learne, that we shall neuer be brought to that which Dauid heere speaketh of, vntil such time as wee are instructed and vnderstande it by the word of God, and the testimonyes of his lawe.

And according too this holy doctrine, let vs prostrate our selues before the maiestie of our good God, with acknowledging of our faultes, beseeching him to make vs so to feele our wretchednesse, as that we may learne too seeke our felicitie in him onely. And because hee so familiarly instructeth vs by his woord, let vs not bee so accursed as too reiect this inestimable treasure whereof wee may be possessed: but that beeing in possession thereof, wee might increase dayly more and more in the knowledge which hee hath giuen vs, and continue therein vnto the ende, and vntill such time as wee shall attaine vnto that Heauenly inheritaunce, and too the full possession of that eternall reste

which

vpon the Cxix. Psalme.

which he hath promised vs, after that we shall be deliuered from all the assaults of this fraile and transitory life. That he wil not onely bestowe this grace vpon vs, but also vpon all people and nations of the earth. &c.

The xiiii. Sermon vpon the hundreth and nineteenth Psalme.

NVN.

Thy woord is a Lanterne vnto my feete: and a light vnto my pathes.

I haue sworne and will performe it, that I wil keepe thy righteous Iudgements.

I am very sore afflicted, O Lord. quicken me according vnto thy worde.

O Lord I beseech thee let the free will offeringes of my mouth please thee: and teach mee thy iudgementes.

My soule is alwayes in mine hand: yet doe I not forget thy lawe.

The vngodly haue layde a snare for mee: But yet I swarued not from thy commaundements.

Thy testimonies haue I claymed as mine heritage for euer: for they are the very ioy of mine heart.

I haue applyed mine heart too fulfill thy statutes alwayes: euen vnto the ende.

F we did throughly consider that it were very requisite for vs too reade the worde of God, and to listen vnto the doctrine taken out of it, wee should not neede to haue the mater to be so much preached off, what profite and vse we receiue by it: For euery of vs should feele the same by experience

experience. But because wee are so colde & blockishe in reading and hearing of that which God declareth vnto vs, it is meete we should be stirred vp therto som other wayes, and be shewed for what cause the word of God shall profite vs, when as we shalbe thus wise and of this mind, throughly to exercise our selues, & to apply our whole study therein. And see why Dauid pursueth this matter so diligently. For besides that which we haue already seene heere before, hee addeth & saith, *Thy word is a Lantern vnto my feete, & a light vnto my pathes.* Wherby he sheweth, that it is an inestimable treasure which we shal receiue when as we be taught by the word of God: to wit, that we shall neuer erre al the dayes of our life, as the vnbeleeuers do, who know not whether they go, but walke at randō. Dauid sheweth vnto vs, that whē as we shalbe guided by the word of God, we shalbe without al danger of falling. Now because it is a very easie thinge for a man to say thus, it seemeth at the first sight that this saying is so common, as that we neede not to stay any longer vpon it. But in the meāne while let vs se how the world practizeth that which is heere spoken, In deed we shall see it all cleane contrary, for there are very fewe that wil abide to be guided by the word of god: but the more part reiect it, & like rather to follow their own wills and desires, or rather can be contented to be gouerned as it pleaseth men, so that they will not suffer God to beare any rule or authoritie ouer them. Therefore let vs well mark what this importeth, when as it is said, That the word of God hath bin as it were a Lantern vnto the feete of Dauid, & as a light vnto his pathes. Nowe hereby he signifieth, that he meaneth not to bee wise in his owne conceite, but hath sought how he ought to be gouerned by the word of God, & so wholy held him self thereto.

Now if this hath beene a necessary poynt for Dauid, let none of vs thinke that we can go beyond him. And see also why S. Peter writing too all the faithful in generall, telleth them, that they should doe very well to be attentiue and to take hede to the word of God, as to a light shining in darke places. By this S. Peter declareth vnto vs, that it is not without

a Pet. 1. 19.

vpon the Cxix. Pfalme.

out caufe that Dauid hath vfed this fimilitude of a Lanterne. And why fo? For he fayth, that we being in the world are as mē in the darke: & to proue it to be fo, I befeech you what wifdom is in any of vs? Although that euery of vs eftemeth of him felf inough, & a great deale more thē needeth, yet for all that when as wee fhall be throughly knowne, we fhall finde all our vnderftanding too be full of vanitie and follie, and although we think our felues to haue a goodly light, yet are we in a deepe dungeon of darkeneffe. And befides, let vs feeke all the meanes poffible too guide and gouerne vs well heere in this worlde, yet fhall it be alwayes but darkeneffe.

Let vs then vnderftand, that it cannot be chofen but that we muft be as ftrayed wilde beaftes without the woorde of God, and that without it there is neither way nor ftay for vs. And although wee thinke our felues to be wife inough, yet fhall wee be altogither abufed: and when as wee fhall thinke vs to be fully refolued, yet fhall all our cafe & eftate be but fmoke. When then we fhall knowe this too be true, we may very well fay with Dauid, that the woorde of God is in fteade of a Lanterne vnto vs. For what is the caufe that we will not be ordered & ruled by God, but either by reafon of our pryde, or elfe becaufe we know not our own want? Some of vs are hindered through a vaine foolifhe opinion which we haue of our felues, that wee are fufficiently learned too iudge of that which is good and profitable. Loe heere is the very caufe why wee will not giue place vnto the worde of God.

There are other fome of vs: that although wee trufte not fo much vnto our owne wifdome, yet knowe wee not what a mifery it is to be heere, as it were in a place of confufion, and that there is no ftay of all the whole courfe of our life. And heerevppon wee contemne the woorde of God, and make no accounte of it. So then, wee muft come too this humilitie that beeing wholly throwne downe as touching the prefumption of our wittes, we muft fuffer our felues too be taught of God.

P, 2.   And

The 14. Sermon of M. Io. Cal.

And besids that we might also know, that our state & condition is too too miserable, vntil such time as we are lightened with this lantern. Now then, like as Dauid sheweth vnto vs by his example, that we ought not to haue any other guide, nor stay, but that which proceedeth frō the word of God: Euen so also sheweth hee vnto vs, that if so be we bee teachable of God & accept him as our scholmaister, & submit our selues to him, that we shall finde light inough in his word, that we nede not to feare to be confouded as though we knew not which way to turne vs. For God will giue vs sufficient light in his word, to lead vs to saluation. And this is such a comfort as cannot be sufficiētly inough expressed: For as it is declared, that we are miserable blind soules, and that whilst we walke in this world, we are but in darkenes, see how God putteth a remedy into our hands: that is, that we should heare him speake, and that we should learne to be ordered by his word: & that then, although this same world be a maze, although we haue many troubles in our life, although the deuil neuer ceaseth craftely to inuent many deceits to turn vs from the right way, yet we shalbe assured to go straight, & to attain vnto saluatiō. And by this wee may see how Satan hath possessed the papists, whenas they say, that the word of God is so darke, that wee are neuer able once to bite at it: and that we ought not to stay our selues thereon, because it is so vncertaine a thing: & besids that it is also a nose of wax, which a man may turne what way he listeth. They shame not to spue out such horrible blasphemies. But contrariwise, let vs trust vnto the spirit of God, speaking by the mouth of Dauid: to wit, that if we be lightened by the word of God, we neede not to feare falling: & that there is no rule so certain. For although the deuil went about with a thousand deceits to turne vs this way and that by crooked bypathes: yet must we be fully assured that the word of God is a lantern vnto our feete, to lead vs the right way. Neuertheles Dauid sheweth vnto vs, howe we shoulde feele such a cōmoditie comming vnto vs by the law of god: to wit, when as we shall receiue it with harty affection. For he saith,

I haue

vpon the C.xix. Pſalme.

I haue ſworne and will performe it: that I will keepe thy righ-teous iudgements.

Nowe heere hee ſheweth, that if there bee a wauering minded ſpirit, which readeth the Scripture for curioſities ſake, the ſame muſt needes remaine and continue alwayes blinde and ignoraunt: as we ſhall ſee many of them which doe nothing elſe but turne ouer the leaues, and wander in ſuch ſorte, as that there is neither firmeneſſe nor yet ſoundneſſe in any of them. And what is the cauſe thereof? For ſooth it is, becauſe they ſeeke not God with a right & earneſt affection. If we then will haue the commoditie, which Dauid heere ſpeaketh of, we muſt come back againe to the woord of God; and apply all our ſtudy ſo couragiouſly, as that wee deſire nothing elſe but too bee inſtructed in this trueth, and to ſubmit our ſelues wholly vnto it. And yet Dauid was not contented to ſay that this was his onely determination: But ſayth, that hee had ſworne and was ſtedfaſtly purpoſed to obſerue it: For the word which he vſeth, ſignifieth, that I will eſtabliſh it: to wit, I will wholly giue my ſelf vnto it: for I am ſo reſolute in this matter, as that I will neuer be turned away from it. Wherby he ſheweth, that there is no queſtion, but that we haue certaine ſmall motions, which ſlip vs, but wee muſt haue ſuch a feruent zeale, as poſſeſſeth our whole minde: and after we muſt with this zeale be conſtant, becauſe then we ſhalbe able rightly to ſee thoſe men which ſo trimly and fairely puf and blowe at vs. But what? This is but a falſe fire as we ſay. Nowe if wee bee truely affected to ſerue God, the ſame our affection muſte be firme and ſure, that we may vnfaignedly ſay with Dauid, that we haue ſworne, and are fully purpoſed too ſtand and abide by this matter. In very deede heere may ſome queſtion ariſe: For it ſhould ſeme that Dauid hath too too much preſumed of him ſelf, to ſweare that he wil keepe the teſtimonies of God. For we are not able to promiſe any thing, which is not in our power and ſtrength. If a man ſhal thruſt in himſelf to promiſe that which he hath not, he of right is to be accuſed of follie: for euery man wil ſay, that it is great

P.3. arrogancy

The 14. Sermon of M. Jo. Cal.

arrogancy in him because he hath passed his bounds. Now when as wee shall haue throughly considered heereof, we shall finde that it is impossible for any mortall man, perfectly to obserue the Commaundements of God.

This should seeme then at the first sight, that the othe which Dauid heere speaketh of, ought rather too be reprehended then commaunded: But heere are two things too be considered of: The one is, that when the faithfull binde them selues so vnto God, they lay not this foundation in their owne proper strength, they looke not into their own abilitie, but they desire of God to accomplish that whiche they haue promised him. And why doe they soe? Now let vs note, that heere he speaketh of the commaundementes of God. And we haue here already declared, that when Dauid nameth the lawe, hee looketh not simply too the Commaundements, but also to the promises: and in these promises it is saide, that God will circumcise the heartes of his children: He sayth, that he wil so liuely touch them, as that he will bring them into his obedience. So then (as we haue already said) the faithfull binde not them selues to God to do any thing of their owne power & strength, but they desire him to fulfil what soeuer is wanting in them, to supply their weakenesse, and to send such remedy as hee knoweth best to be most needefull and expedient for them. See then with what confidence Dauid hath sworne too obserue the Testimonyes of God: hee did it not, I say, of any vaine presumption, that he had conceiued of his owne power and strength, ne yet that he was able to doe it, no, he attributed nothing to his owne strength: But sweareth and doth it, by reaso of the promise of god, by which promise he declareth that he wil by his holy spirit gouerne al those which are his. Loe wherupon Dauid stayed himselfe. Now by & by followeth the second point: to wit, that Dauid hath sworne too obserue the testimonies, yea euen staying himself vpon that which God hath promised, that he wil vpholde vs through his mercye, that although wee halte and that all the obedience which we go about to yeeld vnto him be weake, and

faultie

vpon the Cxix. Psalme.

faultie, becaufe it is done but by halues, yet he not hauing refpect to al our faults, meaneth to make a tafte of the defire which we fhall haue to pleafe him: & in effect, wil accept our feruice as it is, difpenfing with all the faultes which fhall be mingled amongft them. Which thing Dauid confidering, was able to fay that he would obferue the comandements of God. So then let vs note, that when the faithfull binde themfelues to obferue the word of God, they muft not truft to them felues, ne yet be puffed vp with a foolifh opinion, that they haue the power to do it: but they muft fay, Accōplifh thou this, O Lorde, and then I will followe it: write thy lawe O Lorde, in mine hearte, and then fhall I haue a defire to ferue thee: and befides, Let the faithful alwayes remember, that God wil not handle them fharply: yea & although they faile in a great number of pointes, fo that they are not able to obferue one only point, nor iot perfectly: yet wil he fpare them through his free goodnes & mercie, Whē the faithful & childrē of god fhal haue knowen thus much, and fhall fweare that they will obferue the comandements of God: yet let them not ceafe for all that too flie vnto the forgiuenes of their finnes, that they may feele the fame too be a neceffary remedy agreeable to the will of God, for the fulfilling of one parte of his commandements. We fee now then why Dauid hath fworne to keepe the Commaundements of God, and that he wil neuer chaunge this purpofe in his hart. Now he maketh two requeftes immediatly after: whereof, the one is to be quickened and reftored. Wherein he fheweth that which I haue aledy touched: which is, that hee was not ledde with a foolifh prefumption of his owne power & ftregth. For he which defireth god to be reftored, confeffeth that he liueth not as of himfelf, but that he muft needs liue by the grace & goodnes of God. And yet Dauid maketh this confeffion more expreflly; when he addeth the reafon why he vfeth to make fuch requeft: *For I am very fore afflicted O. Lord,* faith he. See then Dauid who confeffing himfelf to be troubled, and as it were vtterly made nothing befecheth god for to reftore him. Shal we fay that he trufted to

P.4.   his owne

The 14. Sermon of M. Jo. Cal.

owne strength? or that hee attributed any thing whatsoeuer vnto him selfe? we se the cleane contrary. So then, according to that which we haue already declared, let vs vnderstand that he sware not vpon any vaine presumptiō: but because he knewe that God would neuer fayle him. And this is the reason why he toke vpon him this boldenes. And that is it which he addeth: *According to thy word*: that is, according to thy promises. Now we ought throughly to consider all what soeuer that is heere said, *Quicken me O Lorde*, saith he. And thus much for the first point. Wherin he sheweth that he liueth not as of him self, but desiereth it of God. And afterward, he addeth the reason, saying after this manner, *I am very sore aflicted*. Whereby hee declareth vnto vs, that we are not able too releeue and maintaine our selues, when as our strength fayleth vs, but that it is God which must put to his helping hand. And besides we may be assured that he will helpe vs, and be ready to restore vs, so that we will desire him, and call vpon him, & haue recourse vnto his goodnesse. Loe heere a mightie comforte for all the faithful, when as they finde them selues to bee so without strength, as that they feele them selues too fainte, too be cleane cast down, and to see nothing else in them selues but death: yet may they be fully assured & resolued, that God will alwayes be their watchman, too restore and quicken them. And why so? To wit, according to that which Dauid addeth when he sayth, *According to thy promises*. Then it followeth, that God hath promised too restore and quicken his, when as they shall be in death. And therefore wee shall neuer be able too make our request in faith, as Dauid heere hath doone, if that wee haue not the promises of God. For, as we haue before said, it is a foolehardines in men to put foorth them selues too pray vnto God as they liste, without beeing sure and certaine of his will before.

See then the cause which mooued Dauid so expressely too sette downe heere the promise of GOD. Nowe this promise was not made too him alone, this is no personall Priuiledge, as wee say, appertaining to one man only: But

vpon the Cxix. *Pſalme.* 117

But it is a generall rule which we muſt holde, that God wil raiſe vp againe from death thoſe which are throwne down, and as it were made nothing: yea euen when as they doe call vpon him, and acknowledge, that it commeth of his owne pure grace that they ought to be ſo reſtored, and not otherwiſe. Nowe here is yet another requeſt which hee maketh,

O Lord, I beſeeche thee let the freewill offringes of my mouth pleaſe thee; and teach me thy iudgements.

Here Dauid deſireth God to accept the praiſes which he ſhall render vnto him. For the oblations whereof Dauid ſpeaketh, are nothing els but prayſe and thankeſgiuing, by which Dauid acknowledgeth the benefites of God. And yet for all that, he in very deede looketh vnto the common order of the lawe: For when a man hath beene cured of a diſeaſe, or hath beene deliuered from ſome daunger, or els that God hath indued him with proſperitie, hee commeth to the Church to make his oblation or offring, for an eſpeciall teſtimonie, and too acknowledge howe greatly hee is bounden vnto God. Dauid had ſmall regarde to any ſuch ceremonies, but yet he noteth and expreſſeth the ende and the vſe, that is, that we ſhould ſtay vs vpon the principal: for if a man ſhould ſacrifice a beaſt, that were nothing at all. And wherefore then ſerued ſuch maner of ſacrifice? Forſooth it was an aide and help: bicauſe it is nedefull that we ſhould be alwayes ſtirred vp. And beſides, this is a good aduertiſement to ſhewe vs, that when we will giue GOD thankes for his benefites which he beſtoweth vpon vs, wee muſt come vnto him by the mediation of our Lorde Ieſus Chriſt: for we are not once worthy to open our mouthes to honour God, bicauſe our lippes are vncleane and defiled. And ſo we thē knowing our vnworthines, muſt come vnto our Lord Ieſus Chriſt, and giue thākes vnto God by him, as alſo the author to the Hebrewes exhorteth vs to do. For he namely declareth that vnto vs, that it is onely Ieſus Chriſte, which giueth vs acceſſe vnto God his father, to confeſſe his bountie towardes vs: and otherwiſe, wee ſhall but profane

Heb.4, 14.&.
16.

The 14. Sermon of M. Io. Cal.

his name, yea he will not accept our praises and thankes giuing, but they shal euē as it were stinke in his nosethrilles. Se then to what ende the sacrifices are. But Dauid notwithstanding sheweth, that the principall ende of the benefites of God is, that our lippes should open them selues to confesse his goodnesse, when as wee haue proued and felte it. And that is it which he speaketh of in the hūdreth and sixteene Psalme, What reward shall I giue vnto the Lord: for al the benefites that he hath bestowed vpon me? I will receiue the cup of saluation: and call vpon the name of the Lorde: as if he should haue said, that he knewe none other waye to please God but to giue thankes vnto him, when as hee had liberally bestowed all the benefites of the world vpon him, in such sort as that he felt himselfe most bounden vnto his goodnesse. Euen so likewise will hee bee contented with vs, when as we render vnto him such thankes. Yea, but in the meane while let vs consider that Dauid knewe, that if God had not freely accepted the praises which hee yelded vnto him, that they had byn nothing worth, as wee haue already declared: but we haue of this here a sufficient and manifest cōfirmatiō. What is the reasō why Dauid besought Gōd to accept the praises which he rēdred vnto him? he did it not like an hypocrite. He cōfesseth then, that whē hee presented him self before God, to magnifie his name, that hee might very well haue byn put by, & his mouth to haue byn stopped. And why so? bicause that we profane the name of God seing there can proceede nothing but filth & stench, from those which are altogether corrupt, neither cā there be any one drop of goodnes in thē. And although God hath put into them any good vertues, yet they are so entermedled with vices, as that it is lamentable. And therfore Dauid knowing this to be so, praieth God that his praises might please him. Now if Dauid knew his vnworthinesse to be such, I beseech you, dareth any of vs to say, that we are of our owne power capable, to magnifie the name of God, & to rēder him such thākes as to him appertaineth, without he of his meere free good wil alloweth thē, not imputing vnto vs the vices and imperfections which are therewithal entermedled? & that

Ps. 116. 11. 12.

he will

upon the Cxix. Psalme. 118

he wil also thinke wel of our praises and thanksgiuing, yea although they deserue it neuer a whit? And besides, it wee need to desire God, to accept our praises which we render vnto him: I pray you what shal become of the rest? For it is most certain, that if ther be any seruice which pleaseth God, it is euen this whē we come to do our homage for whatsoeuer we haue receiued at his hands: and that we confesse & protest that we haue nothing but that we hold of him. Whē as wee doo this homage vnto God, loe this is the seruice, which he chiefly desireth of vs: Loe this is that sweete smelling sacrifice, which the scripture speaketh of. Now so it is, that when we would do this homage vnto God, therby to humble our selues, yet may it be amended: in such sorte as that we deserue to haue it to be put by, & to be disalowed: what shal then become of our other meane seruices, and in effect, of al our whole life? Shal we now go and glorify him with our merites, as the Papists doo, who lift vp their heads against God with an whorish shamelesnes: For they thinke that G O D is beholden too them : or else, although they haue offended his maiestie, yet after that they haue reckened with him, they thinke that they may very well recōpense him with their satisfactions. Go too now, let vs think thus of our selues, that when wee see that in the very best & most requisite, yea and as it were the very flowre of all our good workes, euen of those wherein God guideth vs, that they do nothing else but stinke, except God himselfe clense them too make them sweete, and taketh from them the superfluities and filthinesse which are in them. Nowe if of all our good workes, yea euen of the most excellent we are exhorted to craue pardon of God for them, what shall become of our grosse and ouer manifest sinnes whereof wee are conuinced, and whereof men, yea, and yong children, may reprehende vs? So then, see here an excellent place, which rightly abolisheth al vayne and diuelish confidences, wherewith we deceiue our selues, when as wee thinke too stande before the maiestie of God with our merites, and such other like gewgawes and trifling toyes I knowe not what, thinking thereby to recompense him,

And

The 14. Sermon of M. Io. Cal.

And thus much for this verse. Now Dauid afterward saith, *My soule is alwayes in my hand: yet do I not forget thy lawe. The vngodly haue laide a snare for me: but yet I swarued not from thy commaundementes.*

Here Dauid protesteth as before, that he had such a resolute affection to followe the woorde of God, as that no temptations could withdrawe him from it. And see how we may say, that we serue God, without hypocrisie & in truth. For if we be easily and gently dealte withall, so we haue no affliction, that our God handleth vs as wee would wishe, & leaueth vs to our owne pleasure, or els, if he so much fauoureth vs, as that we are not pressed with any griefes and sorrowes: it is an easy matter then for vs too serue and honour him. But when God afflicteth vs, that it seemeth hee would oppresse and grieue vs euery minute of an houre, when we see death pursuing vs on euery side, that the vngodly are wholy about vs, as it were ready to pull out our eyes, and our life so wretched, as that the world iudgeth vs to be as it were reprobates: when then al these temptations shall touch vs, and yet we remaine still constant prayfing of God, and holding vs vnto him, perseuering in his obedience, and calling vpon him, beeing pacient in all our afflictions, vntill such time as he deliuereth vs: when we haue all this, we may then say with Dauid, that we haue displaied and layde wide open our life to serue God: and this shall be a good and sure profe thereof. But if we haue not this constancie, a great number may make a wonderfull shewe of godlinesse before the face of the worlde, but all that shall proue nothing. And so, let vs well consider of this place: for Dauid spake not this for him selfe, but for our common instruction. And besides, if we will in deede profit our selues by this doctrine, let vs consider that if we sometimes see the apparaunt dangers of death, so that wee be pressed downe on euery side, not to thinke it to be any strange thing. And why so? Bicause the same came too passe as greatly sometimes to Dauid. For he saieth that he was not without continuall trouble. My soule (saieth he) is alwaies in my hand:

my

vpon the Cxix. Pſalme. 119

my life is as it were I can not tell where, it is put foorth to abide all miſchiefe, that it ſeemeth I were at deathes doore euery minute of an houre. If Dauid was alwayes thus troubled, and yet perſeuered in the prayſing of God: I beſeech you ought not we to bee aſhamed to be faint harted, when as it ſhal pleaſe God to exerciſe vs onely but now and then? Euen ſo, although afflictions oppreſſe vs, yet muſt we not ceaſe too fight againſt them, attending and crauing the helpe of God. And thus much for this. And beſides, when wee are thus aſſured, let vs ſeeke our comfort where it may bee founde, that is, in the woorde of God, and to be thus conſtant neuer to forget the lawe of God. Let vs thē conſider and obſerue this doctrine. For it is not without cauſe that Dauid ſayeth, That although my ſoule bee in my hande, yet haue I not forgotten thy lawe. Hee ſheweth vs heereby, that as wee are weake, ſo we ſhoulde be ſoone ſhaken, and in the ende throwne downe, when as wee ſhoulde ſee our ſelues laide wyde open to death. Wee then hauing this vnderſtanding ought to ſtand vpon our guarde, to the ende the diuell might neuer beguile vs, vnder the coloure, that God had as it were forſaken vs, and that we ſhould be as it were in the ſhadowe of death. Moreouer, we ſee what doltiſhneſſe (or rather beaſtlineſſe) this is amongſt the Papiſtes, to take this place for proofe of freewill. My ſoule is in my hand: to wit, I am able of mine owne nature, and of my owne proper ſtrength, to diſcerne betweene good and euill: and to do whatſoeuer I thinke beſt. If brute beaſtes could ſpeake, they would ſpeake a little wiſelier then thus. For to what purpoſe ſhould Dauid ſay, although, O Lorde, that my ſoule is in my hande, yet haue I not forgotten thy lawe? He ſhould altogether ſpeake cleane againſt nature. But as we haue already declared, this is a kinde of ſpeeche much vſed in the ſcripture, to ſay that the life of a man is in his hande, it is as it were in the winde, or I know not where. Let vs now come vnto the proteſtation which he addeth,

The vngodly haue laid a ſnare for me: but yet I ſwarued not from thy commaundementes.

This

The 14. Sermon of M. Io. Cal.

This sentence is like vnto the other which we are about to handle. For hee sheweth howe his life was in his hande: too witte, that ouer and besides the afflictions which were directly sent him from the hande of God, that the wicked also persecuted him aswel: and besides the violences, and outrages, that were doone vntoo him, hee had also secrete ambushes laide for him. See then howe diuersly hee is oppressed, and yet he neuer shronke from the lawe of God. In the ende he addeth and saith,

Thy testimonies haue I claymed as myne heritage for euer: for they are the very ioy of mine hart.

Nowe heere hee sheweth, howe he was able to remaine firme & constant without being withdrawne by any temptations: but that hee alwaies stood stedfastly in the lawe of God: that is, bicause hee alwaies chose it for his heritage, that is for his chiefe felicitie. For this worde *heritage*, in the scripture, is taken for the thing that man moste desireth, and that which moste properly belongeth vnto him. To be shorte, it is such a similitude, as that is which is spoken of the Treasure: as if a man shoulde call it, the souereigne good, the true and perfect felicitie. See then at what ende wee must beginne, if in the middest of death we wil abide so constantly as Dauid hath doone, too keepe the lawe of god: that is I say, to choose it for our inheritance. And how is that? First of al we must vnderstande, that al the commodities whereuntoo wee are ouermuch giuen, are transitory, without certaintie, and without propertie. For wee may want them euery handewhyle: neither can wee enioy any thing be it neuer so iustly giuē, but that we may be robbed of it betwixt this day and too morowe. What is then the surest felicitie which wee can haue, and may enioy for euer? it is euen the woorde of God. And this is it which wee ought chiefely too desire, and wherein wee are especially too reioyce. Lo then how wee must vnderstande that which Dauid heere protesteth. That hee hath chosen the woorde of God for his heritage.

Yea.

vpon the Cxix. Pſalme. 120

Yea and he ſetteth it downe by and by after, that it hath beene the very ioye of his heart. For vntill ſuch time as wee haue had this taſte in the woorde of God, that wee truely ioye in it, it is a ſigne that we neuer yet had any good affection thereto at all. Although wee haue knowne that our chiefe felicitie lieth therein, yet are wee not able well too keepe our ſelues in it, vntill ſuch time as wee haue conceiued, that it is that wherein wee muſt delight, and in none other thing.

Nowe it is impoſsible that wee ſhould euer take any delight or pleaſure in the lawe of God, except we did knowe that he declareth him ſelfe to vs in it, that hee is our father, and taketh vs for his children, that wee haue a teſtimonie that our ſinnes are forgiuen vs, that wee may haue acceſſe vnto him, and bee able to call vpon him in all our neceſsities. If God ſayeth onely vnto vs, loe what it is that I would haue you to doe, I would haue you too take mee for your God, & to ſerue me with all your heart: if we haue but theſe two tables, to looke into, to knowe what wee haue to doe, ſhall the lawe of God delight vs? No, but contrariwiſe, it ſhall feare vs. We ſee then very well when Dauid ſayth, that hee tooke all his delight and pleaſure in the commandementes of God, that he had not ſimply the bare worde of the lawe, to ſay that God commaunded him that which he ought to do. but that he alſo ioyned the promiſes thereto, bicauſe that God willing his children to come vnto him, promiſeth to make them feele his goodneſſe and fatherly loue which hee vſeth towardes thoſe that are his. To bee ſhort, he ſheweth them that all their felicitie conſiſteth in his onely mercie. He ſaieth in the ende,

I haue applied mine heart to fulfill thy ſtatutes alwayes: euen vnto the ende..

Nowe when he ſayeth, that he enclined his heart to obſerue the commaundementes of God: he ſheweth vs, what ſeruice it is that God requireth: that is a voluntary & willing ſeruice. See here yet a point which ought well too bee conſidered off, too the ende wee ſhoulde not thinke

that

that we are euer able to please God, when as wee serue him constrainedly, as wee see the miserable and wretched faithlesse do, which greatly tormēt thē selues. And why so? For all that they do, they doe it cōstrainedly bicause they would the better escape the hande of God, but when they come neere vnto him as well as they may, it is but as it were enforced and constrained, bicause he is their iudge. Nowe if we haue such a constāt desire(as we terme it)that we are enforced to do that which wee are cōmaūded: our whole cace is little worth, and God will neuer allowe of it. And why so? bicause he liketh of nothing els but of obedience, and woulde haue vs come vnto him with franke and willing mindes.

See then why Dauid saieth, that hee hath inclined his heart to keepe the commaundementes of God: not that he protesteth, that he hath done it of him selfe, nor of his own minde: but bicause that God hath giuen him both the will and the power to do the same. And to proue it to be so, wee shall neuer see that Dauid braggeth of him selfe in any one place, that he willed any good, being so led of his own proper minde: he will neuer saye, that it was his naturall inclination, but saieth cleane contrarie, *I was conceiued in sinne*, saieth he, he reserueth nothing to him self but al that which is naught. When then in this behalfe he protesteth that hee had inclined his heart, he onely sheweth what the grace of God was in him. And for conclusion he addeth: *That he did it for euer, or euen vnto the ende*, or, this is it which we haue touched heretofore: to wit, we must be like suddaine blasts which passe by and by, but wee must bee constant: and that when we shall haue once begunne, we must pray vnto God that he will continue the same our well doing which hee hath begunne in vs, and to holde vs by the hand vntill such time as we haue finished our course. After he had sayde, *for euer*, he addeth, *euen vnto the ende*. It is very true, that the saying which hee here vseth, importeth sometimes, salarie or rewarde: But in this place (as in the first verse of the letter,

Psal. 51, 5.

ter. *HE*, he vseth the selfe same saying) it signifieth but too the ende: as if hee shoulde haue saide wee may alter and chaunge our mindes in other thinges: but we must follow vnto the death, when God calleth vs vnto him, beeing assured that in this pursuite wee cannot fayle to come to the true ende, without to fayle and erre for euer.

And according to this holy doctrine, let vs prostrate our selues before the maiestie of our good God in acknoweledging our faultes: beseeching him that it woulde please him too make vs so throughly too feele them, as that wee may in all humilitie bee able too craue pardon of him for them, graoning for all the offences which wee haue committed against him. And that in the meane while also wee may haue recourse vntoo him, beseeching him too remedy all our vices and imperfections: and so too confirme our weakenesse, as that beeing strengthened by him, wee might ouercome all the temptations wherewith Satan can any way assayle vs, that beeing more & more confirmed in his holy dictrine, wee desire nothing els but to submitte our selues vnto it, and too bee squared by none other rule, but by that which he hath giuen vnto vs through his word. That it woulde not please him onely to graunt vnto vs this grace, but vnto all people and nations of the world. &c.

SAMECH.

I hate vaine inuentions: but thy lawe do I loue.
Thou art my refuge and my shield: and I trust in thy worde.
Away from me yee wicked: for I wil keepe the cōmaundementes of my God.
Stablish mee according too thy promise that I may liue: and let me not be disappointed of my hope.
Hold thou me vp and I shall be saufe: yea and my delight shalbe continually in thy statutes.
Thou hast troden downe all them that depart from thy statutes: for their deceipt is vayne.
Thou hast taken away all the vngodly of the earth like drosse: therefore I loue thy testimonies.
My flesh trembleth for feare of thee, and I am afraid of thy iudgementes.

E haue so many lettes and stoppes both from aboue and heere beneath which drawe vs on to doe wickedly, or at least wife which cause vs too slacke our seruing of GOD, that which soeuer of vs that is minded to doe well, must remoue fró him al his wicked & euill affections, and all the temptations, which any waye may come against him. See then why Dauid in this place, meaning to proteste that hee loued the lawe of God, sayeth to the contrarie, that hee

hated

hated high enterprises, or rather wicked and crooked imaginations, or euill considerations. For the worde which is here touched, signifieth a bough or braunch: and by a similitude taketh it for the euill and wicked imaginations and deuises of men which runne this and that way. Now we see what a bottomlesse depth the spirite of man is, and how he wreatheth or windeth him selfe in his fantasies. This selfe same word signifieth, the very height and toppe either of an hie hill, house, or any other hie thing. And therevpon also as by a similitude, the imaginatiue cōceipts of men, whē as they entend to bring them selues into credit, and goe about to aduaunce them selues, euen as ambitiō ruleth our nature, vntill such time as God hath tamed vs by his holy spirite, and humbled and made vs gentle and meeke. And now that wee may haue the true and naturall meaning of this place, let vs see in effect, that Dauid protesting that he loued the law of God, saieth, that hee remoued quite from him whatsoeuer might withdrawe him from it. Nowe hee speaketh not this here to the ende to bragge of him selfe: but rather that this example shoulde bee for our better instructiō. For the spirite of God hath spokē it by his mouth to the ende we might vnderstand and knowe, which is the meane whereby we might be wholy giuen to the seruice of God, and to take holde of the lawe with such an affection, as that our heartes might be as it were euen fast tied thereto. For it is impossible, I say, that wee should euer come or attaine vnto it, vntill such time as we haue cleane cut of the things which withdraw and turne vs away both on the one side and the other: to wit, al our owne fantasies and lustes: we must thrust out frō vs all whatsoeuer, for the loue which we ought to beare to the lawe of God: we must also forget all hawtines or pride, yea euen studying howe too separate our selues from those which any waye might drawe vs too euill: and not too communicate with the vngodly whiche are doublehearted, full of hypocrisie, or else, such as are but vaineglorious and of that pryde which euen moueth thē to lift thēselues vp both against God and men:

Q 2   For

The 15. Sermon of M. Io. Cal.

For their company will so corrupt vs, as that being vuzzeled amongst them, our heartes can neuer be so ordered and ruled in the loue which wee ought to haue to the lawe of God. Now then let vs kepe wel in mind this admonitiō, as a thing most profitable for vs: to wit, as before I haue said, that as we are enclined to committe a great number of offences and villanies, which will withdrawe vs from the loue that we ought to beare to the word of God, let vs so much the more flie from whatsoeuer draweth vs away backward. Yea and let vs vnderstand, that looke howe many our imaginations and affections are, that they are euen so many cartropes to hale & pull vs away from this loue: or els, they are so many poysons which Satan giueth vs, to the ende we should not once taste of the word of God, neither to be so amiable and pleasant vnto vs as it ought: but rather that we might be greeued & lothed therwith, & so to leaue it, as if it were a grieuous matter, & an occasion of heuines. Since then it is so, let vs be well aduised too purge our heartes of all earthly affections, if we will take in had to loue the word of God. And yet it is not enough that wee haue fought against our vngodly lustes, and fleshly fantasies, but we must also as it were gather our wittes together: for hardly can we open our eies to looke about this waye and that waye, but that Satan will laye before vs some euill and wicked stops and encountries. It is very true, that so long as we liue here in this worlde, wee can not but both see and heare a great many of things: but yet must wee bridle our senses. And aboue all the rest, we ought to fight against these strange, & counterfait hypocrisies and affectiōs, wherein we are nuzzeled. We must euen hate deadly al this in our heart, to the ende wee bee not hindred from the loue of the worde of God. And thus much for the first verse. Now in the second, Dauid sheweth howe wee should finde the worde of God pleasant and gratious, that we might loue it, that is, when as we shall trust to his worde. *Thou art*, sayth he, *my refuge and my shield: and I trust in thy word.*

This is not added hereunto without iust cause. For if there

there be none other doctrine in the lawe but too say vnto vs, Loe this must you do, wee can neuer bee comforted For we shal find nothing in it but condemnation. When as god sheweth vnto vs wh: our duety is, we must needs be confounded, and know. hat before him wee are condemned and accursed, seeing that no man performeth that which hee ought. So then, the woorde of God shoulde bee both bitter and grieuous vnto vs, if there were nothing else conteined in it but a rule too liue well: But when God is a testimonie and witnes vntoo vs of his goodnes and mercy, and declareth vntoo vs that from him wee must looke too receiue our chiefe felicitie, that hee is prest and ready too helpe vs, that the treasures of his infinite goodnesse are open vnto vs: when I saye, this shall be in vs, then may wee sauoure and taste his woorde, and conceiue the loue of it, when as we knowe that therein consisteth and lieth all our health and ioye. Nowe then, when as wee would profite in the worde of God, and exercise our selues in it, let vs learne to receiue the promises therein conteined. And let vs not be like vnto them which thinke that God saieth nothing else vnto vs in all the whole scripture, but doe this, or doe that: for then, this were a very thinne and feeble doctrine. For if God were there as a Philosopher, to preache vnto vs of vertues, and to declare vnto vs, that we must be thus gouerned: we shoulde haue but a pitifull colde pull of it: and bicause we are altogether and wholy contrary to the rightuousnesse of God, it is impossible but that wee should bee grieued and troubled with whatsoeuer shalbe said vnto vs.

But I haue already shewed, that the principall matter which God declareth vnto vs in his worde, is this, that hee protesteth howe well he loueth vs in alluring vs vnto him selfe, to the ende we shoulde not doubt, but that he will bee our father in all and through all, and that wee shoulde bee bolde to come before him: that when there is any question of our saluation, and of whatsoeuer els we haue neede off, we should not doubt but that hee is ready to heare all our prayers, that his hande is alwayes liberally bent, to the end

Q3   to giue

to giue vs whatsoeuer we want. When we shall once knowe this to bee true, then, as I haue already saide, the worde of God shall bee pleasaunt vnto vs. Loe nowe why Dauid by & by addeth, *My trust is in thy worde, O Lord.* This is also, in summe, our faith, which bringeth vs to the obediēce of God when I saye that it is faith which bringeth vs into the obediēce of God. I meane, that after we haue vnderstood of his good wil, that we are thē stirred vp to yelde our selues vnto him. And vntill such time as hee hath imprinted in our heartes the testimonie of his loue, and the benefite which hee meaneth vnto vs, wee shall flye from him as much as may bee: and as often as this woorde of God shall sounde in our eares, so often shall it grieue and torment vs, as wee see howe the faithlesse doe feare, when the worde of God is spoken vnto them: it bringeth vntoo them nothing but terrour and feare, as if a theefe or murderer were brought before a iudge. But when as we haue faith to stay our selues vpon the goodnesse of God, too call vppon him as Dauid doth here, our succoure, and shielde: we may call vpon him with such a confidence, as that hee will neuer bee deafe, too heare our prayers: when then wee are thus assured, wee are forthwith wonne to loue him, then delight we to yelde our obedience vnto his lawe. Nowe in following that which wee haue already declared, Dauid againe addeth,

Away from me yee wicked: for I will keepe the commaundementes of my God.

Here hee speaketh of the temptations which come vnto vs by reason of the vngodly who allure vs, as much as in them lieth too make vs too contemne God, and worke so many offences as that they breake all good order, yea, euen to leaue the worlde naked and bare of all goodnesse. For so much then as wee are too liue here amongst contemptuous and outragious people, who haue neither fayth, trust, nor truthe: and that these tēptations are very perilous vnto vs: as wee see what a great number of men are corrupt by them: Dauid saith, *Awaye from me yee wicked, bicause I keepe the commaundementes of my God.* Here wee are to note, as before I haue touched, that hee speaketh not this, too

make

vpon the Cxix. Pfalme. 124

make recitall of his worthinesse, or that hee alledgeth it for his power and strength to wynne him reputation: but speaking by the spirite of God, he admonisheth vs to liue holily: to wit, that if we will walke in the feare of God, and be vnder his yoke, wee must in the first place separate our selues from the vngodly. Nowe this is an easie doctrine to be learned, but it is so slenderly practized of vs, as that we had neede better to thinke of it, then heretofore wee haue done. If there were a great number of offences in Dauid his time, which were to turne the faithfull awaye from the feare of God, and too leade them to doe wickedly, in what case then stande we nowe? It is very true that we are come to the full measure of all iniquitie. For if wee doe beholde at this day the states and conditions of all men, it wil seeme that it is impossible for the world to be worse, that the deuill so possesseth both great and small in townes & villages, as that it is a very hell and tormentory to see it. Euen so the, howe is it possible that a faithfull man can perseuer to liue in the feare of God and in such soundnesse as he hath commaunded, without hee stande very sure vpon his guarde? without he keepe a good watche? and chiefly except he separate him selfe from so great a number of corruptions? For at this daye a man can come in no company, but that the talke shall tende to the dishonouring of God, with all vngodlinesse: or els the talke shall bee so vaine, as that it shall haue no good sauoure, yea, and too make whatsoeuer good seede that is in any man, who is yet teacheable, to bee nothing worth. And yet many times this shall not bee the greatest mischiefe: but a man shall heare the most cursed blasphemies that may be vometed out by these grenning helhoundes at this day, who are growne to the full measure of impudencie, like vnto shamelesse harlottes, discouering their vilanies not onely against God and all true Christianitie, but doe also euen like mastife curres barke against al religion. This we see, let vs then come to the greatest number of those which seeme to bee a little more tollerable, I beseeche you what lesson or fruite shall wee reape by them?

The 15. Sermon of M. Jo. Cal.

We shall finde some of them to vse aboundance of wicked traffique, craftes, deceiptes, or els outrages, violences, opprefsions and cruelties againſt their neighbours. Another sorte shalbe giuen to lechery, and to such beaſtlineſſe: another kinde shall bee gluttons and such like brutish people of life and conuerfation. To be short, turne which way soeuer we will, and wee shall finde nothing but corruption: so that if this doctrine hath beene any time neceſſarily to bee taught, it is at this moſt neceſſary and hie time, since wee are come euen to so full a meafure & bottomleſſe depth of iniquitie, let vs then be well aduifed too departe from all those that worke iniquitie, yea and let vs chafe them farre from vs, if we will faithfully and truely ferue God.

It is moſt fure that we muſt needes be conuerſaunt with the vngodly, or els departe out of this worlde at once: but yet we muſt not keepe them companie so familiarly, as too drawe with them in the same yoke. Let vs take heede that wee in no wayes wynde our felues in with them: but that our life and conuerfation bee so simple and playne, as that they be neuer able to bring vs in, and to bee infected with their vices. For we heare what the holy ſcripture faieth that we had no needc of any thing to corrupt good manners. For as a little leauen sowreth the whole lumpe of dough, euen so when the deuill can thruſt in amongſt vs the leaſt drop of corruption, loe all shall be peruerted and come to naught. We see not at the firſt sight howe the deuill goeth about to beguile vs, and therefore we ought to be so much the more watchfull. Let the vngodly complaine as much as they will, as wee see at this daye the murmurers and grudgers doe, that they thinke them felues to bee ill dealt withall, when as we will not be partakers of their filthines. Nowe wee knowe right well that they feeke none other thing but too make wicked, whatſoeuer is well ruled and ordered, too ouerthrowe whatſoeuer hath beene builded vp in GOD, and too bring foules too deſtruction. All this wee knowe. Nowe if any man keepe him felfe from this, hereat they are all grieued.

Howe

vpon the Cxix. *Pſalme.* 125

Howe ſo? They ſay our company is eſchewed. Yea, but giue you the occaſion that you may be followed, ſeeke the right meane to giue your ſelues to God, and follow you the right way of ſaluation, and the better ſorte will not abſent them ſelues farre from you, but will rather ioyne with you. If they ſhall ſee you ready to march forward, they will ſay, Let vs goe togither: If they ſhall ſee you goe before, they will come after: if they ſhall ſee you tarry behinde, ſo that you be entred into the right way, they will ſtirre you vp too followe them. But when as we ſee ſuch kinde of people to goe cleane backwarde from all goodneſſe, and deſire nothing elſe but to leade vs too wickedneſſe, yea too caſt vs downe hedlong with them into hell mouth, whereinto they ronne like mad men, what ſhould we doe but ſeparate our ſelues from amongſt them, and retire vs from thence, as Dauid ſheweth vs. And namely he ſayth, *For I wil keepe the commaundements of my God.* As if he ſhould haue ſayd, Theſe curſed men doe right well ſhewe that they haue no feeling nor knowledg of euerlaſting life, but that they liue here like to brute beaſtes: Neuertheles for my parte I will not goe one foote forwarde with them, but will goe towards my God. And out of this ſaying we are to gather a good inſtruction, to wit that when we ſee rounde aboute vs all people giuen ouer to wickednes, that it ſeemeth the worlde hath conſpired to make the maieſtie of God nothing worth, that wee declare by our liues and conuerſation, that wee haue no knowledge of euerlaſting life : when as then wee ſhall ſee ſuch impieties, it is euen to this end and purpoſe too withdrawe vs quite and cleane from our God. It is very true, that theſe are very daungerous offences and temptations. But let vs alwayes be ſure to abide firme, and ſtedfaſt, let vs continue conſtant in this trueth which once we haue receiued. See then what Dauid meaneth to expreſſe in this ſaying, *My God.* It is true that the faithfull will often ſay thus. But when there is any queſtion to make theſe compariſons with contrary thinges, the ſcripture vſeth not this ſaying, *My God,* ſo that it is to declare vnto vs, that nothing ought

to

The 15. Sermon of M. Io. Cal.

to make vs wauer: when we see the thinges confused in the worlde, when we shall see all whatsoeuer to be there peruerted and ouerthrowne, that there is neither any more lawe nor order, that it seemeth vnto vs as it were an Hell, let vs not for all that bee shaken: Let vs stande still vppon our guarde, as the Prophet Abacuc thereof speaketh, our faith must serue vs in steade of a Tower, wherein we keepe good watch, and yet too say notwithstanding, no, no, God will tarry with me, and then I neede not to care for the whole worlde. See then that no temptations ought to quaile vs: beeing euen inclosed amidst the impieties and abhominaons of the faithlesse, seeing we cannot otherwise chose but to bec conuersaunt amongest them. It followeth nexte after,

Abac. 1. 12.

Establish me, or stay me, in thy worde that I may liue: and let me not be disapoynted of mine hope.

Although Dauid protesteth heere aboue, that he trusted in God, and that this hope proceeded vnto him from his worde: yet prayeth hee his maiestie notwithstanding too establish him. Wherin he sheweth vs, that we shal neuer haue so well profited neither in faith, nor yet in hope, but that there shalbe alwayes some want, and remnaunt of incredulitie and weakenesse in vs, so that whensoeuer there shall be any question of comming to God, yet shall wee goe as it were halting vnto him. Now if Dauid hath made such a request, I beseech you, haue not wee a greate deale more neede to doe it aswell as hee? It is moste sure, that he neuer spake it hypocritically. When he saith, *Vpholde me, or establish me in thy word*: this is not too make a shewe that his fayth was imperfect, and that hee needed not be strengthened: no, not so, but he knewe well inough his owne infirmitie. If he then who was as it were an Angell of God, had need to profite in fayth, and in hope, and that hee had beene moulten, and beene quite consumed had not God through ly confirmed and established him: I pray you what shall we doe?

So then, when as God shall haue already shew'd vs this
fauour

fauour too bee surely grounded in his woord, so that wee are able to say that we trust in it, let vs not cease notwithstanding to continue this request and say, O Lorde, establish and confirme mee. For when wee shall well consider our weakenesse, wee shall finde that a very small thinge will quayle vs, if God holdeth vs not vp with his hand and power. And afterwarde let vs consider howe boysterous the assaultes of Satan are, what violence he bringeth against vs: and are we euer able too withstand them, if that wee bee not dayly strengthened? They then which shall haue conceiued a true hope in the woord of God, let them knowe that they are yet but in the midde way, and that they must alwayes march furtherforward, vntill such time as they are come to the ende thereof. Which thing shall neuer be, vntill they are vncased of this fleshe, and are departed out of this present life.

Seeing then wee cannot goe forwarde as of our selues, nor yet be strengthened, without God assist vs: Let vs beseech him after the example of Dauid, that hee will confirme vs in his woorde. And afterwarde hee addeth and sayth,

That then he shall liue: and disappoint me not, saith he, *of my hope.*

When he sayeth that he shall liue, It is to shewe vs, that all our felicities lyeth in this, that wee are thoughly confirmed and fully setled in the word of God. When this shalbe so, let vs then feare no more. It is very true, that we shal neuer be but subiect to a greate many of myseryes and afflictions, for it cannot be otherwise but that this life muste be full of afflictions, and many griefes and vexations. Wee are then to fight whiles we liue in this worlde. And so wee shall finde a great number of miseryes, and yet we shall not choose but to liue still, when we shall bee throughly founded vppon the woorde of God: that is to say, our saluation shall be sure and certaine euen amidst all the afflictions which may come vnto vs. And so shall wee haue wherewith to be contented.

For

The 14. Sermon of M. Io. Cal.

For vnder this woorde, *to liue*, Dauid comprehendeth all whatsoeuer concerneth the welfare and felicitie of men. He sayth then, Although O Lorde, I shalbe taken as a miserable creature, and that in deede I shall abide many troubles which shall be greeuous vnto me: yet shall I haue true life and saluation, so I be thus established in thy word. Now he addeth a little more, Let me not be disapoynted of mine hope: wherein his meaning is to signifie, that God neuer suffereth his Children to be disapoynted, when as they put their trust in him: But yet the case so standeth, as that wee must so beseech him by reason of our weakenesse. For although we trust in God, yet for all that we goe coldely vnto him, and wee shall finde our faith to be alwayes too too weake and feeble.

To be short, our heartes shalbe so shutte vp, as that the graces of God, as touching our selues, shall hardly water it by dropmeale. It is very true that God for his parte poureth vppon vs his graces abundauntly: but we therein are nothing capable for the receiuing of them. Wherefore, wee are not worthy to tast and feele his ayde in our neede, What should this then be, if he surmounted not our hope, to help that which therein is wanting? And besides we knowe that the Deuill would soone ouerthrow al our hope, were it not that it is very well kepte by an heauenly power, as also S. Peter maketh thereof mention. For when he speaketh of faith, he sayth not that men are the Gardians or keepers of it. For if that were so, it should oftentimes bee violently taken from them. But that is a treasure which God keepeth in his own hands, and that by his owne inuincible power and strength. See also why our Lorde and Sauiour Christ in the 10. of Iohn, for our comforte saith, That the father who hath vs in his hand, and through whome wee are committed vnto him to be kept, is mightier and greater then they all. Accordingly then as wee knowe, the power of God to be infinite, so must we also assure our selues of our saluation. And therefore it is, that wee are to require of God as Dauid hath done, that we be not disapointed of our hope.

Nowe

2. Pet. 1.

Ioh. 10, 24.

vpon the Cxix. Psalme. 127

Nowe in summe when we make such requests, it is too the end that the promises of God should be so much the more certaine and better ratified vnto vs. See then what God sayth vnto vs. Feare you not when as you shall put your trust in me, for I will nether deceiue, nor abuse you, ne yet shall you be destitute of mine ayde: but be you assured that my hande shall alwayes be streatched out to succour you. We haue this promise made vnto vs which can neuer faile vs. Now it behoueth that it be ratified and sealed in our heartes. And how is that? That in our prayers and supplications, we beseech God to accomplish and performe that which he hath promised, which shall be in steade of a seale sealed within, to the ende we might haue such a certaintie as is requisite: and anon after God sheweth in effecte, that he speaketh not in vaine vnto vs. Loe, say I, what wee ought to note of the accorde that is betwixt the promises of God & the prayers which we make vnto him in desiring to make vs feele by experience, that he is faithfull in whatsoeuer he speaketh. Nowe Dauid by and by addeth,

Holde thou me vp and I shall be safe: yea and my delight shall be continually in thy statutes.

Nowe the word which he vseth, signifieth somtimes to meditate, sometimes to speake: & therfore it may bee said I wil recite ouer thy Statutes. But the most proper sense & meaning is, I will meditate or study in thy Statutes, and therein take delight. In steade that before he hath sayd, *Establish me O Lord, or stay me in thy worde*: Heere hee sayth, *Holde mee vp.* Nowe this is no simple and plaine prayer which heere he maketh, but hauing spoken of the woorde of God, he speaketh of the power which hee sheweth towards his faithfull. It is very true, that when wee thinke that wee haue not one foote of grounde too stand vppon, that there is nothing but the sea vnder vs, and darkenesse ouer vs, that we should be as it were in a bottomlesse pitte, and ouerwhelmed: yet we ought to stay & settle our selues on the worde of God. But when as our hope shall be thus exercised, and that we haue doone God this honor, to hold
him

The 15. Sermon of M. Io. Cal.

him for faythful, although we do not perceiue any succour to come from him: hee will adde a second grace, to wit, he will giue vs his hand, to be releeued by his powre, and to be vpholden by him, and wil preserue vs all the dayes of our life. Loe heere the the meaning of Dauid, whē he desired God to stay him in his woord, he sayth, Holde me vp, yea by thy hand and power. So then, let vs learne to flye vnto God, when as we would be in any good safetie. For without it, as I haue already sayde, wee may very wel for a while assure our selues: and thinke no euill can come vnto vs: But when as we shall be thus foolishly persuaded, too say peace and assuraunce, destruction must needes suddainly come vpon vs, and we to be vtterly confounded. But after we haue wayted and seene God too haue appeared in very deed, let vs learne to seeke all our assuraunce in his woord, to walke in his cōmandements, to take our whole delight in them, and in them to bestowe all our study. In summe, Dauid in this place declareth, That when as God shall haue bestowed any benefites vpon vs, that wee haue prooued his mercie, and fatherly affection: It is to cōfirme vs more and more in his word, to tye all our senses therto: to learne to forsake all vanities, which hinder and occupy our spirits in these wilde affections wherewith wee are carryed hither and thither. That we then beeing retired from them might be inflamed with such a zeale as Dauid was to meditate in the commaundements of God, and in them too take our whole delight. Nowe it followeth,

1. Thess. 5. 3.

Thou haste troden downe all them that departe from thy statutes: for their deceite is vaine.

Heere in this place Dauid considereth of the iudgementes of God, which hee executeth vpon the wicked: howbeit we are not alwayes able to perceiue them. For we shall oftentimes see (as it were against all Gods forbod, as wee say) the wicked to beare auchoritie, and in such sorte to triumph, as that they think it cannot be possibly amended

vpon the Cxix. Pſalme. 128

ded, and ſuppoſe them ſelues to be the moſt bleſſed people in the worlde. And then for the while we ſhall ſee all things goe cleane againſt the haire. But after that the Lorde God ſhall long time paciently haue abidden all theſe abuſers of his mercifull louing kindeneſſe: it cannot bee choſen but that at the laſt hee muſt vtterly deſtroy them. And ſo let vs conſider not too be ſo blockiſh as too forget the iudgements of God: but let them rather inſtructe vs after the example of Dauid, to walke in his feare and to loue his Commaundementes.

Now he ſayth in the firſt place: *Thou haſte troden the vngodly vnder foote, and all them that departe from thy ſtatutes, for they imagine but deceite*, ſayth hee. He addeth one reaſon, which we ought throughly too weigh: For what is the cauſe that the vngodly hearké not vnto God, & ſo outrage againſt him beyond all meaſure: For if at any time GOD mooueth them too repentaunce, through the admonitions of his woorde, they doe nothing elſe but ſcoffe and laugh at him: yea they are ſo ſhameleſſe, as it is pitifull too ſee? What is the cauſe of this? It is becauſe the wicked haue their heartes faſte ſhutte vpp in their backe warchouſes, thinking thereby to beguile GOD, too eſcape his hand through their ſtarting holes, and ſubtile deuiſes, and they ſeeing them ſelues too be braſen faced, to couer their villanyes before men, thinke that they ſhall eaſily inough put of the plagues and puniſhmentes of God.

See howe the wicked doe increaſe in their willes, that they are euen come too this poynte that they feare nothing at all of what ſoeuer they ought too bee affrayde. And this is it why the Prophet Iſaiah alſo ſayth, That they *Iſaiah.* digge Caues in the earth for their defence, thinking that when their eyes are ſhutte vppe, that their ſinnes ſhall be no more ſeene, and that God ſhall not bee able too finde them. Accurſed bee you (ſayth hee,) which thus digge deepe pittes.

Nowe

The 15. Sermon of M. Io. Cal.

Now Dauid sayth in this place, that all the subtiltie of the vngodly is nothing else but vanitie. It shall bee forsooth to great purpose for them, when (as they thinke) they shall through their hypocrisies shroude them selues and couer their wiles and subtilties: yet shall their deuises bee but vanitie: for they shalbe taken in the tripp, as it is sayde in the other place, yea and in the ende shall be fast shutte vp in all their deceits and inuentions. Heereupon he sayeth,

Thou hast taken away all the vngodly of the earth like drosse: therefore I loue thy testimonies.

Heere Dauid declareth vnto vs in breefe by his example, That when God punisheth the Godlesse, he layeth his hand vpon them, in such sort as that we may perceiue that he sheweth him selfe to be their Iudge, to the ende that wee thereby should be the rather stirred vp too loue his Commaundemens, and to be ruled by them in bestowing al our desire and affection vpon them. See then howe the iudgements and corrections which God layeth vpon the vngodly ought to profite vs. And this is it why Saint Paule in exhorting the faythfull to walke holyly, and to abstaine from all pollution sayth, *Take heede that you be not beguiled through vaine woords: For, for such thinges the wrath of God commeth vpon the children of disobedience.*

Ephe. 5.6.

Now it is true, that before God hath executed his iudgementes we ought already to be instructed too walke in his feare. But when God sheweth vs openly howe he putteth to his helping hand, it is good reason that wee should be so much the more attentiue to his Iudgements. And loe why the Prophet Isaiah sayth, That when God executeth his Iudgementes, that the inhabitantes of the earth might learne, that he dooth it righteously. Moreouer, let vs consider how slack we are to come vnto God, that hee is faine to drawe vs perforce vnto him. Ought not we euen to run vnto him, so often as he lifteth vp his finger vnto vs? So often as he shall open his holy mouth to instruct, and shew vs the way of saluation, should we slacke and deferre it from day to day? But what? Marke the peruersnesse, and that not only

Esa. 59.17.18

vpon the Cxix. Psalme. 129

only of the most wicked, but euen of the holyest and perfectest which are intected with this vice. See what Dauid sayth, that he had neede to be pricked forward like an Asse: yea euen Dauid himselfe, who was the most forwarde of all other according to the graces which he had receiued. If it hath so fallen out with him, by reason of the reste of the imperfection which he had, that hee was spurred, and his fleshe pricked like an Asse: what shall become of vs which haue scarcely receiued one drop of the spirit of God, in respect and comparison of this holy mane? And so, let vs consider to be the more watchfull ouer our selues so often as God sheweth vs any token that hee is Iudge, and calleth the vngodly to an accounte: that at the leaste we be stirred vp to run vnto him for refuge, and to loue his word. Nowe in the meane time, to conclude Dauid addeth,

My flesh trembleth for feare of thee: and I am afraide because of thy iudgementes.

Heere Dauid setteth downe two things which seeme at the first sight not to agree togither: For it may bee sayde, that this feare whereof he speaketh can no way agree with the feare of the commaundements of God: but yet there is a sweete hermony betweene the one and the other. And why so? For as the faithles in fearing God wax desperate, & are so thrown down, that they can neuer haue that boldnes to come neere vnto him: Euen so on the cōtrary side, there is a frank & free feare in those which are gouerned by the spirit of God, which beareth a reuerence vnto his woorde, to make them tremble before it. For by the iudgementes which Dauid heere speaketh of, he meaneth not the punishments onely which God executeth, but nowe hee treateth as he doth throughout the whole Psalme, either of Statuts or else of ordinaunces, which are to direct our life: as also the Prophet Isaiah saieth, that the faithfull tremble at the voice of God: that they conceiue his incomprehensible maiestie in his word, and thervpon are humbled: But yet they cease not sot all that, too come boldely vnto GOD, knowing that he wil be their mercifull father and desireth

R. nothing

The 15. Sermon of M. Io. Cal.

nothing else but to receiue them. This humble feare then, may well be conioyned with the loue of God, agree with faith, and with a taste which we might take in the worde of God, in giuing our selues wholy thereto. But the feare, which serueth to none other ende but to astonish the wicked, which onely feele an hell in their consciences, and yet haue no taste of the grace of God: this feare I say serueth to none other purpose, but to shut vpp the gate against these miserable accursed people, without all hope of saluation. Now Dauid speaking of the feare of the word of God, leadeth vs to a deeper and a more weightie consideration. For his meaning is to shewe vnto vs, how that God is our father and Sauiour, and that he freely draweth vs vnto himselfe, as already he hath declared.

According to this holy doctrin, let vs prostrate ourselues before the maiestie of our good God, in acknowledging our offences, beseeching him that it would please him too make vs to feele the sweetenesse of his worde, as his seruant Dauid hath beene thereon throughly setled: too the ende we might haue such a feruent affection to it, as that it might cause vs to forget all the desires of this worlde, wherein wee are too too much plagued: and that wee might cut of all the superfluties of our flesh: to the ende we might be dedicated in all holinesse vnto our God, and to be confirmed more & more in his seruice. And that being once brought by him into the way of saluation, although we must walke in this world, because we are compassed about with so many daungers: yet that he will alwayes stretch forth his hand vnto vs, to keepe and hold vs in his protection vnto the end. That hee will not onely graunt vs this grace, but also vnto all people and nations of the worlde, &c.

The

The xvi. Sermon vpon the hundreth and nineteenth Psalme.

AIN.

I haue executed Iudgement and iustice: giue me not ouer vnto mine oppressors.
Answere for thy seruaunt in that which is good: and let not the proude doe me wrong.
Mine eyes haue fayled in looking for thy saluation: and for thy iust promise.
Deale with thy seruant according vntoo thy louing mercies: and teach me thy statutes.
I am thy seruaunt, graunt mee therefore vnderstanding: that I may knowe thy testimonies.
It is time for the Lorde too lay to his hand: for they haue destroyed thy lawe.
Therefore loue I thy Commaundementes, aboue golde: yea aboue moste fine golde.
Therefore I esteeme all thy commaundements most iust: and all false wayes I vtterly abhorre.

HE holy Scripture oftentimes admonisheth vs, that if wee will haue God to stand with vs against our enemyes, wee must walke perfectly and soundly: For if wee will bee like the wicked, rendering euill for euill, it is in vaine for vs too hope that God will be on our side, either yet fauour vs: But it is meete that he be iudge on both partes, when

vniuſtly oppreſſed, and alſo of the miſerable and afflicted. Now if we haue ſuch wicked hearts, to inforce vs to wicked dealing, how ſhall God put foorth his hand too ayde vs? For then muſte hee intermedle himſelfe with a naughtie cauſe, which is an impoſſibilitie, and altogither contrary to his nature. See then wherefore it is ſaide in this place,

I haue executed iudgement and iuſtice: giue me not ouer vnto mine oppreſſors.

Dauid heere maketh a requeſt vnto God, that he might not bee deliuered into the handes of his enemyes which ſought to deſtroy him. Nowe for the obtayning of that which he demaunded, he maketh this proteſtation, That hee hath walked rightly before God, yea, euen with them which went about to deſtroy him. Moreouer theſe twoo wordes, *Righteouſneſſe and Iudgement:* when they goe togither, importe aſmuch as too doe wrong too none: but too proceede in equitie, and in good fayth (as we ſay) for too maintaine euery good cauſe, and not to ſuffer any wronge to bee doone: For it is not inough for vs too abſtaine from hurting and greeuing of our neighbour. Neither is it enough for vs to goe aboute to diſcharge vs of our dueties? But when wee ſhall ſee any man vniuſtly troden down, and a good cauſe goe too wrack, wee ought too oppoſe our ſelues againſt euery ſuch wicked acte and iniury, and as it were to take parte with God, who as he is the commender of all equitie, ſo will hee alſo haue vs to maintaine it foraſmuch as we are his children. We ſee then in ſumme, the proteſtation which Dauid heere maketh, that is, that he did not only abſtaine from hurting his neighboures, & go about to render to euery man, that which was his: But ouer & beſids al this he ſet himſelf againſt al violences & extortiõs which were

were cõmitted, he would not suffer the innocent to be oppressed to be put forth for a pray or spoyle, but payned himselfe to doe what in him lay to helpe them. Whẽ we may be bolde too make such a protestation in trueth, Let vs not dout but that God will stretch foorth his hand: that if men went about to trouble vs, yea and that wee were as it were in great daunger too fall into their hands, Let vs not doute but that God will haue pittie on vs and ayde vs. For this Prayer which Dauid heere maketh was not made at aduenture: but the holy Ghoste put it into his mouth, to the end to teach vs to walke (as he hath doone) so soundly & perfectly. And heerevpon, if men should lifte themselues vpp against vs, and vse all the outrages and malice they can against vs, Let vs haue recourse vnto God, & be assured that he will be our defendor and protector.

Now we very well see by this, that Dauid made no mention of his merites vnto God, as if he should haue sayde, I haue right wel deserued, O Lord, that thou shouldest keepe and defend me against the wicked, because I haue doone that which is lawfull and right. Dauid spake it not too any such end. But he had regarde (as I haue already said) to the goodnesse of God and to his promisses which are contayned in the lawe, and imprinted in his heart: too wit, That God will vpholde all those that are vniustly troden down, and alwayes helpe those which are outraged and iniuryed: Because that they for their parte haue taken great paine to be at peace withall the world: that they haue not giuen occasion for any to greeue and torment them, and yet that the vngodly haue rysen vp against them. See what a regarde Dauid had. Nowe he addeth,

Answere thou for thy seruant in that which is good: and let not the proude doe me wrong.

The saying that Dauid heere vseth, signifieth sometimes a man to giue his woord, as we say in this countrie: that is, to become a mans suretie, and his pleadge, and some there are which doe so expound it: but the true sense and moste naturall

naturall meaning of it is this, that Dauid prayeth that hee might be giuen to doe good and to delight therein. Wherin wee see this to be a woorke of GOD, and a grace proceeding from him, when we shall desire too be giuen too doe good, so that we haue pleasure in it, and doe taste therof. For this is very certaine, that notwithstanding that men followe the very inclination of their flesh, to hate the good and loue the euil: and when any thing shall be tolde them of God, we see howe it maketh them Melancolique and sorowfull. So then, it is God that muste chaunge and reforme vs, or else we shall neuer attaine to this affection here spoken of, to take pleasure in wel dooing, and so to loue it.

Nowe Dauid was no hypocrite, too make a faire shewe, to desire a thing at the handes of God, which was in his owne hand: But he knewe this too be the manner of men, that it was impossible for him to come to the ful perfection of that, except it were giuen vnto him from aboue. See heere in summe, what we haue to learne and keepe by this. For whē he addeth that the wicked (or the proude) outrage against him, he sheweth that when we shall be so giuen too well dooing, we must trust too the protection of God according to that which I haue already saide. Let vs also note that Dauid in this verse confirmeth the matter already handled. He hath heeretofore very well said, O Lorde, I haue done the thing that is lawfull and right: and yet hee ceaseth not to beseech God too graunt him such courage and strength. And howe is that? Forsooth, that he woulde increase it in him, & giue him the grace to stande stedfastly therein vnto the ende. We see then, that whensoeuer wee shall be the moste desirous in the worlde, to followe sinceritie & equitie: we must vnderstand for all that, that we may yet be amended, and that we are nothing neere that perfection which is requisite.

Wherfore it remayneth that we desire this performance with the graces that Dauid hath heere demaunded: Thy graces O Lord, had neede to increase in vs, graunt vs therfore that we may come too the accomplishment of them.

Wee

him to conserue and increase it, considering that we are very farre from such a perfection as is most requisite: in such sorte as that wee neuer decline from well dooing, which we should doe if he shaked his hande. See then too what end this petition tendeth which is heere placed.

Nowe we must turne againe to the matter, to wit, that Dauid heere repeateth, that they which haue beene thus perfect, & haue loued welldoing, should be vnder the hand and safegarde of God, neuer to be deliuered into the power of their enemyes, so that the proude shall neuer be able to doe them that excceeding great wrong which they had pretended: Not that they shall not be assayled, neither yet that the wicked will not craftely goe about to worke them mischiefe: but yet so, as that God will be their buckler, and defend them with his mightie power. And namely hee sayth, *The proude*. Becaufe that they which are our enemyes, and make warre against vs, haue such an vnbrideled libertie, as that they thinke neither God nor yet any other liuing creature is able to stay them, but that they will bring to passe whatsoeuer they haue determined. Since then it is so, that we haue too deale with such kinde of people as are both stout and cruel, who lifte them selues vpp against all trueth, that neither the feare of G O D, nor yet naturall honesty can stoppe them, but that they will destroye whether it be right or wrong as we say: for this cause Dauid sayth, *O Lord let not the proude doe me wrong*. And so as often as we shall see this boldenesse in men, to lift them selues vp, and to vomit out their pestilent malice against vs, let vs flye vnto G O D, and beseech him too holde his holy hande ouer vs, & to represse so great and insolent arrogancie. This beeing done, although men for their partes make such attempts

tempts, yet shall they neuer bring them to passe. For God will holde them back, as it were with a sharpe brake.

Nowe if this petition came euer in season, it commeth nowe at this day in very good season. For wee see how many the enemyes of God are which bend themselues against the Gospell: wee see the malice and obstinacy throughout the whole worlde. And so, it is not possible but that a man which feareth God, must needes be assayled & troubled on all sides. Seeing then that men are so furious to wrong vs, so much the rather ought we to be carefull to make this request vnto God with Dauid, yea and that with such a confidence, as that we should not doubt but that when wee are vnder his protection, he shall bee sufficient too maintaine and defende vs. Nowe it followeth:

Mine eyes haue fayled in looking for thy saluation: and for thy iust promise.

We shall not neede to stande long vppon this sentence, because it hath beene already handled heere before. Dauid onely protesteth, that he hath looked for such helpe from God, as he desired. And that is to shewe, that he prayed not hypocritically, but faythfully. And this is a thing which we ought throughly to marke. For wee thinke our selues too haue doone very substancially and sufficiently, when as wee haue pronounced and rightly placed our words in the time of prayer: but if wee shall haue spoken neuer so loude, and with neuer so full and open mouth, and yet haue emptie or fast closed vp heartes, emptie I say, and voyde of all trust and fast closed vpp, it is a moste manifest token that wee neuer surely looked for any succour at the hands of God: and therefore beholde why of very right all our prayers are vnprofitable and to no purpose. And so, when as wee wil beseech the Lord our god to take our cause into his hãd to help vs, let vs take this with vs which dauid here sheweth in this place by his example: to wit, let vs attend and looke for our saluation and deliuerance from God: Yea and let vs cõsider of that which is said, & according to the word of thy righteousnes. For by this he signifieth to vs, vpõ whom we

must

must looke and cast our eyes, when as we would throughly stirre vp our selues vnto such an hope: to wit, vnto the promises which God hath giuen vs: for if this be not in vs, it can neuer be said to be any more hope, but a vaine imagination which we haue forged too our selues: for to hope or trust in God, is to be established in his promises. For if a man imagine a thing which seemeth good in his own sight, & after, leaneth thereto, this mā trusteth not in God but in him self. So then, if we looke to haue any help at the hāds of God, we must haue a sure testimonie of his will, we must be sure that he loueth vs, and that when he loueth vs, hee will not fayle vs in our neede. And how shal we be assured of this? It shalbe by the onely meane of his worde. Nowe bicause men are so hard to be brought to rest them selues vpon God, and not to cōtent them with his promises, Dauid saith these promises to be iust, according to the word of thy righteousnesse, saith he. It is not in vayne that hee thus intituleth the word of God. And why so? For he thinketh that if he haue but his bare worde, that it is enough for him. And why so? For God maketh not vnto vs liberall and large promises as men doe, and then deceiueth vs. His wordes are iust. And as he saieth in an other place, his wordes are like to pure siluer which is tried in the fier, and hath beene seuen times purified in the furnace. Euen so is it with all the promises of God, we ought to be very assured of them: Bicause hee is faithfull and iust, and that there is nothing but righteousnesse and truthe in all that he sayth. Now Dauid goeth further on: for he speaketh not of a simple affection: But saith, that his eyes haue fayled, as if he should haue said, that he was hardly so resolued and not without great paine. By this hee sheweth vs, that his faith was so troubled, as that hee knewe not what would become of him, that hee had great and strong conflictes, that he was in marueilous anguishes, & troubles, so that he was as a man halfe dead: and yet that he was armed and fenced amiddest al these hard cases, with the hope & trust which he had in God. See what the wordes import which he vseth, that his eyes fayled for the health,

Psal. 12.6.

R 5 and

The 16. Sermon of M. Io. Cal.

and succoure, which hee looked for at the handes of God. Will we then haue a right hope, and such an one as God alloweth of? Let vs then not trust onely when wee are quiet and at rest, ne yet be throwne downe by any temptations: but when as we shalbe in our extreamest troubles that wee know not at all what shal become of vs, that we shal see nothing els but death before vs and round about vs: here vpon, I say, let vs alwayes be firme and constant, trusting that God will be our sauiour, since he hath so promised vs. Loe how we may make this protestation as Dauid here doeth. Nowe it followeth,

Deale with thy seruant according to thy louing mercies: and teache me thy statutes.

Here it may very wel seeme that Dauid maketh two petitions, but yet they tende both to one ende. For in the first part of this verse, he sheweth, how he desireth, and trusteth to be heard: to wit, through the meere mercy of God. As if he should haue said, O Lorde, teach me thy statutes: and teach mee them, not for that I thinke my selfe worthy of them, but bicause thou art pitifull, and knowest my neede, and hast promised also to helpe all those which call vppon thee. Deale then, O Lorde, with thy seruant according too thy mercie, to the ende thou mightest teache me. By this we see that, which I haue already touched : to wit, that this verse conteineth not two petitions, but one onely. And yet notwithstanding Dauid so setteth it forth, in declaring that when he commeth to God to praye him to teach him, that he doeth it not to the ende that hee presumeth of his merittes, neither yet to make vaunt that hee deserueth any thing of him. Wherefore then? Forsooth bicause hee looketh and trusteth to the meere mercy of God. And in very dede, this is a farre more precious thing then that which Dauid here demaundeth, to be taught the statutes of God, to say that it hangeth not vpon our merites, neither yet of any worthinesse of ours. It is a question to know the way of euerlasting life, and wherein it consisteth & lieth. It is very meete then that God do it, bicause he is pitifull: that he vse

his

vpon the Cxix. Pſalme. 134

his goodneſſe towardes vs, and looketh to none but vnto him ſelfe, bicauſe he is good, and that it pleaſeth him to put to his helping hand to thoſe which are his. Now although he hath here ſpoken of an excellent thing, yet of all the petitions which wee make, were they the leaſt in the worlde, we alwaies ought to laye this foundation, yea, and to ſtaye vpon it, that is, vpon the mercie of God. If we ſhould onely demande but a droppe of water or a morcell of bread, wee muſt not thinke too obtaine, by reaſon of our deſert, as if God paid vnto vs our wages: but his mercy muſt alwaies go before, for that is the cauſe why we receiue ſo many benefits at his hand, and eſpecially that we are taught his ſtatutes.

Now it followeth, *I am thy ſeruaunt, graunt me therefore vnderſtanding: that I may knowe thy teſtimonies.*

This is a more large expoſition of the verſe going before: he hath ſaid, O Lord, deale with me according to thy mercies, & now he ſaith, I am thy ſeruant. And how is this? it ſhould ſeeme that there is ſome diuerſitie betwixt theſe two ſayings. For doth not Dauid in calling him ſelf the ſeruant of God, ſet downe before, what ſeruice he hath done him? Nowe let vs note that for the firſt place that it is not ſaid for any bragge, nor that hee was ſo able a man to attaine vnto any ſuch worthineſſe, neither yet that he deſerued to be preferred before others: hee meaneth not that this honour apperteined vnto him of right. What then? It is as much as if he had ſaid, O Lord, I am thine. Now, commeth it of our ſelues, that wee are the ſeruauntes of God? haue wee obtained this eſtate, or degree as of our ſelues? Alas it is very farre of: for we haue it of free gift. Since the time that we were the bondſlaues of Satan, God hath takē vs vnto him ſelf, to be of his houſhold and of his number. In that then that we are his, it is not bicauſe wee haue deſerued it, but bicauſe hee hath called vs vnto him of his free mercie and goodneſſe. And in deede, if a man who was firſt of a baſe côdition, ſerueth a noble man, he will not ſay that he was worthy of the ſeruice of ſuch a maiſter, nor yet that he was put vnto him therefore: but wil thus ſay, ſir, I côfeſſe that you haue receiued me into your ſeruice of your meere

fauour

The 16. Sermon of M. Io. Cal.

fauour and grace, and haue done me the honour which appertained not vnto me. And thus should wee most wretched wormes of the earth say, Loe God, who ceaseth not still to do vs good: and yet we will bee so arrogant, as too determine to attribute vnto our selues I know not what, as though he had herein nothing to do with vs. Nowe I beseech you tell me whether is this to goe? And that which is more, let vs consider a little, what seruice it is that God might drawe and plucke out from vs, to doe vnto his maiestie. If he shall leaue vs vnto our selues to bee as wee are, about what shall he employe vs, and what seruice can we do him? For loe, both wee and all that is within vs are altogether giuen to wickednesse. Wee cannot once thinke any good: how shall we then do any? Next of all, Dauid meaneth not, that hee beeing called to serue God, was able too discharge himselfe thereof: for he felt him selfe vtterly vnable to do it. And so as touching this place, we must not thinke that he meant to make any vaut of the seruice which he had done to God, but it is as much as if hee had said, O Lord, thou hast shewed me that fauour and grace too bee one of thy number, and hast receiued me into it, through thy bountie and goodnes. I beseeche thee therfore to continue the same thy goodnesse and too heape grace vppon grace in me, as in that behalfe thou art wonted to do.

Let vs now come vnto his petition. He sayeth, *O graunt me vnderstanding, that I may keepe thy testimonies*.

We haue already saide, that hee handled that which he had lately spoken. For by these wordes he meaneth, that we should be alwayes like beastes, vntill such time as God had opened vnto vs the spirite or vnderstanding of humaine things. Wery well, yet shall we learne them according too our naturall disposition. It is very true, that it shalbe according to such measure, as God shall therein giue it vnto vs: but yet it is as it were after a naturall maner. Moreouer, when wee shall talke of the secretes of the heauenly life, & of the wisedome which God sheweth vnto vs in his worde: there must all men confesse, that all their senses faile them, and

and that all their reason is dead and buried. What is then to be done? Let vs come to the remedy which Dauid here giueth vs: to wit, that we desire of God to haue vnderstanding, that we might become very wel learned. For without that, we must continue and remaine still in our beastlinesse. And this prayer answereth and very well agreeth with that which we haue seene in the verse next before, as that matter hath beene already touched. Now it followeth soone after.

It is time for the Lorde to laye to his hand: for they haue destroyed thy lawe.

Here Dauid maketh a petition against the contemners of God, and transgressers of his lawe: saying, That it is time for the Lord to lay to his hād, since that he seeth his law to be so destroyed, that there is no accompt made of it. It is very true, that Dauid greatly desired the conuersion of all men, and by little and little their saluation. And it is no doubt but that hee prayed too God with a good affection, that it would please him to bring to repentance all those which he see to bee lead vnto wickednesse: but yet hee was not without this zeale which wee see in this place: that is, that God would execute his iudgements vpon the obstinate, and vpō all those which were altogether stubburne. And see also howe we ought to temper our affections, that when we see men go to do mischief, let vs haue compassion vpon them: if we se them giuen to sinne and wickednesse, if we see them to be in the way of perdition, let vs trauell too bring them againe into the right way, to procure their saluatiō as much as in vs lieth, and we ought to desire and to pray for it, haue we had any such affection? Then let vs neuer cease to pray vnto God, to stretch forth his hand vpon those his enemies whom he knoweth to be altogether desperat. It is very true we must not condemne them: But wee ought rather, as I haue already said, to vse the effect of charitie towardes all, and pray vnto God that he would saue them: but bicause there are a great number which are stubburne and without amendement, we ought to beseech God, to shewe him
selfe

selfe a iudge ouer thofe whome hee knoweth to bee such. And why so? Bicaufe they drawe the simple and ignoraunt vnto wickednefse, and are an offence vnto them, bicaufe alfo they make the worde of God to be euil spoken of, and are the occasion that libertie is giuen to al euil. When then we see the name of God to be euill spoken of, that there is no reckening made of his word, that all doctrine is cast vnderfoote, we are to praye vnto him to remedie it. It is time, faith he, for God to lay to his hãd: for they haue destroyed thy lawe, O Lorde. He here speaketh in the third perfon: & after directeth him selfe to God. And why doth he so? Although that this order is not alwayes to bee obferued, that he which prayeth vnto God is to continue in one self same person: yet it is so, that in this place, it seemeth that Dauid meant to speake with a greater vehemency, when he sayth, O Lord, lay to thy hand. As if he should haue shewed, what the office of God is: for if hee had simply saide, It is time O Lord, that thou diddest looke vnto the matter, bicaufe thy lawe is destroyed: this had not beene spoken with the like vehemencie, as when he saide it is time that thou O Lorde, lay to thy hande: for by this saying, hee declareth what the office of God is: to wit, to be iudge of the worlde: and befeecheth him to lay foorth his iustice, in punishing the offences, and horrible wickednesses committed here below; that after he had suffered them a long time, he desireth him to prouide for the punishing of all those which had beene so obstinate, and hard hearted against him. Now by this we are admonished, when as we see that the law of God is as it were vtterly cast vnderfoote, his doctrine to be a reproche amongst men, and all right and equitie ouerthrowne, so that there is nothing but confusion throughout: that then we ought to pray vnto God the more earnestly, to the end it might be known that he doth his office. If this euer were necessary, it is at this prefent most necessary. For let vs cõsider the estate of the world I befeeche you, what hauocke is there made of the lawe of God? Are wee not come to the very extremitie, to contemne all doctrine of saluation? When God at this day speaketh vnto vs, what care giue we vnto

vpon the Cxix. Pfalme. 136

we vnto him? and how reuerently? See heere, hee hath beſtowed vppon vs a ſingular grace at this daye, when as his worde hath beene once againe publiſhed. Let vs beholde our vnthankefulneſſe? Let vs lay all theſe things together, and we ſhall ſee that the maieſtie of God his woorde is no more eſteemed then the very pyll of an onion, as wee ſaye. See I pray you too what a point wee are growne and come: euen vnto ſuch an horrible and brutiſhe impietie as is moſt lamétable. Moreouer, let vs looke into the maner of our life and the order of gouernement: ſhall we finde either iuſtice, loyaltie, reaſon, or modeſtie? no: but cleane contrary, wee ſhall ſee the whole ſtate of our life, and order of gouernement, full of treaſon, malice, crueltie, and violence: al full of blaſphemie againſt God: plentie of drunkenneſſe, gluttonie, and diſſoluteneſſe: ſtore of lecherie and all other vyllanies whatſoeuer: To be ſhort, it ſeemeth that the whole world hath conſpired to exceede euen vnto the higheſt degree of wickedneſſe. When then wee ſee the lawe of God to be thus ouerthrowne euery maner of waye, ought not wee to giue our mindes a great deale more then wee doe, to beſeeche God to take order, & to prouide for the ſame. Now when we ſhall haue ſuch a zeale to pray vnto God, as wee ſee that Dauid had, let vs not doubt but that he wil remedy all the confuſions which we ſee to be at this day. And now he concludeth, and ſayeth,

Therefore loue I thy commandementes: aboue gold yea aboue moſt fine golde.
Therefore I eſteeme all thy commaundements moſt iuſt: and all falſe maies I vtterly abhorre.

See here what a notable proteſtation he maketh, & ſuch one as we ought throughly to marke. For whē Dauid hath ſaid here before, that the wicked haue deſtroied the lawe: yea, & ſpeaking of no ſmall number of men, but as of all in general, ſeeing al the world to exceede & to be corrupt: hee addeth: for this cauſe, O Lord, I haue loued thy cōmandements, aboue all gold, yea and aboue moſt fine gold. I haue loued them in all & through al, & haue vtterly abhorred all falſe wayes. Nowe

The 16. Sermon of M. Io. Cal.

Nowe I haue saide that this is an excellent protestation, considering the circumstances. For if Dauid had dwelt amongest the godly faithfull ones, which had serued God, and walked in his feare: then it might haue beene said, that it was an easie matter for him to haue conformed him selfe vnto them. For although we see men alwayes enclined to euill, yet they are many times reduced and framed to goodnesse through good examples. But I pray you in what time was it that Dauid liued? Forsooth in such a time as that he was compassed with the despisers of God, hee see nothing but following of euill throughout the worlde, hee see as it were a madde and diuelish impietie, he see euery thing full of all infection: to bee short, there was neither iustice nor equitie, no feare of God, nor yet any religion. And yet notwithstanding he saith, that he loued the word of God, and his commaundements, and that hee made more accompt of them, then of all the most precious things in the world. Let vs then learne to loue the word of God, not only whē as wee shall be stirred vp by those which keepe vs company to serue God all with one accorde: but also when we shall bee amongest peruerse and frowarde people, that wee bee as it were in hell amiddest all the deuilles, yet to perseuer in this affection, and not to leaue following of the worde of God: that whatsoeuer offences wee shall see committed by men, that they withdrawe vs not from the loue which wee ought to beare to the woorde of God. See then what wee must keepe in minde for the vnderstanding of this text.

And after, we are too note for the last verse., that Dauid saying, that he loued the commaundementes of God, saith not that he did it by halfes, as wee many times doe: but I, sayeth hee, haue loued thy commaundements aboue all thinges. As if he should haue sayd, I am not like vnto those, O Lord, which come to serue thee by halfes: but in all and through all, I loue whatsoeuer that thou hast commaunded. And after this maner it is that we must also do: for it is not in vs to deuide and make a partition of the worde of God, neither yet can wee make it. And therefore, let vs bee

well

wel aduised to obey God, in whatsoeuer he shal commaund vs, and to loue his commandementes from the first too the last: and not to do as a great many do, which wil be contēted to receiue the Gospel, forsooth, so farre foorth as it wil serue their turne and pleasure them. Or els, if they passe ouer this or that: and thinke themselues to giue God greate credit, when as they shall giue him authoritie ouer them in some one point: But if soone after, they shall bee any thing grieued, they wil neuer ouerslip that point. Neuertheles we are there admonished too the contrary, that it is not for vs, as I haue already said to make a partition of that which god hath conioyned: but wee must yeelde our obedience vntoo him euen to the ful: that although whatsoeuer he saieth or commaundeth vs to do, be hard and sharpe too our nature, yet let vs take it in good parte with a gentle and mild mind; and say with Dauid, O Lord I haue loued thy commaundements which thou hast giuen me, not in one, two, nor three points, but in al and through al. According to this holy doctrine, let vs humbly prostrate our selues before the Maiesty of our good god, in acknowledging our offéces, beseeching him that it would please him to make vs better to feele our miseries, to the end we might be grieued with them and to seeke for remedy at his hands: That in renouncing whatsoeuer that is in vs, and whatsoeuer power and strength wee thinke our selues to haue, let vs beseech him to fortifie ys, and so to inlighten vs with his holy spirite, as that wee may more and more draw neare vnto him: And as hee hath already begunne to inlighten vs, that it would please him too cause vs to see his brightnes better than we haue don heretofore, vntil such tyme as we shal come vnto his kingdome, where we shal perfectly see that which now we do but halfe know. And although this worlde be so peruerse & wicked, as that we might take occasion to withdraw vs frō the right way: notwithstanding let vs beseech him, that he wil alwaies vphold vs with a mighty and strong hād, to thend wee may stand stedfastly in that wheruntō he hath called vs, & neuer decline frō it whatsoeuer came of vs. That it wold please, &c

S. The

The seuenteenth Sermon vpon the hundreth and nineteenth Psalme.

PHE.

Thy testimonies are wonderful: therefore doth my soule keepe them.

The entrance into thy wordes: sheweth light, and giueth vnderstanding vnto the simple.

I opened my mouth and panted: bicause I loued thy commaundementes.

Looke thou vpon me and be mercifull vnto me: as thou vsest to do vnto those that loue thy name.

Order my steppes in thy worde: and let no wickednesse haue dominion ouer me.

O deliuer me from the wrongfull dealings of men: and I will keepe thy commandements.

Shewe the light of thy countenance vpon thy seruant: and teach me thy statutes.

Mine eyes gushe out with ryuers of water: bicause men keepe not thy lawe.

IN very deede the sentence cõteined in this first verse of the eight, should be a very ordinarie and common thing with vs. And in very deede there is no man but will confesse it to be true: but yet it is so very far of, as that there is none of vs al which hath the feeling thereof in him selfe: that is, that the lawe of God is a wonderfull wisedome: for we doe see how it is contemned and despised. It is very true that God in all the

the holy scripture speaketh sharpely enough and also humbly: but it is for this cause that he would fit him selfe to our simple capacities. And bicause that wee are blockishe and earthly, it is meete that he should so plainely speake as that wee might vnderstand him. Neuerthelesse, in this speache, which carrieth no great glorie with it, ne yet is coloured with any worldly eloquence, are certaine secretes, which may very well rauish vs with marueilous astonishment. And in deede, the very cause why these faithlesse, and comtemners of God, so little esteeme of the doctrine of saluation, is, for that they beeing brutish, neuer tasted of that, which it meaneth to vtter. See then wherevpon this pride and vngodlinesse ariseth which wee see at this daye too bee in the greater parte of the worlde, so that there are very fewe which beare that reuerence to the woorde of God as they ought: for it is an olde saying, no man can loue a thing, before such time as he knoweth it. They then which are so blockish, as that they haue neither sense nor iudgement rightly to discerne of the truth of God, slippe it ouer, yea, and treade such an inestimable treasure as it is vnder their feete. But they which haue once knowne, what it is that God teacheth vs in the holy scripture, may very well saye with Dauid, that they are wōderful things, and so high mysteries as that we ought to wonder at them, & doe deserue that euery one of vs should wholy apply his mynd thereto. Nowe he sayeth, *That for this cause his soule did keepe the testimonies of God*. This importeth a greater matter, then if he had simply sayd, I haue kept them: for he signifieth that he hath kept them (as we say) with an hartie affection. And loe, howe in deede, we ought to esteeme of the doctrine of God: it is not onely to haue an opinion, that it is excellent, and worthy to be had in soueraigne and high honour: but that we should be very earnestly touched therwith that we might haue such a feare and an obedience rooted in our heartes, as that the saying of the Prophet Isaiah might bee fulfilled in vs, that we might treble at the voice of our God. Loe here in effect the content of the first verse, of these

The 17. Sermon of M. Io. Cal.

eight, which we are nowe about to handle: that is to saye, that the faithfull whose eyes God hath opened, might knowe, that the holy scripture conteineth no common doctrine, but such a wise doctrine as is worthy to be reuerenced and honoured all the world ouer. Nowe when as we shal once haue knowne that God layeth wyde opē his heauenly mysteries in his lawe, it is good reason that wee for our part be touched, & moued to hearken vnto our God when he speaketh vnto vs: yea and that in such sort, as that he handleth no small and light matters, and of no importance: but openeth vnto vs his mysteries, which are farre beyond our reach and capacities, except that of his infinite goodnesse, hee bare vs that fauoure too fit him selfe to our vnderstandings. Now Dauid addeth in the second verse:

The entrance into thy wordes, sheweth light and giueth vnderstanding vnto the most simple.

Wherein he signifieth, that if we vnderstand not all the mysteries of God which he sheweth vnto vs in his worde, we must not straightwayes therefore say, that the doctrine is vnprofitable vnto vs. Why so? Bicause the onely sauoure which we shall feele therein shall profit vs. It is not nedeful that wee bee great clarkes nor perfect doctors to receiue some benefite and edifying from the word of God: for we can not haue so small an entrance into it, but that wee shal become already both wise and well aduised. Loe here in summe the meaning of the second verse. And it is a place which we very well ought to obserue: for like as there are a great sort of people which make no accompt of the worde of God, bicause they neuer tasted of the mysteries therein conteined: euen so also there are some which excuse them selues and say that the worde of God is too too darke and harde, in so much that it maketh them too flie from it, & dare not come neare it.

Alas will one say, I am a very ignoraunt soule, or, I am not so sharpe witted as in deede a man would iudge: or els, I am but a simple scholler, and therefore can not conceiue of so high mysteries. Lo here what excuses a number of men
will

vpon the Cxix. Psalme. 139

will make, bicause they would not be acquainted with the word of God. No doubt of it we shall haue of those people which will vse such excuses and startingholes, onely bicause they would be ignorant, and haue their eyes fast closed vp, although they haue the light of God too shine vpon them. Againe there are another sort which will keepe themselues cleane away from the worde of God, fearing that if they should once enter into it, that it would be like vnto a maze wherein they should be held fast in and so bee vtterly confounded. And therefore, let vs for this cause throughly consider the saying of Dauid: to wit, that although wee attaine not vnto such a perfection, as that wee are able to vnderstand and know whatsoeuer is written in the holy scriptures, and to be so exercised therein euen at the full, as that nothing hath escaped vs: but let vs be throughly acquainted with the law, and haue the very true and vndoubted exposition and meaning of the Prophets, yea and let vs know and vnderstand the Gospel at our fingers endes: and yet although, I say we haue not attained vnto this excellency, let vs not for all this cease to bee inlightened. Let vs then boldly approche, when as we see that God calleth and allureth vs, and is ready to teach vs his word: and let vs know that when we shall haue neuer so little a tast thereof, that it shalbe for our saluation, so that we shall not be altogether blinde, but that we may be able to know which is the right way vnto euerlasting life. To be short, we shalbe inlightened as Dauid speaketh of in this place. And hereby we may see, what a great abuse at this day raigneth in this point in Poperie, when as they shall put by the greater part of Christendome from the reading of the holy scripture vnder a colour, it should thereby be vtterly confouded: and againe being neuer able once to come to haue any tast therof, that it is ouer high a thing for them to meddle with. Now, this is to make the holy Ghost a manifest liar, who hath spoken & pronoūced by the mouth of Dauid, that which we haue already heard, That the first entraunce into the woorde of God sheweth light: in so much that so soone as we shal haue

S 3　　　　　　vnder-

vnderstoode but one onely sentence thereof, the same to be already euen enough to leade and guide vs to euerlasting life. Now sithens then wee see how the deuill possesseth the Papistes, when as vnder such a cloke, they withdrawe the simple people from the reading of the word of God, yea in forbidding it them with such a cruell tyranny: let vs for our part, hauing so good and sure a ground, take great heede how we wauer, and how we alwayes abide wittingly ignorant, considering that God hauing openly and at large manifested himselt vnto vs, cōtinueth still more and more our good God, and giueth vs so great leisure and large a time to profit in his schoole. And why so? Bicause thentree alone is cleare and bright: what will it then bee when as wee shall enter on somewhat further: that euen in the very entrance, we finde saluation? in what case then I beseech you shall we be, when as we shal haue once passed the midway on? And to the ende that Dauid might the better expresse, that the question is not here of the great learned doctors he namely saieth, *That it giueth instruction to the simple and silly soules, to the ende they might haue light and vnderstanding.*

As if he should haue said, that God hath so communicated his word vnto vs, and in such sort framed and wrought it for our vnderstanding, as that there is not the most simple & ignorant which shal not find himselfe capable to bee the scholler of God, yea so that we come vnto it in all lowlinesse and humblenesse. For Dauid, in saying that the word of God maketh the lowly to vnderstand, right wel sheweth, that if we come vnto it in the pride of our own minds, presuming of our own fine heads, as in this point a great nūber of proud and glorious men doe, who wil rather cōtroll God then submit them selues vnto him & to his word: no doubt of it wee shalbee left in the darke. For let vs not bee abashed although such people of whome I haue already spoken, do continually remaine most blockish. But wee for our partes ought to know, that we must be hūbled & throwne downin ourselues, to thend god might lightē vs, And then let vs not dout but that we shal feele God to be euer more ready to play the part of a good schoolemaster vnto vs, whē
as we

upon the Cxix. Pſalme.   140

as we ſhal ſhew our ſelues to bee true and dutiful ſchollers. Now by and by followeth, *I opened my mouth and panted*: he was ſcarſly able to fetch his breath. And by this is ſignified the feruent zeale which he had, which was to be wel inſtructed in the law of God. Now here Dauid ſheweth, how it is that wee ſhould bee enlightened, that is, that after wee are knowne to be lowly and hũbled, feeling our want and neceſsitie, let vs ſigh & groane vnto the maieſtie of our God, in beſeeching him to inſtruct vs. For wee ſhall not neede to be greatly learned for our right and perfect walking, if wee truely and earneſtly deſire to be his ſchollers, & to preferre his word before all other things. Dauid might very wel ſay, O Lord, I haue deſired to vnderſtand that which thou haſt ſhewed me by thy law, and yet contented not hee him ſelfe with this onely ſaying: But ſaith namely, that he opened his mouth, as a forepined ghoſt, who was no longer able to abide it. And afterward he ſaieth that he drew in his breath, that he was ſo zelous, as that it tooke away as it were his very ſpeach from him. There is no doubt that Dauid meant here the very ſingle affection wherewith hee was touched: not for any deſire he had to commẽd him ſelf, but to ſhewe vnto vs by his example what our office & dutie is towardes God: that is, that we ſhould ſeeke too profite our ſelues by his word. Now then we haue here to note, that euen thẽ we ſhall be enflamed with the word of God, when as wee ſhall haue yea euen ſuch a vehement deſire, as hereof is mention made, and as hath byn before ſpoken off. That the word of God ought to be more deare and precious vnto vs then all the riches of the world, & more ſweete then al other ſweetneſſe in the earth. When then we ſhall haue ſuch a deſire as this, we ſhal finde God to bee alwayes ready to accompliſh that which is ſaide in the ſong of the holy virgin, that hee hath filled and ſatiſſied the hungry and empty: God wil ſatiſſie and fil thoſe that hunger after the thinges which concerne but this preſent life. And do you thinke that when we ſhalbe deſirous of his doctrine, knowing it to bee the moſt principal benefite that we can poſsibly wiſh, & whereunto we ought to apply our whole hart, that he wil let vs famiſh?

S 4   Do

The 17. Sermon of M. Io. Cal.

Do you suppose that he will not graunt vs so holy a desire, and such a one as he approueth aboue all the rest? But by the way let vs consider, that we perceiue not at this day, the profit and edifying which Dauid bringeth vnto vs in this place: bicause in deede we are ouer colde to seeke after the will of God. And to say truly, I beseech you can we find one amongst an hundreth which desireth it, I say yea such a one as onely hath that affection to be taught of God? We see to the contrarie, that wee shall not neede the very least trifling toy to keepe vs at the gaze: bicause we are so full of all vanitie as is lamentable: neither can the deuill no sooner set any thing before vs which wee will not runne after, and take occasion to bee withdrawne from all whatsoeuer is good & godly. Now then, when as we shall see our selues to be thus cold, is this to come with such a feruencie, as is here declared vnto vs by Dauid? Alas where shall wee finde it? ought we not then euen to be abashed, when as we shal see so few to be truly taught of God? considering that so small a number of people are touched to the quicke with a true desire of his doctrine? But we ought rather to thinke it more straunge, when as we seeing God to be so full of louing kindnes, as too beare with our negligence that insteede of opening our mouthes, and to desire his heauenly doctrine, as Dauid hath done, wee open our mouthes too craue such things as do nothing els but offende and grieue the maiestie of God: for in that is our whole delight, and vpon it bestowe we all our power and strength. When then wee shall after this sort forsake God, and seeke after the transitorie things of this worlde, yea the which cannot but hurt, and leade into euerlasting destruction, are we not worthy that God should leaue and forsake vs as most miserable and wretched caitifes? And therefore this doctrine is not heere set downe in vayne.

Let vs then vnderstande, that God meaneth here to exhort vs by the exāple of Dauid, that if we wil be wel instructed by his worde, we ought with such an humilitie as here

mention

vpon the Cxix. Pſalme.   141

mention is made of, too come vnto him with an earneſt deſire & zeale, knowing this to be ſuch a benefite as deſerueth to be preferred aboue all the reſt, euen too knowe the will and loue of God towardes vs, conſidering that in it conſiſteth and reſteth our whole ſaluation. Nowe it followeth in the fourth verſe:

Looke thou vpon me, and be mercifull vnto mee: as thou vſeſt to doe vnto thoſe that loue thy name.

Heere Dauid right well ſheweth, what the deſires and petitions of all the Children of God ought to be, to witte that they muſt hang vpon the meere mercyes of God, and to knowe that all their felicitie conſiſteth therein, and ſo to ſtay them ſelues vpon this ground and foundation, That God looketh with his eye vppon them, too guide and gouerne them. Nowe this thing is greatly to be obſerued, becauſe that men commonly make them ſelues beleeue that they ſhall bee bleſſed, if they may obtaine that whiche their fleſhe deſireth. As when the Glutton ſhall haue wherwithal to fill his filthy paunch, ſo that it may ſtand aſtrout: the Whoremonger to inioy all his foule villanyes & beaſtly lecheryes: the Couetous man to be ſo ſcraping as that hee careth not what he getteth nor howe he commeth by his goods, to lay Land to lande, and too bee filled with an other mans blood: Loe theſe are the men, as they thinke, which are bleſſed. Yea, and although they were not ſo giuen to wickednes, as openly to greeue the maieſtie of God: yet for all that ye ſhal haue very few which wil acknowledge them ſelues to be accurſed, but that God hath care ouer them and their ſaluation, & that there is none other bleſſedneſſe nor felicitie but euen this, that they are in the hand of God and vnder his protection. And ſo much the rather ought wee too recorde and haue often in minde this leſſon when as Dauid ſayth, *O looke vpon me O Lord, and be mercifull vnto me*. For by this hee ſignifieth vnto vs, that if we will haue our life to be bleſſed, if we will haue good ſucceſſe in all our affaires, Lo from this fountaine muſte wee drawe all our felicitie: which is the prouidence of God,

S. 5.   becauſe

The 17. Sermon of M. Jo. Cal.

because we should in no wise dout, but that he careth for vs, and bestoweth & imployeth himselfe for our preseruation. When it is thus with vs, all the reste cannot but goe well with vs: but if this point be wanting, we are very miserable, although it seemeth to vs to haue euen asmuch as can bee wished. Nowe by the way let vs note, that Dauid in beseeching God to be merciful vnto him, declareth, that so long as we are in this worlde, that we are subiecte too a number of calamities and afflictions. And so, we haue greate neede of the mercie of God, or else wee shall carry away all the blowes (as we say) amongst so many greeuous encounters, as shall be lamentable. Nowe this may serue vs for twoo purposes: The one is, that wee beeing heere belowe vppon the earth, might make our account that we cannot be here as it were in Paradise, to haue such reste and quietnesse as we would chiefely desire, to lack nothing, and not to bee subiect to any griefe nor displeasure: No, not so: But contrariwise, let vs know that here God subicteth vs to a great number of wretchednesses and miseryes, to the ende wee should be alwayes calling vpon him for his mercie, and too be alwayes running vnto him for it. Lo here the first point which wee are to consider of in this place, that the faithfull to the outwarde shewe shalbe very miserable, and in a most wretched case, so long as they shall liue heere bylowe: and the meaning of God is, to holde vs vnder this condition, to the ende to awaken vs, that we might haue a far greater affection to call vpon him, and to cleaue wholly vnto him.

Now if we shall haue this consideration with vs, we may then in the second place say with Dauid, *Haue mercie vpon vs O Lorde*: that is to say, we may be assured in all our miseryes, that God wil be pitifull and mercifull vnto vs, yea so that we desire him, as we are heere taught too doe by the spirite of God. Namely Dauid addeth, *As thou vsest too doe vnto those which loue thy name.*

This is a sentence of Iudgemēt which is here set downe: But it sometimes signifieth, measure, sometimes, estate, order or fashion: the sense is not darke: for it is asmuch as if hee he had saide, O Lord, haue mercy vppon me, euen as thou art wonted to haue mercy vpon those which call vpon thy name. Now we are to gather from this saying, that Dauid made not this petition only for himselfe: but hath set down vnto vs a general rule, which we may and ought too apply vnto euery childe of God, too the ende that euery one for his owne part might be sure that God wil haue mercy vpō him, and stretch forth his hand to aide him in his neede. And why so? For the holy Ghost namely pronoūceth, that it is the ordinary maner of God to be louing and pitiful to al those which loue his name. What remayneth then for vs to do? Forsooth we must loue the name of God. And heere we are also to consider, what this saying meaneth, too loue the name of God: For wee shal haue some men which wil feare god, so, so, and yet be contented neuer to come neere him, if they could otherwise chuse: yea they wil not sticke to shut the dore against him, and kepe themselues as far from him as is possible.

Nowe Dauid sheweth heere vnto vs, what the true feare of God is. to wit, that we must loue him of our owne good wil, and that with reuerence: and not constrainedly to loue and feare him, but that we desire too come vnto him, and wholy to submit our selues vnto his Maiestie. If we shal do thus: then may we truly say that wee loue him, & in louing him, feare him also. In very deed, these are things that may not be separated, bicause it is impossible for vs rightly too reuerence God, and to feare him as we ought, except (as it is said in the Psalme) that we first acknowledge him to bee our father, loking for al goodnes and courtesie from him. This then affoordeth vs, in the first place, that wee are assured that God loueth vs, that wee must take him as for our father, that wee feele, that hee in the louing of vs, desireth nothing els but our saluation. And thus much for the first point. And after from thence also proceedeth, humilities whenas wee see G O D so too abase himselfe, as too seeke for vs myserable Creatures, wretched wormes of the Earth, yea euen very condemned and vtterly loste
persons,

persons, the bondslaues of Satan, That God seeketh for vs euen in Hell, and draweth vs so louingly vnto himself. And must it not needes be that we are very stubborne, if we bee not touched, and mooued to come vnto him, and yeelde our selues vntoo him, and bee ruled and gouerned by his hand and protection? Loe, say I, how wee ought to loue the name of God, to the ende we might be glad of that felicitie which Dauid heere speaketh of, that is, that God looketh to keepe vs through his prouidence. And although wee are heere compassed with a great number of miseryes, afflicted a great number of wayes, and iudged to be most wretched, yet God is at hand to help our necessities. And namely it is sayd to loue the name of God, Becauſe wee must receiue a testimony from him, to comprehend his good will. Wee see not God in his Essence, or as he is in deede, but he manifesteth himselfe vnto vs by a nother meane: to witte, that wee might beholde him in the glasse of his woorde, where he sheweth himselfe vnto vs openly inough. Nowe Dauid addeth soone after,

Order my steppes in thy woorde: and let no wickednesse haue dominion ouer me.

Heere wee see more cleerely that, which I haue already touched: to wit, what the petitions of the faithfull ought to be, to the ende they should not be giuen to vaine things, For we neede not to haue any thing to make vs by and by to goe astray, seeing our owne nature draweth vs readyly inough thereto. There is no question, but that wee wil go more then a foote pace, when as wee are bent too doe mischiefe: yea we will trot on moste swiftly and violently, euen as wretched men that were bewitched. Wherefore, heere is a remedy set downe vnto vs: considering that our nature is inclyned to all euill, and caryeth vs thereto headlong, that we only ought to indeuour our selues too bridle our vaine and wicked affections: and besides wee ought too desire God to keepe vs through his woord, and not too suffer any iniquitie too reigne in vs. Loe, I say, in what sorte all the faithfull muste order them selues, fighting against all their

fleshly

fleshly lustes: For it is meete that wee vtterly renounce the euill that is in vs, if wee will seeke after God and come vnto him. Nowe heere are two things which Dauid desiereth, To haue his footesteppes ordered according to the worde of God: And afterwarde, that no iniquitie haue dominion ouer him. Which is asmuch as if hee had sayde, That God had conformed him to his word, and giuen him power and strength to withstand all temptations.

Nowe when he sayth, *Order my steppes according too thy word:* he meaneth, that we can doe nothing at all, excepte God gouerneth vs by his holy spirit. So then, it is not enough that we haue the woorde of God preached vnto vs, to heare it, and to be exercised in the reading thereof: But it is God that must put to his helping hand ouer & besids: he it is that must make the preaching of it effectuall, and pearce our eares, to the ende wee might vnderstande that which is set downe vnto vs; and open our eyes when wee reade, and that altogither by his holy spirit. And thus much for this. For although we haue the woorde of God offred vnto vs, yet shall wee profite nothing thereby vntill such time as God giueth vs vnderstanding to see it. And besides, it is not inough to haue the knowledge of the will of God, and to vnderstand the right way to saluation: But God also must leade vs him selfe, and holde vs by the hande euen vnto the ende. And why so? For we will neuer cease drawing backward, when as God shall haue faithfully instructed vs, if so be he himself doth not stil conduct vs, and alwayes holdeth vs with a stronge and mightie arme: because that our rebellious nature will neuer cease too withdrawe vs cleane contrary. For Saint Paule, who had so greatly profited in the feare of God, and was so very forwarde therein as the like was not in his time, yet ceased hee not still too say, *I see two lawes in my selfe: I haue a desire to serue God, but yet there is another thing also which leadeth me to the contrary, so that I doe the euill wich I abhorre, and would not doe: and if I doe any good, it is not doone with so cheerefull an affection as I would.* See heerein what sorte Saint Paule complayneth him *Rom.9.19.*

him selfe, and in the ende concludeth and sayeth: *Alas most wretched man that I am, who shall deliuer me out of this prison?* If Saint Paule vsed this kinde of speech, what shall become of vs, when we shall be no whit guided by the spirit of God? I beseeech you what shall the bare doctrine profite vs? It is meete then, that after God shall haue taught vs, that hee also guide vs, & after, that he giue vs the power and strength to followe him, and too confirme, imprint and engraue his lawe in our heartes, as also it is sufficiently sette downe in the scripture touching the same.

Ephe. 6. 13, 14

Dauid goeth forward and sayth, *Suffer not any iniquitie to haue dominion ouer me.* To what end, and purpose saieth he this? For he had before desired God too order his steppes, to the ende he might serue him in true and faithfull obedience. Forsooth it is, because that when God hath bestowed his grace vpon vs, to be desirous too cleaue vnto him, yet shall we neuer come to the ful ende there of without greate afflictions, hauing so mightie an enemie to stand against vs as we haue. It is very true that we desire nothing else but to be made teachable of God, and to suffer our selues to be gouerned by the great Pastor or Shephearde Iesus Christe: this is already one good steppe: but let vs a little better consider, wherefore such grace profiteth vs not. It is because the Deuil commeth soone after too set it on fire, for hee alwayes findeth good store of Woode in vs according as we are stored with many vices and imperfections in our nature, vntill such time as God shall haue wholy taken vs frō out of this flesh. For all our lustes and affections are so many rebellions against God, as that wee neuer cease to fight against him, that if at any time on the one side we go about to do good, we are on thother side caryed to do euil. What must we then doe? We had neede to haue God too array vs with a power and constancy, to resiste all these contrarietes and wicked lustes which are in vs: that wee bee not onely teachable, and gouerned by him, but also that wee be fenced with such armour and weapon, as are meeete too

fight

fight againſt Satan and all his craftie ſleights and ſtrengths, to the ende our enemie might haue no holde of vs: ſo that wee hauing as Saint Paule ſayth, bothe our headpeece, and ſhielde, might bee armed and appoynted at all peeces, And when as we ſhall be thus armed, then to ſee howe wee ſhould wholly and fully cleaue vnto our God. And whatſoeuer the Deuil ſhall craftily inuent againſt vs, whatſoeuer ſtoppes and lettes are in vs; yet let vs not doubt but too obtaine victory.

So then, it is not without cauſe, that Dauid heere ioyneth theſe twoo thinges togither, to be guided by the maieſtie of GOD, and aboouall to bee ſo mightily ſtrengthened, as that no iniquitie could haue dominion ouer him but that he was well able to ouercome all the temptations wherewith Satan any way coulde aſſaile him. Nowe if Dauid, was faine to make ſuch a petition vnto God, without hypocriſie, by this we may gather of what ſtrength and effect our free will is, which the Papiſtes ſo highly extoll. Whenas we ſhall ſpeake of the ſeruing of God, they ſtraight wayes think that it cōmeth of our owne power & ſtrength. Not that they doe not confeſſe, but that they had in ſome ſorte neede of God his helpe, but yet that they will bee companions and fellow workers with God, and that without they for their parte did ſomething of their owne power and ſtrength, all of it were nothing. And contrariwiſe, excepte the ſpirit of God leadeth and guideth vs, wee muſte needes ſlippe, yea and vtterly fall away. We ſpeake not heere of an halfe ayde onely: But it is GOD that muſt take the whole conducte and leading into his owne charge. And againe hath he taken vs into his hand? Then no doubt of it, there is a ſeconde grace to be looked for: that is to ſay, that we be ſtrengthened with his holy ſpirite, and ſo to be gouerned, as that wee may haue an inuincible power to perſeuer in wel dooing. Howbeit there is yet one point more to be conſidered of in this verſe: And that is, that Dauid deſiereth to haue all his ſteepes ordered according too the woorde of God.

Nowe

The 17. Sermon of M. Io. Cal.

Nowe by this he sheweth that if we be gouerned according to our owne mindes and fantasies, wee will bee very swift to run: But yet not be too seeke our saluation. And why so? because we runne thwart the fieldes, without holding any way and path, Loe heere the maner of the Papists, are they able rightly to say, that their steppes are ordered by the woorde of God? but contrariwise, the abhomination of their Antichrist withdraweth them from the right way, to make them wander and stray heere and there, and in the ende to cast them selues headlong into the bottome of hell: in such sorte, as whatsoeuer they call the seruice of God, when as both the endes shall be brought togither, we shall finde to be so many blasphemyes against God. And if they be asked, Now Sir, I beseech you, frō whom haue you your Masse, your inuocation of Saintes, prayer for the dead, images, your deifiing of Saintes, your erecting of Aultars vntoo them, your torches, candlelights, pilgrimages, and all the rest of your beggerly trash? what aunswere will they make? They are neuer able to answere you one iotte for the maintenance of this their cloutery out of the holy scripture. What wil they thē say? Forsooth, we folow our fathers and their traditions. Yea, but it is heere namely set downe, that we must be ordered by the woord of God. For all our whole life is a very great disorder: and we wander & stray like vnto brute beasts, except the word of God be our only rule and plaine square. Wherefore let vs bee wel aduised not to stray as these miserable accursed people, which close vp their eyes in the cleere day light, yea and which whet them selues and stubbornly stand in opinion against God, when he goeth about to reforme them, and to shewe them that they haue hitherto vainely spente and loste all their time and trauell. And although that they bee altogither so hardened, yet let not vs be so: But let vs knowe that there is none other direction that is good, but the very same which God sheweth vnto vs, as was sayde too Moyses, Loe this is the way which thou must followe. Nowe it followeth soone after,

O del.mer

vpon the Cxix. Pſalme.

O deliuer me from the wrongfull dealings of men: and I will keepe thy commaundements.

Dauid by this manner of ſpeaking right well decʼareth, that the Children of God ſhall alwayes bee aſſayled with many and ſundry aſſaultes, perſecutions & griefes, ſo long as they liue heere in this worlde, and the meaning of God is to appoint him to be as it were a Glaſſe for all the faythfull to looke in. For as we ſee how he hath beene intreated, and do alſo ſee his condition and ſtate, no doubt God hath ſet him as it were vpon a ſcaffolde, to the ende we might be conformed according to his example: as he was alſo in very deede, a figure of our Lord Ieſus Chriſt. Now we knowe that our Lorde Ieſus was a true patron of all the Children of god, according vnto whoſe image we muſt be made like, namely in this poynt, to wit, in afflictions, in anguiſhes, and miſeryes, as Saint Paule therof witneſſeth to the Romanes. Since then it is ſo, let vs know that ſo long as we are to liue in this world, we ſhall be alwayes afflicted and troubled by wicked and vngodly men, neither ought wee too thinke it *Rom. 8. 35.* any ſtrange thing, ſince that Dauid hath ſhewed vs the way: and that God hath purpoſed too haue vs framed after his example, let not the afflictions and perſecutions, which wee muſt abide at this day, ſeeme newe and ſtrange vnto vs.

Nowe heerevpon it followeth, *That he will keepe his commaundements.* Whereby he ſignified, that he will not forget him ſelfe of ſuch a benefite, when as he ſhall haue God too be his protector, to ſuccour him againſt the malice of men that hee will keepe his commaundementes. Let vs learne then, that when God ſhall haue maintained and defended vs, that we ought to be a great deale the more ready too obay and feare him: and that this ought alwaies too ſtirre vs vp to a greater conſideration: that as hee dayly increaceth more and more his benefites vppon vs, ſo ought our affection alſo to ſerue him, increaſe: and beſides it muſte more profite and inflame it ſelfe. Nowe it followeth by and by after,

T. Shewe

The 17. *Sermon of* M. Io. Cal.

Shewe the light of thy countenaunce vpon thy seruaunt: and teach me thy statutes.

By this he confirmeth the matter which he before handled: and therefore we shall not neede to stande much vpon this verse: for he sheweth that he is contented too haue God to looke and care for him. And to proue this too bee true, you may see, that the thing which hee desireth, is that which I haue already touched: that is, the principall safetie which the Children of God ought to haue, is, to stay themselues vpon this prouidence of God, when as they certainly knowe and may boldely say, that God standeth for vs, and will neuer forget vs: and although wee be neuer so miserable creatures, yet for all that he careth for vs, watcheth ouer vs, yea, and also hee hath an eye vntoo vs, neither will he suffer any hurt to come vnto vs, but will prouide for all our needes and wantes. And if we carry this minde with vs, we haue the greatest benefite that is possibly to be wished. And this is it which Dauid speaketh of in this place, when he sayeth, *Shewe the light of thy countenaunce, O Lorde, vpon thy seruant.* For he meaneth that when he shall feele the protection of God, he is then sure that God looketh vnto him, and that the same is it, which shall deliuer him from all cares. Nowe let vs note that this manner of speech is drawne from a similitude, as when wee thinke God his countenaunce to be darkened in the time of our trouble & aduersitie: and feeling no comfort whereby too glad our selues in him, it seemeth to vs by & by, that there are great and monstrous thick cloudes betwixt him and vs, and indifferently we imagine that God seeth vs not. And therefore Dauid so farre as flesh and blood coulde reach vnto, saith, Shewe the light of thy countenaunce, that is, make me to feele that thou hast care ouer me. And in the ende he sayth, *Mine eyes gush out with riuers of water: because men keepe not thy law.*

Here he declareth that ouer and besids the desier which we ought to haue, and wherwith we ought to be affected to cleaue vnto God according to his word, what a great mischiefe chife & grief it should be vnto vs, to see the scorners which so contemne and despise the word of God, too treade the same vnder foote, & besids, to see the wicked to ouerthrow all good order and inftice. See then, that the true childrē of God ought not onely to be contented with their own walking aright, & to be framed according to the law of God: But they ought also by al meanes possible to labor to bring the whole world to that passe with them, too the ende that all the creatures of God might with one accord reuerence and glorifie his maieftie. And therefore when as they see God to be contēned, they should begreeued thereat, & not only to be sory & vexed: but also to bee as it were mortally wounded. For it is not without cause that Dauid saith here *That riuers of water gushed out of his eyes:* He meaneth hereby, that he was so sorrowful & vexed as couldnot be expressed, Now if Dauid had occasion to grone and weepe after this sort, when he see God to be reiected, what shall become of this our time I pray you? to what an extremitie are we cōe? Is not impietie or vngodlines growne at this day to a full meafure? Doe we not see the vngodly exceede in al abundance of wickednes? one forte is fallen out with God and the gospel: Another sort will confesse with the mouth that they allowe of it or desire it: and yet we see them to be an hundreth thousand times worse then the papists: no dout of it we shall find amongst vs of that sort, such deuils incarnate, and so vilanous and deteftable, as that the very aire cryeth out vnto god for vengeāce against them. When then we shall see these accursed monstets to make no account of God nor godlines, muft we not needs be greeued as Dauid was? Let vs know that God wil blesse our crying and groning, when we shall haue this godly sorrowe: as too see his law thus deftroyed and ouerthrown, & not to bee regarded with that reuerence that it deferueth. And yet notwithftanding the contemners of God muft one day come to an account, when as they shalbe mery after another sorte, & then they shalbe assured to make a reckoning for the grones and lamentations of the childrē of God: when they do not only vexe the mortall creatures of God, but euen the liuing

T.2. God

The 17. Sermon of M. Io. Cal.

God him selfe, and his holy spirit which dwelleth in vs, frō whome all such sighes and grones doe proceede. And so, when as we lament, to see the law of God to be so destroyed by the wicked, let vs put them ouer too the iudgement of God, before whome they shall make an accounte of all the grones and sighes whiche wee shall haue powred out, which they thought by their gibinges and laughinges too strangle and choke. For although they treade vnder foote the lawe of God so much as in them lyeth, yet the sorrowe and griefe which we abide for it, shall ascend into the heauens to cry for vengeaunce of them.

According to this holsome Doctrine, let vs prostrate our selues before the maiestie of our good God, in acknowledging our offences, beseeching him that it woulde please him to make vs better to feele our miseryes then we haue heretofore felt them, yea to the end we may lay them open vnto him, and to seeke for remedy where it is too bee founde: that is, that after this our good God hath inlightened vs in his knowledge, that it would please him more and more, to increase the brightnesse thereof in vs, and so to confirme vs, as that wee neuer chaunge from the right way. And although we are too withstand a great number of assaultes, and that the Deuill neuer ceaseth craftely too goe about infinite wayes too trouble vs: yet notwithstanding let vs beseech him too giue vs an inuincible power to resist them, vntill such time as we become fully Conquerors, and bee conioyned vnto him selfe, too liue in his kingdome in euerlasting ioy and felicitie.

The

The xviii. Sermon vpon the hundreth and nineteenth Psalme.

ZADE.

Righteous art thou O Lorde: and true in thy Iudgement.
Thou hast commaunded: iustice by thy testimonies and trueth especially.
My zeale hath euen consumed me: because mine enemyes haue forgotten thy words.
Thy word is proued moste pure: and thy seruant loueth it.
I am small and of no reputation: yet doe I not forget thy commaundements.
Thy righteousnesse is an euerlasting righteousnesse: and thy lawe is the trueth.
Trouble and heauinesse haue taken holde vpon mee: yet is my delight in thy commaundements.
The righteousnesse of thy testimonies is euerlasting: graunt me vnderstanding and I shall liue.

IT is certaine that there is no man but will easily graunte, the lawe of God to be bothe good and holy, and that wee ought not onely to allowe of it: but also to receiue it with all feare and reuerence. Notwithstanding, there are very few touched with this affection, to vnderstand that there is such a perfection in the word of God, as that nothing can bee founde therein, but all puritie and sinceritie: and too

T.3. bee

be so infallible a trueth, & a righteousnesse so certaine as possible can not be more certaine and sure. But very fewe there are which vnderstand this, or at the leaste which are very greatly touched heerewith. And therefore it is not without cause, that Dauid in this present psalme, vseth such a repetitió, that he so highly magnifieth the doctrine which hee hath learned out of the lawe of God: to the ende too declare vntoo vs, that wee haue greatly profited, when wee shall haue such a sauour and iudgement throughly imprinted in our heartes. When as, I say, this righteousnesse, this wisedome, and this sinceritie which is contayned in the woorde of God, shall be very well and throughly knowen vnto vs: then may we be able to say with Dauid, *Righteous art thou, O Lord, and true in thy iudgements.*

Now as the holy spirite of God speaking by the mouth Dauid, hath set down here no superfluous matter, but such as he knewe to be profitable for our instruction: Let vs also diligently weigh and consider all the wordes, which are heere touched. In the first place he sayth, *Righteous art thou O Lord: and true in thy Iudgements.* We haue already heeretofore handled, that the iudgements of God in this Psalme are called, the commandements of the law which he giueth vnto vs, to rule our liues by. Euen so, when Dauid saith, that God is righteous & true in his iudgemēts: It is asmuch as if he had said, That god hath declared what his nature is in his law, that we might behold him in it, as in a glasse. This then is asmuch as if he should haue said, O Lord, wee haue thine Image truely and liuely pictured and expressed in this doctrine which thou hast deliuered vnto vs in thy law, there we see thee to be righteous, and also that thou hast commaunded nothing therein, which tendeth not to the same ende. Wil we thē magnifie God aright? We must know him to be such a one as he sheweth himselfe to be by his word, & not to fashion our selues like vnto a great number of scoffers, which wil not stick to say that god is altogither good, wise, and righteous: but yet they wil separate them selues frō his word: forge theselues a God in the aire, or else they would

be

vpon the Cxix. Psalme.   148

bee contented that there were such a medley as that there were no more diuinitie known. Now see how god sheweth himselfe, as I haue said, by his word. We must then, if wee intend to cōfesse him to be righteous, good, true, & faithfull, to giue these cōmendations vnto his word, wherin he hath once for all declared vnto vs his wil. Now after Dauid hath vsed this word righteous; he addeth, *Thou hast commanded iustice by thy testimonies, and trueth especially.* See thē how Dauid handleth it him selfe, shewing that the lawe of God is wholy righteous, becaufe faith he, that it leadeth vs to righteousnes and trueth. Now when these two thinges are in it, what may we say, but that which hath already beene before said? What is that? It is so far of with a greate number, that when they are cōuinced heerof, are perswaded in good earnest to say Amen without dessēbling. And to proue it to be so, how many men shal we see submit thēselues in this point to the trueth of God, whereunto he desireth to leade vs by his word? How many I say, shal we find, which wil yeeld thē selues teachable vnto it? But contrariwise, we shall finde the greatest part cleane contrary. It is very true we shalbe ashamed, yea euen horribly affraid, to say, that there is any thing in the law of God, which is not true & iust: & yet for al that it may as easily be perceued, that there is no such knowledg ingrauen in our harts, as to be assured therof. To be short, this is fardest of from our mindes, when we shal say thus : I speake now of those which are not yet throughly instructed by the spirit of God. Neither yet let vs think this too be a common & ordinary thing, when as Dauid faith, That the testimonies of God are nothing but true & righteous. For although we haue learned somwhat out of them, yet is not this inough, vntil such time as we are conformed & framed vnto them, that we fully & wholy agree with this saying & cōmendation which is heere giuen to the law of God. Now becaufe Dauid would shew with what affectiō he is moued, he protesteth, that he was not only greued, whē as he felt in himself any rebellion against God, but whē he perceiued it

T.4.   in

in others, that he conceiued a wonderful sorrow and griefe, yea euen a meruelous torment of minde. For hee sayeth, That his zeale had euen consumed him, that he was as one deade, and so throwne downe as hee coulde not be more. Now, he namely speaketh of his enemies, and of such as had afflicted him: But hee signifieth anon after, that all the mischiefes and iniuryes which they had done vnto him, did not halfe so mightily greeue him, as the contempte which he knewe to be in them touching the lawe of God. For hee sayth,

My zeale hath euen consumed me: because mine enemyes haue forgotten thy woordes.

Heere then Dauid sheweth in effect, that hee was not so greatly greeued nor yet so sorrowfull for all the euils and wrongs which he indured at the handes of men, as too see the woord of God to be cast vnder feete and cleerely forgotten. See heere, I say, a moste sure testimony that he highly preferred the word of God, before his owne person: that he had not that pleasure in his life, nor in whatsoeuer concerned the same, as he had in the reuerēce which al the creatures of God ought to haue towards his maiestie. Nowe if he had not had this zeale, he could neuer haue bene thus grieued and vexed, when as men made no reckoning of the word of God, and cast it behinde their backs. And heere we are throughly too consider, that Dauid spake not in this place of a meane sorrowe. For then this had beene inough, to haue said, Alas my God, I haue beene a great deale more greeued to see the wicked cōtemne thy word, then when as they persecuted my self: although that I was sore troubled & greuously oppressed, yet had I greater regard to thy law, then to al whatsoeuer concerned mine owne person. This had bin inough, say I, if Dauid had said but thus much: but he went a great deale farther, saying, *The zeale of the house of God, hath euen gnawne and eaten me vp.* Heere he saith that he was consumed & brought to nothing, so that he had no strength in himself. Now here we must note by the way, that

Dauid

Dauid spake not this to bragge of him selfe: but rather hath set foorth this his example for our better instruction, to the ende we might learne to haue the honour of God and the reuerence of his woorde in such recommendation, as that when we see the worlde to make light of it, and too forget it, we should be grieued and tormented a great deale more, then if we did abide all the griefes, extreeme wronges and iniuries that were possible: yea, that all our particular benefite, or domage, and whatsoeuer is most deare, ought to be nothing vnto vs in respect of this light reckoning of the word of God. Loe here what holsome lessons and instructions, we haue to gather out of this place.

Nowe when he saith, that it grieued him to see the word of God cleane forgotten, what then shall become of the matter, when as men shall not onely forget it, but euen with a most detestable furie oppose them selues wholy against it? As at this day, we shal not onely say that the word of God is forgotten: but men of a set purpose runne violently vpon it vtterly to abolishe it. And to proue it to bee so, I beseeche you, whence commeth this crueltie and furie of the Papistes: but bicause that they are purposed clerely to goe against it? to be angry with God, not abiding too suffer them selues to be subiect vnto him by any maner of meanes? They will not say thus in plaine woordes, but wee may iudge of the matter so farre foorth as wee see it. For, howe should it be possible, that they should so rage against the knowne and certaine truth, if they were not euen the very professed enemies of God? and without they went about to stand against him euē to the hard hedge, as we say? I will not denie but that men many times shall forget the word of God, when as they shalbe carried away with their wicked affections. As thus, when a man is greatly giuen to lecherie, this villainous desire so blindeth him, as that hee clerely forgetteth whatsoeuer he hath heard spoken against it neuer so little before: to wit, they which defile their bodies with lechery, do deface, as much as in them lieth the image of God, pollute his temple, deuide and pull in pieces

T 5   the

The 18. Sermon of M. Io. Cal.

the body of Iesus Christ, shut them selues quite out of the kingdome of heauen, and prouoke the heauy wrath and curse of God against them. And yet an whoremaister forgetteth all these notable sayings, which are set downe too keepe him within his reyne. The couetous man also forgetteth what equitie and right is, let him be admonished thereof neuer so often, as to bee pitifull to his neighbours, to helpe the poore and needy, rather then to take away an other mans goods and substance, and to be so giué to our own gaine: to procure and profit the welfare of our neighbours, rather then to be giuen too seeke our owne priuate commoditie. A couetous man I say, will quite forget all this. And why so? Forsooth, bicause he is blinded with this couetous desire of gayne, and too heape vp together the goods of this world. See then when it is, that the worde of God shall be forgotten: verely euen then when as men shall be drunken with their inordinate greedy passiós. But they which set them selues against God, yea with a fury & frensy vtterly to abrogate his worde, too turne his truth into leasings, these mē, I say, do not onely forget the word of God, but remember them selues of it too too much, euen to sett them selues purposely against it. And we need to go no further but euen into the state of Popery, to see such a villanous and detestable impietie. For we shal see these contemners of God, which are euen here amōgst vs, yea and which come sometimes to defile the temple of God, to thrust in their swynish groynes: and to scorne the doctrine which shalbe read, which maketh euen the very deuils in hell too tremble. Wee shal see then here these contemners of God, which will euen lift them selues vp against him, and powre out their blasphemies, & is it meete that we dissemble this? No, not so, but let vs rather stirre vp our selues to groaning yea to crie out with a loude voyce, beseeching G O D too stretch forth his mighty and strong arme, against such villaines, & fier brādes of hell, such vpholders of Satan, which thus come too defile the sacred and holy things of God, which his maiestie hath set before vs for our saluation. And thus

thus much for this point. And againe let vs not onely bee grieued and sorrowefull, bicause there are in vs rebellious affections which so hinder vs, as that wee cannot take any such taste as is to be wished for in the worde of God: but also when as we see that men so lightly esteeme and forget this word of God, that they outrage in all wickednes, it can not be but that we must be grieued and sorrowefull for the same. And yet there is a further matter to bee required at our handes, which is this, that when wee shall see and heare the name of God to be blasphemed, and his maiestie violated, we should be tormented, and feele a greater griefe for the same, then for all the euill that might come vnto our selues: for it is very good reason that the maiestie of God should be more deare vnto vs without all comparison, then our owne persons and liues. Nowe since it is so, that if wee ought to be sorrowefull, when as we see the worde of God to be forgotten by others, euen to beginne at the best end, if the euill be founde in vs (as Satan moueth vs to fall vnto wickednesse, and we are very farre of from truly seruing of God, and looking to his word, with such feare and humilitie as in deede we ought:) since then, I say, we are so greatly to be améded, that we haue so many sinnes fighting against the lawe of God: euen so much the more ought we to sigh and groane: as saint Paul right well sheweth vs, saying, Oh accursed man that I am, who shall deliuer me out this mortall body. Loe here saint Paul, in shewing their condition & state to be miserable which liue in this world, exhorteth thē to groaning, and to a continuall sorrowe and care, bicause they are not able fully and throughly to yelde them selues to the word of God: so that whensoeuer wee shall doe but euen so much, we shall render a true proufe and testimonie of our faith & Christianitie. Now it followeth soone after,

Thy word is proued most pure: and thy seruant loueth it.

Here it verily seemeth (as we haue before saide) that Dauid bringeth in a most manifest sentēce, yea, knowne euen vnto the simplest, to wit, that the word of God is pure and cleane, without spot and blemishe. But what? let vs see a little whether wee putte this puritie in practize or

not,

The 18. Sermon of M. Jo. Cal.

not, alas, wee are farre from it. For euen then wee may saye the worde of God too bee pure and without spot, when as without any gaynesaying we only trust in him, and that we haue a true certaintie of our saluation, bicause he hath once stretched foorth his hand vnto vs, and promised neuer too faile vs. When then we shall haue such a confidence in God that wee may boldly walke through death, and the very gulfe of hell: that in seeing the bottomles pittes open tco swallowe vs vp, we should not doubt of our saufetie, since that we are in the hand of God: loe howe the word of God shalbe pure vnto vs. But nowe are wee all in a cleane contrary vayne. And from whence commeth this? It is bicause we are full of infinite filthinesse and pollutions: to be short, there is nothing but stenche in vs, and all our senses are defiled. Let vs first beginne at our eyes, and we shall haue such a number of filthy troublesome and gimsing gloatings: to wit, such a number of vanities which hinder vs too knowe the puritie that is in the worde of God, as loe wee haue already lost one of our senses. Afterwarde, we are depriued of our hearing, bicause our eares are so filled with such trifling yea and peruerse matters, that wee can giue no eare vnto God, or els, that which entreth in at one eare, goeth out at another, as we say. Now if this be already a great vice in vs, to be so slacke as to receiue but one good lesson, the second is no whit lesse, that when we shall haue gotten euen a very little, it shall incontinent so melt away from vs, as that wee shall neuer thinke more of it. We see howe iolly and frisking our feete and handes are, when as wee heare any talke of ribauldrie and filthinesse, and altogether dull and sentles when any speach is of vertue and godlinesse. There is neuer a finger in our handes, but will bee as good as a raysour, to cut euen to the quicke, if any talke shalbe had to offend the maiestie of God. And in the meane while we shall not finde one man that will once lift him selfe vp too doe any good. See howe all our senses are corrupt, and howe full of pollutions and filthinesse. And this is it which hindreth vs, that we are not able to knowe howe the worde of God is to be
tried.

tried. Now it followeth,

I am small and of no reputation: yet do I not forget thy commaundementes.

This saying here importeth more then at the first sight it seemeth to doe: It is very true, that it should seeme a farre harder matter for the mightie men of this worlde to serue God then the meaner sort: in so much as wee will neuer accompt it straunge if a man of base condition hath not forgotten the word of God, But what is the cause why wee so greatly prattle, iangle, and lift vp our selues so arrogantly against him, and that we submitte not our selues wholy vnto him? Forsooth euen the very honours and delightes of this worlde are oftentimes the chiefest causes. When a man shalbe in any credit, estimation, and reputation hee imagineth vnto him selfe an idoll In his owne heart: and hereupō forgetteth God, and thinketh him selfo to bee no longer vnder his gouernement. When then our Lorde God holdeth vs in a lowe estate, hee putteth vs in minde, and forceth vs by this meanes not to forget his commandements, and to walke in his feare with all humilitie. But Dauid his meaning tendeth to another ende, that is, although he was as it were contemned, yet ceased he not to loue God. Nowe as I haue said, this is not here set downe without cause. It is very true, that when God liberally bestoweth vpon vs great store of benefites, then are we so blockish, as that we thinke our selues least beholden vnto him. And contrariwise, they vpon whome hee hath not bestowed such graces, thinke them selues for their partes, not so greatly bounden vnto him. And in very deede, the worlde will alwayes finde starting holes, to keepe it selfe out from the seruice and feare of God, or els will be so lightly discharged thereof, as that it may be done without any great paine. As howe I praye you? We see, that they which pretend colour of ignorance, which haue neither knowledge either of God or of true religion, will say, surely for my part I am but a poore simple man, and without learning, and therefore I will leaue this geare to those that are learned. One sort will excuse them

selues

The 18. Sermon of Mr. Jo. Cal.

selues one way, another, anotherway: but yet they all tende to this ende, to exempt them selues from the obedience of God, & not to be subiect either to him or yet to his word. See here the common saying amōgst the Papistes. Ha sirra: This is the office of the priestes & the cloysterers: our prelates haue the charge ouer vs: wee are secular and lay men, we must haue nothing to do with this geare. And besides, euen the meanest sort of vs, haue also our excuses, and will say, I am a poore mā, I must get my liuing with great paines all the day long by my handy worke, I haue scarsly any leysure once to come to heare a sermon on the Sunday. See what startingholes we finde out, to the ende we might followe our vanities, pleasures, and idle times, or I knowe not what other our slouthfulnes, rather then wee woulde heare the word of God and meditate thereon. So then, Dauid contrarily sheweth, that whiles he was small and of no reputation: yet that he neuer ceased continually to be exercised in this lesson, euen to submit him selfe to the obedience of God. And so we see him to be giuē from his childhood: and that he did not onely take pleasure therein, when God had aduaunced him to the kingdome, that hee did not begin then to taste of the lawe of God & to apply his whole study thereto: but when hee kept his fathers sheepe and cattle, and was brought vp in the sheepecoates, before hee came any thing neare the court: euen all that while, I say, he neuer ceased but was wholy occupied in the holy study of the lawe of God. Nowe let vs learne hereby not to exempt our selues by our trifling excuses, as a great number of men do: but let vs vnderstand, that Dauid here exhorteth all the faithfull in general: that the contemptible, base, and simple persons, yea euen as simple as yong children, and that haue no knowledge of that which is most esteemed amōgst mē, that they ought not for all that to forget the word of God. And so, let also both great and smal giue them selues to the study thereof, that we may be all the schollers of the lawe, and of the Prophets, but especially of our sauiour Iesus Christ, seeing that God hath now bestowed a more excellēt

grace

vpon the Cxix. Psalme. 152

grace vppon vs, then euer hee bestowed vppon Dauid. For ouer and besides the doctrine which Dauid receiued from the mouth of Moyses, see how God hath layd open vnto vs, the infinite treasure of his heauenly wisedome, insomuch as we haue the Gospel, out of which the sonne of God hath spoken vnto vs, who is maister ouer the whole houshold, as it is said in the Epistle to the Hebrewes. Now is this the doctrine that must make heauen and earth to tremble; as it is *Heb.3.6.* spoken by the Prophet Haggay: & as this place is alledged by the Apostle, to shew vnto vs that we ought to receiue the *Hag.2.7.* Gospel with greater reuerence, then the fathers did the law, & the Prophets. For God made the earth to shake when he *Heb.12.25.* gaue the law by Moyses, which since that time hath bin co- *26,27.* firmed & ratified by the Prophets: but when as hee opened his holy mouth by his sonne to teach vs: that was to make both heauen and earth to shake, bicause he hath layd open such a wonderfull wisedome, as that it ought to shake & astonish vs, when as God speaketh with such power & maiestie vnto vs. See then as concerning this saying, where Dauid saith, that he did not forget the comandements of God, although he was smal & of no reputation. Now he addeth.

Thy righteousnes is an euerlasting righteousnes: and thy lawe is the truth. Yea in such sort, that when he was afflicted & grieued, that he tooke pleasure in saying, thy righteousnes is an euerlasting righteousnesse, heere Dauid repeateth a word which hath a double significatio. For in the first place Righteousnes, signifieth the law of God, & that bicause it is the rule of all goodnes. And the next, he giueth it the title of righteousnesse, signifying thereby, that this law is so certaine a rule, as that when we shal haue throughly souded it euen to the bottome, we shal finde that God hath set down therein a perfection of all equitie and sinceritie: as if hee should haue said, this is without all doubt a perfect rule of righteousnes. Now he coupleth as hee hath already before done, truth, with righteousnesse. I haue already saide, that these wordes here, are oftentimes repeated: and yet it is no superfluous kinde of speache.

And

The 18. Sermon of M. Io. Cal.

And what is the reason? Because we might fully and wholy confesse that God hath spoken moste wisely, that all mennes mouthes might be stopped, and that we al at once might be silent and stil to heare him. There is no man but will confesse this at the tongues end: But in the meane time for vs to knowe this equitie and trueth, which is contayned in the word of God, Alas we are too too farre off.

So then, let euery man looke well vnto him selfe, and see whether his life be agreeable vnto the word of God or no. And if it be, it is a manifest proofe that the righteousnesse and trueth thereof is deepely imprinted in his heart. Nowe if this be so, then no doubt of it God his woord is honoured as it is worthy. Then let vs render vnto him effectually, the prayses which are heere attributed vnto him, and as they doe appertaine vnto his maiestie. But if wee doe say that the word of God is good and holy, that it is a wonderful righteousnesse and power that cannot fail, and yet despise it in deede, shewe our selues cleane contrary vnto it in our life and conuersation, and making a goodly shewe to honor it, doe spit at it: What a kinde of honor call yee this? Wherfore we are to consider, that it is mete that this righteousnesse and trueth of the lawe of God be imprinted in our heartes, that we may make such a confession thereof, as Dauid heere hath doone. And see why heere hee addeth, *Yet is my delight in thy Commaundements*, Yea when hee was afflicted, and in aduersitie. For it is an easy matter for men to praise God whiles they are quiet and out of trouble, & haue all their heartes desire. Yea wee shall see the very hypocrites cry out with open mouthe, O blessed bee God, and our good God: Forsooth when as hee sendeth them euen their wishe, and intreateth them according too their owne desires. But when God shall afflict vs, so that wee be grieuously vexed, vntill we can no more : Loe heere a good tryall to make vs feele, that we haue willingly and in earnest honored him in his word. And we shall shew it too bee so, when as we shall not chaunge our mindes : but constantly perseuer in it, and say ; whether shall I now runne ? see how

I am

I am afflicted: well, it is my God that must restore me. It is very true that I am not without great stoare of sorrowes and griefes which trouble mee: But yet I will content my selfe with this, that God loueth me. It is true that as touching the worlde I am tormented: but I will comfort my selfe that my God hath called me vnto him, that he sheweth vnto me in deede that he will haue compassion vpon mee, that he taketh me for one of his children, and will extende his fatherly goodnes towardes mee. See here a very good proufe and triall, that we take the woorde of God to bee true and righteous: that is, that if wee bee grieued with trouble and aduersitie, yet that we do neuer forget him, nor it. But what? let vs once come to the practize thereof, and then we shall see howe it fareth with vs. For it is a matter of nothing too lende our eares and saye, surely this is a very good sermō, & that there was nothing taught in it but very good and holfome doctrine, and truely if wee haue once fayde but euen thus much, wee will by and by thinke, that God is greatly in our debte.   A man that commeth thus euen with the eares of an Asse to playe the hypocrite, thinketh verly that God is bounde vnto him, bicaufe hee hath done him thus much henour.

Now this is an ouergrosse and impudent kinde of dissembling, in this maner to thinke to pleafe the maieftie of God. But yet the cafe fo ftandeth, as that the greater part is euen fo giuen: nowe what is the next way for vs too bee ridde of all togither? Forfooth euen this, That when wee for a time fhall make a fhowe to giue diligent eare vnto the worde of God, that all whatfoeuer we haue heard, will incontinent melt and vaniſh cleane away from vs. And hereby wee very well ſhewe, that the truth and righteoufneffe which is in his word, is not fo imprinted in vs as it ought to be. Now Dauid addeth in the ende, *Yet my delight is in thy commaundements.* Whereby he aduertifeth vs, that it is not enough that we cal to minde that we haue vnderftoode the word of faluation, too the ende to profite our felues in the time of affliction: but it muft be of this ftrength and power

V   euen

euen to gladde vs in the middest of our sorrowes. It is very true, that we shall not be senseles and without feeling. And Dauid also hath very well experimented, how greatly affliction and anguish tormented him. He felt then both harde and bitter passions: and yet this hindered him little, to reioyce and to be glad. And although he was greatly vexed as touching the flesh, yet felt he such spiritual ioy in the testimonies of God, that sorrow ouercame him not. Now, if Dauid as before wee haue declared, tooke such pleasure in the law, wheras God only shewed himselfto the ancient fathers, as it were in shadowes I beseeche you, how ought the word of God at this day to glad vs? Where as he sheweth him self so familiar a father towards vs, euē opening vnto vs the very botome of his heart, hiding nothing from vs? When thē our Lord God poureth out the treasures of his infinite loue and goodnes vpon vs so aboundantly: haue not wee a farre greater occasion to reioyce, then the fathers who liued vnder the lawe? Yes verely: but our vnthankefulnesse so hindreth vs, as that in knowing, we know nothing, and in seeing, we see no whit at al. And yet is not this written without cause. Euen so, when as we shall feele the griefes, anguishes, and afflictions of this worlde to trouble vs, let vs haue recourse vnto this word of God: for in it we shal finde him to stretch forth his hand to drawe vs vnto him, declaring that he will helpe the afflicted, haue pitie of the miserable and vexed, ayde the wretched, desireth nothing els but to bring back againe poore sinners which wil yeld them selues vnto him, lay all their cares in his lappe, and that hee will vnburden vs of them all. When then wee are sure, and resolute of such God his goodnesse towardes vs, by his promises, wee ought to come vnto him, to call vpon him, and to reioyce in him: so that we may say with Dauid, O Lord, my delight hath byn in thy testimonies, that they might glad me in the middest of my afflictions. Loe how the children of God, in all the time of their affliction may continually doe, reioyce in the assurance of their saluation, yea when as they shal settle them selues vpon his promises, and recciue them in suoh

sort:

sort as that they may turne to their benefit. Now for a conclusion Dauid saith, *The righteousnes of thy testimonies is euerlasting*: and afterward he maketh his prayer & saith, *graunt me vnderstanding and I shall liue.* See yet againe this worde, righteousnes which is here repeated, and that to very good purpose: For this is according to that which I haue already said, that they which dare not openly rayle & iangle against God to blaspheme his word, yet will they be for all that ful of malice, and treason: or els they wilbe so nusseled in their vanities as that the righteousnes of God shall not appeare in them. So then, Dauid yet setteth it down, to bee an euerlasting righteousnesse: signifying that we ought not to take them as puffes of wynde, as a great number of men haue done, to magnifie God, and after in the turning of an hand to go cleane backward. As at this daye wee shall haue them which will make a shew of great deuotion, and say, O what an excellent sermon, O what notable doctrine was taught this day? But I beseeche you what wil they say the next day? Forsooth they will not for all this sticke too mocke God, make one iest or other at his word: or els, if God send them any aduersitie, they wilbe grieued and angry with him: so that if they be put in minde of that which they before had heard, they will answere, that they haue cleane forgotten it. Dauid therefore meaning to shew, that wee must not bee so slacke as at sometimes to commende the worde of God, sayeth, that it is an euerlasting righteousnes. As if he should haue said, it is very true that men are chaungeable, and this present life also is subiect to very many chaunges, as to daye we shall haue some griefe or other, and to morrowe be well againe: oftentimes many troubles shall come vnto vs: and wee shall see them at last too haue an ende: and yet for all these continuall chaunges, men must not in the meane while be carried away with euery blast of wynde, to bee inconstāt and vnstedfast: but whiles they are sayling through the waues of the sea, they must holde them selues firme and sure in this righteousnesse and sinceritie which is in the woorde of God.

The 18. Sermon of M. Io. Cal.

See then howe we must know the euerlasting stablenes of the righteousnesse of the lawe. And in deede wee shall haue thereof a full feeling and declaration in the worde of God, when as wee shall receiue it as wee ought: but for so much as wee faile herein, and that wee haue not as of our selues the spirite to comprehend this righteousnesse, wherof in this place mention is made, ne yet to attaine thereto: yea, and if that we should attaine therto, so that there were nothing to leade vs to iniquitie, yet let vs pray with Dauid, that it would please God to giue vs vnderstanding. Now it is most true that Dauid had already receiued some portion and measure of vnderstanding: for els he could neuer haue saide, I haue beene grieued and troubled, and yet my delight was in thy lawe. Hee coulde not possibly bee carried with such an affection, but that the word of God had touched the very bottome of his heart: but when he besought God to giue him vnderstãding, he meãt, to haue God to encrease that grace which before he had receiued. Nowe, if he who was so greatly aduaūced: yea that had receiued the spirite of prophecie to instruct others, which is the principall spirite to gouerne the people of God: If hee, I saye, had neede to make such a prayer, what shall wee do, which haue scarsely any one sparke of vnderstanding in our myndes? ought not we, I beseeche you, to praye with a more feruent desire, to haue God to graũt vs vnderstanding? And a great deale the more ought wee to bee stirred vp thereto, when as Dauid sayeth, that wee are not able too lyue, vntill such time as GOD hath so enlightened vs: too the ende wee might conceiue this truthe and righteousnesse which is in his lawe. See here, I saye, howe that the life of men cannot be but accursed, vntill such time as they are come euen vnto this point: And so, let vs not learne too please our selues, as these miserable wretched worldlinges doe; who are euen drunken in their pleasures and pastimes, and thinke that there is no pleasure nor felicitie, without they exceede and outrage in all vanities and follies: But lette vs looke a great deale higher, lette vs seeke

after

after God, & know that then our life shalbe blessed, when as God shall haue deliuered vs from these vayne allurements of this wicked worlde, to make vs feele truth and righteousnes which is in his word: that it may be the onely ende of our life, of all our councelles, and our onely exercise and study: To be short, the very summarie of all whatsoeuer we take in hande.

According too this holy doctrine, let vs prostrate our selues before the maiestie of our good God, in acknowledging our offences, beseeching him that it woulde please him to make vs to feele them better then heretofore wee haue: that we knowing our owne wretchednesse and miseries, & what neede we haue of his assistance, might haue recourse vnto him, hauing our whole refuge to his goodnes and mercy, and stay our selues vpon his promises, not douting but that as he is true and faithfull in all that he sayeth, so also that he will fulfill whatsoeuer hee hath shewed vnto vs in his worde: to wit, that he wil so vnite vs vnto him self, as that after he hath separated vs from all the filthinesse of this world, he will make vs partakers of his righteousnesse, and finally of his glorie. That he will not onely graunt vs, this grace, but also all people and nations of the earth. &c.

The nineteenth Sermon vpon the hundreth and nineteenth Psalme.

COPH.

I haue cried out with my whole heart: heare me O Lord, and I will keepe thy statutes.
Yea euen vpon thee haue I called, helpe me, and I wil keepe thy testimonies.
Early in the morning I cried vnto thee: for in thy word is my trust,

The 19. Sermon of M. Io. Cal.

Mine eies preuent the night watches: that I might be occupied in thy wordes.

Heare my voyce (O Lorde) according vnto thy louing kinduesse: quicken mee according too thy iudgement.

They drawe nigh that followe after malice: and are farre from thy lawe.

Thou art nigh at hande, O Lorde: for all thy commandementes are true.

I haue knowne long since by thy testimonies: that thou hast grounded them for euer.

Orasmuch as the most requisite thing that wee can possibly desire for our saluation, is praier vnto God, and bicause we are so slacke and colde therein, or els that a very small matter will make vs colde: we are to consider of the examples which the holy scripture setteth forth vnto vs of the children of God, & of the faithfull in deede, how they continually were exercised in prayer. Euen as in this place Dauid his meaning is to set before our eyes, not that he meant to glorifie him selfe of his owne strength, thereby to get him estimation, but to the ende that this example might direct vs the right waye. We see then howe carefull Dauid was to call vpõ the name of God, how he applied his whole affection, and continued therein, bicause that euery of vs might doe the like. Nowe in the first place he sayeth,

I haue cried out with my whole heart.

Whereby he signifieth vnto vs, that he babbled not euē as the hypocrites doe, or els that he cried not out vppon

God

God for a fashion or coldely, but prayed with a true & earnest zeale. Neither do we any otherwise but euen prophane the name of God, when as wee pray vnto him without attentiue mindes hauing our thoughts wandring this waye and that waye, and on euery side. Let vs then consider, what it is principally to be required in our prayers, which is, that we must not only wagge the tongue, and open our mouth, with an intent to pray vnto God: but we must pray sincerely and purely also vnto him from the bottom of our harts. Now in very deed we ought to bring this into a more plaine order: But yet according to the manner which wee haue heretofore kept in handling of this Psalme, it shal suffice that we set down euery thing briefly in certain articles. It remaineth then for this tyme that euery one priuately by himself doth more diligently meditate & bestow his whole studie herein. Nowe let vs see how we ought too make our prayers to God, to wit, our prayers must not proceed from the midst of our mouth, but from a godly minde, and pure truth. This word to cry out, importeth vehemency, as shall again soone after be spoken of. Nowe Dauid meaneth not that he strained his throate to cal and cry out, but he rather signifieth that he went not coldly vnto it, as they do which pray vnto God, they know not why nor wherfore, without it be for a fashion or if they be pressed through any neede, yet are they no whit at al rightly moued, bycause they doo not assure themselues that hee will heare and receiue them. Dauid then sheweth that he was not so blockish, but that he had such an earnest desire as pusshed him thereto as S. Paul saieth, that when we come to pray vnto God, wee ought to approch with groaning harts, which no toung cā expresse, by which we are pusshed forward by the spirit of god. Se then the 2. cōdiciō which is required in our prayers, that is, that we must lift our harts & minds vp into heauen, when as wee pray vnto God. For we knowing what great need we haue of his help, must pray that he wil haue cōpassiō of our miserable estate, yea & cōfesse that we are the childrē of perditiō, if hee stretched not foorth his merciful hand vntoo vs: and

Heb.5.7.

V 4   therfore

The 19. Sermon of M. Io. Cal.

therefore that hereupon, we ought to set out and call vpon him with an earnest affection. Nowe in the third place Dauid telleth vs that he was very diligēt in praying vnto God: to wit: that he hoped euen vnto the last cast, as there are very many which doe so, when as they see welynough that they can go no further, except God help them: and yet for all that they steppe backe from him as much as in them lyeth, and are neuer carried to the very point, with all their heartes to call vpon God, without it bee that they can neither will nor choose, and are driuen euen too their wittes ends, as we say. Dauid declareth that he was not so drowsy, for he saieth, that he preuented the night watches, that hee occupied him selfe, seeing that it was the true, and onely refuge of the children of God, and the very faithfull, to recommend them selues into his protection. Nowe he lastly declareth, that he continued it, that it was no suddaine motion or blast, and afterward to waxe colde againe, as some do: and I would it pleased God that we might not practize it so often as wee haue done. But there is not that hee amongst vs which hath not founde by experience that wee are by and by tyered in praying to God, and that wee waxe very colde so soone as we haue poured out one onely sigh and groane. For we thinke it inough, if we haue set down our whole summe to God in a worde, and do suppose, that if we haue made one onely prayer, that we are discharged of all together, and that God will helpe vs, if hee thinke it good. Nowe Dauid sheweth vnto vs, that hee perseuered in calling vpon the name of God. Loe heere the foure pointes which we haue to note in this place, to the ende that euery of vs might discharge our selues of them. For see from whence we must learne the maner to pray wel: to wit, in the first place, not with hauing our mouth going, but we must lay open our heartes, and all our affections before the maiestie of God, and pray in spirituall truth: and not onely so, but we must also be enflamed with such a zeale, as that wee be fully assured that he will both heare and helpe vs. And for performance hereof, we must be touched to the quick

with

vpon the Cxix.Psalme.

with the knowledge of our sinnes: and knowe that our estate is moste accursed, if God hath not pittie on vs: and also what the saluation is which he hath promised vs: wee must haue alwayes these things in minde, to the ende wee might be the more carefull, watchfully to call vppon him: and not to waite vntill God constrayneth vs through extreeme necessities, but to be alwayes in such a readinesse, as Dauid heere speaketh of, we must day and night, and euery minute be occupyed to looke vnto God, and too call vpon him: and to haue this vnderstanding with vs, that whensoeuer any of vs shall wake in the night, that it be to this end to poure out some sighes vnto our good GOD for our sinnes and transgressions. And also when as wee shall be alone by our selues, wee muste doe the like knowing right wel that God seeth vs, and that we are alwayes as it were in his presence. Lastly we must perseuer heerein, & not take vp the Bucklers, and by and by lay them downe againe, and be soone wearyed: But we must still continue in our prayers, as Dauid heere sheweth vs an example. Nowe after hee hath made these protestations, he goeth on and sayth,

That after he shall be hearde, and shall haue obtayned his requests, that he wil keepe the testimonies of God.

Heere Dauid sheweth that he will not be vnthankfull for the grace which was bestowed vpon him. And this is a poynt which ought greatly to be considered of by vs. For what is the cause that God so easily graunteth vnto vs whatsoeuer we demaund according to his holy will that he so louingly intreateth vs, yea that his hands are continually open vnto vs, to the ende liberally to bestowe his benefites and riches vpon vs? Wherefore sheweth he himselfe so liberall euery way vnto vs? It is to the ende that wee might haue wherefore to yeelde him our heartie thankes, and too glorifie him. Let vs then learne, that it is impossible for vs rightly to pray vnto God, except we be already prepared to acknowledge his benefites, and too haue this full resolute minde that Dauid had: to wit, to glorifie God, when as he shall haue hearde our prayers.

As also we see these two things to goo togither in another place, where it is said, *Call vpon me in the day of trouble, and I will deliuer thee, and thou shalt gorifie me.* See then what we haue to note vpon this saying where Dauid sayth, *That hee will keepe the ordinaunces and testimonyes of God.* But wee are to consider in the seconde place, what the thankes are which God requireth of vs, after he hath holpen vs, & that we haue felt his goodnes in not reiecting our prayers. Now this is true, that it is meete that the mouth doth his office to magnifie the name of God, in confessing how greatly we are beholden vnto him: and yet it is not inough that our mouth hath spoken, but wee muste glorifie him with the whole action of our life, and too shewe this acknowledgement, howe greatly we are bounden vnto him, in seruing & honowring him in all and through all. Dauid then in saying, That he would giue thanks vnto God because he heard him, sayth not, that he wold do it only with the mouth, but sheweth that he will passe farther: that is, to keepe the testimonies of God, and to submit him vnto his ordinaunces.

See howe the glory of God ought to resound, not onely at the toungesend of the faithfull, but also in the whole action of their handes and feete, and whatsoeuer else ought to apply them too honor this good God, that wee should doe him homage all our life longe, considering that wee holde all of him: and not onely for our creation, but also for our maintenaunce and conseruation, and for that hee continually sheweth him selfe too be our protector. For there passeth not one hower ouer our heads, wherein God deliuereth vs not from one mischiefe or other. We haue then a large matter to thanke him for, not onely with the mouth and in words: but also in making protestation therof all the dayes of our life. Wee see nowe the summe and effect of that which is heere spoken, to witte, *I haue called vppon thee with my whole hart, O heare me, and I will keepe thy Statutes.* And afterwardes, *I haue called vpon thee, saue me, and I will keepe thy Testimonyes.* And after that, *I haue preuented the dawning of the day.*

I haue

I haue called vppon thee, yea in trusting in thy worde. Now heere he againe repeateth the point which wee haue noted in the other Sermon: that is, that for our well praying vnto God, we muste builde vppon the trust of his promises. And this is the true preparation which wee ought to make, euen such a one as this. It is true that we had neede to feele our miseryes and necessities, as it hath beene before declared. For wee shall neuer pray vnto God with a right affection, and from the hearte without this. And besides it is very needefull also that we so lay open our heartes, as that we come boldely too presentthem before our good God too discharge and vnburthen those our heartes of all their cares and sorrowes. But in the meane while, howe is it possible for vs, so watchfully and carefully too pray vnto GOD, and to be at full libertie to come before him, if wee had not this hope that hee woulde heare vs? And howe coulde wee haue any hope, if hee had not giuen vs his woorde which witnesseth vnto vs his will, and certifieth vs that wee shall not lose our labour in praying vnto him? The firste laying open then which is requisite for rightly calling vppon GOD, is, that wee come vntoo him in full asuraunce that he will heare vs. And why so? Because hee hath promised vs.

They then which shall pray at all aduenture, shall gaine nothing, as the scripture sayeth: For it is doone but in hypocrisie: when as wee assure not our selues that God will heare vs. We must, as the Apostle sayth, in drawing neere vnto God, knowe that it is GOD which calleth vs vnto him. And they which haue not this knoweledge, shall be voyde of their hope. And therefore euery man must looke into him selfe, to be thus resolued and say, Wel, since it is God that calleth and biddeth me to come vnto him, I must not stand in doubt of obtayning that which I shall aske of him, yea because I trust to his woorde. When then wee shall be thus fully assured, we may very well beginne too pray: But if this be not in vs, we may bestow great paines in

praying

praying vnto God, yea from morning vntill euening: wee may continue all the whole night in babling, but wee shall get nothing at all by it: although we had some desire and zeale, we should neuer know what gaine we should haue by our prayers, because wee trust not to the promises of God nor yet stay our selues vpon them.

Let vs then not dout but that hee will helpe vs, and that we shall feele his ayde in time conuenient. Heereby wee see, that we could neuer duely and truely pray vnto God in all the Religion of Popery, I say according too that doctrine which they hold. And why so? Because they teach the wretched world to be alwayes in doubt and wauering. See then that a meere and professed Papist can neuer bee able too make one prayer to pleafe God: and cannot choose but to prouoke the wrath of God against them selues in all their Prayers. And why so? Forsomuch as they looke not vnto his promises, vpon which we must settle our selues, to be assured: but that which is worse, they teach that in their prayers they must alwayes stand in doubt. So much the more then ought this doctrine rightly too be considered of vs, where it is declared, that the key which openeth the gate for vs to approch vnto God in calling vppon his name, is this, that we must haue the promises contained in the holy Scripture, & to learne such an affiaunce out of it, as that we doubt not that God regardeth vs: and that so oftentimes as we pray vnto him, that our prayers enter into him, and that he will receiue them, declaring that hee is ready too graunte vnto vs what soeuer wee shall craue of him in his sonnes name according to his wil.

Nowe in the meane while, because that God ordinarily heareth not vs at the first chop, that is to say, sheweth not it according to the outwarde shewe, and as we would wish, heere is required patience to remaine constant in this assuraunce, and too retaine and nourish it in our heartes after the example of Dauid. For hee sayth not, that hee prayed onely vnto God for a time: but sheweth that he continued therein, and that hee preuented the night watches. See then

then what perseueraunce was in him as touching prayer. Nowe it is a signe that God shewed him not too haue obtayned the thing that he prayed for. It falleth out then that Dauid his patience was troubled in that that hee languished: and yet for all that he alwayes trusted to the woorde of God. Nowe wee for our partes are to doe euen the like. For although God sheweth not himselfe to be mercifull vnto vs so soone as we would wish, and too graunt vs our requests, yet ought we notwithstanding too builde heerevpon that hee will bee faithfull, and shewe him selfe so in the ende. Although he prolongeth it for a time, he doth it because he knoweth it to be very profitable for vs to humble vs, and to proue our patience. It followeth soone after,

Mine eyes preuent the night watches: that I might be occupyed in thy worde.

This verse is not put to without cause. I haue already sayd, that we can haue no accesse vnto God in our prayers, without we trust to his word. For it is a very harde matter for vs to stay vpon God, if we onely consider of him according to our naturall reason, whether he bee neere vs or no, and whether he putteth foorth his hand to help vs. When then we shall not perceiue this power and grace of God, as we would wishe, it is a very hard thing for vs too beleeue in him, and therefore wee must stoutely striue in this behalfe. And see why Dauid sayth, *That his eyes preuented the night watch*, to be occupyed in that which might confirme him. As if he should haue sayde, O Lorde, I haue beleeued thy word, but it was with greate paine, and with many harde conflicts. For I am a weake man, and of mine owne nature inclyned to distrust, and besides I am assayled with a greate number of temptations: But yet haue I remedied all this geere, when as I occupyed my selfe aboute this continuall meditation of thy word, which I did not onely bestowe on the day time, but also in parte of the night. See heere what we are in very deede to gather out of this place. But first we must mark the proceeding of Dauid. For after hee hath spoken of the hope wherein he was setled, to pray vnto God too God without doubting that he would heare him, hee sayeth,

That he carefully meditated on his woord.

And why did hee so? Shall that which was necessary for Dauid to doe, bee superfluous for vs? God forbid. For if such a Prophet as hee, had neede too arme himselfe against the temptations of his fleshe, against the infirmities wherwith he might be assayled, I pray you how quickly shal he be ouerthrowne, if we haue not the same remedy which we vsed, and the courage also which he heere exhorteth vs vnto?

Let vs then consider, that if we will be stayed vpon the promises of God, becausewe would call vppon him in the time of neede, we ought many times to meditate vpon his woords both day and night: and to set all our study and affection therein. And see what the cause is why there are so fewe which be disposed to pray vnto God. Yea, and when they are thereto inforced, they knowe not which way too beginne, because they cannot be fully resolued, to say, It is very requisite that when I shall call vpon my good God, that I be fully assured that hee will not refuse to heare me. What is the cause of this vncertaintie? It is because they are not wel acquainted with the promises of God. For a man will thinke that it were euen inough sleightly and lightly to beleeue, that God will heare those that are his. And when we come to prayer with this thought, we thinke that if we haue said, but a word or two: that it is too much. Yea and if wee come to a Sermon, and heare the promises of God spoken of, we thinke it by and by too bee an vnprofitable speach, and will say, that it is more then needeth, for what is he that vnderstandeth not that well inough? And in the meane while, beholde a mightie great temptation, like vnto a boysterous whirlewinde and tempest euen at hande: and then he which thought him selfe so able a man, is become a very Milkesop: He will looke whether God wil haue pitie of him: He will possibly imagine, that he hath turned his back, yea or else hee will doubt of his prouidence, whether

ther he hath any care of the worlde or no, there are a thousand fantasies which the Deuill goeth about to put in our mindes. And when we are in this case, see we are so astonied, as that there is no comming for vs too pray vnto God. And what is the reason? It is because wee haue not beene carefull to meditate vpon his promises.

And therefore we ought so much the more, throughly to consider of this lesson, when as it is said, That Dauid his eyes preuented the night watches, too meditate vppon the promises of God. Let vs nowe compare our selues with him. But it is so farre of that any of vs in particular hath this care, whereof mention is heere made, as that wee cannot by any meanes possible bee trayned ynto it. And although God biddeth vs to come vnto him, yet cannot wee be brought to come any thinge neere him. See howe the Bel shal ring euery day to moue vs to come to the Sermon: God there telleth vs of his will, hee declareth vnto vs that he is ready to receiue vs to his mercie, as often as wee shall call vpon him.

Nowe euery of vs may very well see, that wee passe not of his helpe one minute of an houre. And yet howe many are there notwithstanding which will vouchsafe too steppe one foote, too come to occupy them selues aboute the promises of God, that their memoryes might be refreshed in them to thend they might so much the better be remembred of them? Nay we shall sarcely haue a number of them com to it on the Sunday, yea, and if percase they come once, they thinke it too bee as it were ouer much. And forsooth they muste not come thither neither euery Sunday, because their eares will bee ouer much filled with noyse: and againe such as doe come too it, with what affection come they, thinke you? Verely, because that they cannot deny, but that there must bee one day in the weeke for them to meete togither: and besides, they will for once come thither: but it shall be to sleepe, so that they vnderstand and carry away asmuch as these pillers, or else the stoles whereon they sit.

Los

The 19. Sermon of M. Jo. Cal.

Loe heere, howe a great number of the people come to the Sermon. Yea and there are no small number which wil come thither, euen to mock God, as we see these scoffers and gibers, who come to none other ende, but too dispite him, bring with them whorishe and shamelesse faces, and such a beastly impudencie as cannot bee greater. All this we see. Nowe let vs consider that it is so farre of that our slouthfulnesse should be excused, as that God cannot but iustly punish vs, in that we shall be depriued of the abilitie to call vpon him in our neede, and shall haue our mouthes also stopped. And afterwarde the mischiefe shall increase dayly more and more, vntill such time as we are come euen to the deapth of the bottomlesse pittes: that is to say, wee shall be vtterly excluded from the help of our good God, that he will retire him selfe from vs, and cleerely banish vs his kingdome. Beholde heere the fruite which commeth by our negligence, when as we shall make no accounte of the exercising of our selues in this study of the promises of God. Nowe Dauid addeth,

Heare my voyce, O Lord, according vnto thy louing kindenes: quicken me according to thy iudgement.

Heere Dauid declareth yet more plainly, vppon what ground he layde his foundation of praying vnto God: to wit, he brought no kinde of presumption with him, thinking to make account of this or that, and so to be thought very woorthy that God should heare him: but he preferred the goodnesse and faithfulnesse of God aboue all his owne woorthinesses. Loe heere, wherevnto wee must looke if wee wil haue God to be merciful vnto vs. And whē as we would profite our selues by our prayers, wee must not once talke of bringing in of any thing of ours with vs, ne yet alledge this thing nor that, as thinking too binde God vnto vs for some good turne that wee haue doone him: but too haue this principall regarde with vs, God is good, and faithfull, and iust.

See then wheron it is that we must settle our confidence, if we will be resolued that he will heare vs. And this is such

a doctrine

a doctrine, I tell you, as we ought well to holde and keepe. For in very deede, vnder this worde, Promise, this must altogither be vnderstoode. For what is it that induceth God to helpe vs, and to saye, come vnto me, without hee looke that wee would craue something at his handes? What is the cause that our God presenteth himselfe thus vnto vs? Are they our merites? haue we any wayes on our parte deserued, that he shoulde be so louing and kinde vnto vs? No without all doubt. We must then needes conclude, that the promises do spring out from this fountaine, euen his meere mercie. And therefore it is not without cause that Dauid, after hee hath spoken of the promises of God, declareth heere that he desireth not to bee heard, but in this respect, *That God is good and merciful.* As if he shoulde haue sayde, O Lorde, if any man inquire the cause why thou hast hearde me, and haste pittie on me, I am able to say nothing as touching mine owne person, but that I iustly deserue too bee reiected of thee, but thou hast taken the matter and cause vnto thine owne goodnesse and righteousnesse. Now it followeth soone after,

They drawe nighe that followe after malice: and are farre from thy lawe.

Thou art nigh at hand, O Lord: for all thy commaundements are true.

Heere Dauid complayneth vnto God, and desireth him to helpe him against the wicked and vngodly contemners of his maiestie: As if he had said vnto him, O Lorde, I can alledge nothing at all for mine one defence, but that they which draw nigh vnto me to hurt me, are so much the farther off from thy lawe, and I the neerer thy commaundements. It is a common entendement, that they which doe imagine malice, are farre from God, in withdrawing themselues from his lawe: but when as wee shall narrowly looke into the matter, that is the very true and naturall sense of the Prophet which I haue already touched, that they which imagine malice or deceit, are farre off: that is, they are retyred from the lawe of God, to persecute those which drawe

X. nigh

The 19. Sermon of M. Io. Cal.

nigh vnto it. And see how Dauid hath taken for his aduantage, that, that the wicked are farre from God, bicause hee did very well see, that he had beene ouerthrowne through their malice, without God had holpen him. Which thing he sheweth by this cōplaint, that the wicked troubled him euen to the vttermost. And so much the more ought wee to consider of this, bicause we being so womānish as possibly may be, do by & by think that if the wicked beare the sway, and craftily goe about too deuise any thing against vs, that all is loste, and that God hath giuen vs ouer for a spoile. We can in no wise abide that God should exercise our patience nor yet humble vs. Let vs then throughly consider of the example of Dauid. For although that God had specially chosen him out, amongst the rest, and had bestowed so many excellent graces vpon him: yet for all that hee was contented that the vngodly shoulde persecute him, neither could he make them stande aloofe off, for hee had neither Rampares or Bulwarkes, that he was able to saye you shall not come neare me. For he saieth that they drew nigh him. So then, when God giueth such leaue to the wicked, as too haue the raines at will, so that it should seeme, that they had the power euen to set their feete on our throates, yea and to swallowe vs cleane vp, Let vs consider, that it hath beene the will of our God in all ages, to haue his children subiect to the malice of their enemies. Let vs also haue a further cōsideration of this which he sayeth, that they are farre from the lawe of God. For this importeth, that they neither had truthe nor equitie in them. When then the vngodly, shall with the contempt of God, and an extreeme impietie, euen rushe vpon vs to ouerthrowe vs, let vs then, I say, remember thē example of Dauid and saye, wherefore doe the wicked thus persecute vs, without any regarde too him, who ought and will when it pleaseth him both with force and violence represse them? It is bicause they are both blynde and blockish, and are without all truthe and equitie. But on the contrary side, let vs not be afearde, bicause wee knowe that God is nigh vs; & let vs continually cal vpō him, to the

ende

ende he may be alwayes nearer and nearer vnto vs, too put him selfe betwixt vs, and make him selfe our buckler to put backe the attemptes, and to beare the blowes wherewith the wicked shal assail vs. Moreouer, let vs be sure & resolute, that notwithstanding that the vngodly shall thus oppresse vs, yet that God is not farre from vs, although that we can not perceiue it. For God will oftentimes be neare vs, when as we shall thinke that he is cleane hidden: that is to say, he sheweth not vnto vs his power and vertue, neither laieth he it open at the first chop. For we must also call vpō him, that we might shew what honour wee beare him: that although hee prolongeth the time, and tarrieth longer before hee helpe vs, then we would, yet must we notwithstāding tarry his good leisure. In summe we must alwayes bee resolute in this which Dauid here speaketh of, saying, are the vngodly nighe? very well, and God is at hand. That is to say, God is not asleepe in heauen, whiles these men are maliciously imagining to do vs hurte. God his armes are not a crosse, neither are his handes closed, notwithstanding that these men, seeke nothing els but to deuoure vs. God is not yet blynde, whyles these vngodly awake, to destroye and confounde vs. Se then howe God, according to the necessities which he knoweth to be in vs, will alwayes be at hande, so to assist vs, as that whatsoeuer mischiefe is neare vs, it shall neuer be able to ouercome vs, yea, inuent the wicked what they can on all sides. This is it that Dauid meaneth to signifie in this place.

Nowe he also sayeth, *That the commaundements of God are true.* Wherein he exhorteth vs to haue recourse vnto the worde of God, for although wee are thus tormented and fast closed vp in sorrowe and griefes: yea and that we looke this way and that way for helpe, and yet see not God to remedie the same: then I saye, hee teacheth vs too haue recourse vnto his worde. And this is a most profitable admonition. For when we seeke after God, we must not haue regard to our own fantasies, nor to any worldly maner, as we are accustomed, nor too looke that hee submit him selfe

The 19. Sermon of M. Io. Cal.

vnto our will, to shewe him selfe vnto vs after a visible sort, to haue him come downe from heauen in his maiestie, too consume with fire and brimstone all our enemies, to set vs aloft, and to beare vs such fauour, as that wee might haue all things at our owne desire: Loe I beseech you howe wee desire to haue G O D to shewe him selfe, for like as wee are fleshly, so also would we haue him to shew him selfe vnto vs in a visible maner. All this while, his worde is of no great authoritie with vs: for if hee shewe vs not why and wherefore, we are not contented with that which hee hath spoken, but we would forsooth see his hande altogether open. Wherefore, this admonition which Dauid here giueth vs, is very necessary: to wit, that the commandementes of God are true. As if he should haue said, O Lorde, I haue already said, that thou art neare vnto vs, for as much as thou seest vs to bee persecuted and troubled by the wicked, and how they come vpon vs to destroye vs, and that thou arte right before them and against them to beate them backe, and to beate their blowes. All this do I confesse, O Lorde, But yet I see not this after a visible & worldly maner. Howe then? It is bicause thy commaundements are true. Dauid then knewe that God was neare vnto him, bicause hee settled him selfe vpon the lawe, and the promises which were giuen him. And euen so must we do, although it seeme very hard, as we haue already touched. It followeth,

I haue knowne long since by thy testimonies: that thou hast grounded them for euer.

    In this latter verse, for a conclusion, Dauid sayeth, that he was not like a nouice, to bee nowe too learne to knowe what the commaundements of God were, but hee was resolute that God was neare him, bicause hee had his worde, from which he could not starte. He sheweth then, that the faithfull ought not too bee as it were in their A. B. C. but must bee long time exercised: as Dauid protesteth of him selfe, I haue knowne them, sayeth hee, long since.

    Now here he setteth downe a woorde which signifieth
conti-

vpon the Cxix. Pſalme.

continuaunce: *From the beginning haue I knowen* ſaieth hee, *long ſince thy commaundements which thou haſte grounded for euer.*

So then, let vs learne that if wee will boldely ſtriue againſt all the aſſaultes, wherewith wee may bee aſſayled, wee muſte continue in this knowledge of the woorde of God, and we ſhall alwayes finde him ready to be neerehand vs: ſo that we may be ſure of his protection, not for a day onely but all the dayes of our life. And ſo let vs throughly recorde this leſſon, to the ende we may ſay with Dauid, that wee haue the teſtimonyes of GOD ſo deepely imprinted in our heartes, as that wee haue longe time ſince knowen what is already in them, too witte, that God hath eſtabliſhed them: That is to ſay, that although we ſhall ſee a great number of chaunges in this world, that all things are chaunged and turned, yet that God is no chaungeling, that hee neuer altereth his minde, that his woorde is, as it was from the beginning, and as it ſhall continue for euer: that it ſhall neuer be ſubiect to al the turnes and chaunges of this worlde, but ſhall euer abide in his ful ſtrength and vertue, becauſe that God hath eſtabliſhed it for euer. And this is euen ſo, as that we ought to bee prepared to call vpon God, to witte, when as we ſhall be ſetled vpon the true confidence of his promiſes: that we ſhall haue knowne the euerlaſting power & ſtrength which he hath giuen to his woorde: that is, that he will remaine alwayes like vnto him ſelfe. When, I ſay, wee ſhall haue knowen this, we may boldely come and preſent our ſelues before him, beeing aſſured that hee will make vs feele by proofe, that which he promiſeth vs, ſo oftentimes as wee ſhall haue recourſe vnto him, truſting heerein that he hath rendered vnto vs a teſtimonie of the loue which hee beareth vs.

Nowe let vs proſtrate our ſelues before the Maieſtie of our good God, and father, in acknowledging our innumerable offences, which wee dayly commit againſt him: Beſeeching

The 20. Sermon of M. Io. Cal.

seching him that he will so touch vs, as that in steede that wee haue beene ouer much giuen to our fleshly affections, and vanities of this world, that nowe we seeke none other way but wholy too order our selues according to his good will, beeing assured that although we bee feeble and weake, yea and vtterly voyde of all strength, so that wee cannot stepe one foote forwarde without stumbling, or else in going backwarde we bee farre from him, yet let vs not doute but that hee will be neere at hand too helpe vs: And also that when hee hath made vs too feele his helpe, that he will giue vs that grace that wee may bee so thankfull vnto him, as hee deserueth, desiring nothing else but too glorifie him all the dayes of our life, for so many his benefites as he dayly giueth vs, and liberally bestoweth vpon vs.

That hee will not onely graunt vnto vs this grace, but also vnto all people and nations of the earth, &c.

The xx. Sermon vpon the hundreth and nineteenth Psalme.

RESH.

Beholde mine affliction, and deliuer mee: for I haue not forgotten thy lawe.
Pleade my cause and deliuer me: quicken me according vnto thy woorde.
Saluation is farre from the vngodly: because they seeke not thy statutes.
Great are thy tender mercyes O Lord: quicken me according to thy iudgements.
Many there are, that trouble me, and persecute mee: yet doe I not swarue from thy testimonies.

It

vpon the Cxix. Pfalme.   164

It greeued mee when I sawe the transgressors: because they kept not thy lawe.

Consider, O Lorde, howe I loue thy Commaundementes: quicken mee according vnto thy louing kindenesse.

Thy worde is true from euerlasting: & all the iudgements of thy righteousnesse inudre for euermore.

F wee might haue whatsoeuer we would desire & wish, in very deede wee should bee the better at ease, and without any griefe. And this is it that man naturally desireth. But in the meane while wee are to consider, that God wil exercise vs with diuerse afflictions, so long as we are in this worlde. Wherefore such is the condition and state of Christians, so long as they shall liue heere vpon the earth: That is, they must striue, & be exercised with diuerse sortes of greeues, sometimes of the body, and otherwhiles of the soule. And therefore for this cause must we arme our selues to the ende we be not ouercome in the midest of our conflicts. Now the principal peece of our armour is, to pray vnGod, and to call vpon him to helpe vs. And to bring this about, we are throughly to consider howe all the faithfull which liued long before our time, proceeded heerein, too the ende we might order our selues after their example, as in this texte heere, we see howe Dauid was euen extreemely afflicted. Againe, wee see also howe he behaued him selfe in all his afflictions, which although they were very vehement, yet did they not hinder him too haue recourse vntoo God, and of him he was rescued and saued. See then what we haue to meditate vppon, too the ende that wee might doe the like.

X.4.   Beholde

The 20. Sermon of M. Io. Cal.

Beholde mine affliction, and deliuer me: for I doe not forget thy lawe.

When as he desireth God to looke vnto his afflictions, it is euen the same which wee haue already saide: too wit, That although God loued him, yet would he not but that he should be subiect, too a greate number of miseryes, torments and griefes. Let vs not think then to be priuiledged, so long as we are to walke heere bilowe on the earth, but that God will exercise vs and assay and proue our patience, as he hath prooued Dauids, whome he so greatly loued, as the scripture witnesseth of him.

Nowe heere we are to note two things, The one is, that when Dauid desired God to looke vpon his afflictions, and to deliuer him out of them: hee confesseth that hee was astonyed, as if God had turned his backe vpon him. It is very true, that Dauid considered not of all that was too bee considered neither did he conclude, that God would cast off his children in such sorte: But yet so farre forth as naturall reason coulde reach, see howe he might iudge of his estate.

And at that pointe also are all the Children of God. For on the one side, whenas they shall looke vppon their owne state and condition, they cannot chose but that they must be forced to say, what a thing is this, Surely, if God hath any compassion vpon vs, and that he seeth vs, is it possible that euer wee should bee thus cruelly handled, will not he take some better order for this: See then, that wee cannot choose, but to conceiue these and such like imaginations in our heartes, when as wee are greeued and persecuted, and looke into out owne present estate: yea, euen as I haue already sayde, we cannot choose euen too feele our selues as it were to be forsaken of GOD. And yet for all this, wee muste bee fully perswaded and resolued, that GOD beholdeth vs: and although it seemeth, that hee hath turned his backe vppon vs, yet that hee ceaseth not too helpe vs, and is carefull for our saluation, yea on, yea and though wee see nothing, yet let vs holde this for a certaine and an vndoubted trueth, in oure heartes. And therfore so often as we shall be thus troubled to thinke that God hath no lenger care ouer vs, but that he hath clerely forsakē vs, yet let not this hinder vs from praying, after the example of Dauid: neither let vs be slacke, but euen say, O Lord, beholde me. In the second place we haue to note, the reason which Dauid here setteth downe. For I do not forget thy lawe. If then wee will haue God to heare vs, wee must haue his lawe as it were fully settled in our heartes. And howe is that? Forsooth, wee must thinke and study vpon his promises, we must know him to bee louing and mercifull, to helpe all those that are his, and too ayde them in all their necessities, and besides, this must bee oure sure foundation that his promises are infallible, and that he will not suffer his children to goe emptie away, when as they shall tende them selues thereto.

See then how we must meditate vpon the lawe of God that is to say, vpon his word. For vnder this worde, the law, there is no doubt, but that Dauid comprehended the summe of al the doctrine which God gaue vnto his church. Euery of vs then must be exercised in this study, and we hauing the lawe thus imprinted in our heartes, may bee certaine and sure that God beholdeth vs, and will helpe vs in all our afflictions: yea although it seemeth, and wee may iudge according to our carnall senses, that hee hath turned his backe vpon vs, or that he hath closed vp his eyes, and sleepeth, and as a man would saye, neuer thinketh more of vs. Now it followeth in the second verse,

Pleade my cause and deliuer me: quicken me according vnto thy worde.

Here Dauid expresseth what this his affection is, whereof hee hath spoken: to wit, howe that the wicked vniustly persecuted him, as againe hereafter shall more at large bee declared. Now wee knowe that the griefes which the children of God doe suffer in this worlde, are diuerse and sundrie: For sometimes God will lay his heauy hande vppon them, without any man his touching: sometimes also men shall persecute them with vniust actions, so that the wicked shall torment and grieue them. Dauid then sheweth that the affliction which he endured, was of this second kinde, to wit: that hee had enemies which did vniustly trouble him. And see wherefore hee desireth God, too pleade his cause, and restore him. By this wee are admonished, according to that which I haue already saide, that when we haue liued in a good conscience, and haue trauelled euen to doe good vnto euery man, so that no man hath any cause iustly to complaine of vs, yet although wee are persecuted and troubled wee must not for all that bee ouermuch abashed: bicause as great matters as al these were layde vpon Dauid. For this is most sure, that hee walked so maruelous soundly as that euery man had occasion too loue him. And yet notwithstanding hee was not without troubles amongest men. And why so? Bicause of their vnthankefulnesse. Let vs then vnderstande that this vice began not first in these dayes, (I meane the vnthankefulnesse and iniquitie of men:) But long time a goe, and therefore as much as in vs lyeth, let vs seeke after peace: but if so be wee shall procure to doe any wrong, the worlde will neuer giue ouer hating of vs, and procuring of our hurte, yea, and goe about euen to destroye vs. But as I haue already saide, let not that seeme straunge vnto vs, seeing it came so to passe in Dauid. And thus much for this. Nowe in the second place, wee are to beseeche God too auenge our cause, too comfort vs, when we see our selues to be wrongfully dealt withal, when as we are oppressed with false and slaunderous reportes, that we are euill spoken of without iust desert: we must the desire God to be our warrant and deliuerer: and let vs not dout but that he will take our cause into his owne hand, & shewe him selfe to be more then a protector & lawyer. For he saieth that he is the aduerse partie for the maintenance and defence of the causes and quarrels of all his, when as they shall haue walked sincerely before him selfe & before men. Loe here a notable, and very profitable admonition:

That

That is, we must cast all our care vpon God, when as we are wrongfully accused, iniuriously dealt withall, troubled, and oppressed: and beseech God to take the cause into his own hand, and to auenge it him selfe. Nowe this may serue too make vs patient: for what is the cause that men so trouble and torment them selues, waxe so fierce, and cruell, vse reuenge, or els, growe to be very cowardes when any wrong is done them, but bicause that they haue not recourse vnto God, put not thē selues vnder his protectiō, & pray him not, to holde his holy hand ouer them, and to defend their cause? Now if wee knowe this, it is most certaine, that oure heartes shall incontinent bee a great deale more quiet, and let vs not haue such boyling affections as wee haue, to be a-uenged of them which trouble vs, but let vs followe the doctrine which is here set downe vnto vs: to wit, that when we are vniustly entreated, let vs pray vnto God that he will auenge our cause. And besides also, let vs learne to stay our selues of the promise, which is made vnto vs thereof: for like as a Dauid maketh here such a request, so also we are to consider, that he made it not of his owne head, nor at aduenture, but he knewe it to bee the office of God: That is, *That he will auenge all outrages*, as it is said in the song of *Exo. 15.* Moyses, *That if men oppresse any vniustly, our Lord sayeth, that it is he which auengeth the cause of the innocent, and of him that is troubled without a cause.* Dauid then knowing, that God hauing taken this title vnto him selfe, and declared that he will not suffer the throates of the righteous too bee thus cut, to be tormented, and troaden vnderfoote, but that hee will stretche foorth his hand too helpe them: hee hauing knowne this calleth vpon God with a sure constancie, that will receiue him. Wherefore it is meete that we looke vnto this promise when as wee praye, to the ende wee praye not doubtfully but in full assurance, that God will be incontinent ready to helpe our necessities. And this is it why Dauid by and by after sayeth, Quicken mee according vnto thy worde. It is not without cause that this saying was added. For as I haue already said, when as we will beseeche the

Lord

the lorde our God to take vpon him our quarrell, and too afsiste vs in our afflictions: and then we in the meane time shall stand in doubte of his so doing, wee shall profite our selues little in so praying. But we must bee fully assured that he will deliuer vs. And whensoeuer it shall come too passe, that we shalbe destitute of all mens ayde, yea that it shall seeme that all the whole worlde had conspired our destruction and decay, then should we chiefliest assure our selues, that God will auenge our cause: and not onely serue vs in steade of a proctour, but will be altogether also our iudge, & aduerse partie against our enemies, and against all those which haue vniustly afflicted vs. For he it is that must take in hand all iust causes. Wee had neede then too assure our selues of this. But from whēce shal we learne this? euen out of the worde of God, bicause hee hath lefte vnto vs a testimonie thereof in it: as wee see that Dauid speaketh not here at a wilde aduēture, but hath already groūded him self vpon a good foundation, whereon he hath settled him self. Now it followeth,

Saluation is farre from the vngodly: bicause they seeke not thy statutes. And afterwarde hee sayeth, *Great are thy tender mercies, O Lorde: quicken me, according to thy iudgementes.*

Nowe here are two thinges to bee considered off. The one is, that Dauid telleth the reason why all the contemners of God, and all that rebell against his maiestie runne headlong into destruction, and that hee forsaketh them: that they feele no taste nor ease in their afflictions, but that God clerely forsaketh them. Dauid setteth downe here the cause of all this: it is, saith he, bicause they haue not sought after thy lawes, and therefore are farre from thy saluation. Nowe he cleane contrary, protesteth of him selfe, that hee followed the lawe of God, and kept it in his heart. So then we must needes conclude, that he could not be estraunged from it. In very deede, this sentence at the first sight is somwhat darke, but I will make it plaine in three woordes, and then by little and little shewe what doctrine wee are too gather out of this. When any telleth vs of our saluation, wee

must

must in the first place know, whence it proceedeth: to wit, from God, and that there is no saluation but in him: in so much that so long as God is good and gracious vnto vs, it must needes be that all must goe very well on our side, and be assured that our life is blessed, and that we shall want nothing that is meete for our welfare and felicitie. So then, our saluation, and all fulnesse and perfection of benefites consist in this one onely pointe, that God loueth vs and receiueth vs vnto himselfe. And since it is so, let vs nowe consider, what he is whome God will forsake. Once, we are his creatures, and euen as he hath created and fashioned vs, so also will he continue his goodnesse towards vs. Now, seeing that his mercie extendeth euen to brute beasts, euen to the moste vile and abiect thinges, yea euen which wee contemne, and disdaine once to looke on, seeing the mercie of God extendeth so farre, as the holy Scripture teacheth vs, how can it be that he wil forsake vs, yea vnto whom he hath graunted so great dignitie and excellencie? For wee haue a thing excelling all other his creatures, which is this, that God hath imprinted his owne similitude and likenesse in vs: Now when as he hath exalted vs vnto so highe a degree of honor, will he, thinke you, now forsake vs? Hee will not without all doubt. What is the cause then that wee see so many caitifes, and miserable wretches which are euē giuen ouer, so that God sendeth them not so much as the leaste ayde and comfort, that it seemeth, that he hath set them as it were vpon a stage, to be a shame and rebuke to the whole worlde? Whence commeth this? Forsooth because they withdrawe them selues from God: for when as they withdrewe not them selues from him: it is most sure that then he shewed him selfe vnto them, such a one as indeede hee is of his owne nature, that is, louing, kinde, pitifull, gentle, & mercifull. To be short, so long as we will be ordered by him as his children, it is most sure, that he will play the parte of a father towards vs: so long as we will yeelde our obedience vnto him, he wil intreate vs gently. But when we are so peruerse as that wee will not submitte our selues neither vnto

him

The 20. Sermon of M. Jo. Cal.

him selfe, nor yet vnto his word, but contemne his loue & grace offered vnto vs: is it reason that God should put forth his hand to helpe vs? is it meete he should entreat vs as his children, and accompt vs in the number of those which wholy dedicate them selues vnto his maiestie? No not so. But we rather are worthy to be set farre from him, and too haue nothing at all to do with him. Loe here the meaning of Dauid in this place, when he saieth, *O Lord, helth is farre from the vngodly bicause they regard not thy statutes*: As if hee should haue said, we ought not to be abashed, O Lorde, although thou giuest vs ouer, and that we feele no succoure of thy goodnes, but that we languish in al miserie and calamitie. And why so? Bicause wee haue forsaken and refused thy grace: and therefore of very right we ought to be confounded and come to naught. Now I pray you tell vs, what meaneth it that God will not be nigh vs, but by meanes of his word? we must needes feele his goodnes by the effect, yea forsooth, and yet God commeth nigh vnto vs by his word: for that is a preparatiue by which he fashioneth our heartes, to the ende he might shewe him selfe to be a mercifull father vnto vs. And so he maketh an entrance into our heartes for his mercie, that we might be capable to enioye his benefites. Seeing then it is so, that God by his worde, sheweth him selfe and also commeth nigh vnto vs, we must not be abashed, although they which refuse his worde, yea, which so vilananously and contemptuously reiect it, as wee see: we must not, I say, thinke it straunge, although that they feele no help at the hand of God in their afflictions, & that his mercifull goodnesse stretcheth not it selfe vnto them. Now Dauid returneth to this sentēce which we haue seene, and desireth to be quickened according vnto the worde of God. It is very true he vseth the word, *Iudgement*, but al cōmeth to one, as we haue already heretofore declared. *Quicken me then according to thy iudgements*, sayth he, *yea which I haue loued*. But yet notwithstanding, he sheweth vs how it is that God hath promised to quicken vs, and why hee attributeth it vnto his onely mercie.

Nowe

Nowe this is a saying which importeth a very good and excellent lesson: for they which confesse, that they can not be saued but by the grace of God, yet notwithstāding how soeuer it is, they cease not to ouerthrow the grace of God, in extolling their merites, or els in making them selues beleeue that God hath promised them to bee so kinde vnto them, bicause they haue deserued it. It is requisite then that we know with Dauid, what it is that hath moued and stirred vp God to promise to quicken vs: to wit, to mainteine vs. For this worde to Quicken, importeth all whatsoeuer concerneth our estate & saluation. It is bicause he is good, and neuer sought the cause otherwise but in his goodnesse. When then we are enforced to cōfesse that it is God which mainteineth vs, we must also forthwith confesse that God hath done it for his promise sake, and for that he hath reueled it as a testimonie in his worde. Moreouer, see wherein a great number of people are too too grossely deceiued: that is, that God promiseth too mainteine and conserue vs, accordingly as we are worthy thereof, or accordingly as euery man shall deserue. And hereupon, as I haue already said, we darken the grace of God, and faine through arrogancie, I know not what presumption, that it seemeth, that wee our selues are the cause why God fauoureth vs, and that the same commeth at the least, partely of our selues. And therefore we ought so much the more throughly to consider of that which Dauid speaketh of in this place. *Thy mercies, O Lord, are great, O quicken me according to thy testimonies.*

He sayeth not onely, O Lord, I am conserued by thee, bicause thou hast promised: but meaning to declare that it commeth altogether freely, hee sheweth that God was not moued too make any such promise, ne yet was induced by any occasion that he found in vs, or that he tooke it on our behalf. No, no: but bicause his mercies are great. So then, by this saying Dauid teacheth vs, that the promises of God are altogether free, that they hang not of our worthinesse, ne yet bicause God found some thing in vs, why to loue & succour vs so: but bicause he is good, & pitieth our miseries.

Loe

The 19. Sermon of M. Jo. Cal.

Loe what made him to offer himselfe so liberall to vs, & consequently to perfourme his promise. Wee must learne then to glorifie our selues in the meere grace of God, and not to attribute any thing whatsoeuer, either to our owne persons, or yet to our merites, for there is nothing at all in vs. Nowe it followeth,

Many there are that trouble and persecute me: yet doe I not swarue from thy testimonies.

Here Dauid maketh a protestation and complaint, too the ende God might the rather encline him selfe to heare, and helpe him. And that is, according too that which hee hath already said. For if we will haue God to helpe vs, it is good reason that wee should patiently attende his leisure. And in very deede hee that shall presume to aduaunce him selfe, or thinketh that God will haue mercy vpon him, and then letteth him selfe to be ouercome with temtation, and becommeth altogether desperate: hee by this meanes suffereth not God too exercise his goodnesse as he hath promised: but in thus doing, shutteth the gate against God as it were. Wherefore if wee be moued to be reuenged of our enemies, to be our owne caruers, as we say, in reuenge and not tary vntill God doth his office, doe we thinke that hee ought to helpe vs? Hee that will doe iustice with his owne hand, and of his owne priuate authoritie, will hee come to craue aide of the Magistrate, after that hee hath killed his enemy? If so be then there be any man which thinketh to be saued of him selfe, and yet sayeth vnto God, Saue me O Lorde, this a very mockery. And therefore for this cause Dauid saieth in this place, *Many there are, O Lorde, which trouble and persecute me: yet do I not swarue from thy statutes.* Dauid speaketh not here to boast him selfe, but it is to declare that he wayted for the help of God: and putting him selfe vnder his protection, trusted to obteine his request, bicause he might boldely craue it of him. See then what a full boldnes we may conceiue to haue in calling vpon God, & not to dout but that we shal obtain whatsoeuer we pray for vnto him according to his wil: that is, he hath pitie of vs: so

that,

that, I say, we must alwayes stay our selues vpon his promises, as we see Dauid here hath done. So then, let vs here consider in the first place, that so often as we come vnto God, we must come vnto him attending his good leysure, and not to be shaken with whatsoeuer temptations shall come vnto vs, but we must alwaies seeke after God, meditate continually vpon his promises, & haue them alwayes in minde: we must, I say, haue all this, if we will haue God to help and defende vs. Now, as I haue already said, Dauid bragged not here of his vertues, but meaneth onely that hee was not caried away with the iniquitie of men, to be euen with them, or to crie quittance, as wee say, that hee was not in haste to haue that which was promised him, but helde him selfe continually quiet and still, attending paciētly to haue God to accomplishe that which he had promised, touching the reuenge of his enemies: euen so, when as any shall grieue & trouble vs, yet must we not leaue to followe our vocation, and to perseuer in the feare of God. For the greater part of vs will alwayes be full of malice and vnthankefulnesse, vntil such time as God hath refourmed vs. So then, when as wee shall not haue hurt any man, if they ryse vp against vs in armes, let vs not be astonied thereat. And thus much for this. Nowe the other is, that when our enemies shalbe infinite in number, wee must not be troubled for all this: but let vs knowe what the power of God is, and glorifie him as he ought to be glorified. And this is a very necessary point for vs to learne: For wee must not bee afeard of our owne shadowes, as we say. And therefore, if there be two or three men which are in credit and authoritie, that shall make warre against vs, wee are so faint hearted before the blowe come, as that it semeth vnto vs that we are vtterly vndone: euen as though God were not strong enough to helpe vs. See how we through fond ignoraunce glorie in the power of men, and vtterly ouerthrowe the power and might of God. And therefore wee ought a great deale the better to consider of this place, where it is saide, *Many there are, O Lord, which trouble and persecute me: yet doe I not swarue from thy lawe, thy lawe, neither yet haue I forgotten it*: That is to saye, that although wee see an infinite number of people too rise vp against vs, that wee see a generall conspiracie of the whole world, and of all the creatures therein, yet let vs not be too too much afeard, knowing that the power of our God shal be sufficient inough to saue & defend vs. See what we haue to note out of this place, where it is said, *It grieued me when I sawe the transgressors: bicause they kept not thy lawe.*

Here Dauid sheweth that, which we haue already seene before: to wit, that it greeued him more, to see the offences which were committed against God, then all the outrages which he bare in his owne person. And this is also it, which we ought to haue in great recommendation. For if we bee so fine and as it were womannish, that wee can abide nothing, and yet in the meane while haue no care howe God is dishonoured, his iustice violated, and his commaundements broken: I beseeche you do we not right well shewe, that wee are so giuen too please our selues, as that wee euen contemne his sacred maiestie. If a man, meaning to defende his honour euen with tooth and nayle as we saye, and maketh no accompt too see the glorie of God troden vnder feete: if he bee so gallant and hawtie, as to bee reuenged for euery iniurie, and can abide too heare the holy name of God to be euill spoken off, his lawe to be cast vnder foote, doth he not right well shewe him selfe to be a very sensuall and fleshly man? Yes surely, hee is no better then a brute beaste. And therefore for this cause let vs learne, after the exãple of Dauid to be chiefly grieued and vexed, whẽ as we shall see the commaundements of God to be broken. It is the common and ordinarie fashion amongest vs, too bee extreemely vexed when as any iniurie is done vnto vs, as if the honour or credit of any of vs be touched, we are by and by in a great heate, and desire nothing els but too followe the matter hoatly. And why so? bicause we haue no regarde but to our owne person. If one man shall robbe another, his choler or anger will not be apeased: hee looketh to his purse, his medowes, his possesions, and to his houses, euen as he shalbe hindered either in this thing or in that. Now, a

man

man that can well rule his affectious shall neuer haue so great regard to his honour, nor to his goodes as hee shall haue when as hee shall see the righteousnes of God to bee violated. What? (shall hee saye, euen groning in him selfe) ought men in this sort to peruert the righteousnes of God? shall men breake and corrupt all order and equitie? Loe, say I, what it is that ought to touch vs, and to make vs very angry: that is, when we see offences committed against God, and not that which toucheth our owne persons. But what shall we speake of this: for very fewe there are which haue any care hereof. And yet for all that it is not in vaine that Dauid hath set downe vnto vs this example; but to shewe how the children of God ought to moderate their pasiós: that is, they should alwaies beginne at this end, to be grieued and sorrowfull to see the transgressors, which breake, contemne, and treade vnder foote the worde of God, and this should bee their chief grief and sorrowe which should crucifie them, and not to haue such regarde to their owne persons as they haue, but to let God alwayes to be preferred before them selues, and to let him to haue the most soueraigne degree, as he is most worthy. Now if it grieueth vs to see the transgressors, which teare in pieces, and breake al iustice and pollicy, it is certaine, that we should also be grieued at the euil which we know to be in our selues. For euery man is to iudge of him selfe without exception. As for those which will say, Oh see, I am not grieued as touching mine own person: and in very deede, I care not so much for my selfe, as I am grieued to see men thus horribly to offend the maiestie of God, and yet they themselues will take leaue to cōmit as great or els greater villanies & wickednes, thē the rest: and yet when they haue thus said, they will couer their own vices, & flatter thē selues when they haue offended his maiestie, wheras they should lay thē wide ope: now in deede these men shew thē selues to be right hypocrites. And why so I beseech you? bicause they are not grieued at the transgressors, when as they see the glorie of God impaired, his seruice not obserued and his righteousnesse contemned:

Y 3 But

But rather persecute the persons, and hate not the vices which are nourished, and purposely mainteined in them. For what shewe soeuer they make of condemning the euil, yet it may bee easely seene that they are no whit touched therewith. And by this they right well shewe, that they know not what it is to be grieued as they ought. Now this is not to do as wee ought: For whatsoeuer shewe wee shall make of the great zeale wee haue to the honour and glorie of God, we shall very well see, that there is nothing but hypocrisie and dissimulation in vs, if wee looke indifferently into the matter. Loe here what we haue to note out of this place. Now Dauid saieth in the ende.

Consider, O Lord, how I loue thy commaundementes: quicken me according vnto thy louing kindnesse.

Here Dauid doth nothing els but setteth downe more manifestly that which was spoken of heretofore, Consider O Lorde, I loue thy commaundementes, hee speaketh not onely of that which is said vnto vs, that wee must loue our neighbour, liue chastely, honour our father and mother, do wrong to none: but vnder these wordes, hee comprehendeth all the doctrine, wherewith God meaneth to gouerne his people, and church, as we haue already handled. Nowe in this doctrine, are conteined the promises, which witnesse vnto vs his goodnesse: yea and they haue the chiefest place, bicause that God shewing himselfe vnto vs to bee our father, wil not giue vs ouer for any thing: forsomuch as we be assured of our eternall saluation, and that in this worlde he hath care ouer vs, and our life is as it were committed vnto him, so that herein lieth the whole substance, that after hee hath pardoned vs of our sinnes, hee alloweth vs for righteous, and will also gouerne vs with his holy spirite. See then what it is, that is conteined in the testimonies of God. And so Dauid in summe, protesteth in this verse, that he alwaies walked in this loue of God which hee founde in his promises. This is it which he protesteth, and thereupon sayeth, *Quicken me according vnto thy mercy.*

vpon the Cxix. Pfalme.

If Dauid then loued the commaundement of God and his teftimonies, wherefore defireth he not to be quickened according to his merites? And if it be so that he hath deserued, why hath he recourse to the mercie of God? Nowe he very well sheweth, that he meant not too boaste of his vertues, neither yet of any such, I know not what perfection, to haue fulfilled the lawe of God: but he had a speciall regard, as I haue already saide, to the content of God his promises. He alledgeth not here that he had deserued to bee holpen: but he desired to bee defended according to the mercie of God. In this point he setteth before vs his example, to the ende wee might followe him, as this is also the meaning of the holy Ghost, when as he spake by the mouth of Dauid. Now he goeth on for a conclusion and saieth,

Thy word is true from euerlasting: and all the iudgementes of thy righteousnes endure for euermore.

That is to say, thy iust iudgementes are euerlasting: or els, thy iudgementes are alwayes righteous. Heere Dauid, in summe, meaneth to signifie, that hee so stayed him selfe vpon the worde of God, as that he had set his heart vpoon it, yelded him selfe wholy vnto it, and bestowed all his thoughtes & wittes on it. And why did he so? sayth he, *The beginning of it is true, and the righteousnesse thereof endureth for euermore.* As if he should haue thus said, Thou, O Lord, art true in thy word, & shalt alwayes bee found so, & afterward, It is nothing but righteous, it is true from the beginning & thy righteousnes shall endure vnto thend, and without end. See how the two borders or limittes of the worde of God are layde out. When as we shall seeke for this word, wee must make a destinction and difference, betweene truthe, and righteousnes, with this resolution, see how God sheweth him selfe true and righteous. And the farther we go on, the better shall we finde his worde to bee such: so that after we haue throughly vnripped and examined it we shall not haue one syllable, where righteousnes & truth, wil not shewe them selues. Euen so may wee alwayes attribute this title to the woorde of God, as Dauid here sheweth vs. In

Y 3 summe,

The 20. *Sermon of* M. Io. Cal.

summe, when as wee would haue a perfect assurance, to be confirmed, and strengthened in all temptations, so that the deuill shall neuer be able to take fast holde vppon vs: let vs haue this regard, to stay our selues chiefly vpon the worde of God, and therewith to arme vs, attributing thereto these true titles which are here set downe, that there is nothing in it but all truthe and righteousnesse. And therefore this ought greatly to content vs, to assure onr selues of God, not doubting but that hee will graunt vs the grace, that when he hath once brought vs into the waye of saluation, that he will continually conduct and gouerne vs, and hold vs with a mightie strong arme, vntill such time as hee hath brought vs to that ende whereunto he hath called vs.

According too this holy doctrine, let vs prostrate our selues before the maiestie of our good God, in acknowledging our offences, beseeching him that it would please him to make vs better to feele our miseries then wee haue heretofore felt them, to the ende we may laye our selues open vnto him. And that we may in the meane while attaine too that remedy, as to craue pardon of him for them: not douting but that he will graunt vs pardon for them according to our desire, through the death and passion of our Lorde Iesus Christ, albeit we are miserable sinners: And also that he wil through his holy spirite so purge vs frō our sinnes, as that we desire nothing els but to be cōfirmed vnto his righteousnesse, to come vnto him, & to aduaūce vs thereunto daily more and more, vntill such time as he hath coupled vs vnto that holinesse of life, whereunto he continually exhorteth vs. That hee will not only graunt vnto vs this grace, but also vnto all people & nations of the earth, &c.

The

The xxi. Sermon vpon the hun-
dreth and nineteenth Psalme.

SCHYN.

Princes haue persecuted me without cause: but my heart standeth in awe of thy worde.
I am as glad of thy worde: as one that findeth great spoiles.
I hate falshood and abhorre it: but thy lawe doe I loue.
Seuen times a daye doe I prayse thee: bicause of thy righteous iudgementes.
They that loue thy lawe, shall haue great prosperitie, and they shall haue no hurt.
Lord I haue trusted in thy sauing health: and haue done thy commaundements.
My soule hath kept thy testimonies: and I loue them exceedingly.
I haue kept thy commaundementes and testimonies: for all my wayes are before thee.

Hen as men shall trouble vs, and do vs many iniuries, or els any waye grieue and vexe vs, yet are there twoo thinges too leade vs too walke wickedly without the feare of God. The one is, that it wil seme that God hath not compassion of vs, to helpe vs. The other, that wee will bee more afearde of men then in deede wee ought:

For

For we imagine that all is in their hand, and that they may doe all thinges at their owne pleasure and as them selues liste, doe God what he can to the contrary. Lo heere, I say what it is that he hindereth vs frō perseuering in the feare of God: That is, That when men trouble vs with iniuries, violences, & extortions, we are straightwayes discouraged. And so we are heere throughly too consider of this place where Dauid saith that hee stoode in awe of the woorde of God, although princes persecuted him without a cause: & in deede, wee ought euen then most specially too weygh it, when as we see the mightinesse of men to astonish vs, & our enemies to be in great credit and authoritie, yea that it seeme we are euen as sheepe in the iawes of woulfes, that we haue no meane too resist their violence, but that they may do whatsoeuer seemeth good vnto them, in so much that no man dareth once to open his mouth against them. When as, I say, our enemies shall haue all this, and bee thus highly lifted vp ouer vs, that wee knowe not what shall become of vs: then it is a harde matter for vs too conceiue, what the helpe which God hath promised vs is worth, so that we are ouertaken with this feare, to say, O, see wee are vtterly vndone, all our cause is cleane cast to the grounde. And yet in the meane while we neuer once thinke, that they are but Gnattes, or els when wee shall esteeme most of thē, that they are but Frogges leaping and skipping vp and downe heere belowe. Neither yet haue they so mighty thighes and legges as that they are able too iustle against God: but that whensoeuer he shall stretche forth his hand, it shall throwe downe euen into the depth, whatsoeuer mē shall of purpose with all their complices, craftely or wickedly deuise, and whatsoeuer power they shall be any waye able to make. See then what wee haue here especially too note: that is, that whensoeuer we shall fall into the handes of our enemies, and that it shall seeme they might at their pleasure bring to passe whatsoeuer they listed, so that there remained no way to withstande them: yet let vs looke vnto this infinite power of God, and not too doubt, but that

when

vpon the Cxix. Pſalme. 173

when it ſhall pleaſe him to deliuer vs, that the Deuill ne yet all his rable of maintayners ſhall be able to doe any thinge againſt vs. And although all the creatures in the worlde lifted them ſelues vp againſt vs, yet are they not able too doe vs any hurt ſo long as God is on our ſide. And thus we muſt I ſay, receiue the grace of God, which hee hath promiſed vs, to the ende we might not doubt, that all the world can doe vs any harme, when as he ſhall haue taken vs into his protection. And ſee alſo I pray you whether it is that the Scripture leadeth vs, *Although*, ſayth Dauid, *an hundreth thouſand men did ſet them ſelues againſt me, yet will not I bee afrayde. And why ſo? Becauſe the Lord is with me.* And againe, *If I ſhould walke in the ſhadowe of death, ſo long as I ſhall looke vnto God, and ſee his Sheepcrooke before mee, I will not bee afrayde, but be aſſured that I ſhall liue.* Saint Paule alſo comprehendeth all this, ſpeaking not onely of this preſent life, but of the health of our ſoules likewiſe, when as he ſayth, *If God be on our ſide, who ſhall be againſt vs.*   *Pſal.*3.6.

*Pſal.*23.4.

*Rom.*8.13.

I cannot deny, but that wee ſhall haue a greate number of enemyes, and Satan will labour by all meanes poſſible to hurt vs: we ſhall haue great ſtore of his ſupporters to goe about to caſt vs downe headlong into the bottomleſſe pit: and yet all they ſhall doe nothing, when as wee ſhall bee in the ſafekeeping of our God. Nowe this is the ſumme, which we are too gather heereby, in the firſte place of this text. But yet we muſt goe on a great deale farther. For Dauid doth not onely ſhew vnto vs, that we ought highly too eſteeme of this mightie power, and greate goodneſſe of God, wherewith he hath promiſed to helpe vs in our nede: but alſo aduertiſeth and exhorteth vs not too turne aſide from his obedience, for any hurte that men can doe vntoo vs. Nowe it is very true, that the one hangeth vppon the other. For how can it be that wee ſhould haue heartes too ſerue G O D, when as wee ſee the whole worlde too bee againſt vs, and we alwayes in daunger to be hurt: That is to ſay, Let vs put our truſt in God, although the allarme and aſſaultes bee giuen vs on euery ſide: For otherwiſe it
Y.5. ſhall be

shalbe impossible for vs too stand: stoutly to it, without we be throughly perswaded, that God is sufficient to defende vs: yea when as we see all the men in the world, to set them selues againſt vs: but that we trusting in his power, cease not to followe that which he hath commaunded vs: notwithſtanding all the lets that men can possibly lay before vs. Moreouer, we muſt giue our minds to this word of God, as here it is said, *I ſtand in awe of thy word*. For Dauid meaneth not that he would haue God to shew himſelfe in a viſible manner, that he might come vnto him to doe him homage: but he is contented that God hath shewed vnto him his will & pleaſure, and holdeth him ſelfe well pleaſed therewith. And euen so muſt wee alſo doe. For there are a great many of people, which wil brag that they feare God, and profeſſe it with open mouth. And yet notwithſtanding, see how God calleth vs vnto him by his word, & we for al that are no whit moued therwith: yea we ſcarcely vouchſafe once too open our mouthes to declare that we are contented to obay him. Where then is that feare wherof we so brag, ſince the word, wherin the maieſtie of God appeareth, is so contemned of vs? See then wherefore we ought a great deale the more to conſider of this manner of ſpeaking which Dauid heere vſeth, that he ſtandeth in awe of the woord of God, and that he deſired none other viſible preſence: but it ſufficed him that God had onely ſpoken, and hee made good accounte thereof. Now, if we doe not thus, we ſhall euer be letted frō following that which God hath commaunded vs, neither ſhall we euer haue the harts, to diſcharge our ſelues perfectly of our dueties. Contrariwiſe, they that ſhalbe reſolued as Dauid was, only to giue their mindes to the word of God, ſhall ouercome all lets & ſtops: Moreouer after they haue walked aright, doe they ſee that men murmure againſt thē for it, that it ſeemeth that they for their wel dooing ſhalbe recōpenſed with euill, and that this thing & that is miſcheuouſly wrought againſt them? that they muſte needes languiſh in long attending without ſparing, yea that they haue kindled the fury of men againſt them, without any occaſion

vpon the Cxix. Psalme.   174

occasion giuen by them? doe they see, I say, all this? And if they doe thus, it is very well: for then stande they in awe of the word of God, knowing that they shall not be without the help of God, as also our sauiour Christe exhorteth vs. *Feare not* saith he *them which may kill the body: but I wil shewe you whome you ought to feare*, to wit: *feare him who hath both soule and body in his subiection*. *Mat.* 10.28.

When as then you shall looke vnto your God, then shall you not neede to feare whatsoeuer men goe about to cause you to turne aside, & to withdraw you from the right way. And thus we see in summe, that it is our infirmitie, or rather our infidelitie which hindereth vs, when as men threaten vs, when as we see the wicked practizes which are imagined against vs, and that wee are troubled and tormented without cause. For if wee still looked vnto God, this should neuer be able to withdrawe vs, but that wee should alwayes remaine constant to doe that which hee commaundeth vs. And by this also we may see, how al to the cōtrary raigneth at this day in the world, and that there is very little feare of the word of God: For so that wee can holde the fauour of men, in doing our duetie any way, wel, this goeth for payment: But if there bloweth an ill winde, and that wee perceiue any euill practise, or that we bee threatened, and that the vngodly beare the sway: we are incontinent astonyed, yea and that in such a feare, as that we are not able once to stirr a finger. And that which is more, to gratifie the wicked whom we see to be in authoritie, we will make no bones at it, as we say, to offend the maiestie of God: And frō whence commeth this? but that we loke not vnto his word, as here it is set downe? We are then euen conuinced of infidelitie when as we assure not our selues of the helpe of our God, to do that which he hath ordayned, and that which is our duty to doe: that we haue not this inuincible power to resist the assaultes of men. And why so? Because it is most certaine, that we haue not earnestly stoode in awe of the word of God, which ought to be as an assured fortresse, and not to make any account of whatsoeuer that Satan can any way craftely inuent against vs.   Now

The 21. Sermon of M. Io. Cal.

Now after that Dauid hath thus spoken, hee goeth on and sayth,

I am as glad of thy worde, as one that findeth great spoyles.

That is to say, he gladded more in the promises of God, then in all the riches in the worlde, as wee haue seene in the nienth parte, beginning with the letter TETH, which hath beene in that place song, That hee esteemed more of the worde of God, then of all the golde & Siluer in the worlde. And heere he sayth, that he reioyceth to heare God speake, more then if hee had founde all the goods in the worlde, that all the riches in the worlde were nothing to him in respect of it. It seemeth greatly at the first sight that heere is some contrarietie, as to stand in feare & awe of the word of God, & also to reioyce in it. For ioy & feare are meere contraryes. But we haue already declared what it is that Dauid meaneth by this feare: not that hee was abashed too serue God; ne yet that he douted of his saluation: But it was to bridle him and to holde him in obedience, and also to declare, that God gaue him such a constancy against all the men in the worlde, as that when hee seeth all the creatures of God to lifte theselues vp against him, yet that hee ceased not to goe on to doe that which God had committed vnto him, and that which he saw was his duetie to doe. To be short, let vs then holde this for a resolute point, that Dauid had not such a feare as made him fierce and cruell, ne yet which made him to flye from the presence of God: but he so reuerenced that, which God spake, as that hee stoode boldly at defyaunce with all men, declaring that hee made no rekoning of their fury, poyson, nor yet of all their deadly enmities. Dauid, I say, cared for none of all this, And why so? Because he so reuerenced and honoured God, as that He fully reposed himselfe vpon his worde.

Nowe, when as we haue such a feare, it is nothing contrary to the ioy which Dauid heere speaketh of: But it is rather an excellent accorde, or sweete hermony: for it is impossible for vs rightly to giue our selues vnto God, and to obay him in such sort as we ought without we loue him,

and

and that his word be pleasaunt and sweete vnto vs. And see wherefore Dauid doth not onely say, that the woorde of God was more deere vnto him, then either golde or siluer: but he sayth, that it was sweeter vnto him then hony. Hee setteth downe these two thinges which ought too be coupled together: to wit, that the word of God ought too be more deere and sweete vnto vs, then all other thinges, and that we ought to take all our delight and pleasure therein, desiring nothing else, but to order and holde our selues to it: knowing that whatsoeuer God hath, is to this ende, too communicate the same vnto vs, that wee might taste of his bountie and loue.

Nowe wee see that Dauid did not without cause ioyne this ioy: which he conceiued of the woorde of God, with feare: signifiing that he stoode not in awe of God perforce, and with a slauish feare, as we say: but he did it in acknowledging him too be his God and Sauiour, and setling him selfe wholly vpon his promises. And thus much for this second verse. Nowe he addeth soone after:

I hate falshod and abhorre it: but thy lawe doe I loue.

This verse is not heere added but to good purpose: For Dauid sheweth that we can neuer be glad (as hee hath declared how he hath beene) neither yet stand in awe of the word of God, without we detest falshod. Now, we of our owne nature are so nusseled in vanitie, as that it is lamentable. The lawe of God then shall neuer come so fully home vnto vs, as that we may iustly say, that we earnestly heare it, and receiue it from the hart, vntil such time as we haue striued against our fleshly affections, that is too say, against all whatsoeuer is in our nature, because it is all but vanitie. In summe, Dauid, after hee had spoken of this ioy, which hee had conceiued of the promises of God, wherein hee declareth vnto vs his goodnesse: after he had spoken of the feare which we owe him, to become subiect vnto him, and after that he had giuen him the authoritie which hee deserued aboue all other men and creatures: for a conclusion hee addeth, the meane howe to attaine to all this: to wit, that

we must

we must eschewe falshod, and not onely eschew, & hate it, but also detest it: yea, signifying that wee must greatly abhorre it, so that wee ouercome all our wicked desires and tame them, and all other our lustes which cary vs away too wickednesse, & withdraw vs from the obedience of God. So then, we see nowe, that naturall men can neuer be disposed to serue God, vntil such time as they haue striuē against the vanitie of their owne nature, and that not onely once, or twise, but also too continue it all the dayes of their life. For what are the lustes which are in vs, and which doe wickedly leade vs from the right way? In very deede, the more parte are so preuented with them, as that they feele them not: or else thinke, that it is nothing so meruelous thicke darkenesse remaineth in them. As for those which haue a desire with all their hart to forsake them, yet shall we finde them also to be ouermuch nusseled in them. Moreouer, if all the men in the worlde were examined, and an inquisition made, I confesse that wee shall finde the moste wicked sometimes to be remorsed and stoong, and to be inwardly pricked and constrayned mauger their hearts to haue loathing to doe euill. They haue an eye vnto it by fittes: and yet they cease not too followe the euill with a continuall course, although betweene whiles they haue a lothing of it. And we must not greatly meruell at this: For carnall men which are not gouerned by the spirit of God, are carryed away with their wicked affectiōs, as with a fury, so that their whole reason is altogither brutish. And euen they shal very wel haue an hatred of their euill, but yet not so flye frō it, as that wee shall not be able to say, that they haue such a feare of God as is to be required, too forsake them selues, and wholy to submit themselues vnto his will.

Se heere what we haue to consider out of this place. But in the meane while one thing is to be obserued, that Dauid maketh a comparison betweene the lawe of God, and all whatsoeuer that men can imagine on their owne head, with all their reasons and desires: as if he should haue said,

That

vpon the Cxix. Pſalme.   176

That there is but onely rule that is good, and worthy to be beloued, to wit, the lawe of God. When then our life ſhalbe conformable to the word of God, all ſhall goe wel: But wee ſhall not withdrawe our ſelues neuer ſo little from it: as that we ſhal not by and by royle ouerthwart al the fields. And why ſo? For all our trueth and ſinceritie is incloſed within this rule which God hath ſet downe vnto vs. Wee ought then to beare this honor vnto the word of God, too heare it as it is layde out vnto vs, and to follow it in all ſimplicitie: or elſe ſo ſoone as we ſhall decline from it neuer ſo little, ſee, we are quite out of the way of ſaluation, ſo that we cannot choſe but to be confounded, vntill ſuch time as we are entred againe into the way, which God hath ſhewed vs. Now hee addeth:

> *Seuen times a day doe I prayſe thee: becauſe of thy righteous iudgements.*

Heere we may take this word *Iudgement*, for the manner which God holdeth in gouerning the worlde, and the puniſhments which he layeth vpon the vngodly: as alſo for the grace which he cauſeth them to feele which call vppon him, and which walke ſincerely before him.   For the holy Scripture oftentimes when it ſpeaketh of the Iudgementes of God, meaneth al this. But becauſe that in this Pſalme, the Iudgements, are for the moſt parte taken for the ſtatutes, & ordinaunces that are contayned in the law of God: I gladly meane to ahandle it at this preſent thus: that is, That Dauid prayſed G O D becauſe he had giuen vnto his people a lawe which was bothe iuſte and full of equitie, and that therein hee had whereof to bee glad, and to prayſe and magnifie him.

Lo: heere a place well woorthy the noting. For by theſe woordes Dauid doth vs too witte, that wee cannot prayſe G O D, ſo longe as wee are not inſtructed in his woorde, our mouthe ſhall bee cloſed vppe, and our hearte looked faſt vppe, ſo that a man ſhall not pull from vs one good woorde, which may turne too the prayſe of God.

And

And to proue this to be so, we see that the vnfaithful shal not onely bee dumbe too praise God: But they will also fall out with him, that whatsoeuer shall come from their mouthes, shalbe to blaspheme God, & to murmur against his diuine maiestie. As for the ignorannt, they shalbe so blockish as that they shall haue no desire to prayse God: & if they doe prayse him, it shall bee but for fashions sake, because it is but a mocking of God and his word. How then may we praise God in good earnest & without hypocrisie? Forsooth, euen when as wee shall be instructed in his ordinaunces, when as we shall haue knowen what care he hath of our saluation, how he gouerneth his Church, howe hee embaceth him selfe, to apply him self vnto our grosse capacities, & to make himself to be familiarly acquainted with vs. When then we shal see God to haue such a care ouer vs to instruct vs, that he hath so rightly ruled our life, that hee so purueieth for al our necessities as that we want nothing: ought not we to giue our mindes vnto him, yea euen to be inflamed wholly to magnifie his holy name, and to bee rauished with that desire which Dauid heere speaketh of.

Let vs now see what we haue to gather in summe out of this place: and thereby we may see how slenderly wee haue at this day profited in the Schoole of God. For, whence commeth this circumspection? Where is that zeale of ours in praising of God, which Dauid sayth, that he had? Seeing that sarcely one word can bee pulled from vs, when any speech shalbe of praysing God, yea, were it not for fashion sake and contenaunce onely. This is farre from continuing in it, and farre from extending our whole study thereto, as to make it the most principall thing that ought to bee in our whole life. Now we are heereby conuinced of our slender studying and meditating in the worde of God because we are so colde and negligent in praysing of him, and without hauing a greater care in acknowledging his benefites bestowed vpon vs. And that which is more, Let vs throughly consider that Dauid sayeth not onely, that he was stirred vp to prayer vnto God for once, & so continued it for certaine

taine dayes, but hee sayth *dayly*, & after, *seuen times:* that is, that he cōtinued in it all his life long. For this word *Seuen*, is taken in the holy Scripture for a meruelous perseuerance, when as men continue it, and are not drawne away for any cause whatsoeuer, but do alwayes holde thē selues therto. And this is the meaning of the Scripture, for this number of Seuen. Nowe Dauid protesting that hee dayly prayfed God seuen times, meaneth that he exercised him selfe therin, from the morning vnto the euening. And after that, hee exhorteth all other men too haue the like desire and zeale too praise God. So then, let vs compare our selues with Dauid, and we shall finde, that wee haue learned very little out of the word of God, considering that we are so slouthfull in prayfing of him. And yet for all that wee are greatly too giue him, yea infinite thanks, when as wee shall haue knowne his grace and goodnesse towards vs, in that hee is so carefull to gouerne and order our life, and too shewe vs the way of saluation. The Papistes haue applyed this saying to their set houres: and haue layde holde onely on the first parte of the verse, saying, That they prayse God seuen times a day, when as they sing their Mattaines, Primes, their third houre, sixth houre, at midnight, their euensong and Compline. See heere how God shall be well prayed seauen times a day as they thinke. Yea, yea, good inough, As though God would call back that, which hee hath pronounced by his prophet Isaiah, *This people*, saith he, *honor me with their lips, but their hearts are very farre from me.* He goeth on farther and sayth, that hee will shewe them that hee cannot abide such mockeryes, and to be so dallyed withall. See heere howe God threateneth the Iewes with an horrible vengeaunce, because they onely prayfed him with the mouth. Nowe, we knowe, what their set houres which their Monkes, Fryers, and Priestes doe sing, or rather which they bleate and houle out in their Churches, are that they are without either vnderstanding, deuotion, and any good desire whatsoeuer. And they thinke it not inough that they

Isai.29.13.

Z. shewe

shewe them selues in deede openly to mock God: but their deuilish doctrine also emporteth the same, that they cannot but merit, hauing this finall meaning to prayse God. So that when a Chanon hath put on his Grayamisse, and Surplisse, and going out of his Chamber with this finall intent: and yet anon after thinketh of his Gossip, his cheere, and his pastime: yea that he play the Hypocrite there, yet forsooth he must needes merit. It is very true, that they will confesse, that there is veniall sinne entermedled amongest: but yet that the same cannot hinder them from meriting, when as they had this finall intent to prayse God : yea and so also, as that when they come home againe vntoo their house, they think them selues to haue discharged their dutye. To be short, so that at the beginning and the end, they had some motion to deuotion, it is inough. And is not this wholly to mock God, and to dally with him, more then a man would dandle a young Childe. But see how this miserable cursed people haue peruerted all the holy Scripture, in mingling it with so shameful thinges that euen the very Heathen, when as they shall haue gotten the vnderstanding of the least sparke of trueth, will bee ashamed too see such seruice in the Papacy too bee called godly seruice. When it is all after this manner, I pray you what praysing of G O D shall there remaine ? Let vs then vnderstande, that these people are very farre from Dauid : and that if wee woulde take example by them, they right well shewe, that they knowe not what it is too prayse God, but rather prophane his holy name, when as they wil thrust in such abhominatiõs amongst, as we dayly see them to commit against his worde. Now Dauid addeth soone after:

They which loue thy law, shall haue great prosperitie, and they shall haue no hurt.

Heere Dauid beeing led by the spirit of God, as a true Prophet, contenteth not him selfe with speaking of the benefites he had done: but it was needefull that he might be let as a Glasse before our eyes, to the ende we might be ledde too followe him. But yet in this verse, he more expressely setteth foorth the office and duetie of a prophet, when as hee sayth, They which loue thy lawe, shall haue great prosperitie, and they shall haue no hurt.

Nowe by this he sheweth vnto vs that wee are euen in good earnest accursed, when as wee giue our selues vp vnto our owne fleshly liking, because we would bee esteemed amongst men, and take pleasure in our pastimes and delightes. And why so? Because we shall be alwayes tormented with vnquietnesse and griefe, so that we shall neuer be at peace and rest. And although wee veryly thinke our selues to be assured of victory all the dayes of our life, yet shall we reele this way and that, and willingly hurt our selues, so that it shoulde seeme we had a will too breake both our armes and legges, & in the end, neck and all. And the reasōis, for that we follow not the way which God hath set before vs. Let vs then cōsider, what the meaning of Dauid is, to wit, that we must not make reckoning of any assurāce heere in this worlde, except we loue the woorde of God: yea and that so to, as that we desire nothing else, but to be wholly ordered by it, to submit and holde our selues therto, without beeing withdrawen by the intisementes of Satan, and with all the temptations of our corrupte fleshe and nature shall laye before our eyes. In very deede it may very well seeme at the firste sight, that experience teacheth vs the contrary of that which Dauid speaketh. For who are moste greeued, vexed, and troubled? Forsooth euen the children of God, who haue al the shame & offences doone vnto them? Euen the selfe same men. For it is saide, That

That our sauiour Chrift is as it were a badge and marke of all thefe contrarieties, we muft then haue all the vngodly to be our enemyes. In fumme, all they which intend too ferue God, cannot efcape from fhame and flaunderous reportes, from beeing defpifed, troubled, and outraged, & to indure great numbers of iniuryes and violences: Loe howe the Children of God are intreated and handled in this prefent life. And fo by this reafon, it feemeth that Dauid promifeth vs heere, that which we haue not. But we are heere too confider, that Dauid promifeth vs not fuch a reft, as fhalbe as it were an earthly Paradife. Hee fpeaketh of this true profperitie, which the Children of God haue, when they are contented to ferue him: that in all their griefes: yea in all their anguifhes and troubles, they runne onely vntoo him, and lay all their cares vpon him, not doubting but that he will helpe them: and afterward, heerevpon not too feare, whatfoeuer that mortall men can imagine or deuife againft them.

When as then wee fhall haue fuch a peace as this, although our eftate and condition be in the viewe of men the mofte miferable in the whole worlde, yet ought we too bee throughly contented, knowing that God will raife vs vp, and make vs to tryumph ouer all our enemyes, although we thought we fhould fall euen to bee cruffhed and vtterly beaten too poulder, yet will God bee ready too vpholde vs, and make vs to be bleffed. As it is faid in the 91. Pfalme, That God will not fuffer his faithfull too tumble ouer and ouer, neither yet fo to fall as that they fhall not be able to releeue them felues againe: but will rather fende his Angels to lifte them vpp into the Ayre. In very deede, yet fhall it not bee fo, as that we fhall not fometimes hurt our felues: howbeit the affaultes fhall not be fuch as to frufh vs deadly: howe euer it bee wee fhall in the ende feele in what fort God fhall haue affifted vs by his Angels. This is the meane and the manner too feele by effecte, that which Dauid fpeaketh off.

Now

Now in trueth, the wicked shal neuer be able to take any such holde: becaufe they are not worthy of it. For by reason they know not what God, nor his worde is, without it be to hate him, and too anger him: it is meete that they proue by experiment the contrary of that which is heere spoken of by Dauid: to wit, becaufe they loue not the lawe of God, it is good reafon that they shoulde bee inwardly troubled, and greeuoufly tormented without end. Now it followeth,

Lorde I haue trufted in thy fauing health: and haue done thy commaundements.

Heere Dauid more liuely expreffeth and declareth that which I haue already touched: to wit, that our affection in feruing of God, proceedeth of the truft which wee haue in him, in beleeuing his promifes. If then we conceiue not that God is our fauiour, and fo by that meanes trufte that hee will help vs, it is impoffible that we fhould be inflamed too ferue him. It is true, we may very well haue fome feeling of the duetie which we owe vnto him, and be fome what touched therewith, although in deed few there are which think therof: but admit it be fo, yet will no man for all that freely and of his owne accord, fay, O come, Let vs ferue, yea let vs ferue our God, euen vntill fuch time as we are fully affured of the good which he meaneth, and is ready to procure vs, and of the true and full hope of our faluation, throughly imprinted in our heartes. And fo let vs rightly confider, that they which remember no more of that which is preached vnto them but this, to fay, Loe this is it which GOD commaundeth vs: we muft either doe this or that: Truely this is no pointe of true Chriftianitie. And why fo? Becaufe the principalleft pointe of Chriftianitie, is to knowe the goodneffe of God, and the mercie which hee vfeth towardes vs.

Loe, this is I fay, the true knowledge which wee mufte learne in the Schoole of our Lorde Iefus Chrifte, and holde vs to that which he hath declared vnto vs. And befides, we are alfo to confider of that which he commaundeth vs: but

his

his promises must be preferred, & haue the cheefest place. And by this also we are shewed, that in the popish religiō, the principall doctrine of Christianitie is put out & made nothing: Because that when the Papistes creake and chatter their prayers, making as though they presented their supplications vnto God, they say, that they must neuer assure them selues of that which they pray for. And the cause is, for that they looke not vnto the free promises of God. And how so? Beholde an hypocrite shall step vp and preach nothing else but that which euery man is bounde to doe. Hee will preach vnto you of Chastitie, he will make you another Sermon of Almes, one of this matter, another of that: and yet for all this, we knowe not what it is to beleeue in God. Then doe we a great deale lesse know what it is to call vpon him in full assurance, to say, God is our father, he alloweth vs for his children, because he hath vs as he would wish, & that our sins are forgiuen vs through the grace of our lord Iesus Christ. There is no whit of this in popery: &therfore it is impossible that there should be one word of good and sound doctrine in it, and profitable vnto saluation. Let vs then well consider of this saying of Dauid, O Lorde, I haue trusted in thy sauing health, and haue doone thy Commaundements. Nowe in the ende he sayth:

My soule hath kept thy testimonyes: and I loue them exceedingly.

I haue kept thy commaundements and testimonies: for all my wayes are before thee.

After that Dauid hath sufficiently protested, that hee loueth the word of God, that it was so sweete and pleasant vnto him, as that all his study and delight consisted therin: he concludeth and saith, That his soule had kept it, as if he should haue said, O Lord, in that I was giuen to serue thee, it was not with my hands and feete onely, but because I loued thy word, yea and that with all my soule, and I take my whole delight therein. For when the Hebrewes meane too shewe a pure and sounde lyking, they say, My soule hath done this, or that, that is asmuch to say, as I haue doone

it with

it with all mine hearte. Loe then an heartie seruice which Dauid heere expresseth: & this is yet a point which ought throughly too be considered of: For wee see howe men are giuen to play the hypocrites: euen too set a very fayre outwarde shewe of the matter, and by that meanes thinke them selues to be discharged before God.

Nowe wee must beginne farder of, as Dauid heere sheweth vs, that is, wee muste keepe the woorde of God in our heartes. Wherein hee confirmeth the matter, which we haue already heeretofore handled: to witte, that the question is not, to haue GOD simply to teach vs, whereby wee might know what he requireth at our hands, & what our duetie is towards him: but he buildeth vpon his promises. Howbeit Dauid hauing said, that his soul kept the cōmādemēts of God, becauſe he loued thē, by this which he addeth ſone after he ioyneth the promises with the cōmandemēts, saying *For al my wayes are before thine eyes*, It is true, that he sheweth by these words, that except he had byn sure that god protected him, it had not byn possible for him to haue had that true lyking to haue serued his maiestie. And hereupon hangeth the seconde pointe, that God helde him alwayes in his presence, becauſe hee should not haue leaue to doe euill: as if hee shoulde haue saide, O Lorde, becauſe I knowe that no man is able too hide him selfe from thee, Loe why I giue my selfe wholly too feare and serue thee. And too say the trueth, what is the cauſe that the vngodly take such libertie, to commit and deuise such vilanous and greeuous Actes, as that they them selues are ashamed off, yea that it maketh the very heares of their head to stand vpright: What is the cauſe of this? The reaſon is, for that they knowe not that God seeth them, for if they were sure of that, they would be somwhat moued with the feare of his maiestie. So then, in that the faithles war thus against God, and take libertie too doe wickedly: it is, bicauſe they think that God seeth them not, according too that saying in the Scripture, *The wicked man hath said, God seeth not, hee knoweth nothing of that which is doone heere on the earth*.

Z.4.

I meane

I meane not that the wicked doe thus openly speake: yet for all that they think no lesse: as by experience wee see, for they thinke that God marketh not all their iniquities, neither yet that it is needefull for them once too make any account of their sinnes. Howbeit Dauid sayth cleane contrary, That because hee knewe that all his wayes were before God, therefore he kept his commaundements. See also why the scripture, in speaking of the holy fathers which liued sinceerly, sayth, That they walked before God: to wit, they had this consideration, that they knew that God did see them: and therefore they walked, as if they had beene in his presence. And this importeth, that they toke not such liberty as they theselues thought good, but that they wholy ordered them selues according to the will of God, as hee had declared it by his worde. See then Dauid his meaning. And euen so must we also doe, if wee will haue our life and conuersation to be well ordered: to witte, to know that God seeth vs, and therefore that we cannot flye from his hand, but must submit our selues vnto it, albeit wee wil not doe it freely and of our owne accorde. And so let vs willingly be contented to be, ruled by him, beeing certifyed of his loue and goodnesse towards vs, to the ende wee might in trueth make this protestation which Dauid heere maketh.

According too this holy doctrine, let vs humbly prostrate our selues before the maiestie of our good god, in acknowledging our offences, beseeching him that it woulde please him to make vs to feele the power of his woorde, in such sort, as his holy Prophet heere sheweth vs, and so too feele it, as that wee may wholy submitte our selues vnto it: Knowing that when it shall come in question for vs too remitte our selues, and cleaue vnto him as hee requireth, that wee must forsake the whole worlde, and all our carnall affections which any way hinder vs from comming vnto him: to the ende wee may so climbe vp vnto his maiestie, as that not fearing the world nor all his assaultes, wee may putte our whole confidence in his mercifull goodnesse,

nesse, and boldly present vs before his face: to the ende he may receiue vs, so that wee might alwayes bee gouerned through his holy spirit, vntil such time as he hath brought vs vnto that perfectiō, wherevnto he calleth and biddeth vs. That hee will not onely graunt vnteo vs this grace, but also &c.

The xxii. Sermon vpon the hundreth and nineteenth Psalme.

THAV.

Let my complaint come before thee, O Lorde: and giue me vnderstanding according to thy word.
Let my supplication come before thee: and deliuer me according vnto thy worde.
My lippes shall speake of thy prayse: when thou hast haft taught me thy statutes.
My tongue shall treate of thy worde: for all thy cōmandementes are righteous.
Let thine hande helpe me: for I haue chosen thy cōmaundementes.
I haue longed for thy sauing health, O Lorde: and in thy lawe is my delight.
Let my soule liue, and it shall prayse thee: and thy iudgementes shall helpe me.
I haue gone astray like a sheepe that is lost: seeke thy seruaunt for I doe not forget thy commaundementes.

These

These eight last verses, which ar the knitting vp of the whole Psalme, do shew vnto vs that, which we oftentimes haue before seene: to wit, that Dauid his chiefest desire was this, to be duely and truely instructed in the word of God, and therin to be cōfirmed: for he tooke such pleasure in it, as that all the rest was little, or nothing worth vnto him in respect of the same. Now it is very true, that he hath already sufficiētly spoken of this matter: and yet that which he presently addeth is not supperfluous, especially, if we consider in what sort our carnall desires rule vs. For that is it which letteth vs that we can not onely haue that feruency which Dauid had, to seeke throughly to profit in the schoole of God: but we scarsely haue so much as any small desire. And therefore as I haue already said, we are too too much nuzzeled in our earthly affections: Wherefore this is a lesson which ought many times too put vs in minde: that if wee will pray vnto God according vnto his will, wee must not come vnto him with a desire of our owne, to saye whatsoeuer commeth in our brayne, yea and to leaue out the most principall parte: but we must beginne with this saying: to wit, that it would please God so to instruct vs, as that our life may be squared according to his law, and we to cleaue so vnto it, as not to come with a double and twyfold heart. Although we are to striue against the worlde, and our owne nature, yet must we remaine constant in this: chiefly to loue the woorde of God. And therefore for this cause Dauid here sayeth,

Let my Complaint come before thee, O Lord: and giue me vnderstanding according vnto thy word.

When he speaketh of his complaint which hee maketh vnto the Lord, he sheweth that he made no cold prayer vnto God, as we many times, and as it were daily do. but with great vehemency. I can not deny but that an hypocrite may

may very well make complaint with a loude noyse, and thrust out his weasaunt. But Dauid hauing here consideratiō of God, meaneth not to make an outward shew before men. Wherefore, That he cried out aloude, importeth as much as an earnest testimonie wherewith hee was pricked forward. Now by this we see, that he chiefly desired that which he craueth: to wit, to haue God to instruct him, and to giue him vnderstāding. And in desiring this gift of God, he cōfesseth that he was of him selfe a very wretched blind soule: that hee neuer vnderstoode any thing, yea although he had the lawe in his hands, which he might reade, wherein was conteined a true perfection of all wisedome, yet that he still continued euē like a poore miserable blind wretch, except God enlightened him. So then, let vs vnderstande that this is an especiall gift which God bestoweth vpon vs, when hee openeth our eyes, too make vs vnderstande that which is shewed in his word, whether we reade it, or that it be preached vnto vs. Yea, and let vs not here make any exception, thinking our selues to bee more sharpe witted, or abler then Dauid was: but let vs rather knowe, that if hee needed to beseech God to giue him vnderstanding, that we for our partes haue as great neede. So then, it can not bee chosen but that whē God hath deliuered vnto vs his word, and declared his will therein conteined: and for performance hereof inlighteneth our hearts by his holy spirite: for other waies we shal haue our eares beaten in vaine; and then the doctrine which we haue heard will do vs no good. Now that which followeth, *According vnto thy worde*, may two wayes be set forth, According vnto thy word: that is to say, that thou wilt make me wise. And after what maner? That I be altogether ruled by thee, and do that which thou commaundest. This is a very true saying, for by this wee are admonished to heare God speake, and we againe must suffer him to haue dominion ouer vs: and not to be ouertakē, with this fooolish arrogancie, and saye, I haue knowledge inough, I neede not so much teaching. Wherefore, when as God shall haue spoken the worde, let vs passe it simply and without gainesaying. This

The 22. *Sermon of* M. *Io. Cal.*

This sentence then which I haue spoken, is very true: but yet it agreeth not with the meaning of Dauid, ne yet with the plainenesse of the text. For he craueth here two things, the one in the first verse, the other in the second. He sayeth in the first verse, Let my complaint come before thee, that I might be instructed according vnto thy worde. And afterwarde he addeth,

Let my supplication come before thee: and deliuer me according vnto thy worde.

It is very true that he vseth two sentences: but yet they are not without a marueilous grace in one selfe same signification: and by this repetition we may the better perceiue that Dauid meant not, but to haue God to graunt either of both his requestes, according to the promises which he had made him. See then, what the naturall sense is of the first verse, O Lord, giue me vnderstanding as thou hast promised. And this is according vnto the rule which wee haue heretofore touched, that wee ought not too craue of God any thing whatsoeuer, without it bee that which hee hath promised, yea so that we be assured of his wil. It is very true, that God dealeth very familiarly with vs, when as hee calleth vs, to come vnto him, as the father calleth his childrē, suffereth vs to poure abroade all our affections vnto him, and to vnburden them as it were in his lappe, as the scripture maketh mention: and yet hee meaneth notwithstanding that wee should holde this modestie, not too craue of him any thing whatsoeuer that seemeth good in our owne eyes: but to discerne of that which best liketh him. And howe shall wee knowe that? Forsooth by his promises. Wherefore we must be well assured of our prayers, and not to craue of God at a wilde aduenture, this thing, or that: but we must beseeche him, and be certaine and sure that he will heare vs. And how may this bee done, seeing that no man hath beene of his counsell, too saye that wee haue any such certaintie, except hee him selfe had tolde vs, that it is his pleasure to graunt vs? So then, it is requisite that al our prayers be conformable vnto the promises of God, that

we gawe gather together, I say, out of the holy scripture, al whatsoeuer he hath promised vs, to the ende wee may that waye haue an entrance to make our supplications, and prayers vnto him. Now it remaineth for vs to knowe, whether Dauid had the promise alone made vnto him by God, or els, whether it bee common vnto vs all. No doubt of it God spake not to Dauid as to a priuate man: but too declare in generall that he would not misse to instruct all those which come vnto him in humilitie, and to aske nothing, but according vnto his worde. Since then it is so, that God hath spoken to vs in generall, declaring that he is ready to playe the part of a schoolemaister, if we will become as his schollers: we may then say with Dauid, O Lorde, giue me vnderstanding according to thy promise. Now we are here briefly to marke two notes. The first is, that we are aduertised to acknowledge our ignorance and rudenesse. For if we craue of God to bee made wise, and then we thinke to become wise through our owne industrie and power, this is a meere mockerie. We must then acknowledge our selues to be vnprouided both of wit and reason, if wee will make this request in truth: to wit, to haue God to giue vs vnderstãding. And thus much for the first point. For the rest, we ought to know, that God desireth but to receiue vs with this condition: to wit, euen when we shalbe humbled and cast down, For otherwise we will neuer abide to bee instructed, whatsoeuer holy scripture we haue, bicause that in it hee sayeth, that it is his office to teach the humble and meeke, that it is as it were his very proper nature to open the eyes of the blinde, and to instruct those which are altogether ignorant, to gather together the strayed sheepe, and to bring them to the hauen of saluation, when as they are in the way of perdition. Since then it is so, that God taketh all this vpõ him selfe, let not vs doubt but that he will heare all our requestes. But what? We see howe colde we are. For we are so hindered with the things of this worlde as that wee leaue out the principal. Now after that Dauid had declared what he chiefly desired, he goeth on and sayeth,

My

The 22. Sermon of M. Io. Cal.

My lippes shall speake of thy praise: when thou hast taught me thy statutes.

Here he prosecuteth that which he began withall at the first: that is, to shew that he would not be vnthankefull, but that he would acknowledge the benefites of God. It is very true that whē we come vnto God, it is not any thing nedefull for vs to make great outwarde shewes, as though hee knew them not perfectly inough as of him selfe: but thus he meaneth, that when we pray, hee would haue vs to saye, that we will neuer hereafter be vnthankefull vnto him: and this needed not neither but to the ende, the better to stirre vs vp to do our dueties. And this also maketh vs to praye with a boulder courage, to feele the fruite which shall come vnto vs, when as we shal haue obtained that which we haue craued and desired. Dauid then, in saying here, My lippes, O Lord, shall speake of thy prayse, when thou hast taught me thy statutes: kee meaneth that hee shalbe disposed to praise God with open mouth. Nowe why speaketh Dauid after this maner? In thus doing, he taketh vppon him, and stirreth vp him selfe too such an acknowledgement, as hee protesteth to make: and it is, as if he had said: Goe to nowe, when as God shall haue shewed me this fauour to instruct me, what is then my dutie to do? Forsooth, I must euen thē prayse him, for that I ought to be thereto the more stirred vp, and to be greatlier occasioned therein. And since I desire God too teach mee, what fruite shall I reape thereby, when as he shall haue called me vnto the waye of saluation? I shall then haue wherefore too sing prayses vnto his holy name, knowing the grace which hee hath bestowed on me. See then how that in this protestation Dauid speaketh not to bynde God, through any recompense or seruice: but onely stirreth him selfe vp, and pricketh him selfe foreward as it were with a spurre, to the ende he might be the better disposed, too receiue the benefite which God had promised him: and that he might knowe, that this benefite ought not to be an occasion to make him vnthankefull vnto him

from

from whom he receiued it. Howebeit we are here briefly to confider of two pointes. The one is, that as God hath liberally beftowed vppon vs his graces, fo much the more ought we to be ready to prayfe, and magnifie him for e-uer. For furely this is all the recompenfe that wee are any way able to yelde him, if fo bee, it may bee called recom- *Pfal.116.* penfe: howebeit hee accepteth it thankefully vnder this title, as the fcripture thereof maketh mention. Since then it is fo, if wee will not that the benefite which God hath be-ftowed vpon vs, turne it felfe into condemnation by reafon of our vnthankefulneffe, let vs be well aduifed to difcharge our felues towardes him: and fo, when as hee fhall haue layde open his goodneffe vpon vs, let vs not bee forgetfull of it, neither yet let our mouthes be clofed vp, but euen to acknowledge the fame vnto him.

And thus much as touching the firft point. The fecod is, That he which fhalbe wel and duely inftructed in the word of God, let him fhewe it, yea in glorifying his name all the daies of his life. They then which are fo colde in praifing of God, do right wel fhew, that they neuer felt what the power of the worde is. And why fo? Bicaufe it is impofsible for vs to haue any tafte of the worde of God, to receiue thereby any inftruction, but that wee muft needes bee moued and rauifhed therewith to fing prayfes vnto his glorious name. Whatfoeuer hee bee then that fhall fhewe him felfe negli-gent herein, fufficiently inough declareth that hee know-eth not what the worde of God is, albeit hee proteft him felfe to be a Chriftian. Let vs nowe come to thofe, which are not onely dumbe them felues: but that, which is alfo worfe, which would fhut vp the mouthes of others, to the ende it might not bee lawefull for them too prayfe God. And yet forfooth thefe men are fo fhameleffe, as that they woulde notwithftanding bee taken for good Chriftians: but by thefe meanes they declare them felues too bee the deadly enemies of God, yea worfe then the very deuilles.

And

And why so? Forsooth they thinke it not inough that they haue nothing profited in the schoole of God, neither yet are they contented to shewe the waye, to doe well, vnto others: but they would haue al the world to be like vnto thē selues, that there should neuer mention bee made of praysing God, & yet in the meane while, as I haue already saide, this word Christian shall stand them in neuer a peny. Nowe without all dout. God disaloweth of all those, which will not giue them selues to sing praises vnto his maiestie, and that will not stirre vp their neighbours to doe the like, that they might shewe them selues to haue studied his woorde. But let vs bee well assured, that it is not inough, too open our mouth and to sing praises vnto him with the tongue: but it must also come from a well affected heart. For Dauid telleth vs not here, that hee will solemnize the praises of God: but in addressing him selfe vnto God, hee protesteth before him, that he will sing prayses vnto him. And in speaking this, he right wel knoweth that his heart must needes be disposed thereto. Wherfore, when as we would magnifie the name of God as appērtaineth, let vs not deliuer it out with the mouth onely: but our heart also must be set thereto, and that it agree therewith to make a sweete hermony. If this be so, all our life by litle and litle shalbe answerable thereto, that it shall bee no vntruthe which wee haue pronounced with our mouth. Now he addeth a sentence which is very short: to wit,

My tongue shall treate of thy word: and why? bicause all thy commaundementes sayeth he, *are righteous*.

In this verse he sheweth that after he hath beene well instructed, that he him selfe will also trauell to bring others by little and little, to the like knowledge.

Loe here his full pretence. But yet the better to expresse his affection that hee hath too drawe on his brethren and neighbours, to the knowledge of God, and of his truth, hee vseth this word, to Sing, not contenting him selfe to speake after a plain maner: but expressing, that he wil sing alowde and cleare: that he will make his word to resounde, that it might

might be heard, yea that it should be a thing as notoriously knowne, as the very common songes. Nowe since it is so, that Dauid speaketh after this sort, let vs nowe see what our duetie is. For as I haue already said heretofore, he bragged not of his owne power: but the holy Ghost hath set him before vs in steade of a glasse, to thend it might serue vs for our better instruction. Nowe when as we shall haue knowne the truthe of our good God, what is there then for vs to do? Forsooth, we must not holde fast this treasure as it were lockt vp in a cheste, but communicate his graces vnto others: yea and doe the best wee can, to drawe on the miserable ignoraunt people, too the seruice of God: and too carry about with vs the doctrine, to publish it to all men, when as it is committed vnto vs as a treasure, and to bestowe the gifte which we haue receiued, vpon our neighbours, according to that measure of faith, which God hath giuen vs. Howebeit this order is farre of from vs: For if there be but three wordes of the worde of God spoken, we wil soone be wery of it, nay, we shall not heare it spoken of at this day. It is so farre of, that it is talked of, both at the table, in the waye, and euery where, as that we can hardly abide, that euen for fashions sake, the preaching of it be kept: and although it be here lawefull too speake in the pulpit one houre in the name of God, yet shall you haue a great number of dogges which will not sticke euen to gyrne at it, as if God were too too much priuiledged. It is very farre of to haue euery man to apply him selfe to sing the commaundementes of God, and his whole worde, and for vs to haue our eares beaten with it. Nowe whence commeth this vnthankefulnesse? verely bicause wee neuer tasted of that which Dauid here addeth, *All thy statutes* sayeth hee, *are righteous*. If wee did throughly know, what equitie and purenesse there is in the statutes of God, without dout we should be more earnest, to learne, holde, and shewe them, vnto others, then heretofore we haue beene. So then, all they which make no accompt too instruct their neighbours, and do not esteeme of the knowledge and faith which they haue receiued: doe

Aa hereby

hereby shew, that they will not render the righteousnesse to God as to him appertaineth, accordingly as it is conteined in his word, and as he him selfe sheweth it therein. Nowe Dauid by and by addeth,

Let thine hand helpe me: for I haue chosen thy commaundementes.

He yet returneth too that which before hee had sayde of deliuerance. For after he had required to be taught of god, he saide, O deliuer me: yea hee right wel knewe that if hee had not him for his protector, that hee shoulde alwayes remaine as it were in death. Now he addeth, *Let thyne hand helpe mee*. And why so? *For I haue chosen*, saith hee, *thy commaundements*.

When hee desireth God too helpe him with his hande, he confesseth his want, and that hee was as a man which needed help, euen as though he had neuer had more need: and that it was not in him, to deliuer himself, neither could he find it in any of his creatures. And therfore except God had stretched foorth his hand, see howe Dauid had beene vtterly cast away. Nowe, this confession here is very profitable for vs. For which of vs is he, that can be without afflictions? and that is able to saye, I haue all things that are necessarie? It is most true, that we are more carefull for that which concerneth our bodies, and this present life, then for that which is required for the saluation of our soules. If we stand in neede of meate and drinke, if wee be sicke, if we be in daunger of any plague or warre, that stirreth vs, and toucheth vs too the quicke: but when wee are pressed with any euill, we abuse our selues, and lifte our selues vp in such a fond presumption, as that we thinke wee haue some power to do this, and that we then make our selues beleeue, that we are very well able to defende our selues, although not wholy, yet at the least partly. And therefore wee ought so much the rather rightly to marke, the sayings of the scripture where it is saide vnto vs, that it is the hande of GOD that must helpe vs, to the ende that euery man may learne to knowe his neede, and that we had all neede too bee defended

fended by this heauenly power: so that we are all cast down into the bottomlesse depth, without it pleaseth G O D to stretch forth his hande to helpe our necessities. And thus much for this. Now when Dauid setteth downe the reason, that he had chosen the commaundements of God, he did it not to extoll any dignitie or worthinesse of his owne. Wherefore then? Forsooth, euen to shewe that he wayted for his ayde and helpe, from the hand of God. And therefore they which perswade them selues at aduenture that God heareth their prayers, and yet haue this foolish hope with them, to finde helpe at the handes of his creatures: refuse the hande of God as much as in them lieth: and so by that meanes shall neuer finde him to bee fauourable vnto them. And for this cause Dauid saith, *I haue chosen the commaundementes of God*, that is to saye, that all his whole liking was in them. And this saying importeth a very great matter, and much greater then at the first sight it seemeth. Why doth Dauid rather set downe this worde Election, or choise, then any other? I haue chosen thy commaundementes. It is bicause wee are alwayes carried with peruerse affections, and bicause we cannot make choise, neither can we hold vs to that which is best. Euery man wil gladliest desire that thing which is meetest for his own ease, and quietnesse: to be short, euery man desireth to be happy. Wee are nothing indifferēt herein: for the very wicked in the world, and the most vile persons, wil saye, I would haue that which were good and meete for me: howbeit wee can not chose: but euen the very worst. Wee shall very well haue a naturall desire, which shall carry vs as it were to one selfe same end: but we cannot keepe the waye. Euery man goeth out of it. One mā will chose this thing, another that: & in this choyse we are all confounded. One will chose, goodes, landes, and possessions: another, great trade of marchandise: another to come vnto dignitie and into credit: some one man will be giuen to lecherie, and bee wholy carried that way: another will yelde him selfe, too some other filthinesse, as too drunkennesse, intemperancy, and wantonnesse,

Aa 2   See

See then, how we al make choise of that which is naught, And for this cause Dauid saieth, that he chose the commã-dementes of God: to wit, that although hee was a mortall man, subiect too a great number of wicked affections, yet that he neuer trusted his owne flesh, neither yet obeied his lustes, to chose nothing but vanitie, and that which might withdrawe him from the right way, and leade him too destructiõ: but that he made a good wise choise: to wit, that he helde himselfe to the commandements of God. So then, let vs learne to make a good choise: when as God shall present vnto vs his worde, when as he shall offer him selfe so liberally on his part, as to looke for nothing at our handes but that we should come to seeke him, and that hee presenteth him selfe before vs: let not vs be deceiued nor carried away by the deceiptes of Satan, through the corruptions which he layeth wyde open before our eyes: let vs not be so foolish as to stay our selues vpon matters of nothing, and to leaue that which ought to bee the most principall, and wherein lieth all our felicitie and saluation. It followeth,

I haue longed for thy sauing health, O Lorde, and in thy lawe is my delight.

This sentence comprehendeth all whatsoeuer wee haue already touched, and is the onely confirmation thereof. For he sayeth, that he hath longed for the sauing health of God. And howe is that? For it seemeth that euery man might say as much: and so, that Dauid had no more then the very faithlesse. For if wee shall aske a desperate man, yea euen a very halfe deuill, and saye, wouldest not thou haue God to be thy sauiour? he will make answere and sayē, yes forsooth. Loe what answere wee shall finde in the mouthes both of great and small, of good and bad.

Nowe Dauid his meaning is, to make a great protestation, and such a one as a very fewe can make in truthe. For we suppose him to be all our Sauiours: and yet we seeke our sauing health at a wilde aduenture, and euery man will haue regarde to his owne considerations and prouidence. When

When there shall arise any question of our maintenaunce here in this present life, do we beleeue that God must keep and preserue vs, & that it is hee in deede which mainteineth vs herein? whence commeth it that wee haue so mighty euill consciences? whence commeth all deceiptes, fraudes, excesse, cruelties, iniuries, violences, and all such like? What is the cause that maketh vs to liue with such euil cósciences? but bicause wee do not beleeue, that God will giue vs our daily bread? Wee desire God to feede vs, and yet wee will haue the deuill to do it: in so much that there are very fewe which at this day thinke, that that which they haue, commeth from God. So then, it is very farre off frō the thought of our heartes, to saye, O Lorde, I haue desired thy sauing health. For in steade of attending vppon God, to haue him too guide, defende, and helpe vs at all times whensoeuer that wee haue neede: in steade of this I saye, what doe wee? Euery man as I haue saide, seeketh for his sauing health at a wilde aduenture. We should rather seeke for it in hell, then to haue our eyes lifted vp into heauen to call vpon God, & to seeke for our sauing health both of body and soule in him. So then, there are very fewe which are able to saye as it is here set downe, O Lorde, I haue longed for thy sauing health: if they will not lye. As we see the impudencie of hypocrites which will make mighty great bragges inough: but yet for all that, it is no small matter, as I haue already sayd, to trust altogether in God, and to saye, that it belongeth to him to guyde vs, that wee runne to him, and haue there our refuge both for soule and body. Nowe then hee addeth, *In thy lawe is my delight*: To signifie, how we ought to demeane our selues, not to hope for saluation, nor yet to wishe for it otherwise then from God alone: to wit, when as we haue taken delight in his lawe.

It is meete then that we tame and brydle our affections, that we seuer them from all other our desires, and saye, that in looking vpon his word, and in cleauing thereto, we take there our repast, and in it doe truely ioye.

A a 3

For whensoeuer we shall be brought vnto this point, it will stande vs in nothing to seeke our sauing health in God. And why so? bicause wee see none other thing in all the holy Scripture, but so many promises where God so gently biddeth vs, and where hee declareth vnto vs that hee is most ready to receiue vs, that hee looketh for none other thing at our handes but that we should seeke him, and that he thrusteth him selfe forwarde, and presenteth him selfe euen before vs. The Scripture, I say, is full of this doctrine, to shewe vnto vs that God is ready prepared too helpe vs when as we shall take pleasure in his lawe. We may very wel then long after the sauing health of God when as wee shall in truthe haue sought him. But what? wee see very fewe whose heartes are so confirmed, as too saye that they will holde the right way, whatsoeuer commeth of it. And therefore see heere consequently why God disapointeth vs, & helpeth vs not, as wee gladly desire to bee holpen. Nowe he addeth,

Let my soule liue, and it shall praise thee: and let thy iudgementes helpe me.

He alwayes pursueth his purpose, but here hee coupleth together two thinges which before he seuered. When hee sayeth, let my soule liue: that is alwayes, as he hath sayd, that he seeketh his sauing health of God, and longeth after it. He sayeth not, I will that my soule liue: but hath recourse vnto God, knowing right well that hee is the keeper of his life: and therefore putteth it into his handes, and leaueth the keeping thereof vnto him, as appertaining onely vnto him: and after he sayeth that hee will giue him thankes, for that his life shall bee prolonged.

Nowe heere wee see too what ende the faithfull ought to desire too liue in this worlde: to wit, that they might prayse GOD: as it hath beene also spoken in the other places. And chiefly without going farre, in the song of Ezechias For there, as in the hundreth & thirteenth Psalme, and as it were in the song of Ionas, it is shewed, that if we must liue, wee must not liue, for too liue (as wee saye)

Psal. 113.

and

and to haue none other regarde: neither yet, too say, I will onely liue to eate and drinke and to dwel heere in this present world. But we must goe yet farther: to wit, wee must liue, to the ende to prayse God: so that if this bee wanting in vs, Let vs wish to be a hundreth feete vnder the ground, that we may be neuer more spoken oft. Loe, I say, how our life shall be blessed, and agreeable vntoo the wilt of God: to wit, when as we bend our selues to none other ende, but to prayse and magnifie his holy and blessed name.

Now in the meane while Dauid addeth, *O let thy iudgements helpe me.* This is it which he had in effect before spoken of the sauing health of God. For he setteth the Iudgements of God against all the helpes which men and the faithlesse are any way able too inuente for the seeking of God. For they suppose that they shall bee very well holpen else where, when as they shall haue their prety shiftes too think that the creatures shall be sufficient inough to helpe them. When then these worldlings think too bring it so about, to be defended without the ayde of God; they must needes be deceiued in forgetting the iudgements of God: to wit, his prouidence, whereby he vseth to rule the world: as we must be fully assured that he holdeth the vngodly in a bridle, when as they skirmish, & forcibly set them selues to hurt the good and innocent: and that it is too represse the malice of all those which torment his, because he hath taken them into his hand, and protection. See then, how the faithfull ought to put them selues to the Iudgementes of God, to wit, to this prouidence, by which all is disposed and gouerned. It is very true that God may very well arme all his creatures to defende and maintaine vs: but yet must we not cease for all that to feele his hand, and too beholde it by faith when as it shall helpe vs. Wee must not cease too see this prouidence which is hidden from the faithlesse, because their spirites are wreathed vpp in horrible darkenesse.

To be short, let not vs cease too attribute all the helpe
which

which we shall feele from the hand of God, vnto his iudgementes, although hee hath inferior meanes too helpe vs. Nowe in the ende Dauid concludeth,

I haue gone astray like a Sheepe that is loste: seeke thy seruant for I doe not forget thy Commaundements.

Heere wee might thinke it very straunge why Dauid sayth, that hee hath strayed like a loste sheepe, seeing that he addeth, That he hath not forgotten the Commaundementes of God, and that wee haue already seene by so many goodly protestations, that it was his whole delight to serue God: yea and that it was too him more deere then Golde and Siluer. And howe is it then that he now compareth him selfe vnto a loste sheepe. For to make plaine this hard point, it is commonly said, that Dauid confesseth him selfe to be a strayed sheepe, yea notwithstanding the great desire that he had to please GOD, too gouerne his whole life aright, and yet that he ceased not to erre. This saying is very well verified in him selfe. For although that this appertaineth not vnto the whole life of Dauid: yet he had a terrible fall, and was like a pore loste beaste in the sin which he committed with Bethsabe, Vrias wife: For it seemeth that he had then forsaken God, and that he was as it were a lost man. He might then very wel say, that hee had highly and mightely erred like a loste sheepe. But this might be taken more properly, That Dauid respected not the time wherin God had called him, & set him in a good way: but rather respected his owne naturall estate and condition, and saith, O Lord, what am I of my selfe, without thou guidest me? Alas what had become of mee? In what case had I beene? Where should I haue first begunne? Dauid then might very well make heere protestation of such his condition as is common with vs. For this is a generall thing amoongst vs all, that wee all go astraye like wilde and forlorne beastes, vntill such time as GOD repayreth and amendeth vs. For in what case shall GOD

finde

wee are loſt ſheepe, vntill ſuch time as God ſheweth him ſelfe to be our Shephearde, and giueth vs the grace too followe him. And yet there is another reaſon which made Dauid to cal[him ſelf a loſt ſheepe: & this is the very true meaning, and the moſte naturall: to wit, becauſe he was deadly purſued of his enemyes, and was ſo hardly and greeuouſly perſecuted by them, as that he was like vnto a poore chaſed ſheepe: Who ſeeing the Woulfe to purſue him fleyeth from him into the Mountaines, thinking there to hide him ſelfe. Loe heere a poore ſheepe which ſhall eſcape the throte of the Woulfe: he is ſo hartely afrayd, that if he finde a wel, he wil ſooner leape into it, then too goe on any farder: for hee knoweth not what to doe, nor what ſhall become of him: beeing thus mortally purſued. And therfore Dauid ſaying, that hee erred like a loſt ſheepe referred it not vnto his ſins, to ſay, O Lorde, I haue offended, I haue ſtrayed from the way of ſaluation: but he ſayeth, O Lord, I know not what ſhall become of me. Heere then wee nowe ſee what the naturall meaning of this text is, wherevpon we muſt chiefly ſtay our ſelues. Although the doctrine which I haue already touched be very good and profitable, yet muſt wee haue reſpect vnto the meaning of Dauid. I haue then erred ſaith he, like a loſte ſheepe. Nowe he ſayth,

O ſeeke thy Seruaunt, for I doe not forget thy commaundements.

When as we ſhall ioyne theſe twoo things togither, That Dauid forgot not the Commaundements of God, and that he hath erred: we ſhall finde, how greatly he was giuen to the ſeruing of God, that he deſired it from the bottome of his heart: and yet was he not without extreeme affliction: yea he was ſo voyde of helpe, as that it ſeemeth hee coulde not

not choose but despaire of his sauing health. When then wee see such an example, haue not we very good occasion to take courage, although God suffereth vs many times to bee euen extreemely persecuted? For if this came to passe in Dauid who was so excellent a man, as we haue spoken off: Let not vs think to be greatlyer priuiledged then he. But let vs chiefely consider to be patient in our afflictions, seeing that GOD thereby meaneth to make proofe of our faith and patience, and will cause it all too turne vnto our saluation. And this is it which Dauid concludeth withall, O Lorde, seeke thy seruant: signifying, that he stayeth him selfe chifely vpon the protection and sauegarde of God. And see howe wee must order our selues in this behalfe: For if wee can stay our selues vpon him, when as wee shall be persecuted, and beseech him to seeke vs, wee must not doubt but that hee will make vs too feele his helpe, yea, and that wee shall obtayne our saluation when as wee shall there seeke it.

According vntoo this holy Doctrine let vs prostrate our selues before the maiestie of our good GOD, in acknowledging our offences, beseeching him, that it woulde please him to make vs feele them better then heeretofore wee haue doone. And in the meane while that it woulde also please him to helpe all our miseryes, and too giue vs this soueraigne remedy, to witte, to be purged of all our wicked affections, that the lawe might raigne wholy in vs, haue full possession both of our thoughts and desires, and of all whatsoeuer else there is in vs : and we too bee so gouerned by it, as that forsaking all the things of this world, and of this present life, wee craue and desire none other thing but to cleaue vnto our good GOD, and too bee wholy conformable vnto his holy will. And although we are nowe nusseled in a greate many of vices and imperfections, and subiecte too a great number of calamities: yet for all that, let vs knowe that wee are very happy

so

vpon the Cxix. Psalme.

so longe as wee shall bee vnder his protection and sauegarde, looking alwayes for the saluation which hee hath promised vs, vntill such time as hee hath graunted vs a full inioying thereof, too beholde him face too face in his heauenly kingdome, which nowe wee see heere belowe as it were in a duskishe Glasse. That hee will not onely &c.

FINIS.

Imprinted at London
at the three Cranes in the Vintree by Thomas Dawson, for Iohn Harison and Thomas Man.
1580.

www.ingramcontent.com/pod-product-compliance
Lightning Source LLC
Chambersburg PA
CBHW030341230426
43664CB00007BA/493